COLLECTED WORKS OF ERASMUS

VOLUME 3

THE CORRESPONDENCE OF ERASMUS

LETTERS 298 TO 445

1514 TO 1516

translated by R.A.B. Mynors and D.F.S. Thomson

annotated by James K. McConica

University of Toronto Press

Toronto and Buffalo

The research costs of the Collected Works of Erasmus
have been underwritten by the Canada Council.

Toronto and Buffalo
Printed in Canada

Library of Congress Cataloging in Publication Data
Erasmus, Desiderius, d. 1536.
The correspondence of Erasmus.
Vol. 3 annotated by J.K. McConica.
Translation of Opus epistolarum Des. Erasmi Roterdami.
Includes bibliographical references.
CONTENTS: [1] Letters 1 to 141, 1484–1500. –
[2] Letters 142 to 297, 1501–1514.–
[3] Letters 298–445, 1514 to 1516.
1. Erasmus, Desiderius, d. 1536 – Correspondence.
I. Title.
PA8511.A5E55 1974 199'.492 [B] 72–97422
ISBN 0-8020-2202-2

The Collected Works of Erasmus

The aim of the Collected Works of Erasmus is to make available an accurate, readable English text of Erasmus' correspondence and his other principal writings. The edition is planned and directed by an Editorial Board, an Executive Committee, and an Advisory Committee.

Contents

Illustrations

Preface

The interest of this volume centres on Erasmus' work at the press of Johann Froben in Basel. Erasmus made his first journey to that city in the late summer of 1514, when the first letters presented here were written. It was his purpose to arrange with Froben for the printing of a greatly revised and expanded version of the *Adagiorum chiliades*, which had been published first in 1508 by Aldus and again in 1513, in a pirated version, by Froben himself.[1] It seems altogether likely, however, that Erasmus was also interested in the Amerbach project for a complete edition of the works of St Jerome,[2] in the possibilities of Froben's Greek type, and in the impressive quality of the press's productions, for he was now ready to publish the fruits of his extended labours in Cambridge – chiefly the letters of Jerome, his revised text of Seneca, and his new translation of the New Testament. In the event these and other lesser works were soon to issue from Froben's press with astonishing rapidity.[3]

Although in Basel Erasmus found the nearest thing to a permanent home that he would ever know, he continued his travels. After wintering in Basel he left for England sometime in March 1515, chiefly, no doubt, to gather further materials for his work on the letters of Jerome and the New Testament.[4] By the end of May he was once more on his way to the Froben

* * * * *

1 Cf Ep 283:181–96; Phillips chap 4 and especially 119–20.

2 Cf Epp 263:31n; 396 introduction.

3 *Adagiorum chiliades* 1515; Seneca's *Lucubrationes* August 1515 (Ep 325); the epistles of Jerome 1516 (Epp 326, 396); a revised edition of the *De octo orationis partium constructione libellus* August 1515 (Ep 341); the *Novum instrumentum* 1516 (Epp 373, 384); the *Institutio principis christiani* 1516 (Ep 393); a revised edition of the *Grammatica institutio* of Theodore of Gaza November 1516 (Ep 428). At the same time Matthias Schürer brought out the first edition of the *Parabolae sive similia* (Ep 312) and the second edition of the *Lucubrationes* (Ep 343).

4 Ep 326B introduction

press. He arrived again in Basel in mid-summer after an extended tour through the cities of the Rhine where he had enjoyed such a resounding welcome the previous summer. Once more ensconced in Basel, he set himself this time to the immense and gruelling task of printing both the New Testament and the edition of Jerome. It was not until May 1516 that he took to the road once more, this time to confirm his appointment as councillor in the Netherlands to Prince Charles, the future Emperor Charles v. It is at this point that the present volume ends, just as he is renewing contact with his old associates in the Netherlands, and on the eve of a further journey to England. Erasmus' travels thus confirm what the contents of his letters suggest, that at this time the centre of his familiar world of patronage and friendship is located in the old Burgundian territory of the Rhine.

He had travelled almost unwittingly into a region of profound religious and intellectual ferment, and found that he had already won reputation there as a hero of German letters.[5] The welcome he received from men like Wimpfeling, Pirckheimer, and Zasius, not to mention Froben himself and the Amberbachs, was as reassuring as it was apparently unforeseen. It is reflected later in the warm sentiments Erasmus expressed to his friends in the north about the delights of life in Upper Germany.[6] Many of these new acquaintances were – like Pirckheimer himself[7] – evangelists of the patriotic tradition already established by earlier German humanists such as Rodolphus Agricola and Conrad Celtis, and Erasmus was willing to indulge the notion of his German identity.[8] It is doubtful however that he appreciated the full significance of the sentiment he encountered in these Rhenish cities: a regional self-awareness nourished by growing material prosperity, by the legacy of conciliarism, and by long-standing resentment of the ecclesiastical and cultural dominance of Italy. This complex sentiment would find violent expression in the writings of another correspondent introduced in this volume, Ulrich von Hutten, as it proved a potent factor in the career of a man whose acquaintance Erasmus had yet to make, Martin Luther.

* * * * *

5 Epp 302 introduction; 321:16n

6 Epp 411; 414:13–15; 416:7–9

7 Pirckheimer encouraged younger men to continue the investigation of German history and himself contributed, among other things, the first historical geography of Germany, *Germaniae ex variis scriptoribus perbrevis explicatio* (Nürnberg: Johann Petreius 1530); cf L.W. Spitz *The Religious Renaissance of the German Humanists* (Cambridge, Mass 1963) chap 8.

8 In his youth 'Germania' signified to him only the lower Rhine region (Ep 23:57–74), but in Basel the term took on a wider significance; cf Ep 307:15–20 and J.D. Tracy 'Erasmus Becomes a German' *Renaissance Quarterly* 21, 3 (1968) 282.

Others among his new correspondents attest to the highly personal and intimate character of the humanist world. Among the new friends of distinguished reputation was Reuchlin, and we now have Erasmus' own account of their first meeting in 1515 from a newly edited letter.[9] Lefèvre d'Etaples greeted Erasmus from Paris, welcoming his decision to leave England for the wider opportunities afforded by a good publishing house.[10] Beatus Rhenanus and Oecolampadius added their own testimony that Erasmus had become a figure of international importance. Some men of modest reputation and ambition wrote letters whose whole object was to elicit a reply, but distinguished correspondents too, like Zasius or the youthful Zwingli, introduced themselves to seek his friendship.[11] In April 1516 Johann Witz of Sélestat, known to his fellow humanists as Sapidus, penned the phrase that summed up this striking phenomenon when he sent greetings to Beatus Rhenanus 'and all the Erasmians.'[12] The acclaim is the more remarkable when one realizes that, of the works Erasmus had so far published to attract this reputation, only one – the *Praise of Folly* – would eventually rank with his greatest achievements.[13]

Away from his admirers in Basel and the Rhenish Oberland Erasmus maintained his former contacts with highly placed figures in England and in Rome, and in France he himself sought out the friendship of the eminent Guillaume Budé, almost as if to confirm to himself the reputation attributed to him by other men.[14] Their correspondence discloses, amidst much rhetorical flattery and self-deprecation, the iron core of scholarly discipline that underlay their eloquent achievements.[15]

Not all the exchanges were so amiable. The slender but ominous thread of controversy in the letters with Maarten van Dorp of Louvain reminds us of the *Praise of Folly*'s hostile public, and, like Erasmus' occasional contacts with Reuchlin's troubles, foreshadows the bitter disputes that lay ahead. On the whole, however, Erasmus' critics and detractors are not conspicuous in this volume, where the mood is set by incessant schol-

* * * * *

9 Ep 326B

10 Ep 315

11 Epp 303, 401; Johann Kierher (Ep 355), Nikolaus Basellius (Ep 391), and Georgius Precellius (Ep 398) exemplify the first category.

12 Ep 399:13

13 The *Enchiridion* of 1514, the *Adages* of 1508, *De copia* (1512), and Erasmus' edition of Valla's notes on the New Testament (1505) were perhaps the other works chiefly responsible for his reputation at this juncture.

14 Ep 403 introduction

15 Cf CWE I xii on this aspect of the humanist epistle.

arly work accompanied by high optimism. This mood is best characterized by Erasmus' appointment as councillor to Prince Charles, by the compliments of such learned and noble patrons as Hermann, Graf von Neu,[16] and by the attempts of Duke Ernest of Bavaria to lure him to Ingolstadt as an ornament for his university there.[17] The courteous exchanges with the new Medici pope, Leo X, also point to Erasmus' good repute in Rome.

This volume differs importantly from its predecessors in one respect: many more letters from this period have survived. The first volume in this series contained one hundred and forty-one letters written over a period of sixteen years; and the second, one hundred and fifty-five from some thirteen years. This volume contains one hundred and fifty-one letters written during two years, from 1 August 1514 to 5 August 1516. They appear with remarkable regularity over the months between those dates, and there is a reasonable balance between letters from Erasmus' hand and those sent to him, so that the flow of comment and event reported here is correspondingly more vivid and continuous. This change coincides with Erasmus' departure from England and with his busy preparations in Basel to publish the major scholarly works he had ready in manuscript. The feeling that we now meet the mature Erasmus, and that what has gone before is prologue, is consequently difficult to resist.

The survival of so much of the correspondence of this period results, in part, from the preservation of the Deventer Letter-book in which Erasmus' servant-pupils copied out his correspondence in the years 1517–18. Most of the letters so recorded were letters Erasmus received; some few were letters he had written. Almost half of the letters in this volume, apart from those published as prefaces or dedications in Erasmus' printed works, were gathered by Leclerc in 1705 from this early manuscript and published – with few exceptions for the first time – in the Leiden *Opera omnia*.[18]

For most of the letters by Erasmus himself we are indebted to printed sources: the steady production from the Froben press of volumes furnished with dedicatory and prefatory epistles and the early printed collections of letters. Erasmus' first personal intervention in the latter enterprise occurred when he arrived in Basel and inserted four important letters, including his long reply to Dorp's criticism of the *Praise of Folly*, into Froben's *Jani*

* * * * *

16 Ep 442

17 Ep 386

18 CWE 1 xi–xii; Allen I 603–9. Epp 319, 355, 409, 423, and 425 have manuscript authority in the Deventer Letter-book but first appeared in collections other than LB, as is noted in the introductions to those letters.

Damiani Senensis ... elegeia (August 1515).[19] The occasional production of larger collections also began at this time through the initiative of Pieter Gillis and Thierry Martens at Louvain. Of the more extensive collections later printed by Froben, it is the *Farrago epistolarum* of 1519 that is most frequently drawn on here.[20] These early printed collections are all discussed in the appendix to this volume, where the prefaces published by P.S. Allen at the end of his second volume are also translated: prefaces to the *Epistolae ad Erasmum* (Louvain: Martens October 1516), to the *Epistolae elegantes* (Louvain: Martens April 1517), and to the *Auctarium* (Basel: Froben August 1518).

While there is obvious appeal in a correspondence as continuous and extensive as this one, there are also certain dangers for the reader interested in reconstructing the world of Erasmus. A modern critical edition will give far more information about the world framed by his pen than was available to any of his contemporaries, or even to Erasmus himself. To allow the interested reader at least to rediscover the sequence in which these letters became known, therefore, the introduction to each letter cites the first collection in which the letter was printed, along with the manuscript source, if one exists. Where the introduction to any letter is silent about both the manuscript source and the collection in which it was first published, the letter is in the Deventer Letter-book and was first printed by Leclerc in the Leiden *Opera omnia*. If the letter was first published by Allen, the manuscript alone is cited. All of the printed letter-collections, which are described in the introductions by short titles, are listed in full among the Works Frequently Cited.[21]

The translation in this volume is the work of R.A.B. Mynors, who wishes to thank his colleagues for their help, and to acknowledge his indebtedness to Mme Marie-Madeleine de la Garanderie for her edition of the difficult correspondence with Guillaume Budé.

Each volume of the correspondence will contain an index to the persons, places, and works mentioned in that volume. When the correspondence is completed, the reader will also be supplied with an index of topics, and of classical and scriptural references. The index for volume 3 was prepared by James Farge CSB. The footnotes dealing with technical problems of coinage and moneys-of-account were supplied by John H. Munro.

* * * * *

19 The letters were Epp 333, 334, 335, and 337; see appendix.

20 See appendix and CWE 1 xix–xx.

21 References to the Gouda MSS are to two manuscript collections of letters in the town library at Gouda which are very important for the early correspondence, and which were described by Allen (1 app IX 613–15).

I would like here to record my personal debt to my colleagues on the Editorial Board who have been unfailingly generous in supplying counsel from their own special fields of competence. In addition, I would like to acknowledge the valued assistance of Reverend James J. Sheridan of the Department of Classics, University of Toronto; Reverend Adolar Zumkeller OSA, of the Augustinus-Institut, Würzburg; Reverend Dr Stanley Greenslade, Christ Church, Oxford; and others whose help I have acknowledged where appropriate in the notes.

The editors again wish to record here their personal gratitude to the Canada Council, the generous patron of this extensive undertaking, and to University of Toronto Press.

JKM

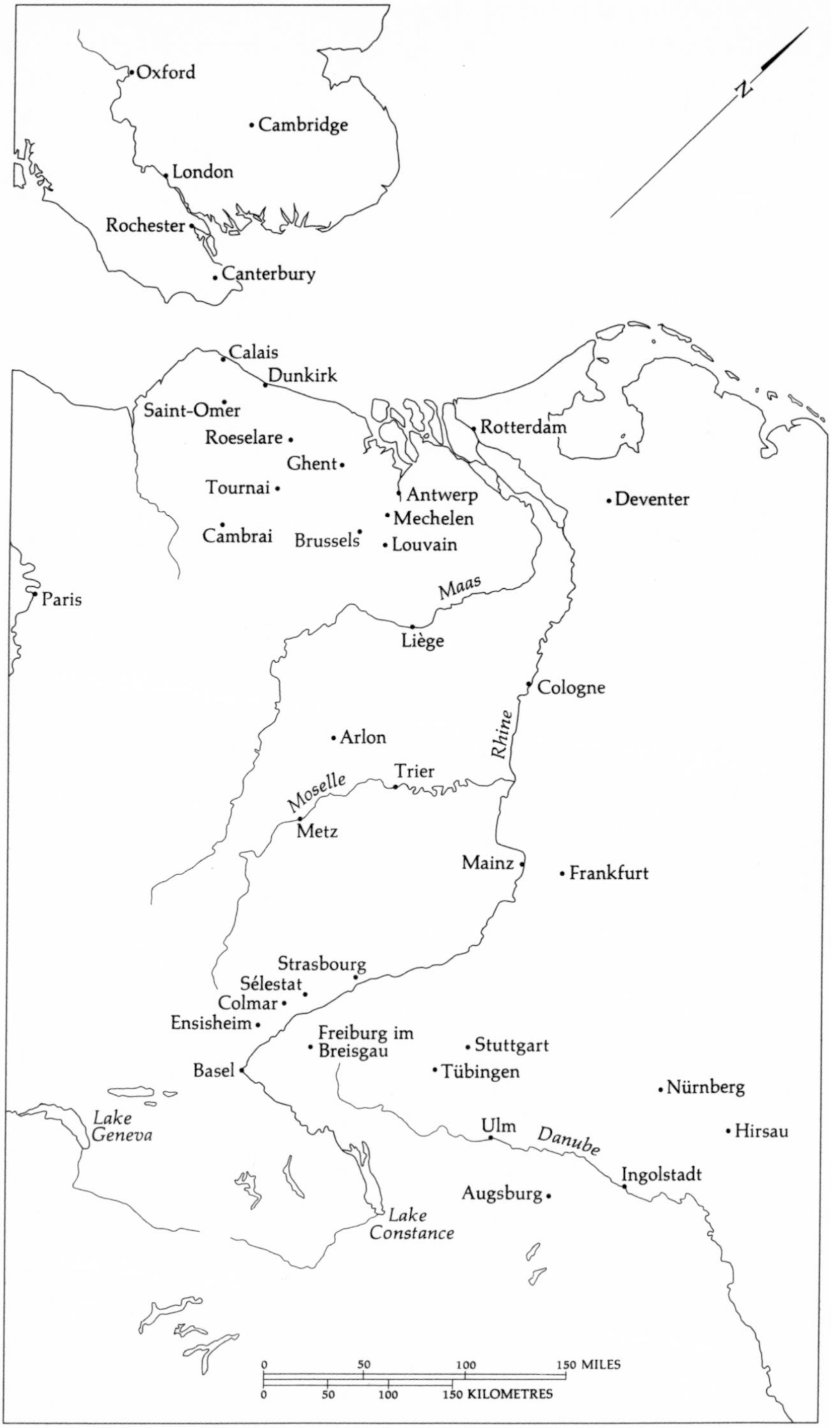
Oxford
Cambridge
London
Rochester
Canterbury
N
Calais
Dunkirk
Saint-Omer
Roeselare
Ghent
Tournai
Cambrai
Brussels
Antwerp
Mechelen
Louvain
Rotterdam
Deventer
Paris
Maas
Liège
Cologne
Rhine
Arlon
Trier
Moselle
Metz
Mainz
Frankfurt
Strasbourg
Sélestat
Colmar
Ensisheim
Freiburg im Breisgau
Stuttgart
Tübingen
Basel
Nürnberg
Lake Geneva
Ulm
Danube
Hirsau
Ingolstadt
Augsburg
Lake Constance
0 50 100 150 MILES
0 50 100 150 KILOMETRES

THE CORRESPONDENCE OF ERASMUS

LETTERS 298 TO 445

298 / To Jean de Nève Louvain, 1 August 1514

This is the dedicatory preface to *Opuscula aliquot Erasmo Roterodamo castigatore*, which included *Catonis praecepta, Mimi Publiani, Septem sapientum celebria dicta*, and *Institutum christiani hominis carmine pro pueris*. The first edition was printed at Louvain by Thierry Martens in September 1514 (NK 534); it was reprinted at Cologne in November by Martin von Werden and by Martens in September 1515 (NK 2603). In October 1515 Matthias Schürer published a new edition revised by Erasmus at his request, and many editions followed from the presses of Schürer, Martens, Josse Bade, and Froben during Erasmus' lifetime. The last edition produced by any of Erasmus' authorized printers was brought out by Froben and Episcopius in 1534. The collection continued to enjoy great success and was still being printed in London in the seventeenth century; see E.J. Devereux *A Checklist of English Translations of Erasmus to 1700* (Oxford 1968) 28–9.

Having left his friend Mountjoy at Hammes, Erasmus now went on to Louvain where he had stayed earlier during most of 1502 to 1504; cf Ep 171 introduction and the letters following. His host there was Jean Desmarez (Paludanus), to whom the *Panegyricus* was dedicated, as was Erasmus' translation of Lucian's *De mercede conductis* (Ep 197). In 1502 the magistrates offered Erasmus a lectureship, but he turned it down, chiefly in order to devote all his time to the study of Greek (cf Epp 171:13 and ff; 172:11–12; Ep 266:14–15). While there, he became acquainted with a group at the Collège du Lys – the college of the lily – and among them Jean de Nève of Hondschoote, near Dunkirk.

De Nève was a graduate in both arts and theology of the Collège du Lys, where he became a reader about 1498, and taught logic and physics for years with great success. Eventually, after a disputed regency at the college, he became rector of the university in 1515. Among his pupils was Maarten van Dorp (cf Ep 304 introduction), with whom Erasmus left the text of his *Opuscula aliquot*. Erasmus stayed with de Nève during his residence in Louvain from September 1517 to October 1521 and the two men became close friends. After de Nève's death in 1522 Erasmus wrote a letter of regret (Ep 1347) which was published in 1524 by Froben with the *Exomologesis*. Cf Epp 304:158; 643; 651; and 696; and de Vocht *Literae* 68–9.

ERASMUS OF ROTTERDAM TO JEAN DE NÈVE OF HONDSCHOOTE, REGENT OF THE COLLÈGE DU LYS AT LOUVAIN

Dear de Nève, leading light of theologians, the moral couplets which pass commonly under the name of Cato I have in the first place carefully revised, comparing with them the version of Planudes, although as a mere Greek he often falls short of the meaning of the Latin lines. I have also added notes which are very brief, but will be found, if I mistake not, somewhat more serviceable than the commentaries with which two persons have disfigured this small work, one of whom is full of pointless points of rhetoric although he is quite incapable of self-expression, and the other of misplaced philosophy, so that neither offers anything to the purpose. For that matter, the identity of the author, and whether he was one person or more than one, I take to be a question of small importance; I see no reason why they should be called Cato's, except that the sentiments are not unworthy of a Cato. To these I have added the *Mimes* of Publius, wrongly known as the *Proverbs* of Seneca. These too I have corrected, for I found them heavily corrupt, and I have added very brief notes, casting out spurious additions taken from the books of other men and appending a few from Aulus Gellius and the *Controversiae* of Seneca.

'But what is this?' I hear some trouble-maker cry. 'You, a theologian, wasting time on such trumpery stuff!' To this I answer, first, that I think nothing beneath our notice, however elementary, that contributes to a good education, not least lines such as these which combine a neat Latin style with the implanting of high moral standards. Although, for that matter, why should I be ashamed to spend a few short hours in a field of literature in which not a few Greek authors have distinguished themselves? We still possess the moral precepts of Theognis, and the maxims of Phocylides and Pythagoras which well deserve their name, the Golden Verses. And then again, if they think it beneath me to have corrected and explained such modest works, how much more discreditable that they should have been corrupted and that (as is clear from their commentaries) these childish works were not understood by men who thought they knew everything!

* * * * *

298:5 Planudes] The Byzantine scholar (c 1255–1305) whose numerous translations from the Latin included the *Disticha Catonis*, published by Aldus in February 1496.

8 two persons] Which commentators these are must be left to conjecture. Cato was printed almost two hundred times in the fifteenth century, often with notes.

11 anything to the purpose] *Adagia* I v 45.

27 Theognis] The moral verses ascribed to Theognis and Phocylides and the 'Golden Verses' of the pseudo-Pythagoras had been printed for the first time by Aldus in 1495/6.

Who dares despise the *Mimes* of Publius, when Aulus Gellius calls them most elegant and Seneca most expressive, and when, as Seneca also tells us, the most eminent orators were ready to try and match his pithy style? I have added also the celebrated *Sayings of the Seven Sages*, and the pattern of a Christian, expanded by myself, in verse which aims at clarity rather than polish, from an English text written earlier by John Colet, in my opinion as religious a man and as true a Christian as the flourishing realm of England has to show.

This work, such as it is, I have decided to dedicate to you, my honoured de Nève, partly to give you something to read with those pupils of yours whom you guard from any taint of barbarism in education or in character, and partly that this small token may preserve our friendship from decay. Nor have I any doubt of my success in this, given your inborn kindliness and your long-standing feelings towards me, and also because in this modest undertaking I meet a wish you once expressed. Long ago, as my friend Dorp has told me, you voiced the earnest wish to see a scholarly edition of the maxims of some standard author that might shape the minds of the young for a life of virtue and their lips for correct and fluent speech; and if this double purpose is not met by these precepts of Cato and Publius and the Seven Sages in their revised and annotated form, it never will be. Farewell.

Louvain, 1 August 1514

299 / To Andreas of Hoogstraten — Liège, [August 1514]

The recipient of this letter evidently belonged to a younger branch of the family van Borssele who acquired the lordship of Hoogstraten in 1437. Eras-

* * * * *

33 Publius] Publilius Syrus

33 Aulus Gellius] 17.14.3

34 Seneca] *Controversiae* 7.3.9

36 pattern of a Christian] The *Christiani hominis institutum*, Reedijk poem 94

45 Nor have I] In Erasmus' revised edition of October 1515, by which date the regent had become rector of Louvain university, the words 'leading light of theologians' were added to the first sentence, and the rest of the letter was replaced by this: 'It is not concealed from me how trivial my offering is and how unworthy of the exalted position of one who, with singular learning and a marriage of integrity and charm, adorns the distinguished faculty of theology and adds fresh lustre to the famous university of Louvain. But I was confident that, humble as my book might be, so good a man would accept it, just because it would be useful.'

48 Dorp] Cf Ep 304 introduction.

mus' visit marks his long-standing friendship with Andreas, which may have dated back to his Tournehem days. Cf Epp 80 and 93 introduction. This is evidently the letter referred to by Andreas in Ep 381. It was first printed in the *Epistolae ad diversos* in 1521.

ERASMUS OF ROTTERDAM TO ANDREAS OF HOOGSTRATEN

I went somewhat out of my way to see an old friend like you and to enjoy a glimpse of such a famous city, but through some adverse fate I failed of both. You were not at home, and the city made such an impression on me that I never left any place with greater pleasure. Farewell.

Liège, [1517]

300 / To Johann Reuchlin [Basel, August 1514]

The reference to Froben, the request for a codex of the Greek New Testament, and the proposal to move on to Italy in September suggest that this letter is one of the first written from Basel, where Erasmus found the nearest thing to a permanent home. It is probably the reply to Ep 290; cf the note to line 39 below. Like Epp 324, 457, and 471 it was printed not by Erasmus but by Reuchlin in *Illustrium virorum epistolae ... ad loannem Reuchlin Phorcensem*, published in Alsace at Haguenau by Reuchlin's friend Thomas Anshelm in 1519. Its publication was part of an attempt by Reuchlin to make known his support from members of the learned world, and, in particular, the general satisfaction among men of letters at the decision of the bishop of Speyer, who had upheld Reuchlin's case in the condemnation of his *Augenspiegel* by the Inquisition of Mainz (1513) and the theological faculty of Cologne (February 1514); cf Ep 290 introduction.

ERASMUS TO JOHANN REUCHLIN

While I was living in England your letter reached me, accompanied by the favourable verdict of the bishop of Speyer, and I showed these to several learned friends, not one of whom but has a high respect for such a gifted and prolific scholar as yourself. They were all smiles, and were very insis-

* * * * *

299:3 city] Erasmus' caustic observation provoked the courteous defence of Liège in Ep 381.

300:3 bishop of Speyer] A papal bull of 17 November 1513 had committed the question of Reuchlin's *Augenspiegel* to the bishop of Speyer. A verdict favourable to Reuchlin, denying that the *Augenspiegel* was heretical, was given on 29 March 1514. Cf Ep 290:12n and 27n.

View of Basel
From the ms Chronicle of Lucerne by Diebold Schilling, 1511–13, f 113[v]
Zentralbibliothek Lucerne
Photograph courtesy Schweizerisches Landesmuseum, Zürich

tent that I should produce the book which had been condemned, supposing it to be a remarkable piece, if for no other reason, from the quality of the men it had offended. First among them was the bishop of Rochester, a man of singularly high character and a most accomplished theologian; after him John Colet, dean of St Paul's in London. For my own part, I still retained some misgivings that you might have expressed yourself rather incautiously, for I scented a certain timidity and almost uneasiness in the bishop's judgment, when he spoke of 'open heresy' and 'with the addition of the treatise,' until when I was in Mainz I secured the book itself and read those same heretical, irreverent, and impious paragraphs, upon which I could contain my mirth no longer. And once I had read that famous condemnation (a pretty piece of work, in heaven's name), I acquitted you and accepted it as a complete defence of what you had written, wishing particularly that it might find itself in the hands of all good scholars. When I had read your Defence, written with such energy, such confidence, such flashing eloquence, such piercing wit, such manifold and copious erudition, I seemed to hear the accents not so much of a culprit making his apology as of a conqueror triumphing over his defeated foes. One complaint I had to make, my dear Reuchlin, for I will speak frankly as a friend should: I wish you had diverged rather less into general considerations or at least had not spent so long on them, and also that you had refrained from open personal attacks. But the first, if it is a fault, is the fault of a man abounding in scholarship and literary gifts; and on the second point it is hard to lay down limits for another man's resentment. You will give great pleasure to all good scholars if you will have the book sent to England, either to John, bishop of Rochester, or to Colet, the dean of St Paul's. I will send my own copy too, if I can, although it is the only one I have.

I have written annotations on the entire New Testament, and so have now in mind to print the New Testament in Greek with my comments added. They say that you have a very accurate copy, and if you will give

* * * * *

6 the book] *Augenspiegel*

8 Rochester] John Fisher; cf Ep 229 introduction.

10 Colet] Cf Ep 106 introduction. Colet was, however, uneasy about Reuchlin's cabbalistic studies; cf Ep 593.

14 Mainz] Cf Ep 314:5.

20 your Defence] *Defensio Joannis Reuchlin Phorcensis LL. Doctoris contra calumniatores suos Colonienses* (Tübingen: Thomas Anshelm March 1513)

33 annotations] Apparently the first reference to the annotations on the New Testament; cf Ep 305:229n.

35 copy] Basel MS AN IV 2: cf Ep 384 introduction. This was a twelfth-century Greek minuscule MS borrowed by Reuchlin from the Dominicans at Basel in

Johann Froben access to it, you will do a service not only to me and to him but to all students of the subject. The volume shall be returned to you intact and spotless. Farewell, and pray let me hear from you.

I answered the letter sent to me in England, but whether it reached you or not I do not know. I shall look for a letter from you. Farewell once again. All Germany can show really nothing like you, the brightest ornament she has. I wish very much that I could speak with you but, as far as I can see, this will not be possible. For about the end of the second week in September I leave here for Italy, unless something new turns up before then. Once more, my very best wishes.

301 / To William Blount, Lord Mountjoy — Basel, 30 August [1514]

1514 is the only year in which Erasmus travelled to Basel at this time. He apparently wrote the main part of the letter while he was in Ghent during the summer, adding the postscript after he arrived at Basel. Mountjoy (see Ep 79 introduction) had been appointed lieutenant of the castle of Hammes in October 1509 and held the position until 1531, three years before his death. Hammes was one of the English garrisons of the region, along with Calais, Guisnes, and Rysbank. From 1514 to 1517 Mountjoy was also lieutenant of Tournai. After the capture of Tournai in September 1513 Mountjoy was made the city's administrator, and in January 1514 he took the title of bailiff of Tournai; cf LP II i 41; E&C 156. As Erasmus' chief lay patron in England Mountjoy had received the dedication of the *Adagiorum collectanea* in 1500 (cf Ep 126) and that of the much enlarged version of 1508, the *Adagiorum chiliades*; cf also Epp 71 introduction; 117; and 125 introduction. On his role as a patron of humanism see McConica 56–7, 60, and passim. The letter was first printed in the *Farrago* (1519).

* * * * *

1488 and not returned to them until after his death. It lacked only the Book of Revelation. The Dominicans had obtained it in 1443 from Cardinal Ivan Stojković of Ragusa, who bequeathed his library to them; nothing is known of its earlier history. For a full description of the MS see Kirsopp Lake *Codex I of the Gospels and Its Allies* Cambridge Texts and Studies vii 3 (Cambridge 1906) ix–xiv. See also A. Bludau *Die beiden ersten Erasmus-Ausgaben des Neuen Testaments und ihre Gegner* (Freiburg im Breisgau 1902); B.M. Metzger *The Text of the New Testament* 2nd ed (Oxford 1968) 99–100, 269; and C.C. Tarelli 'Erasmus's manuscripts of the Gospels' *Journal of Theological Studies* 44 (1943) 155–62, 48 (1947) 207–8.

39 letter] Perhaps an indication that Erasmus had already replied to Ep 290; cf Epp 324:2; 573 introduction. Ep 290:25–8 may refer to previous correspondence with Reuchlin.

ERASMUS OF ROTTERDAM TO WILLIAM MOUNTJOY

Greetings, my best of patrons. I spent a couple of days with the abbot, and very cheerful days they were. He sent me away by no means empty-handed, with many kind promises of more to follow. In a word, all seemed set fair, when suddenly misfortune laid me low, showing that one should never trust things when they go well. Scarcely had I left an inn somewhere about half-way between Roeselare and Ghent when my horse was frightened at the sight of some linen sheets spread on the ground, and, as I bent over and was about to say something to my servant, the horse took fright again and shied in the opposite direction, twisting the base of my spine so severely that the sudden torment was unbearable and wrung cries of anguish from me. I tried to dismount. It was impossible. My servant took me in his arms and lowered me to the ground. The agony was indescribable, especially if I bent down. When I stood up, the pain was less, but once I bent over I was unable to straighten my back. There I was in the open country, not an inn except of the most cheerless and primitive kind, and six very long miles from Ghent. I felt my trouble somewhat relieved by walking, but the remaining distance was too great to be accomplished on foot even by a man in perfect health.

Imagine my feelings. I made a vow to St Paul that I would complete a commentary on his Epistle to the Romans if I should have the good fortune to escape from this peril. A little later, faced with despair, I was forced to try whether I could mount my horse. To my surprise I found I could. I set off at a slow walk – it was bearable. I told my servant to go rather faster – still bearable, though not without great pain. I reached Ghent, dismounted, and went to my room; there the pain returned in full force, especially if I remained motionless. Stand I could not, without two people to hold me up, one on either side, using considerable force; and if I relaxed even a little, the intolerable pain returned. Nor could I sit down, and if I lay down, I could not move at all. I sent for a physician and an apothecary. So overcome was I that I could think only of death.

In the morning, preparing to relieve nature, I made some effort to move myself in bed. It worked; I stood up, moved, sat down, all unsupported. I returned thanks to God and to St Paul. I could feel the trouble still there, especially if I turned my body. And so I stayed in Ghent several days, being detained by friends, and my trouble making this advisable, nor am I

* * * * *

301:2 abbot] Antoon van Bergen of the monastery of St Bertin in Saint-Omer. Cf Ep 143 introduction.

7 Roeselare] 51 km west-south-west of Ghent and 31 km south of Bruges

21 commentary] Cf Epp 164:41–2 and n; 296:166–8.

Anna van Bergen (1492–1541), wife of Adolph of Burgundy
The portrait is apparently contemporary, possibly a copy after Jan Mabuse.
Isabella Stewart Gardner Museum, Boston

yet free of the anxiety. Whatever it was, it was no ordinary affliction. Here I found the president of Flanders, a very well-read man, and two councillors, Antonius Clava and Willem van Waele; de Keysere and some others I knew before. I shall now go to Antwerp, if only the state of my health permits; and wherever I am, and wherever I may be, you shall hear how I am. Farewell.

The heer van Veere was at Bergen, and I paid my respects to him, together with his mother; but I found him preoccupied, for his wife was by no means well after childbirth and the news from Zeeland was not good. I gave him greetings from you, and pointed out what favourable treatment you had given to his dependants. I reached Basel after the Assumption.

* * * * *

38 president] Jean Le Sauvage, lord of Schaubeke (1455–1518), was a Flemish jurist who had been prominent since 1494 in the diplomatic dealings with France. In 1506 he was president of the Council of Flanders, and on the death in 1507 of the old chancellor Thomas de Plaine he became *chef et président du conseil privé*, a position equivalent to chancellor during the minority of Charles V. In 1509 he became chancellor of Brabant, in 1515 chancellor of Burgundy, and in 1516 chancellor of Castile. He accompanied Charles V to Spain in 1517 and died at Saragossa. He was a liberal patron of Erasmus (cf Ep 436) who dedicated to him a new edition of the *Institutio principis christiani* (Ep 393). Cf Ep 410.

39 Clava] Antonius Clava (Colve) was an alderman of Ghent and a close friend of Erasmus during his years in Louvain; cf Ep 175:13n. He was also a friend of the printer and scholar Robert de Keysere (see note below) and of Pieter Gillis, who dedicated to him Erasmus' *Epistolae elegantes* (Louvain: Martens April 1517; NK 819). Erasmus' epitaph for Clava is printed by Reedijk (poem 129). See also Allen Ep 2260:39–47 for Erasmus' tribute to Clava in a letter of condolence to Gillis.

39 Waele] Willem van Waele, heer van Hansbeke and a prominent citizen of Ghent; see de Vocht CTL II 190, IV 524. On 4 June 1532 he was created a member of the Council of Flanders, succeeding his father and grandfather. He died in 1546.

39 Keysere] Robert de Keysere was a scholar and printer who had also been a schoolmaster at Ghent. He printed the first edition of Erasmus' *Concio de puero Iesu* on 1 September 1511 (NK 2887), and, according to the editor J.-C. Margolin, an edition of the *De ratione studii* at about the same time; see Reedijk introduction to poem 85; Ep 175 introduction; NK 2975; and ASD I-2 91–4. At this time he was about 44 years of age and was shortly, in 1517, to become tutor to Leopold of Austria. He was unsuccessful as a proponent of a university at Tournai, latterly through opposition from Louvain.

42 Veere] Adolph of Burgundy, heer van Veere, and his mother Anna van Borssele, vrouwe van Veere. Adolph was grandson and heir of Anthony of Burgundy, le Grand Bâtard (1421–1504): cf Ep 93 introduction. The child here referred to was Adolph's eldest son Maximilian.

46 dependants] At Tournehem; cf Ep 266:5n.

Germany has given me such a distinguished reception that I was almost embarrassed. Now I am shut up in these German hot-houses, seeing my wretched stuff through the press, and no less at sea in this business than ever Caesar was in his conquest of the Veneti. I will return to you just as soon as ever I can. God send I find you all safe and sound.

Basel, 30 August [1515]

302 / From Jakob Wimpfeling — Strasbourg, 1 September 1514

This letter was written in the name of the literary society – the *sodalitas literaria* – of Strasbourg, after Erasmus had departed from the city for Basel, where he arrived apparently about mid-August. In the surviving correspondence this is the first record of Erasmus' visit to Strasbourg on this occasion. He there received a great deal of flattering attention, and his journey to Basel to oversee the publication of the *Adagia* took on something of the character of a triumphal progress. The Strasbourg printer, Matthias Schürer, had already reprinted some of Erasmus' works, including the *De copia* (Strasbourg January 1513), and a prefatory address in this edition hailed Erasmus as a hero of German letters. Erasmus probably entrusted the first edition of the *Parabolae* (October 1514) and a revised edition of the *Moriae encomium* (November 1514) to Schürer at this time. Farther up the Rhine, at Sélestat, Erasmus was equally well received by the literary community there, while the master of the famous town school, Johann Witz, called Sapidus (cf Ep 323 introduction), accompanied Erasmus as he continued his journey to Basel (Ep 305:182–4). This evidence for the strength of Erasmus' reputation among the scholars and reformers of the Upper Rhine was an auspicious introduction to the scholarly community at Basel itself, the cultural capital of the region. See Gerhard Ritter *Erasmus und der deutsche Humanistenkreis am Oberrhein. Eine Gedenkrede*, with appendix by Josef Rest 'Die Erasmusdrücke der Freiburger Universitätsbibliothek' (Freiburg 1937); E.W. Kohls 'Erasmus und sein Freundkreis am Oberrhein' in *Hommages à Marie Delcourt* (Brussels 1970) 269–78; James Tracy 'Erasmus Becomes a German' *Renaissance Quarterly* 21, 3 (1968) 281–8.

* * * * *

47 Germany] Cf Epp 302, 305; preface xii–xiii.

50 Caesar] In his *De bello Gallico* 3.9.4 Caesar describes his difficulties in the tidal creeks (*aestuaria*) of the Veneti on the Atlantic coast. There may be a punning allusion here to Maximilian's war against Venice in the League of Cambrai and the subsequent complications through Julius II's withdrawal to form the Holy League (1511). But *aestus* means 'heat' as well as 'tide,' and Erasmus' *aestuaria* are also the rooms heated by the German stoves he so much disliked; cf Ep 360:2–4.

For Wimpfeling see Ep 224 introduction; together with Sebastian Brant he founded the *sodalitas literaria* in Strasbourg in 1510. Cf P.A. Wiskowatoff *Jacob Wimpfeling* (Berlin 1867); Charles Schmidt *Histoire littéraire de l'Alsace* (Paris 1879; repr Nieuwkoop 1966) I 1–188; Joseph Lefftz *Die gelehrten und literarischen Gesellschaften im Elsass vor 1870* (Heidelberg 1931); and Otto Herding, 'Erasme et Wimpfeling,' a communication delivered to the *colloque* organized by the university of Strasbourg, 20 November 1970, and printed in *Erasme, l'Alsace et son temps* Série 'Recherches et Documents' VIII (Strasbourg 1971).

The best text of this letter and of Erasmus' answer (Ep 305) is found in Gouda MS 1323 f 24^{v} and 25; see Allen I app IX. They were first printed in Schürer's edition of the *De copia* of December 1514.

TO DESIDERIUS ERASMUS FROM JAKOB WIMPFELING

A nag scarcely fit to ride is sometimes loaded with boxes and bundles, and I, who am getting on in years and not really the man for it, have been charged by the literary society of Strasbourg with the duty of greeting you on behalf of us all, of sending you our best wishes, and of urging you to write without delay and tell us how things are with you. We suppose that you will have had a kindly welcome from the literary society of Basel, and are being hospitably entertained as a great scholar among your lesser kindred. In particular, we hope that in that society of philosophers you will be denied nothing that you need for a pleasant life by Beatus Rhenanus, who is in any case your great admirer and your faithful servant.

Our society as a body presents its compliments to you and offers its devoted services, if there is anything it can do for you: Sebastian Brant,

* * * * *

302:4 literary society of Strasbourg] Beatus Rhenanus at the same period listed as members of the society: Ottmar Nachtigall, Sebastian Brant, Nikolaus Gerbel, Hieronymus Gebwiler, Jakob Sturm, Johannes Rudolfinger, Thomas Rapp, Johann Guida, Stefan Tieler, and Matthias Schürer. See BRE Ep 54, Rhenanus to Ottmar Nachtigall, 31 December 1515.

7 literary society of Basel] *gymnasio*: The printing firm of Froben and Amerbach was itself a great focus of intellectual activity in Basel, bringing together such scholars as Beatus Rhenanus, Heinrich Loriti (called Glareanus, as a native of canton Glarus), Wolfgang Capito, Ludwig Baer, and Bruno Amerbach, son of the firm's founder; see E. Hilgert 'Johann Froben and the Basel university scholars 1513–1523' *The Library Quarterly* 41 (April 1971) 141–69.

13 Brant] Sebastian Brant (c 1458–1521) of Strasbourg, author of the famous *Narrenschiff* (Basel 1494), was a student with Reuchlin at the university of Basel, where he later (in 1492) became dean of the faculty of law. In 1501 he returned to his native Strasbourg. See Schmidt I 189–333; NDB. On his relations with Reuchlin see E.H. Zeydel 'Johann Reuchlin and Sebastian Brant: a study in early German humanism' *Studies in Philology* 67 (April 1970) 117–38.

Sebastian Brant
Albrecht Dürer
Staatliche Museen Preussischer Kulturbesitz
Kupferstichkabinett, Berlin

Jakob Sturm, Thomas Rapp, Thomas Vogler, Matthias Schürer, Johannes Rudolfinger, Stefan Tieler, Petrus Heldungus, Johann Guida, Hieronymus Gebwiler, Johann Ruser, Ottmar, and all the others whose names it would take too long to set down – not least myself. Farewell.

Strasbourg, 1 September 1514

* * * * *

14 Sturm] Jakob Sturm von Sturmeck (1489–1553), of an old and wealthy family in Strasbourg, was both a kinsman and pupil of Wimpfeling. He had studied at Heidelberg from 1501–4 and then at Freiburg under Zasius. As a diplomat and later as a member of the Council of Strasbourg he played an important part in the politics of the Reformation. Bopp 5160.

14 Rapp] Thomas Rapp was vicar of Strasbourg cathedral and a friend of Beatus Rhenanus, whose edition of Seneca's *Ludus de morte Claudii Caesaris* and of Erasmus' *Moriae encomium* (Basel: Froben 1515) was dedicated to him. He helped to obtain a manuscript of Tertullian for Beatus' edition of 1521. See BRE Epp 44, 179, and 207.

14 Vogler] Thomas Vogler ('Aucuparius') of Obernai, who died on 4 March 1532. He was almoner of Strasbourg cathedral after 1501, and editor of some unpublished writings of Poggio and of a Terence for schools. In 1524 he was nominated by the citizens of Strasbourg for a committee of the bishop to participate in a colloquy with the Reformers, and he apparently spent his last years in the convent of Stephansfeld, near Strasbourg. Cf Schmidt II 149–54.

14 Schürer] Matthias Schürer of Sélestat; cf Ep 224:49; Ritter 160–70.

15 Rudolfinger] Johannes Rudolfinger was vicar of Strasbourg cathedral, to which he presented a collection of MSS in 1505. He was well known as a musician and as a friend and patron of the learned community in Strasbourg; cf Allen III xxv. The name may indicate a connection with the village of Rudolfingen in canton Zurich, but there was no noble family to justify the appelation 'von Rudolfingen' applied by nineteenth-century historians.

15 Tieler] Little is known of Stefan Tieler, who is mentioned also in the list of members of this society by Beatus Rhenanus; cf note to line 4 above.

15 Heldungus] Petrus Heldungus (c 1486–1561) of Obernai, a layman, became steward to the cathedral chapter of Strasbourg.

15 Guida] Johann Guida of Sélestat was a pupil of Wimpfeling, whom he assisted in the production of Aeneas Sylvius' *Germania* (Strasbourg: Beck 16 June 1515). He appears in the *Epistolae obscurorum virorum* as a defender of good learning.

16 Gebwiler] Hieronymus Gebwiler (c 1473–21 June 1545) of Horburg near Colmar. He received his BA at Paris and then matriculated at Basel (1492) where he studied with Brant. He subsequently returned to Paris for his MA (1495). He embarked on a career as a schoolmaster and in 1501 became master of the famous school at Sélestat, where his pupils included Bonifacius Amerbach, Beatus Rhenanus, and Johann Witz. In 1509 the humanist party in Strasbourg persuaded the cathedral chapter to appoint Gebwiler as director of the cathedral school, after attempts to persuade the *magistrat* to start a gymnasium or Latin school had failed. Like Thomas Vogler (see note to line 14) he

303 / From Udalricus Zasius Freiburg im Breisgau, 7 September 1514

This distinguished teacher and scholar (1461–1535) was born at Constance and matriculated at Tübingen on 27 April 1481. His early career was divided between the practice and study of law and schoolmastering, but legal studies carried the day, and he became a DCL of Freiburg at the turn of the century. In 1508 he was named an imperial councillor, and for almost thirty years, until his death, he held a chair of civil law at Freiburg. His *Lucubrationes aliquot*, published by Froben in 1518 and introduced by Erasmus (cf Ep 862), was the first contribution of German scholarship to the humanistic revival of jurisprudence. His teaching was highly influential: see Erik Wolf *Grosse Rechtsdenker der deutschen Geistesgeschichte* 3rd ed (Tübingen 1951); G. Kisch *Erasmus und die Jurisprudenz seiner Zeit* (Basel 1960); Hans Thieme 'Les leçons de Zasius' and 'L'œuvre juridique de Zasius' in *Pédagogues et Juristes*, Congrès du Centre d'Etudes Supérieures de la Renaissance de Tours: Eté 1960 (Paris 1963); Pierre Mesnard 'Zasius et la Réforme' *Archiv für Reformationsgeschichte* 52, 2 (1961) 145–61. Among Zasius' pupils were Basilius, Bonifacius, and Bruno Amerbach, sons of the Basel printer, Lukas Klett, Onuphrius, son to Sebastian Brant, Urbanus Regius, and Jakob Sturm. See Hans Winterberg *Die Schüler von Ulrich Zasius* (Stuttgart 1961).

Respectful greetings. I thought I had summoned up sufficient effrontery,

* * * * *

was among the scholars nominated for the bishop's conference with the reform party in 1524: see Schmidt II 167. In the same year, after the attempt at reconciliation failed, he moved to the school at Haguenau, where he later died.

302:16 Ruser] Johann Ruser of Ebersheimmünster, who worked for the press of Matthias Schürer of Sélestat. He was a friend of Beatus Rhenanus, who dedicated to him an edition of Pliny's letters (Sélestat: Schürer February 1514). He became a priest of the order of St John and died in their house at Sélestat on 28 October 1518.

16 Ottmar] Ottmar Nachtigall of Strasbourg (c 1487–1537) was a pupil of Wimpfeling who studied at Paris about 1508 under Publio Fausto Andrelini and Girolamo Aleandro. His travels took him as far as Hungary, Greece, and Asia Minor. In 1510 he returned to Augsburg, and in 1514 to Strasbourg where he shortly became organist and vicar of St Thomas' church. He was the first to teach Greek at Strasbourg and his publications included books on music and law. With the advent of the Reform he withdrew to Augsburg and eventually died in the charterhouse in Freiburg. Cf Schmidt II 174–208. He wrote a preface to a 1523 Augsburg reprint of the *Colloquia*; cf *Bibliotheca Erasmiana* (Ghent 1897) I 133.

303:1 effrontery] *Adagia* I viii 47

great Rotterdam, to write you at least a brief letter, but was held back by increasing awe at the thought of your more than human learning, which rose before my eyes and sapped my courage. How could one like myself, who have never undergone proper initiation into any subject, dare to set my unhallowed foot within your sacred precincts? But I took heart from the encouragement of that excellent young man Bonifacius, who speaks continually of your exceptional kindness, and have written you these rustic lines, only begging you to enrol me not among your immediate disciples (of such an honour I count myself not worthy), but at least among the menials of your household. Your footman, hall-porter, sweeper, swabber, broomsman I will gladly be, and turn up my nose at nothing that falls from your table, if I may have leave to sweep before your door.

Farewell, glory of the world, and not the German world alone, for you are the shining light of all living men. The civil law is my profession, and I am engaged on sundry modest pieces in defence of true interpretations against the accepted opinions of other men, in which I make mention of your name as of a god among mortals. Farewell once more.

Freiburg, 7 September 1514

Your sincere admirer Udalricus Zasius, doctor and professor of law in the university of Freiburg

304 / From Maarten van Dorp Louvain, [c September 1514]

The friendly but cautionary warnings of Dorp (1485–1525) introduce an exchange of opinions that tells us much about the attitudes both of Erasmus and of his critics to the *Praise of Folly* and to his edition of the New Testament yet to come. Dorp was a graduate of Louvain and professor of philosophy in the Collège du Lys. He later completed his doctorate in theology and in 1523 became rector of the university. He acted at this time to advise Erasmus of the objections of the theologians of the university, and, despite clear differences of opinion, their relations remained friendly. On Dorp's death Erasmus wrote an epitaph for him. See Erasmus' important reply to this letter Ep 337 (May 1515); cf Pierre Mesnard 'Humanisme et théologie dans la controverse entre Erasme et Dorpius' *Filosofia* Anno XIV, Suppl. al fascicolo IV (November 1963) 885–900. The text of this letter was first published with Ep 337 in Marten's reprint of Erasmus' *Enarratio in primum psalmum* (October 1515; NK 814), and

* * * * *

7 Bonifacius] Amerbach; cf Epp 307:59n, 408 introduction.

10 not worthy] Virgil *Aeneid* 1.335

16 sundry modest pieces] His *Intellectuum singularium libri II* (*Opera* V), first published by Cratander at Basel in January 1526

later by Bade (again with Ep 337) in his printing of the *Moriae encomium* (June 1524), but the best text is in Gouda MS 1324 f 51v (see Allen I app IX).

MAARTEN VAN DORP TO ERASMUS OF ROTTERDAM, DOCTOR OF DIVINITY AND LEARNED IN MANY FIELDS

You must not think, my dear Erasmus – to the bare name I need add nothing, for it has now become synonymous with scholarship and high standards – you must not think, I repeat, that among all your friends whom your universal learning and your friendly sincerity have secured for you in such numbers in almost the whole of Christendom there is anyone who feels a more sincere affection for you than myself, first because we have known each other well for a long time, and second because of late, since you have been here, you have most kindly given instructions for me to be invited almost by myself; last but by no means least because I am your fellow-countryman too, not to say a very great admirer of your gifts and a promoter of your reputation second to none. And so anything I write to you, however outspokenly, comes – you must please remember – from one who is your devoted friend, and its object is to take steps to preserve your name and fame. I think you ought to know how people feel about you in your absence.

The first thing you should know is that your *Folly* has aroused a good deal of feeling, and that too among your oldest and most faithful supporters. Who would not be a sincere supporter of a man whose mind the Muses have chosen as a favourite haunt, and philosophy and theology the same? Although there were some people, and still are, who made vigorous excuses for it, yet those who approved it at all points were very few indeed. It is all very well, they say; but even if what he says were perfect truth, surely it is madness to wear oneself out with the sole purpose of making oneself unpopular. Surely it would be folly to act a play, however well written, which no one could see without taking offence, and by which many people are very greatly offended? Then take the faculty of theology, for which it is so important to retain the respect of common folk; what good did it do, indeed how much harm it will do, to attack it so bitterly, however much we may grant at the same time that what you said about some individuals is the truth. And then Christ, and the life in Heaven – can the ears of a good Christian endure to hear foolishness ascribed to him, while life in Heaven, it says, is likely to be nothing but a form of lunacy? We know that it is not

* * * * *

304:9 for a long time] Cf Ep 337:8–9; perhaps in the Low Countries 1502–4.

25 madness] Sallust *Jugurtha* 3.3

33 ascribed to him] LB IV 498A

34 lunacy] LB IV 500A

only what is false that is a stone of stumbling, but anything that may prove a cause of undoing for the weaker brethren for whom, no less than for great wits, Christ laid down his life. Many things of the sort have been condemned in the majority of councils, although in other respects they were perfectly true (as was clear at the Council of Constance); we have the authority of the famous doctor Jean Gerson. For my part, dearest Erasmus, the way I have answered these arguments would take too long to tell; at least I have never held my peace, I have never let things pass, because I thought it in your interests to watch in all prudence, not only what is said of you by people who may not be gifted but are free of malice, but also the outpourings of the lowest class of men, that it might be refuted either by your friends who are here or by you in writing if you are far away.

And please do not take refuge in asking 'What business is it of mine what objections are raised by these illiterate and barbarous busybodies? My conscience is clear: enough for me that I and what I write should enjoy the approval of all the best scholars, although they may be fewer than those who condemn me.' What has prevented even men of small learning, not to say barbarians, from admiring your scholarship and praising you to the skies, as they used zealously to do before? What gain can there be – surely there is a great loss – if those same people eat their words, if they say hard things about you and accuse you falsely and, turning against you one and all, do their best to obscure your reputation? Astringent pleasantries, even when there is much truth mingled with them, leave a bitter taste behind. In the old days everyone admired you, they all read you eagerly, our leading theologians and lawyers longed to have you here in person; and now, lo and behold, this wretched Folly, like Davus, has upset everything. Your style, your fancy, and your wit they like; your mockery they do not like at all, not even those of them who are bred in the humanities. And that is the point, Erasmus my most learned friend: I cannot see what you mean by wishing to please only those who are steeped in humane studies. Is it not better to be approved rather than rejected, even by rustic readers? We like it, surely, if even a dog wags his tail at us as a sign of friendship. But (you will say) that you should be a good man and do what is right – that is within your responsibility; that other men should think well of you and never speak against you is not in your power to secure. And so like Christ you spurn the

* * * * *

40 Gerson] The early editions of this letter (which Allen prints from Gouda MS 1324 f51v) run, 'as the famous doctor Gerson asserts of the Council of Constance.'

52–3 to the skies] *Adagia* I v 100

56 astringent pleasantries] Tacitus *Annals* 15.68.4

60 Davus] Terence *Andria* 663

Pharisees as moved by ill will, the blind leading the blind. I hear you saying that, Erasmus dearest of men. But those who condemn you and your work are only human; they do it from weakness and not wickedness – unless you think nothing but the humanities, not even philosophy or sacred study, can make a good man. They do it for good reason, not a reason they have simply picked up, but one they have been provided with by you, it seems, although it was in your power not to. 'And what, pray,' you will reply, 'am I to do? What's done cannot be undone. I wish I could change my policy, I wish that everyone who once thought well of me should do so once more.' O sweetest Erasmus, if only I could persuade you to think like that and to talk like that! A man of your active mind cannot fail to know what to do; not for me to tell you, like Minerva and the sow. But I hope, so far as I understand it, that the easiest way to put everything right will be to balance your *Folly* by writing and publishing a *Praise of Wisdom*. It is a prolific subject, worthy of your genius and your favourite studies, and will be delightful and universally popular; and it will bring you far more popular acclaim and friendship and good repute and (I might add) profit, even if you despise that, than your *Folly* which, as it seems, was so ill-judged. Whether you approve this idea or no, at least I am entirely devoted to you, and always shall be.

Now for the rest of what I had to say in this very long letter. I hear you have purged St Jerome's letters of the errors in which they abounded hitherto, killed off the spurious pieces with your critical dagger, and thrown light upon the dark places. This was a task worthy of you, which will earn the gratitude of all theologians, especially those who hope for a marriage between Christian literature and elegance of style. I understand that you have also revised the New Testament and written notes on over a thousand passages, to the great profit of theologians. This raises another point on which I should like in the friendliest possible spirit to issue a warning. In the first place I say nothing of the efforts of Lorenzo Valla and Jacques Lefèvre in the same field, for I do not doubt that you will surpass

* * * * *

70 blind] Cf Luke 6:39.

81 Minerva and the sow] Minerva taking lessons from a sow is the ancient equivalent of teaching your grandmother to suck eggs: *Adagia* I i 40.

91 St Jerome's letters] Cf Ep 296:162n.

96 New Testament] Cf Ep 296:164–6.

99 Valla] Cf Ep 182; presumably a reference in particular to his comparison of the Vulgate and Greek texts in his *Collatio Novi Testamenti* of 1444.

100 Lefèvre] His edition of the Epistles of St Paul (Paris: Estienne December 1512) from the Vulgate text carried emendations and a paraphrase which

them in every respect. But what sort of an operation this is, to correct the Scriptures, and in particular to correct the Latin copies by means of the Greek, requires careful thought. If I can show that the Latin version contains no admixture of falsehood or mistake, will not you have to confess that the labours of all those who try to correct it are superfluous, except for pointing out now and again places where the translator might have given the sense more fully? Now I differ from you on this question of truth and integrity, and claim that these are qualities of the Vulgate edition that we have in common use. For it is not reasonable that the whole church, which has always used this edition and still both approves and uses it, should for all these centuries have been wrong. Nor is it probable that all those holy Fathers should have been deceived, and all those saintly men who relied on this version when deciding the most difficult questions in general councils, defending and expounding the faith, and publishing canons to which even kings submitted their civil power. And that councils of this kind duly constituted never err, in so far as they deal with the faith, is generally agreed among both theologians and lawyers. If some new necessity should arise and require a new general council, this beyond doubt is the text it would follow whenever a knotty problem arose touching the faith. We must confess therefore either that the Fathers were ill-advised and will be ill-advised in the future if they follow this text and this version, or that truth and integrity are on its side. In any case, do you believe the Greek copies to be freer from error than the Latin? Had the Greeks any greater concern than the Latins for preserving the Scriptures undamaged, when you think of the blows Christianity has suffered among the Greeks, and how they firmly hold that everything except St John's Gospel contains some error (to say nothing for the moment on other points), while among the Latins the Bride of Christ, the church, has continued always inviolate? And how can you be sure you have lighted on correct copies, assuming that in fact you have found several, however readily I may grant that the Greeks may possess some copies which are correct?

These arguments move me, my dear Erasmus, not to set a very high value on the work of Lorenzo and Lefèvre; for I do not like to condemn

* * * * *

Lefèvre justified on the ground that the Vulgate text was not the work of Jerome: see E.F. Rice jr, ed *The Prefatory Epistles of Jacques Lefèvre d'Etaples and Related Texts* (New York 1972) Ep 96.

102–3 by means of the Greek] Dorp later retracted this objection in his *Oratio in praelectionem epistolarum divi Pauli* (Antwerp: M. Hillen van Hoochstraten 27 September 1519, NK 739; repr by Froben March 1520); cf Ep 438 introduction. He there asserted the need for a grasp of the languages and made clear his debt to Erasmus; cf Ep 1044 (28 November 1519).

outright anything that is not wholly bad. Nor do I see what they have contributed with all that labour, except that, whenever they point out, as I said, that the translator might have given the sense more fully, I gladly accept this also, when they note that the translator is affected by the Greek or has given a barbarous rendering. That the version could have been much more elegant is common knowledge. If however they contend that a sentence as rendered by the Latin translator varies in point of truth from the Greek manuscript, at that point I bid the Greeks goodbye and cleave to the Latins, for I cannot persuade myself that the Greek manuscripts are less corrupted than the Latin ones. You may say that Augustine tells us to fill our Latin water-channels from the Greek springs. Very true, in his own generation, when as yet no one Latin version had been adopted by the church and the Greek sources were not as corrupt as they probably are by now. But you will say 'I should not like you to change anything in your text, or to suppose that the Latin is in error; I merely display what I have found in the Greek manuscripts that differs from the Latin ones; and what harm will that do?' My dear Erasmus, it will do a great deal. For a great many people will discuss the integrity of the Scriptures, and many will have doubts about it, if the presence of the least scrap of falsehood in them becomes known, I will not say from your work, but simply from some man they have heard holding forth. Then we shall see what Augustine writes in a letter to Jerome: 'If falsehoods were admitted into Holy Scripture even to serve a useful purpose, what authority can they still retain?'

All this has moved me, dearest Erasmus, to beg and beseech you in the name of our mutual friendship, which you preserve when you are far away, and by your natural courtesy and friendly frankness, to emend only those passages in the New Testament where you can retain the sense and substitute something that gives the meaning more fully; or if your note says that the sense simply must be changed, to answer these arguments in your preface.

This is a long and foolish letter, but you cannot be sorry to get it, for it comes from one who is very fond of you. Dirk van Aalst the printer, who printed your *Enchiridion* and *Panegyricus*, has asked me to remember him to

* * * * *

144 Greek springs] This precise reference has not been traced: cf *De civitate Dei* 8.10; Augustine *Epistulae* 118.10.

154 Augustine] Ep 28.3.4; PL 33:113

165 Dirk van Aalst] This is Dirk or Thierry Martens; cf Ep 263:10n. He published the *Enchiridion* first in the *Lucubratiunculae* of 15 February 1503, and reprinted it on 6 November 1509 (NK 836); cf Ep 164 introduction. He printed the *Gratulatorius panegyricus ad Philippum Archiducem Austriae* (NK 837) in 1504; cf Ep 179.

you. He wanted very much to see you, and indeed to entertain you in a friendly and hospitable fashion, and set off to Antwerp for the purpose; when he heard you were not there, but at Louvain, he came straight back, and by travelling all night reached Louvain the next day about an hour and a half after you had gone. If there is anything he can do for you, he makes every promise, and I doubt if there is a man anywhere who is more devoted to you. The Cato you corrected and entrusted to me he has printed very accurately, and I corrected the mistakes. I dedicated the work, as you told me to, to Jean de Nève, regent of the Collège du Lys, who is so much attached to you by this kindness that on your return you will be fully conscious of this. If you have anything to be published that you could dedicate to Meynard, abbot of Egmond, my patron, I know for certain that he will be delighted and will reward you generously. So I beg you earnestly to do this. He is a Hollander and the leading churchman in Holland, a well-read man, but more a man of religion than a scholar, although he has a great affection for all scholars; and he might be helpful to you in many ways, should it so fall out.

Farewell, very learned and to me very dear Erasmus. From Louvain

305 / To Jakob Wimpfeling — Basel, 21 September 1514

Erasmus' lengthy reply to Ep 302, which contains careful courtesies directed to each member of the circle that had welcomed him in Strasbourg, is indicative of the importance he attached to the recognition of his 'fellow Germans.' The best text of the letter is that of the Gouda MS 1323 f 25; cf Ep 302 introduction. This letter was first printed, like Ep 302, in Schürer's *De copia* (December 1514).

DESIDERIUS ERASMUS TO JAKOB WIMPFELING GREETING, AS FROM ONE GERMAN TO ANOTHER, FROM THEOLOGIAN TO THEOLOGIAN, AND TO A MAN WITH GREAT KNOWLEDGE OF THE HUMANITIES FROM ONE THAT THIRSTS FOR THEM

What is this, my dear Wimpfeling? You call it putting pack-saddles on the

* * * * *

169 not there] Erasmus had gone from Ghent to Bergen; cf Ep 301:42.

173 Cato] Cf Ep 298.

175 Nève] Cf Ep 298 introduction.

178 Meynard] Meynard Man (d 1526) was thirty-sixth abbot of Egmond, near Alkmaar, from 1509 until his death. Dorp was indebted to him for a benefice. He received the praise of several humanists from the Low Countries: see de Vocht *Literae* passim, and de Vocht CTL I 490.

305:5 pack-saddles on the ox] Proverbial for entrusting work to the wrong man; *Adagia* II ix 84

ox if you of all men are given the task of writing to me? Now I should have thought that was clearly, as the Greeks put it, to bid the horsemen scour the plain. On whose shoulders could that burden more fitly have rested? And your Strasbourg literary society, as you call it – and as courteous as it is literary – to what better person could they entrust this duty than to Wimpfeling, the unquestioned leader of the humanities in his own city and a champion of all sound learning? I should not have allowed you to pay me the courtesy of writing first, had not this labour of revising and enlarging the annotations which I have written on the New Testament kept me so completely tied down, so chained to the treadmill, that I scarcely have time for meals. Your friend Erasmus is not too insensitive to appreciate this unheard-of kindness, nor so forgetful that he has no memory of it, not such a boor that he tries to conceal it, or too ungrateful to try and answer it to the best of his ability. For whenever I recall that well-attended gathering of excellent scholars, how they welcomed me, an unknown guest, with (as they say) open arms, the exceptionally delightful society with which they relieved my weariness, the kindness with which they looked after me, the warm feelings with which they surrounded one of their own kindred, the modesty and friendliness of the respectful reception they gave even to a creature like myself who cannot aspire to mediocrity, the honourable and almost onerous attentions they lavished on me, and the hospitable feelings with which they took leave of me and politely saw me on my way – all these fill me with a kind of embarrassment, knowing as I do how little my modest gifts measure up to such lavish hospitality and, as Persius puts it, 'how scant the gear I have at home.' Yet at the same time I share the joy of our native Germany which has borne and bred up so many and such excellent men, not merely outstanding in every branch of knowledge but distinguished no less by high character and high simplicity.

In fact I reflect with a certain self-satisfaction (for why should I not unburden myself of my feelings privately to you?) on the thought that men who enjoy universal approbation should have, I will not say given me their approval, but at least not disapproved of me. For I have not yet sufficient effrontery to accept as my due the tributes which you offer me. And yet I think there is something to be said for your praise of me, which I at least interpret as intended to spur me on in idle moments, to rouse my courage in

* * * * *

7–8 scour the plain] To tell someone to do what he is good at; *Adagia* I viii 82

21 open arms] *Adagia* II ix 54

29 Persius] 4.52 (a very favourite quotation)

38 effrontery] Cf Ep 303:1n.

moments of despondency, or to equip your poor ill-found friend and furnish him forth from your own stores, as though it were right that friends should hold not money alone but reputation in common. Such men are too well educated to make a mistake, too friendly to play a trick on me, too honourable to flatter, and too much the true German to pretend. I would say that you were misled by affection, were not your very affection for me the offspring of judgment; you did not owe this opinion of me to excessive affection for me, you conceived the affection because you judged I was that kind of man. I only wish I could claim some right to enjoy your favourable judgment too; there is no tribute I would value more than approval by the votes of such men. But the debt I owe you for your kind words is all the greater, the less I deserve them; for praise well and truly earned is sometimes conceded even between enemies. The principal reason for my gratitude must be that your gift was quite unsolicited. But enough! Did you mean to spur on the idler? Thank you for your enthusiasm. To rouse the pedant to higher things? Thank you for your kindness. To adorn the naked crow with your own plumage? Thank you for your generosity. If it was some warmth of affection for me that made me seem the man you think me, I owe a still greater debt for such good will; if I do possess any of the qualities you credit me with, I am your debtor for such frank recognition of them.

Again, I am well aware that I owe it to you, if the two distinguished magistrates at the head of the city of Strasbourg, who gave me such a warm welcome when I was with you and treated me with no common respect, honour me with their good wishes now that I am absent and indeed far away. You say it is impossible that they should ever forget me; say, rather, that I myself shall never cease to remember those truly noble characters and to sing their praises in conversation and in print to the utmost of my power; for, my life upon it, never did I find greater kindness or see anyone more richly endowed with all the virtues. Believe me, my dear Wimpfeling, no words of mine – still less, a letter – could do justice to the happiness I felt, or the pleasure I took in what I saw. There was the image of one of those cities we read of in the ancient philosophers, with its noble citizens displaying at first glance (as they say) and in their whole deportment exceptional wisdom, complete integrity, and almost a kind of majesty, tempered however

* * * * *

45 German] Cf Ep 269:43.

57 crow] From an Aesopic fable, eg Babrius 72; cf *Adagia* III vi 91.

63 magistrates] Cf line 128n.

74 at first glance] *Adagia* I ix 88

with admirable discretion. Agamemnon in Homer thinks he would be fortunate to have ten counsellors like Nestor. How many times more blessed his imperial majesty Maximilian, who possesses in one community so many Nestors – or rather, men like Scipio and Cato, or anything wiser and more upright than they. As I watched their serious demeanour, I seemed to see those ancient senators of the Areopagus; their integrity recalled Aristides; their calm and regulated behaviour was pure Fabius. Again, when I considered the sober neatness, the neat frugality, of their dress and way of life, an image of the early Lacedaemonians rose before my mind. Finally, as I watched the admirable balance with which in turn their strictness was rendered agreeable by obliging manners and their friendliness ennobled by a touch of severity, there came into my head that famous city-state of ancient Massylia, which is said to have achieved a wonderful balance between Roman severity and Greek refinement, and to have enjoyed institutions of such a kind that from this one city examples of every civic virtue could be derived.

It was possible, when I was with you, to see in one city the virtues of all the most celebrated city-states: Roman severity, Athenian wisdom, and the self-restraint of Lacedaemon. I was especially delighted by the remarkable harmony of different qualities, as very different notes make a single harmonious chord. I saw there so many men old but not peevish, well-born but not proud, influential but not conceited, commonalty adorned with all the virtues of distinguished nobility, a great throng of men but no crowd. And I saw the rule of one man without tyranny, aristocracy without faction, democracy without civil strife, wealth without self-indulgence, success without insolence. What could be imagined more blessed than such a harmony? O divine Plato, how I wish that you had had the good fortune to light upon a city-state like this! Here, if anywhere, you might have installed your ideal and truly happy commonwealth. St Jerome, in that most spirited and yet most learned letter that he wrote to Gerontia on monogamy, men-

* * * * *

76 Homer] *Iliad* 2.371–2

81–2 Aristides] The Athenian politician of the fifth century BC, known as 'the Just'

82 Fabius] Quintus Fabius Maximus Cunctator, the Roman general in the second Punic war, who became proverbial for 'slow but sure'

88 Massylia] The modern Marseille; *Adagia* II iii 98

105 letter] Jerome Ep 123 in CSEL 56 72–95. The letter is the eleventh in Erasmus' edition of 1516 (vol I, folios 41–4) and the reference to Strasbourg ('Argentoracum') is at folio 44A (CSEL 56 92). Erasmus' scholia complimenting the city are at folio 40D.

tions your famous city, which shows that it was already celebrated long ago, and deplores its destruction by the barbarians. What if he could see it now? – one city watered by three rivers, nobly fortified, flourishing rich and populous; above all, distinguished by such admirable institutions and governed by such admirable leaders. Surely he would change its name and call it Aurata instead of Argentoracum, a city not of silver but of gold. Besides which, it has enjoyed for so long the blessings of peace, untouched by sack, untouched by the raging tumults of war which for some years now have thrown almost the whole world into confusion. And in Maximilian it is blest with the mildest of princes, whose power it never feels except when it receives some benefit from his wisdom and generosity. And here we have a noble quality, worthy only of a truly great emperor; for as this world of ours experiences the power of God in no other way than through his goodness towards it, so the noblest empire is the one which protects instead of oppressing the liberty of its citizens, which fosters instead of driving away its people's wealth, and makes all things flourish. Such is the rule of the supreme deity over the world, such the rule of the spirit over the body, always beneficial, hurtful never.

But there will be another opportunity to speak of these things more fully and in greater detail. My letter has long been demanding to be brought to a close; I hear the call of my interrupted labours. And so pray give my greetings in return to those leading citizens who are so distinguished and have been so kind to me, especially his worship Heinrich Ingolt, burgomaster of the city of Strasbourg, and the other members of that most civilized council; and should there be any service that my devotion, my writing, or my industry can render them, you may boldly promise it all on my behalf. Next, I beg you to return greetings in my name with especial care to your most elegant society, that company of all the Muses and the Graces, and particularly to that incomparable young man Jakob Sturm, who adds lustre to his distinguished family by his own high character, crowns his youth with a seriousness worthy of riper years, and gives great charm to uncommon learning by his incredible modesty. Then Thomas Rapp, whose glance and expression suffice by themselves to show his charming open-hearted character. Thomas Vogler too, whom I would think worthy of the laurel wreath, if for no other reason, because he is so very far from any kind of conceit, the besetting sin of men of his profession. Much as I value him, it is

* * * * *

128 Ingolt] Ingolt (d 1523) was in 1491 a member of the town council of Strasbourg, and Ammeister in 1509 and 1514.

134 Sturm] Cf Ep 302:14n, as to subsequent notes there for other members of the literary society mentioned here by Erasmus.

Jakob Sturm
Portrait drawing
Cabinet des Estampes, Strasbourg

his own doing that I must moderate my praises, for he has praised me in one of his poems, without much truth perhaps but with great affection, and we must avoid the old taunt that one mule knows how to scratch another. Besides, there is Matthias Schürer, a man to whom I am much attached on many other grounds, but still more as a son of Sélestat, that town so fertile in learned and gifted men to which I owe also Beatus Rhenanus and Johann Witz and Wimpfeling himself. And so, were I not deeply attached to Matthias, I should rightly be accused of having iron and adamant where my heart should be, such was his initiative in offering by acts of kindness to become my friend. Nor will I so act as to fall short in spirit at least and in readiness, although it was he who began it; one day I will repay what he has done for me, if only my spirit is matched by my capacity.

Next, you must be most careful to greet Hieronymus Gebwiler, the most civilized person I ever met, who exalted me to the skies with compliments which were very eloquent but also, if I may speak frankly, as one German to another, highly misleading. And the magic of his eloquence so imposed upon me that I really thought I was somebody, and scarcely came to my senses after a couple of days and recognized what I was. Then Johannes Rudolfinger, that master of harmony not only in his music but in his character, a most cheerful and orderly man, who accompanied me with Hieronymus to my next night's lodging. Do not forget Ottmar, a man who seemed to me well read without ostentation, who with the rapid trilling on his pipes that outdid the very nightingale so ravished me that I seemed rapt in ecstasy. At the same time please greet that promising young man Johann Ruser, who seemed so much attached to me; also those elegant characters Stefan Tieler, Johann Guida, Petrus Heldungus, and (for I must make an end) all the rest; for, although their names have slipped my memory, the remembrance of them is inscribed in my inmost heart and always will be. Sebastian Brant is a man apart; I set him outside any classification and beyond all hazard. I think so highly of him, my dear Wimpfeling, I like and respect and venerate him so much, that it seems to add greatly to my happiness to have been allowed to see him face to face and converse with him.

And now, since you want to know how the rest of my journey went,

* * * * *

142–3 one of his poems] See line 267 below.

144 one mule] *Adagia* I vii 96

147 Rhenanus] Cf Ep 327 introduction.

147–8 Johann Witz] Cf Ep 323 introduction.

157 German] Cf line 45 above.

here is the story in few words. Your native town of Sélestat I reached successfully. There the town magistrates, hearing I know not how of my arrival, immediately sent me three flagons of really excellent wine as a present by the hand of the town crier, and such flagons as might hold up to ten two-gallon measures. They asked me to dinner next day, but I sent my excuses, for I was in a hurry to start on the work upon which I am now engaged. Johann Witz, your old pupil in the humanities, who is remarkably like you in character as well and loves and respects you like a father, came with me as far as Basel. There I had told him not to advertise my arrival, on the ground that I like few friends but rather special and select ones. So to begin with I saw no one except the men I really wanted to see: Beatus Rhenanus, whose unassuming wisdom and keen literary judgment are a great pleasure to me, nor is there anything I enjoy more than his society every day; Gerard Lyster, a physician of no common skill and a good knowledge of Latin, Greek, and Hebrew besides, and a young man born to be my friend; the learned Bruno Amerbach, who also has the three tongues. I gave Johann Froben a letter from Erasmus, adding that I was very closely acquainted with him, that he had entrusted to me the whole business of publishing his work, and that whatever steps I took would have the same authority as if they had been taken by Erasmus himself; in fact, I said, Erasmus and I are so alike that if you have seen one, you have seen the other. He was delighted later on when he saw through the trick. Froben's father-in-law, after paying all that was owing in my inn, took me together

* * * * *

176 Sélestat] In acknowledgment of this hospitality Erasmus wrote a panegyric on Sélestat, printed in *Jani Damiani Senensis elegeia* (Froben August 1515); Reedijk poem 98. See also Ep 328 introduction.

189 Gerard Lyster] Lyster (c 1490–after 1522) came from the province of Utrecht, and studied at Louvain and Cologne. While studying medicine at Basel in 1514 he contributed some Greek verses to the title-page of Erasmus' translations from Plutarch. See Ep 495 introduction.

191 Amerbach] Cf Ep 331 introduction.

192 Froben] The printer who, on the death of Johannes Amerbach in 1513 took over his press in partnership with Amerbach's sons, to complete the great edition of Jerome in 1516. Cf Ep 419 introduction.

198 father-in-law] Wolfgang Lachner (c. 1465–1518) of Neuburg on the Danube, and long a bookseller and publisher in Basel. In his later years he was closely associated with Froben and managed the publishing branch of his printing business. His daughter Gertrude (d 1560) married Froben as his second wife in November 1510, and became the mother of Erasmius Froben. On Froben's death in 1527 she married Johann Herwagen who carried on the firm together with Froben's son Hieronymus (d 1563) and Nicholas Episcopius, her son-in-law. See AK I 221n.

with the horses and the baggage to stay in his house. A couple of days later the doctors of this university, through the dean of the faculty of theology and another man, invited me to supper next day. All the doctors of all the faculties, as they call them, were there. Ludwig Baer (Ursus, if you prefer it in Latin) was there too; he is rector of this university, a distinguished graduate in theology from Paris, a man still in the prime of life, but so well-read, of such high character and such wisdom, that I reckon he must bring no common distinction to his native Germany. For he is a native of Basel; and the city, which has other claims to fame, has also acquired lustre from the character and learning of Guillaume Cop, the new Hippocrates of our age, to such a degree that it need yield to none of the most famous cities. They were preparing to burden me with some kind action every day, had I not begged them to leave me to myself as I was now all ready for my programme of hard work. There has also come here on purpose to see me one Johannes Gallinarius, a man of wide learning with a character to match. And a poet laureate is here, Henricus Glareanus, who has an admirably frank and gay disposition and is a young man of high promise. I have had two or three letters from Udalricus Zasius, the well-known professor of civil law at Freiburg, in which I seem to detect a man who not only is learned and

* * * * *

200 dean] Moritz Fininger of Pappenheim in Franconia, an Austin friar, was dean for eight annual terms between 1502 and his death in 1520.

201 Baer] Ludwig Baer (1479–1554) was a theologian and friend of Erasmus who was born at Basel and studied theology at Paris (MA 1499). After obtaining his doctorate in theology (1512) he returned to Basel, where he joined the theology faculty. Through the favour of the bishop, Christoph von Utenheim, he also became provost of the collegiate church of St Peter. Cf Allen Ep 488.

208 Cop] The physician (c 1466–1532). Cf Epp 124:18n and 50:6n. Erasmus expressed gratitude for Cop's ministrations often, and he dedicated to him his important poem on growing old, *Carmen ad Gulielmum Copum medicorum eruditissimum de senectute* (August 1506); cf Reedijk 122 and poems 83, 131. Cop also treated Lefèvre d'Etaples (c 1505) and defended the cause of Reuchlin. His humanist learning was demonstrated in his translations of Greek medical classics.

213 Gallinarius] A kinsman of Wimpfeling, also known as Johann Henner, from Heidelberg. He matriculated at the university there in 1495 and received his MA. He was later involved in publishing in Strasbourg, where he was also a schoolmaster. He subsequently became a priest. Cf Schmidt passim. On his involvement with Wimpfeling in the production of the *Adolescentia* see Otto Herding ed *Jakob Wimpfelings Adolescentia* (Munich 1965) passim.

214 Glareanus] Heinrich Loriti of Mollis in canton Glarus matriculated at Cologne and Basel. Cf Ep 440 introduction.

216 letters] Ep 303 and, apparently, Ep 306

eloquent but has a rare sincerity of nature and uncommon wisdom. I hear that distinguished scholars are to be found in many places among the Germans, which makes me more and more charmed and attracted by my native Germany, so that I am ashamed and annoyed to have so long put off getting to know it. And so I can easily be induced to stay here for the winter until the middle of March; and then, when I have finished the business I want to do in Italy, I will return to you about the middle of May. And this I would do the more readily, if it should prove possible to get all my works out in these winter months with the same labour and lamp-oil, as the saying goes.

My *Adagia* has now begun to be printed. There remains the New Testament translated by me, with the Greek facing, and notes on it by me. Then the letters of St Jerome with the text corrected by me and the spurious and wrongly ascribed pieces removed, also with explanatory comments of mine. Besides those, all the works of Seneca the orator corrected by me with the greatest efforts; to which I shall perhaps add something in the way of notes if I can find the time. There are other small pieces as well, about which I am less concerned; and if the printer here will undertake them, I shall retire into myself like a tortoise, not to go to sleep but to be completely free for all this work. On my return from Italy, or so I hope, I shall take some days for paying my respects to the German princes and getting to know them. The real princes I consider to be not those who wear gold chains round their necks and decorate their chambers and their entrance-halls with paintings of their ancestors, but those who use the advantages which are genuine and are really theirs – learning, high character, eloquence – not merely to adorn their country and its citizens but to be some use to them. To Christoph, bishop of Basel, I have not yet delivered your letter, which contains, I can easily guess, nothing more than well-meant falsehoods about your friend Erasmus (you see how much I wish to court favour!); but to begin with he was not in the city, and now I am avoiding every engagement that might

* * * * *

221 native Germany] *mea Germania*; cf lines 45 and 157.

222 to stay here] On 24 September 1514 Bruno wrote to Bonifacius Amerbach: 'Dominus Erasmus apud nos hyematurus est.' See Ep 500:5–6 in AK II, where the date 21 September is accepted. Erasmus stayed until mid-March 1515 (cf Ep 332).

226 labour and lamp-oil] Cf *Adagia* I iv 62.

229 translated by me] This is the first mention of his intention to publish his Latin translation along with his Greek text and annotations; cf Ep 384 introduction.

243 Christoph] Christoph von Utenheim (c 1450–1527), a bishop of noble Alsatian birth, was strongly committed in favour of reform. Cf Ep 598 introduction.

take me away from my books. Will you not congratulate your poor friend on being, by grace of Juno and Ilithia, so successfully brought to bed? You have heard how productive I have become; I breed faster than a rabbit; and, what deserves your sympathy still more, I have also given birth, after most exhausting travail, to a stone. My dear Wimpfeling, may Lucina ever be equally gracious! What, you say, can you make a jest of anything so painful? Why less so than Socrates, who jested as he drank the hemlock, and died with a jest on his lips?

That really accomplished person, Johann Reuchlin, endowed as he is with such a range of literatures and languages that one might think he has more hearts than Ennius, in my opinion the supreme glory and shining light and ornament of the whole of Germany, is so far from here that it is hardly possible to converse with him in letters; and this I much regret. Johann Witz, since I saw that he could hardly be torn away from me, I have consoled with a quatrain; and to make the keepsake of more value to my admirer, or more truly to one who is head over heels in love with me, I have written it out with my own hand. Here it is. I send you also what I had written on the journey to that incomparable man Sebastian Brant; for I have changed a few words in it of no importance. I have added the nonsense I scribbled rather than wrote to Vogler. Beyond that, time and opportunity will one day produce the appropriate occasion for expressing my feelings towards the magistrates of the city of Strasbourg. Give my greetings to the venerable prior of the Hospital of St John, your friend and mine. Farewell, my honoured brother and most sincere friend.

Basel, 21 September 1514

* * * * *

249 Juno] Juno was the Roman, Ilithia a Greek goddess of childbirth; Lucina (line 252) was a cult-title of Juno as the same goddess.

258 Ennius] The early Latin poet, who said he had three hearts (the heart being the seat of the intelligence) because he could speak Greek, Oscan, and Latin (Aulus Gellius 17.17.1)

259 so far] Reuchlin was in Stuttgart; cf RE Epp 188ff.

262 quatrain] Reedijk poem 97

264–5 what I had written] Reedijk poem 95

267 Vogler] Reedijk poem 96

270 prior] Allen, following Ingold's edition of Grandidier *Ordres militaires et mélanges historiques* (Colmar 1900) 44, suggested that this might be Thomas Erber, shown as prior 1492–1539. Erber's name does not seem to appear in the correspondence of the *sodalitas literaria*, however, and it is notable that the commander of the Knights of St John in Strasbourg at this period (1511–32) was Balthasar Gerhard, who wished to establish a readership in theology and wrote to Wimpfeling in 1513 about the matter. Perhaps it was to Gerhard that Erasmus meant to refer, in a slip about his office, as 'amicus tuus et meus.'

306 / From Udalricus Zasius — Freiburg im Breisgau, 21 September 1514

Zasius' concern at Erasmus' evident failure to reply to Ep 303 suggests the intensity of his desire to make his acquaintance. For Erasmus' comment see Ep 307:10–14.

Respectful greetings. Although, great man that you are, – and great I will call you, since everything about you achieves the highest level of greatness – although, I repeat, I might have known that I did not deserve the privilege of interrupting you with my humble literary attainments, yet the love I bear towards great souls, and you especially, has urged me on to write. And so, since you remain silent and indeed may perhaps reject my letter as ill-digested, I felt the need to defend myself against any charge of temerity in approaching your precincts, unhallowed as I am. I beg you to believe that I have no object except to satisfy my own heart, which leaps up with desire at the mention of your name. I know what Vatinius wrote to Cicero: great men should not be approached except for suitably great reasons. If I have approached you for reasons so insignificant, my only purpose is to seek an outlet for the burning enthusiasm I feel for you. Farewell, great man and glory of the whole world.

Freiburg, 21 September 1514

Give my greetings on many grounds to Gerard, a man of solid learning. I hope that one day he and I shall live nearer and see more of one another.

Udalricus Zasius, doctor and professor of law

307 / To Udalricus Zasius — Basel, 23 September [1514]

This letter was first printed in the *Farrago* (1519), and an imperfect copy, possibly from the autograph, is in Clm 1470 f 199[r] in the Bayerische Staatsbibliothek, Munich; cf Ep 313 introduction.

ERASMUS OF ROTTERDAM TO UDALRICUS ZASIUS, DISTINGUISHED DOCTOR OF LAWS AND INCOMPARABLE GLORY OF GERMANY

The fame of your eminent learning and the eloquence that matches it have reached me lately through two men learned and eloquent themselves,

* * * * *

306:11 great reasons] A reminiscence of Vatinius' appeal to Cicero; cf *Epistulae ad familiares* 5.11.2.

16 Gerard] Gerard Lyster; cf Epp 305:189 and 495 introduction.

Beatus Rhenanus first and then Johannes Gallinarius. That you have no mean sense of humour I gather from your letters. First of all, a man of all-round endowments such as you are does not think it beneath him to offer his friendship in a most elegant letter to a nobody like myself, which is a piece of good fortune I would never have dared to hope for; and then in a second letter you beg that you may not be thought impertinent in writing, poor creature that you are, to such a great man. Let us have none of that exchange of compliments with which scholars in Italy habitually regale one another, and speak the honest simple truth as one German to another; I measure myself, as they say, by the length of my own foot, and know well 'how scant the gear I have at home,' so far am I from accepting the tributes which you offer me. But I do sincerely congratulate our native Germany which, having so long enjoyed great glory in the wars, is now distinguished everywhere by all these men of eminence in every field of learning, which is the truest and most enduring sort of glory. Greatly as I respect them all, as is only right, yet there is no one whose style attracts me more than yours, not only because it is so classical and free from all disfigurement, but because it reminds me so much of the delightful cadences of Poliziano, whose gifts I have always admired above any other man's. And while his style was Poliziano's great claim to fame, how much more should one admire such a thing in you, my dear Zasius, for in you what was supreme in him is an accessory, a mere addition.

And so I owe much both to Beatus and to Gallinarius, through whom I first came to know of you, but still more to you, whose most generous and elegant letters co-opt me into the number of your friends, which is a pleasure and an honour above anything that could happen. Nor should I have left you to take the first steps, had I not been so tied and bound to this treadmill that I scarcely have any time for meals. My volume of *Adagia* is being so much enriched that it might be thought a new book. Jerome is being got ready for the press with my summaries and notes. The New Testament is being prepared, revised, and expounded in my notes. The *Copia* is being published with my own revisions, and a volume of *Parallels*

* * * * *

307:6 Gallinarius] Cf Ep 305:213n.

14 German] Cf Epp 269:43; 305:45, 157, 221; 310:18.

15 my own foot] *Adagia* I vi 89

16 how scant the gear] Cf Ep 305:29.

23 Poliziano] Angelo Ambrogini of Montepulciano (1454–94), the eminent humanist to whom Erasmus often refers as an admired model of style

37 Parallels] The *Parabolae sive similia* (Strasbourg: Schürer 1514)

will follow it. Those works of Plutarch which I had translated are now printed. Anneus Seneca is also in hand, corrected with immense labour by myself. Since any one of these works is capable of absorbing an entire man, and no Erasmus either but a man of adamant, you can easily guess how little spare time I have. And so you must please forgive me, first if in return for your polished letters I send such an unfinished reply, truly giving bronze in exchange for gold; and after that, if in the future I seem to write to you more seldom or more briefly than you would wish. As soon as I have extricated myself to some extent from all these labours, it will be a pleasure to match my friend Zasius with full-scale volumes if he pleases.

Your plans for the exposition of the civil law will, I hope, receive the blessing of the Muses; you know, I expect, that Budé in Paris has attempted something of the kind, and Cuthbert Tunstall, chancellor to the archbishop of Canterbury, a man of great experience in both Greek and Latin, has made notes on innumerable passages. You say that you mention my name in your notes, and prepare to make me immortal; a great satisfaction it is to receive praise from a man whom all men praise. One thing I would beg of you, not to load my poor self in future with invidious titles that can only give small sneering men an excuse to laugh at me. Who would not laugh to see Erasmus called a great man, when he is the least of men in every way? and fortunate, although to Fortune I owe nothing? Pray be so good as to give my greetings to Bonifacius, a young man as modest as he is learned. My friend

* * * * *

38 Plutarch] A reference to the *Plutarchi opuscula* (Basel: Froben August 1514). Cf Epp 272, 297.

39 Seneca] Cf Ep 325 introduction.

44 gold] *Adagia* I ii 1

48 exposition] Cf Ep 303:16 and n.

49 Budé] *Annotationes in pandectarum libros* (Paris: J. Bade 17 November 1508); cf Ep 403 introduction.

50 Tunstall] If Tunstall (cf Ep 207:25n) ever composed such a work, it does not seem to have survived. He did compose a compendium of the Nicomachean Ethics (Paris: Vascosan 1554) and wrote the first treatise on arithmetic to be printed in England: *De arte supputandi* (London: Pynson 1522; STC 24319); it was dedicated to Thomas More. In 1518 Pynson published his *In laudem matrimonii oratio* (STC 24320), and in 1519 the work was brought out by Froben. His *De veritate corporis et sanguinis Domini nostri Jesu Christi in eucharistia* (Paris: Vascosan 1554) was written when he was imprisoned by the government of Edward VI; cf C. Sturge *Cuthbert Tunstal* (London 1938) app 26.

59 Bonifacius] Amerbach, who was studying law under Zasius; cf Ep 408 introduction.

Gerard Lyster returns your best wishes most sincerely; devoted to you as he is, he fully deserves the mutual affection which I know you feel for him. Very best wishes.

Basel, 23 September 1514

308 / To Gregor Reisch [Basel, September 1514]

Gregor Reisch (d 1525) of Balingen in Wurtemberg was a graduate of Freiburg in 1489 who became a Carthusian monk of the Mount of St John Baptist, near Freiburg. Johann Eck was one of his pupils there. Before that time he had composed his *Margarita philosophica* (Freiburg: J. Schott July 1503), a kind of encyclopedia for educational purposes with chapters on arithmetic and geometry. By 1510 he was Visitor of the Carthusians in the province of the Rhine, and he was confessor to Maximilian, to whose deathbed he was summoned in 1519. He seems to have been involved in work of a preparatory kind on the great edition of the letters of St Jerome planned by Johannes Amerbach; cf Ep 396; K. Hartfelder 'Der Karthäuserprior Gregor Reisch, Verfasser der *Margarita Philosophica*,' *Zeitschrift für die Geschichte des Oberrheins* ns 5 (1890) 170–200. The autograph original of this letter is MS G II 13^{a} 55 in the Öffentliche Bibliothek of the university of Basel.

Greetings, reverend Father. With very great effort I have been, and still am, trying to publish a correct text of St Jerome's letters, which are more corrupt than one can imagine or describe, although in my judgment Jerome is almost the only author who deserves to be universally read, at least among the theologians who wrote in Latin. I have decided on the following order. I shall place first what is really his; second, what is wrongly ascribed to Jerome, but none the less is worth reading. Third in order I shall append the spurious works which some witless and shameless rascal has fathered on him. I shall add reasons why these do not seem to me to be Jerome's. Two ends will thus be served: the reader will not be taken in by false ascriptions, nor will anyone interested in such crazy stuff fail to find in the volume what he wants. I have detected the pen of one worthless fellow, who made many additions to Augustine's works as well, for example the eremitical sermons, and foisted onto the works of Ambrose the sermon in which Ambrose congratulates Augustine on his baptism.

I see that you have the same feeling for this more than human author as I have, nor do I disapprove of your order, but I could not follow it myself without great labour, for I should have to undo everything. Besides which, my classification would disappear. A final argument: there are many letters

The figure of Grammar
From Gregor Reisch *Margarita philosophica* Basel 1508
Fisher Collection, John Robarts Library
University of Toronto

which in a different scheme of arrangement belong together; for Jerome himself gave instructions that the treatise he addressed to Nepotianus should be coupled with the one he wrote to Heliodorus. And so I shall follow the traditional order except for the spurious pieces, and to replace the order designed by you I shall construct a table to show both orders and provide the convenience of both. I have supplied introductions to the individual letters and notes, so that only moderately good scholars may be able to read him without stumbling. I have explained the allusions to Holy Scripture, those at least which might not be obvious to any student of theology.

I rejoice at the good fortune of this most saintly author, in that he begins to see the light of day after such scrupulous correction by those very scholarly young men the Amerbachs. You will be ready, I am sure, reverend Father, to allow me the use of any correct manuscript that you may possess, or any felicitous notes on individual passages.

In the letter to Heliodorus which begins *Quanto amore* there are various readings in the passage *cui nos morituros relinquis?* and what follows. Tell me, if it is not tiresome for you, what you think. In the letter to Rusticus beginning *Nihil christiano*, etc, I am much puzzled by the reference to the sons of Jonadab, of whom he says it is written in the Psalms that they were the first to suffer captivity. I find a mention of them in Jeremiah, but in the Psalms I do not remember anything. In the letter to Nepotianus beginning *Petis a me* I am much exercised by *Testudineo Grunnius incedebat gradu* for several lines, especially at *Hic bene nummatus*, etc. In the letter to Letha I am held up by the words *Quibus corax niphus miles.* I have made many conjectures, but cannot do everything. Again, in the same letter for *Cibus eius olusculum sit et simila caroque et pisciculi* I conjecture that we ought to read *Cibus eius olusculum et e simila garoque pisciculi.*

There are others too; for everything is corrupt; but I have no leisure to go into details. Farewell, reverend father.

Your sincere friend Erasmus

* * * * *

308:39 Jonadab] In the scholia Erasmus explains this difficulty by reference to the Septuagint title of Ps 71; edition of 1516, folio 19 (Allen).

41 Nepotianus] A wrong reference to Jerome's letter 52; the words come in his Ep 125.18.2; CSEL 56 137–8.

44 *Quibus corax*] Erasmus' conjectures are on folio 24 of the 1516 edition (Allen); cf Ep 107:5; CSEL 55 292.

309 / From Gregor Reisch

Freiburg im Breisgau, 4 October 1514

GREGOR, PRIOR OF THE CHARTERHOUSE, TO DOCTOR ERASMUS WITH EVERY GOOD WISH FOR HIS ETERNAL SALVATION IN THE LORD

Most courteous and learned of men, I am delighted that the Jerome we have in hand is to enjoy the benefit of your well-known and authoritative scholarship. I think it providential that the work we had already planned should not see the light until your gifted and experienced hand can elucidate and restore with the skilled tools of criticism what would no doubt remain for ever missing or defective and obscured by error. I heartily approve that works falsely ascribed to Jerome and spurious pieces should be separated from others that are really his. But as to my arrangement, which is really that of the late lamented Amerbach senior, if you change this you will in many people's opinion inflict no small loss on the booksellers, and equally perhaps on readers too; for the letters are mingled in great confusion among the books and shorter treatises in the printed editions of other men, as you can see well enough. I often hear criticisms from better scholars than myself of this way of grouping things and giving them titles, which results in a whole book being numbered as a letter, although it is not usually so referred to, and printed as a letter, and little or no classification of the subject matter is maintained, while the arrangement of Augustine's works in distinct volumes or parts has given general satisfaction, including those who bear the cost of the work; for this kind of arrangement has proved of very little use.

Consequently I hope that you will preserve, if possible, the traditional order of the various parts, except that letters necessary for the understanding of works or treatises should stand in front of them; and then let what is wrongly attributed follow. The old introductions I never found satisfactory; you are right to add others, and the same with the notes. I have nothing here

* * * * *

309:12 Amerbach senior] Johannes Amerbach, who died in 1513, was born about 1430 in Lower Franconia. He was a graduate and MA of the university of Paris, who learned his trade as corrector in Koberger's press in Nürnberg. He set up his own press in Basel about 1475, and published his first book in 1478. He was dedicated to the production of scholarly works, as was Johann Froben, who took over his press in 1513 after more than a decade of collaboration. Amerbach's particular ambition was to publish scholarly editions of the four Latin doctors of the church: Gregory the Great, Ambrose, Augustine, and Jerome. Ambrose appeared in 1492, Augustine in 1506, and at his death the edition of Jerome, already planned, was well on the way to completion. See AK I (Basel 1942) XIX–XXIII.

in the way of good manuscripts, and have not written any notes, if you except the Hebrew words found in the printer's copy. The passages you indicate in certain letters I have put into shape, but the printer is away and I have not been able to look them up. I have no confidence, however, in my being able to discover anything that is too much for a man of your great learning and experience. With my very best wishes.

In haste, from the Charterhouse of Freiburg, St Francis' day 1514

310 / From Udalricus Zasius — Freiburg im Breisgau, 11 October [1514]

This letter was first printed in the *Epistolae ad Erasmum* (1516).

UDALRICUS ZASIUS, PROFESSOR OF CIVIL AND CANON LAW AT FREIBURG, TO ERASMUS

At this very moment, great Rotterdam, the Varro of our age, I have happened on the courier who brings you this, and could not let him depart without a letter from me to keep him company, although I am now at a crucial point in my lectures on civil law, and my ears hum with Bartolo and Baldo and other unclassical authors of the kind. Your most elegant letter has made me truly happy, if there is any happiness to be found when scholars converse; and so much material is offered me there both for enjoyment and for a reply, that I feel I must choose a different time and place for the purpose. One thing I would have you know. Your letter – yes, that sweet letter from you – is being passed from hand to hand all round our university; the faculty are clamouring for it, full of admiration for such a great fountain of the purest style, for the genius of the divine Rotterdam, and for the fire of inspiration that comes down from heaven. Even a Zasius is highly esteemed; people point me out: 'This is the man,' they say, 'who has had a letter, a kind and friendly letter, from Rotterdam, the Cicero of our modern Germany.' Happy, they think, is he whom Fortune counts worthy of the honour of being praised by Rotterdam; no less fortunate than Achilles who had Homer to trumpet his praises, Augustus who had the clarion of Virgil, Scipio who had Silius' bugle-call – no less, I say, than any man who

* * * * *

310:3 Varro] Marcus Terentius Varro (116–27 BC), the most learned man of antiquity, of whose enormous output a partial list was transmitted by St Jerome

6 Bartolo] Cf Ep 134:30–1n.

18 Germany] Cf Epp 269:43; 305:45, 157, 221; 307:14; and the preface xii.

21 Silius] Caius Silius Italicus (died c AD 101) wrote an epic, the *Punica*, on the second war between Rome and Carthage, of which Scipio Africanus was the hero.

has been praised by one whom all men praise. So much has this one letter increased my reputation, secured me the friendship of a great man, and made me rich beyond the wealth of Croesus. Imagine then, dear Rotterdam, how grateful I must be to you.

But that, as I say, is for another occasion. This clumsy letter of mine, precipitate as it is, serves none the less as forerunner and prelude, and earns me time to think how I can find some other way to give you pleasure. Farewell, and come some day to visit me at home, if you are not too grand, like great Jupiter visiting the cottage of some country faun, for you will be a most welcome guest.

Bonifacius sends you his warmest greetings. After the green pleasance of the humanities he has had to learn the uphill path towards the rocky summits of the civil law, but he will win his way by brains and industry and the steadfast help, such as it is, of his instructor. Farewell, you idol, mine I will not call you, although it is true enough, but of the whole world of letters. From Freiburg, 11 October 1514

Pray do not answer when you are tired with such important business; enough for me that you should even glance at my foolish letter.

Your sincere Udalricus Zasius, doctor of laws

311 / To Matthias Schürer Basel, 15 October 1514

This is the preface to Schürer's edition (Strasbourg, December 1514) of the *De copia*, which he published together with the letters between Wimpfeling and Erasmus (Epp 302, 305) and the *Parabolae* (cf Ep 312). Josse Bade, the original publisher (Paris 15 July 1512), found his own sales hurt by this transaction and complained of it to Erasmus; cf Epp 346, 434, 472, and 260 introduction. It may be noted that Schürer alone published editions of the *De copia* in January 1513, January and December 1514, February and October 1516, December 1518, and March 1521.

ERASMUS OF ROTTERDAM TO MATTHIAS SCHÜRER OF SÉLESTAT

A good proportion of those who print books, Matthias Schürer, either from ignorance and lack of judgment undertake the worst authors by mistake for the best, or from greed of gain reckon the best book to be the book from which they expect the most profit. And so we see the same thing happen in the art of printing that is so familiar in other walks of life, that an invention designed to be the greatest blessing to learning and education tends through the errors of those who misuse it to become a serious threat. Now

* * * * *

24 Croesus] *Adagia* I vi 74

in this matter you seem to me to deserve credit on two separate grounds: first, because as an uncommonly well-instructed man and a man of keen discernment you choose works which will contribute to the genuine advancement of knowledge and, second, because you have a natural love of good literature and are happy to consider these studies of ours and not your own coffers. Your one purpose is to publish the best books very accurately printed.

And so I have sent you my *Copia*, which I have most carefully revised and purged of errors, that a book conceived in England long ago and published after a fashion in Paris, but now entirely renewed and polished as though it had cast its slough, may come before the public once again under happier auspices in your famous city of Strasbourg. Provided you think it not unworthy of your press, this in itself will commend it to lovers of good letters, when they see it issue from the house of Schürer; for there is now a general conviction that nothing comes from that address that is not a finished product of the author's brain, as correct as your expert hand can make it. I have added a book of *Parallels* hitherto unpublished, which comes to you, as they say, fire-new from the mint.

The works of Rodolphus Agricola, a man of more than human stature, we await with impatience; for whenever I read anything he wrote, I feel fresh admiration and affection for that inspired and soaring mind. Farewell.

Basel, 15 October 1514

312 / To Pieter Gillis — Basel, 15 October [1514]

This is the preface to the *Parabolae sive similia*; cf Ep 311 introduction. Gillis was one of Erasmus' closest friends and their friendship dated back to the early years of the century; cf Ep 184 introduction. Although now chief secretary of the town of Antwerp, Gillis worked – as he had before – as a corrector and editor for the press of Martens.

ERASMUS OF ROTTERDAM TO PIETER GILLIS, SECRETARY OF THE FAMOUS CITY OF ANTWERP

Friends of the commonplace and homespun sort, my open-hearted Pieter, have their idea of relationship, like their whole lives, attached to material

* * * * *

311:26 fire-new] Literally 'straight from the (blacksmith's) bellows'; not a classical allusion

27 Agricola] A project never realized; see P.S. Allen 'The Letters of Rudolph Agricola' EHR 21 (1906) 302–17.

things; and if ever they have to face a separation, they favour a frequent exchange of rings, knives, caps, and other tokens of the kind, for fear that their affection may cool when intercourse is interrupted or actually die away through the interposition of long tracts of time and space. But you and I, whose idea of friendship rests wholly in a meeting of minds and the enjoyment of studies in common, might well greet one another from time to time with presents for the mind and keepsakes of a literary description. Not that there is any risk that when our life together is interrupted we may slowly grow cold, or that the great distance which separates our bodies may loosen the close tie between our minds. Minds can develop an even closer link, the greater the space that comes between them. Our aim would be that any loss due to separation in the actual enjoyment of our friendship should be made good, not without interest, by tokens of this literary kind.

And so I send a present – no common present, for you are no common friend, but many jewels in one small book. Jewels I well may call them, these parallels selected from the richly furnished world of the greatest authors of antiquity. Of late, as I reread Aristotle, Pliny, and Plutarch for the enrichment of my *Adagiorum chiliades*, and cleared Anneus Seneca of the corruptions by which he was not so much disfigured as done away with altogether, I noted down by the way these passages, to make an offering for you which I knew would not be unwelcome. This I foresaw, knowing as I did your natural bent towards elegance of expression, and perceiving that not polish alone but almost all the dignity of language stems from its metaphors. For the Greek *parabolê*, which Cicero latinizes as *collatio*, a sort of comparison, is nothing more than a metaphor writ large. Of the other ornaments of style, each makes its own peculiar contribution to its charm and flexibility; metaphor taken alone adds everything in fuller measure, while all the other kinds of ornament add one thing each. Do you wish to entertain? nothing adds more sparkle. Are you concerned to convey information? nothing else makes your point so convincingly, so clearly. Do you intend to persuade? nothing gives you greater penetration. Have you a mind to expatiate? nowhere is plenty readier to your hand. Or to be brief? nothing leaves more to the understanding. Have you a fancy to be grand? metaphor can exalt anything, and to any height you please. Is there something you wish to play down? nothing is more effective for bringing things down to earth. Would you be vivid and picturesque? metaphor brings it

* * * * *

312:22 *Adagiorum chiliades*] Cf Ep 269 introduction.

22 Seneca] Cf Ep 325 introduction.

28 Cicero] *De inventione* 1.30.49

before one's eyes better than anything else. What gives their spice to adages, their charm to fables, their point to historical anecdotes? metaphor, which doubles the native riches of a pithy saying, so that Solomon himself, an inspired author, chose to recommend his wise sayings to the world by calling them *Parabolae*. Deprive the orators of their arsenal of metaphor, and all will be thin and dull. Take metaphor and parable, *parabolê*, away from the Prophets and the Gospels, and you will find that a great part of their charm has gone.

Someone will say, perhaps, 'This man has a pretty knack of making his work sound important, as though it were really difficult to produce parallels, when they lie to hand everywhere.' But I have not chosen what was ready to hand, nor picked up pebbles on the beach; I have brought forth precious stones from the inner treasure-house of the Muses. The barber's shop, the tawdry conversation of the marketplace are no source for what is to be worth the attention of the ears and eyes of educated men. Such things must be unearthed in the innermost secrets of nature, in the inner shrine of the arts and sciences, in the recondite narratives of the best poets or the record of eminent historians. In this field there is a twofold difficulty, and double praise is to be won. That first task is already something, to have tracked down what is really good. But it is no less labour to arrange neatly what you have discovered, just as it is something to have found a precious jewel in the first place, but there is credit to be won from its skilful mounting on a sceptre or in a ring. I will add an example to make my point clear. Hemlock is poisonous to man, and wine neutralises hemlock; but if you put an admixture of wine into your hemlock, you make its venom much more immediate and quite beyond treatment, because the force and energy of the wine carries the effect of the poison more rapidly to the vital centres. Now merely to know such a rare fact in nature is surely both elegant and interesting as information. Suppose then one were to adapt this by saying that adulation poisons friendship instantly, and that what neutralises that poison is the habit of speaking one's mind, which Greek calls *parrhesia*, outspokenness. Now, if you first contaminate this freedom of speech and put a touch of it into your adulation, so that you are flattering your friend most insidiously while you most give the impression of perfect frankness, the damage is by now incurable. Would this win no credit as an ingenious application of the parallel? I think it would.

* * * * *

45 *Parabolae*] Cf 1 Kings 4:32.

72 outspokenness] This information about hemlock and wine and the analogy with parrhesia come from Plutarch *Moralia* 61B, and are developed by Erasmus in *Parabolae* LB I 565 F.

Yet I do not mean to fish for gratitude where I deserve none. In anything under the heading 'From Aristotle and Pliny' the application of the image is my own invention. For anything taken according to the rubric from Plutarch and Seneca I claim no credit, except for the labour of collection and exposition and such praise as is due to brevity and convenience. I am well aware what an ocean of parallels could be got together from the whole realm of nature, from all the fields of knowledge, all the poets, the historians, the orators. But an attempt to pursue the infinite would be mere madness. I wished to give at least a taste, and thus to arouse young men's minds to find such things for themselves. Of Plutarch I have made a very full survey, partly because he wrote in Greek, partly because in this field he is such a leader as to defy comparison even with the greatest authors. From Seneca, since my work on him at the time had a different purpose, I have not gathered so much. It will not be found out of the way to attach this book to my *Adagia* or, if so preferred, to my *Copia* as a kind of supplement, since it has so much in common with the former and contributes eminently to abundance of style. If your epithalamium is not yet finished and published, the fault lies with my servant, who left the text in Louvain, of which I was unaware. Farewell.

Basel, 15 October 1514

313 / To Udalricus Zasius Basel, 18 October [1514]

The reference in line 4 of this letter to the 'third' edition of the *Adagia* provides the year date for the letter. The 'second edition' was the *Adagiorum chiliades* of 1508, an extensive revision of the original *Adagiorum collectanea* of 1500. This 'third edition,' Erasmus' first revision of the *Chiliades* (for which work we reserve the short form *Adagia*) was published by Johann Froben in 1515; cf Ep 326B:33n. It contained over 3,400 adages and showed once again extensive rethinking and expansion. For the first time Erasmus' comments on proverbs were sometimes turned into sharp critical essays of considerable length, some of them of great importance, like the 'Sileni Alcibiadis,' 'Dulce bellum inex-

* * * * *

78 heading] Erasmus refers to the cross-headings which name the classical sources of his material, Plutarch, Seneca, and the writers on natural history.

93 epithalamium] A work to mark the occasion of Pieter Gillis' marriage to his first wife Cornelia Sandria, about this time. Erasmus was often a guest in their house in Antwerp. See Ep 184, and Reedijk appendix I.2 for the text of the epithalamium. The verses were printed in the colloquy 'Epithalamium P. Aegidii' in the September 1524 edition of the *Colloquia*, which is how they became well known.

pertis,' and 'Scarabeus aquilam quaerit': see Phillips pt I c 4. The source of this letter is Clm 1470 f 199v in the Bayerische Staatsbibliothek, Munich, and it was first printed in Josef Neff's *Udalricus Zasius* pt 2 (Freiburg 1891), not entirely accurately.

TO THE EMINENT PROFESSOR OF CIVIL AND CANON LAW UDALRICUS ZASIUS FROM ERASMUS OF ROTTERDAM

If I did not answer your letter, Zasius my learned friend, what prevented me was my *Adagia*, which is now coming to birth for the third time, and goes one better than Bacchus who was born twice. And in its new-born form it is so much enlarged and enriched that it might be thought an entirely new work. An even greater obstacle was St Jerome, for it has cost me considerably more labour to correct and annotate his works than it cost him to write them. And then you told me in your letter not to answer. But the same letter in which you tell me not to reply spurs me on to do so; you have found a new art of saying 'no thank you' so that it sounds like 'please'; your 'you are excused' means 'you are expected'; and 'do as you please' means precisely 'do what I want.' This is the picture of my Zasius that your letter draws so vividly – the picture of a man who unites in equal measure three outstanding qualities, in any one of which one can find few who excel: what stores of learning, what genuine eloquence, what courtesy and frank good will! Happy the university of Freiburg in her possession of a man who can match style with scholarship and scholarship with style as he dispenses light and learning, and in her enjoyment of true culture in such accessible form! I may rather say happy is Germany in an ornament so incomparable! When you say that my letter is being passed from hand to hand in your society, in other words that my foolish nonsense is exposed to universal view, I could bear this with less discomfort if I knew that all had Zasius' readiness to think well, for, however slovenly the picture drawn of you, you take it in good part. Farewell.

Konrad is a friend of mine and a seeker after good literature; be kind to him, if he needs it.

Basel, St Luke's day

* * * * *

313:5 Bacchus] Cf Ep 269:6.

26 Konrad] Probably Konard Brunner of Wesen, known as 'Fonteius,' who was born about 1495 and was a contemporary of Bonifacius Amerbach at the university of Basel (MA 1513). He later worked with the Amerbachs and with Froben, in part as a book-buying agent. He succeeded Heinrich Loriti (Glareanus) when the latter gave up teaching in Basel in 1517, and he died shortly afterward (October 1519) in the same plague that took the life of Bruno Amerbach. See AK I 241.

314 / From John Colet London, 20 October [1514]

This is a reply to a letter which Erasmus evidently wrote at about the same time as that to Mountjoy (Ep 301) and in which he narrated the same events. For Erasmus' earlier relations with John Colet, beginning in October 1499 in England, see especially Epp 106 and 260.

JOHN COLET TO ERASMUS

Dearest Erasmus, the letter has arrived which you wrote from Basel on 30 August. I am glad to know where you are and under what sky you are now living, and glad too that you are well. You say you have made a vow to St Paul; do not fail to keep it. That in Mainz they thought as highly of you as you say, I can well believe. I am glad that you will come back to us one day; but I cannot hope to see it. As to a better position for you, I know not what to say, except that those who have the power have not the will, and those who would, have no power. Your friends here are all well: the archbishop of Canterbury is as sweet and good as ever; my lord of Lincoln now reigns as archbishop of York; he of London still plagues me. I think daily of retiring and taking refuge among the Carthusians. My nest is nearly finished. When you return to us, as far as I can guess, you will find me there dead to worldly things. Look after your health, and let me know your movements. Farewell.

London, 20 October

315 / From Jacques Lefèvre d'Etaples Saint Germain des Prés, Paris, 23 October [1514]

Lefèvre d'Etaples (Faber Stapulensis), a Picard, was the greatest exponent of humanistic reform in France at this time. He was born about 1460 and died in

* * * * *

314:4 vow] See Ep 301:20ff.

10 Canterbury] Warham; cf Ep 188 introduction.

10 my lord of Lincoln] Wolsey. This was the time of his most spectacular preferment, from the office of royal almoner to bishop of Tournai (1513), then of Lincoln, and within a few months to archbishop of York and cardinal, on the unexpected death of Christopher Bainbridge (14 July 1514); cf Ep 333:22n.

11 he of London] Fitzjames; cf Ep 270:53n.

12 Carthusians] The Carthusian house at Sheen, near Richmond on the Thames, was a twin foundation with the Brigettine monastery of Syon at Isleworth, both having been established by Henry v in 1414. For Colet's connection see J.H. Lupton *Life of John Colet* (1887) 217–19; for the involvement of the house with reform circles see McConica 56.

1536. After graduating from the university of Paris he taught philosophy and the liberal arts, probably at the Collège du Cardinal Lemoine, and during the winter of 1491–2 he travelled in Italy especially to meet Pico della Mirandola and Ermolao Barbaro. He published a number of studies and editions of the philosophical and scientific writings of Aristotle, Dionysius the Areopagite, Boethius, and others. After his retirement from teaching in 1508 his studies were chiefly of the Bible. Under the patronage of his former pupil, Guillaume Briçonnet, he was established at the abbey of Saint Germain des Prés. In 1521 Briçonnet, now bishop of Meaux, called him there to help in a comprehensive scheme for reform of the diocese. Lefèvre contributed to this a French translation of the New Testament and Psalms, and in 1530 published in Antwerp the first complete version of the Bible in French. This letter of greeting to Erasmus indicates an attitude of respect which was to yield to one of sharp contention: cf Allen Ep 597:5n. See Margaret Mann *Erasme et les débuts de la réforme française, 1517–1536* (Paris 1934); Renaudet *Préréforme*; and Ep 304:100n. The text was first printed in *Epistolae ad Erasmum* (1516).

TO ERASMUS OF ROTTERDAM, LUMINARY OF LEARNING, FROM JACQUES LEFÈVRE

Yesterday about nightfall the bearer of this came to see me, and brought me greetings from you which could not fail to be most welcome, but filled my mind with gladness all the more as I understood that you were in Germany busy with the printers. The public good (as I realised at once) and your passion for the successful spread of the humanities have induced you to leave England, and, so far as we are concerned, nothing could be more wished for and more fruitful. What else should you do, full as you are with good literature in every form, except spread it abroad, not for your own profit but for the public good – taking the sun as your example, who gives light to all? For so does the sun in heaven, full of such brilliant radiance, hide none of it within himself, but displays it and presents it before the eyes of all mortals, not for his own benefit but for theirs. Who can fail to respect, admire, and love our Erasmus? No one who has any claims to either character or education. May He therefore who can prolong our days grant you as long a thread of life as possible, that, after a long career spent in piling one good deed upon another, you may pass on in old age to a more blessed realm, leaving the whole world in your debt – not merely bequeathing a glorious name to posterity, but sharing henceforward in the life of gods and heroes. Long may you prosper for the benefit of all of us and this world of ours; and pray keep a warm corner for one that feels so warmly towards you.

From the monastery of Saint Germain, hard by Paris, 23 October

316 / From Lukas Klett [Basel], 1 November 1514

Klett (fl 1509–38), whose father was a schoolmaster of Rufach near Colmar in Alsace, was a graduate of the university of Basel and himself a schoolmaster who returned to the study of law. He took the humanist name 'Paliurus,' the Latin translation of his German name, which meant 'burdock.' It seems likely that it was in connection with his desire to leave schoolteaching and take up legal studies, which he did about this time, that Klett wrote this letter to Erasmus. He went first to Paris with the Amerbach brothers and Onuphrius Brant. In 1510 he took his BA at Basel, and in 1515 his doctorate in laws. By 1517 he was chancellor to the bishop of Basel, Christoph von Utenheim (Ep 305:243n), and in 1520, 1523, and 1527 he was dean of the law faculty. For an epigram by Erasmus addressed to Klett see Reedijk poem 101; see also Winterberg 48.

TO ERASMUS, MOST LEARNED OF MEN, FROM LUCAS PALIURUS

Forgive me, dear Erasmus, if I intrude upon your noble self with my unpractised wit; support from you carries great weight and authority everywhere, and I have brief need of some such assistance. I know the very high opinion of you entertained by Zasius, the most accomplished jurist of our generation. Would you please write him a letter in support, not so much of me, as of a piece of business in which I am concerned? The reason why I need your recommendation will be explained to you by your friend Froben. If you are willing to lend an ear which is not deaf to these prayers of mine, which come from a heart that is humble enough, heaven knows, you will bind me to your distinguished self by such a debt of gratitude that there is nothing I would fear to undergo on behalf of great Erasmus, my most kind and learned teacher. Farewell.

Written at home, which is a seething whirlpool of worries, this All Saints day 1514

317 / From Udalricus Zasius Freiburg im Breisgau, 7 November 1514

At the moment, dear Erasmus, greatest of the great, I have no time to write at length and so, tied as I am by lack of leisure and by official duties, you must make do with this modest effort. For our friend Lukas, that excellent and well-read man, I am most ready to do what I can, for besides being a man of no ordinary promise he is recommended by an eloquent letter from you – and you are one whom I venerate as a light sent down from heaven.

* * * * *

317:3 Lukas] Cf Ep 316.

Your gift of your Plutarch in Latin dress is not the sort of thing I can do justice to in words: my starveling style could never achieve the flow of language needed for an adequate reply to a work so gratefully received, so delightful, and let me add, so scholarly. And however eloquent I might be, it is in deeds, not in words, that one ought to show at least an outline of one's gratitude. In your last letter you uttered such fulminations – it might have been Jupiter with his thunderbolt – when I called you great and fortunate, that I am stricken, and now withdraw what I wrote and call you the greatest of the great instead. How else am I to put it? What other title can I give you, rising as you do above all mortal praise, the one man in a thousand years to show the true greatness which makes you little lower than the immortals? I know you will say that this is only Zasius lapsing into girlish adulation, and flattery of one German by another, which is improper; for this is a black mark you gave me once before, being the upright, inflexible, serious, energetic man you are. But I could do no different, my whole self being carried away by enthusiasm and affection. How is it possible not to praise on every count a man like you, who are, to use Cicero's phrase, great in repute, in action greater still? Counting in fact will have no place; in praising you, not only number but weight and measure too confess themselves exceeded.

But I must call a halt and go and lecture on the *Digestum vetus*. More, and at more length, later, for I love to gossip with you as with a man abundantly blessed. Farewell, my life, my glory, or rather the glory of philosophy and encyclopaedic knowledge; forgive me if I misuse the Greek word, for in this field I am a stranger.

From Freiburg, 7 November 1514. Your Zasius

Your friend Bonifacius, ours I should say, dares not write, for your thunderbolt has paralysed his hand, but he asks me constantly to mention him to you and send you his respects; which, having so far forgotten myself as to send you my unwashed letter, I gladly do, both to give my imperti-

* * * * *

7 Plutarch] The *Plutarchi opuscula* (Basel: Froben August 1514), the first book printed for Erasmus after his arrival in Basel. Cf Epp 272, 297.

20 black mark] *Adagia* I v 54

24 Cicero's phrase] 'An allusion to Virgil, *Aeneid* 11.124, which Macrobius (*Saturnalia* 6.2.33) notes to have been imitated from Cicero's lost work on Cato' (Allen).

27 *Digestum vetus*] The medieval title of the first division of Justinian's *Digest*, as far as book 24.2

30–1 Greek word] Zasius had written *philosophiae encyclicae*.

36 unwashed] *Adagia* I ix 55

Willibald Pirckheimer
Medallion by Albrecht Dürer
Victoria & Albert Museum, London

nence free rein and to oblige a friend who is as dear to me as anyone in Freiburg. So kindly accept respectful greetings from your humble servant on behalf of Bonifacius.

318 / From Willibald Pirckheimer to Beatus Rhenanus

Nürnberg, 9 December 1514

This letter was evidently written during Erasmus' first visit to Basel. Pirckheimer (1470–1530) of Eichstadt studied in Italy from 1490 to 1497: Greek at Padua and law at Pavia. He became town councillor of Nürnberg, imperial councillor to Maximilian, and, after his retirement in 1522, a leading patron of letters in the city. Like More he was famous for the careful humanistic education he provided for his five daughters, while he himself published translations from Lucian and Plutarch and historical writing on Germany and on the Swiss wars. He was also patron to Albrecht Dürer. This letter is BRE Ep 41, WPB Ep 342. See W.P. Eckert 'Erasmus von Rotterdam und Willibald Pirckheimer' in *Willibald Pirckheimer 1470/1970* Dokumente Studien Perspektiven (Nürnberg 1970) 11–22.

WILLIBALD PIRCKHEIMER TO BEATUS RHENANUS

You remember, I expect, my good sir, that I made your acquaintance some time ago with an introduction from our common friend Konrad Peutinger. I now need the same assistance, and very much in the same line of business, so I now make bold to address you in your turn. I hear that Erasmus Rotterdam, a name not to be mentioned without great respect, is now living in Basel, who of all the men I have never met is the best known and the one whose friendship I am particularly anxious to secure. For although I have earned the emperor's approval, am on good terms with various magnates, am admitted to the society of eminent and learned men, and reckon myself in other respects pretty well provided for in the way of friends, yet the friendship of such an eminent scholar would be by no means the least among my blessings; in fact I should value it above the most precious things I possess. Do your best, I beg you, to enable me to make friends with the great man; it will be the most acceptable service you can render me. You

* * * * *

318:3 Peutinger] Konrad Peutinger of Augsburg (1465–1547) had studied law in Italy, and in 1490 entered the service of Augsburg, where he became town clerk, an office which took him on many diplomatic missions. He made the first attempt to study Roman inscriptions in Germany (*Romanae vetustatis fragmenta in Augusta Vindelicorum et eius diocesi*, Augsburg: Erhard Ratoldt 1505) and was learned in Roman law. He was also imperial councillor to Maximilian, and after 1534 retired to devote himself entirely to his studies.

promised once in a letter to pay us a visit here. How I wish you could bring with you such a guest! Think what good will and affection I should greet him with. For I hope and believe that I shall not depart this life before I have seen him and enjoyed the privilege of his conversation. You must satisfy your friend's longing, for nothing could make me more grateful. Farewell, and when the moment comes that you have transcribed the rest of what was left me in the will of our kind and learned friend Johannes, take steps to see they reach me. Farewell again.

Nürnberg, 9 December 1514

319 / From Udalricus Zasius Freiburg im Breisgau, 22 December 1514

This letter was first printed in the *Farrago*, and there is manuscript authority in the Deventer Letter-book.

Respectful greetings. You must not be surprised, Erasmus my great hero, if I have written to you rather seldom; you will find it more surprising that I should ever have written at all, so dazzled are my eyes and my mind by the brilliance of your reputation. A man whom Plato himself and Cicero and Quintilian and their like would have admitted to their roll of fame and for whom they would have found a seat among themselves – where shall we place him, how show him respect and honour, we who are speechless, tongue-tied, barbarian? In fact, had I not been encouraged by your wonderful kindness (which our friend Bonifacius Amerbach, a young man distinguished alike in character and abilities, never tires of praising), and did not the generous and ever-welcome present with which you honoured me invite, or rather, urge me on to write, I should never have taken pen in hand; you must take it in good part. My modest education, if it gave me

* * * * *

21 Johannes] Johannes Conon (or Kuno) of Nürnberg (c 1463–1513) was a Dominican and a Greek scholar. He studied Greek with Reuchlin at Heidelberg after 1496, and by 1504 was a member of the Aldine circle in Venice. He then became a pupil at Padua of Marcus Musurus and Scipione Fortiguerra (Carteromachus). He returned to Germany late in 1510, and by 1511 he was working at the Amerbach press in Basel. He helped extensively with the edition of Jerome, and edited the pseudo-Gregory of Nyssa. He worked at various tasks connected with editions of the Greek fathers, and also taught Greek to Bruno and Bonifacius Amerbach and to Beatus Rhenanus. The epitaph on his tomb in the Dominican church in Basel was written by his pupil Beatus; for the text see H.D. Saffrey 'Un humaniste Dominicain, Jean Cuno de Nuremberg, précurseur d'Erasme à Bâle' BHR 33, 1 (1971) 38. For Erasmus' tribute to his learning see Ep 335:322–5.

319:9 kindness] Cf Ep 303:8.

11 present] The gift of his translation of Plutarch; cf Ep 317:7n.

very little in the way of polite learning, did at least equip me with enough discernment to know, for all my lack of skill in speech, the difference between assailing the ears of great men in their presence and dwelling on their praises when they are not there; for the first is only for those who are within the pale of a higher culture, while everyone may do the second. And so, if I keep silence, it is respect for you that make me tongue-tied, not ingratitude that turns my attention elsewhere. Whatever place may be my home and wherever I may go, Erasmus will ever be on my lips and in my conversation. His greatness haunts me everywhere; he is the man I celebrate with praise however inadequate; his awe-inspiring knowledge, the marvel of our whole generation, I extol, and bid men reverence it as something divine; he is, I maintain, no man of mortal clay, but fire come down from heaven.

This the most learned jurist of our age, Pius Hieronymus Baldung, counsellor to his imperial majesty and officiating principal of the consistory court of our province, will confirm. Within these last few days he had invited me, as an old friend, to dine with him in the town of Ensisheim, where he lives; and to contribute to our entertainment I recited, as I always do, your incomparable gifts – recited them indeed to such a tune that although the dinner of itself was resplendent with dishes of every kind, yet your name added something to the splendour, and something not easy to forget. Hieronymus was unaware that you are living so close at hand, and seemed ready to pick a bone with Fortune because so great a man had been concealed from him all this time, which should never have happened. This man desires to be better acquainted with you, longs to become your friend; he is an enthusiast for your letters, and I beg you, I urge you, to send him one. He is a distinguished lawyer and, besides that, equally at home in every field of humane studies; to put it in a word, you will find Hieronymus a man for whom, in view of his youth (for he is not yet thirty), our Upper Germany will hardly find you a match.

As far as I am concerned, pray use your Zasius as your footboy. I shall think my prayers have been answered, if I find myself thought worthy to be counted among your minor camp-followers. The glosses which I am planning on certain parts of the civil law, the summary of the *Digestum vetus* which is now almost finished, the *Truth* of certain interpretations in the

* * * * *

27 Baldung] Pius Hieronymus Baldung of Schwäbisch-Gmünd (fl 1506–32), a doctor of laws of Freiburg. Cf Ep 400 introduction.

42–3 Upper Germany] The region of the Upper Rhine, including the Vosges and Black Forest, and extending to Mainz

48 certain interpretations] Cf Ep 303:16n.

civil law which will shortly appear and oppose the accepted opinions of the experts, a respectable book on the profession of an advocate, all of which are red-hot on the anvil at the moment – these will say things of you which modesty forbids and shame deters me from writing to you in the flesh. Farewell, O luminary of learning, of which posterity will hardly see the like.

From Freiburg, 22 December 1514

Your sincere Udalricus Zasius, doctor of laws

320 / From Jan Becker van Borssele Arlon, Luxembourg, 4 January 1515

Jan Becker was a graduate of Louvain who studied at the Collège du Lys, taking his BA in 1497 and his MA the following year. He was reputed an excellent Latinist, and from 1502 was a member of the Council of the Faculty of Arts. He also tutored boys from wealthy families, and in 1507 had become tutor to a nephew of the Busleydens, whom he apparently accompanied to Luxembourg. In the spring of 1513, possibly through the influence of Jérôme de Busleyden, he was appointed canon in Middelburg, whence he wrote to Erasmus on 19 April 1514 (see Ep 291 introduction). About this time he accepted the task of tutoring another nephew of Busleyden, François, a son of the recently deceased Valérien de Busleyden, and for this reason he removed to Arlon. See H. de Vocht *Jérôme de Busleyden* Humanistica Lovaniensia 9 (Turnhout 1950) 342–3; de Vocht CTL I 256–68.

JAN BECKER VAN BORSSELE TO ERASMUS OF ROTTERDAM

I had made up my mind never to lose any opportunity of writing to you, my most respected master, and so, since I now have the chance of a messenger who is setting off for your part of the world, I could not fail to write you at least these few lines, although I have no idea whether you are at home still, or have already set out for Rome, as I very strongly suspect and am much afraid you have; for I would certainly write at much greater length if I were sure that you had not yet left. And so, since I have to send this letter to an uncertain address, I have chosen to write in brief, and only what I could easily allow anyone else to read, for fear my letter might be sent back to me without an answer from anyone, as happened to a letter I sent you in England. First, then, I have to report that I have left home, and all my friends and relations, besides my fellow-students and all the advantages of

* * * * *

320:6 Rome] Cf Ep 300:43–4; it was originally intended that the stay in Basel would be short, but the journey to Italy (cf Epp 323:22, 324:27) was finally abandoned.

11 letter] Perhaps that referred to in Ep 291:54

home, at the invitation – the orders almost – of my old benefactor, Jérôme de Busleyden, and have migrated to this country of Luxembourg, to instruct his nephew in civilized manners and in a liberal education; and I am living with the boy's mother, a most worthy lady, at Arlon and sometimes at Luxembourg, for we move house from time to time; and my living conditions are very creditable and reasonably lucrative, but I find them a little tedious, having to live for the moment out of touch with literary society and almost in solitude, until he and I are sent to some public school. For my lady cannot yet be persuaded to part with her son, who is still of tender years and her only consolation for her husband's death.

I long to hear in return what books you have sent to the press in those parts; for I understood, both from a letter of yours and from the people who met you when you were leaving for Basel, that you have decided to hand over a critical edition of the New Testament and another of St Jerome's letters to your local printers or typesetters before you move to Rome; and several other things besides, which I learnt that you had written from the letter you sent me last summer. If only on your way back from England you had met me too at Middelburg, as I very much wanted you to, and you had said you would if you conveniently could, I should have known much more definitely about them all, and even seen some of them with my own eyes. But now I should be most grateful if you could tell me what books you have sent to your local printers, and how much each costs, and even how I can get them sent to me in this remote place. If only the man who brings you this letter had been willing to take on the task of bringing me the books or even despatching them to me somehow or other, I should have given orders for the purchase of everything that has been printed. If however they could be sent to some bookseller in Trier or Metz, since printers and booksellers have so much business in common, so that I could get them from there at a definite price, that is what I should really like; for I want, as I say, to have everything you have published in Basel. If you have published anything small, which this man could and might be willing to bring with him without inconvenience, I should like it to be sent by him. Farewell, and do not forget that your friend from Borssele will always be devoted to you even in absence.

From Arlon or, as students of antiquity would have it, Aralunum, a town in the country of Luxembourg, 4 January 1515

* * * * *

15 Busleyden] Cf Ep 205 introduction.

16 nephew] See introduction.

30 letter] Evidently a lost reply to Ep 291; cf Ep 573 introduction.

Your sincere friend Jan Becker van Borssele

If Erasmus is away, and someone else who loves his name and admires his learning opens this letter, as I have asked should be done in the address, I beg him in the name of our common devotion to Erasmus to send me a brief answer, and take Erasmus' place in this respect; and although I cannot thank him in person, being a stranger and far away, I shall always feel and be most grateful.

321 / From Heinrich Bebel — Tübingen, 20 January 1515

Bebel (1472–1518) of Justingen, near Ulm, was of peasant stock. He was lecturer in poetry and rhetoric at Tübingen and author of several treatises on Latin style. He was popularly known however through his *Facetiae* (Strasbourg 1506). Melanchthon was among his pupils.

HEINRICH BEBEL OF JUSTINGEN TO MASTER ERASMUS

The other day, when Beatus Rhenanus, who was the victim of some false rumour, published in a letter the news that you had been taken from the land of the living, I was very sad on your account, and very sad at the loss that had befallen equally the world of letters and the reputation of Germany. Now that I learn that you are at Basel and in good health, and busy in the cause of good literature, I am filled with joy, nor can I refrain from sending you my greetings, somewhat uncouth though my letter may be. For, to say exactly what I think (and every educated man in Swabia agrees with me), I believe you are the one person to whose gifts, with your many-sided learning and your exceptional skill in both ancient tongues, all other living men must yield; so that, being far in advance, as you are, not only of all Germans but of the French and Italians as well, you can be equated as a man of letters with the famous names of antiquity, and must be enrolled among their number. I have therefore one request to make of you: declare yourself in your writings to be a German so openly that neither the

* * * * *

321:3 letter] Cf Ep 270 introduction; the dedicatory epistle itself is BRE 35 (13 August 1513).

16 German] For references to this continuing allusion see Ep 310:18n. For the French claim to Erasmus see Beatus Rhenanus to Lefèvre d'Etaples BRE 24 (1 March 1512). The identification of national territory in this region is discussed by Werner Kaegi in his essay 'Die Rheingrenze in der Geschichte Alemanniens' *Historische Meditationen* I (Zurich 1942) 41–76; cf J. Huizinga 'Erasmus über Vaterland und Nationen' *Gedenkschrift zum 400. Todestage des Erasmus von Rotterdam* (Basel 1936) 34–49.

English nor the French, who as nations are eloquent in their own praise, can pride themselves on possessing you or boast of you excessively as a fellow-citizen. Farewell, learned sir, and take it in good part if I bombard you with an ill-written letter, for its source is a great reverence and admiration for yourself. Farewell once more.

Tübingen, 20 January 1515

322 / To Willibald Pirckheimer Basel, 24 January [1515]

The earliest text of this letter is in the Department of Manuscripts of the British Library, in a volume containing miscellaneous writings by Pirckheimer: MS Arundel 175 f 17. It was first published in M. Goldast ed *Bilibaldi Pirckheimeri Opera* (Frankfurt 1610) 267; WPB Ep 349.

ERASMUS TO WILLIBALD

I had long had a burning desire for your acquaintance, and had conceived no small affection for you as a result of reading your collected pieces, in which I seemed to recognize a kind of express image of my Willibald; and it was the image of a man, a great man not easily matched, in whom a distinguished position in the world and literary gifts shed lustre on one another, and both were rendered more remarkable by integrity, enhanced in its turn by an equally courteous and friendly nature. This flame was further kindled by the commendation of Beatus Rhenanus, your most zealous supporter who, as the Greek proverb has it, added fire to fire. The almost daily enjoyment of his society – for he is as well read as he is charming – is such a pleasure to me that I feel it truly gives me the beatitude suggested by his name. He talks to me of no one more often or with more respect and affection than of his friend Willibald. On top of that came your letter, not indeed addressed to me, but all about me; and yet it was written to me too, inasmuch as it was sent to a man who I can truly say has one soul with me. You are eager that we should become acquainted and wish that we may be friends, two things which I myself have for long greatly desired without much expectation of success. Distant as we are from one another, that is no reason why we should not be very close friends, and we must do what we can to achieve a meeting.

* * * * *

322:9 Rhenanus] See Ep 327 introduction.

10 proverb] *Adagia* I ii 8

15 letter] Ep 318

My *Adagiorum chiliades* is being republished, so much corrected and enriched that it might be taken for a new work. So are the entire works of St Jerome, with summaries and notes by me, and corrected with great labour, all the spurious additions having been detected and separated out. I have corrected the whole New Testament and added notes, and am working at other things too on the side. These labours have so overwhelmed me for nearly six months now that I can scarcely keep my health. All the same, I could not refrain from addressing you in these worse than hasty and pointless lines. I knew how a man of your position and your learning should properly be approached; but you must take in good part what was dictated rather than suggested by the wish to know you. The opportunity of this courier was quite unforeseen, and I thought it better that he should bring with him a foolish letter from me than none at all. I shall soon be allowed a little more spare time, and then I shall approach you not in letters but in whole volumes. I only wish you were not so far away, for in March I return to England. Farewell, chief glory of our native Germany. Basel, 24 January

To the right honourable Willibald Pirckheimer, councillor of his imperial majesty, senator of Nürnberg

323 / From Johann Witz — Sélestat, 31 January 1515

Witz (1490–1561), called Sapidus by his fellow-humanists, was a native of Sélestat and a pupil there of Hieronymus Gebwiler, who directed the school from 1501 to 1509 and developed its programme along the lines set out in Wimpfeling's *Adolescentia*. In 1508 Witz received the degree of MA from the university of Paris, where he studied both with Lefèvre d'Etaples and Fausto Andrelini. He then returned to Sélestat to assist Gebwiler, and became headmaster in turn in December 1510. He became an enthusiastic follower of Luther, as well as a member of the literary society founded at Sélestat by Wimpfeling in 1517, and under his energetic direction the school reached a peak of prosperity. The growing atmosphere of religious contention in the 1520s clouded the peaceable atmosphere, and in 1525 Witz took the opportunity afforded by a minor quarrel with the *magistrat* of the city to resign his post;

* * * * *

22 *Adagiorum chiliades*] This reference determines the year-date of the letter, since on 24 January 1515 Gerard Lyster (cf Ep 495) wrote to Bonifacius Amerbach hoping that the *Adagia* would be finished by 2 February.

37 England] Cf Ep 323:22, where it appears that he had fixed the date for departure to Italy. The only explanation seems to be that he was undecided; cf Epp 300:44; 301:40; 324:27; and 326B.

a year later, in October 1526, he withdrew to Strasbourg for the rest of his life. He first met Erasmus on the occasion of the latter's triumphant welcome to Strasbourg in 1514; cf Ep 302 introduction; Reedijk poem 97 (*Ad Ioannem Sapidum suum, in discessu*, August 1514); Lefftz 11 and ff; and Adam 21–3 and passim.

JOHANN WITZ TO MASTER ERASMUS

For a long time now I have passed over in silence many opportunities of writing to you; so much I freely admit. The reason, I would have you know, was not only the press of business both at home and in the school, which demands all my time and scarcely allows me any leisure or breathing-space. There was also my reluctance to interrupt with trifling chatter of my own those studies of yours and all your labours for the cause of literature and religion, which are so great that every educated man will some day sing their praises and make your name famous. But I would not have you suppose from this silence that I have forgotten you, when I can scarcely pass one short hour without recalling and indeed mentioning your honourable and beloved name, and since I never cease to win fresh admirers for Erasmus. Among these, to name no others, is Dr Jakob Spiegel, one of the secretaries of the emperor Maximilian, a man of great learning and wonderfully high character, who returned some time ago from Vienna in Austria to his native town. Provoked by me, he has a great desire to see you, and has promised that he will visit you as soon as a suitable moment of leisure permits. Meanwhile he begs you to be so good as to add his name to the roll of your friends.

* * * * *

323:13 Spiegel] Jakob Spiegel (c 1483–after 1547), a distinguished scholar and statesman, came from an old family of Sélestat. He was a pupil at the Latin school there under Crato Hofman, who directed the school from 1477 to 1501 and was Gebwiler's predecessor. On the early death of his father, Spiegel joined his uncle Wimpfeling at Speyer, and was sent by him to study at Heidelberg. After receiving his BA there in 1500, he studied law at Tübingen and Freiburg. He spent a period in the imperial chancery, where he continued his legal studies, proceeding as a doctor of both laws (canon and civil), and in 1513 he became professor of law at Vienna, where he published a translation of Isocrates' *De regno gubernando* (1514). In these years he lived continuously at the imperial court, but made frequent visits to Sélestat, where he was an active member of the literary society. With the death of Maximilian (12 January 1519) his appointment lapsed, but he remained a counsellor of Charles v and of the archduke Ferdinand. In 1526, after an unfavourable turn of fortune at the court, he settled at Sélestat. Among other things he wrote a much reprinted *Lexicon iuris civilis* and scholia for Erasmus' hymn in praise of St Anne (cf Reedijk poem 22), and he published Wimpfeling's autobiography with his version of Isocrates. See Reedijk poem 98 n21; Adam 68.

If you ask why I write to you now, when you are no less busy than of old with your literary labours, the answer is that I have not forgotten the first of March, which may perhaps set you soon on your way to Italy. I decided therefore that it would be best for me to write before your departure, that my letter might revive your memory of me, the most devoted of all your friends, like the opening of an old wound, and give it new life. No words of mine can ever express my satisfaction and delight that the friendship of great scholars should have fallen to my lot, tongue-tied as I am. So I congratulate myself all the more on yours, inasmuch as you surpass all other men in learning, wisdom, and integrity; so far in fact do you outdo them that, although you are a match for them all, it is impossible to find your fellow. But why am I holding a candle to the sun?

Farewell. 31 January 1515, from Sélestat in haste

324 / To Johann Reuchlin [Basel], 1 March [1515]

This letter was printed in *Illustrium virorum epistolae* in May 1519; cf Ep 300 introduction.

ERASMUS TO HIS FRIEND REUCHLIN

I have written to you twice already, perhaps with less elegance than was proper considering the man you are, but in a simple friendly style; and you send not a word in reply. I can have no suspicions of you except such as are suitable to a very good scholar and a very civilized man. The bishop of Rochester, a most accomplished person, speaks of you in a letter to me: 'That you should have thought of me,' he says, 'and sent me greetings, I take very kindly, and particularly that you give me such a full account of Reuchlin, whom I think very highly of although I do not know him.' And a little later: 'To return to Reuchlin, if he has published anything which I may not have here, please have it sent me. I find his type of scholarship very congenial; in fact, I know no one else who comes closer to Giovanni Pico. I wish, my dear Erasmus, you would write and ask him, if you do not happen to meet, where he found that genealogy of the blessed Virgin Mary which

* * * * *

22 first of March] Cf Ep 322:37n.

31 a candle to the sun] *Adagia* II v 7

324:2 twice] Ep 300 and the letter mentioned there, line 39

6 Rochester] John Fisher; cf Epp 229 introduction; 300:8.

14 genealogy] In Reuchlin's *Rudimenta hebraica* (Pforzheim: Thomas Anshelm 27 March 1506). Reuchlin used it as a convenient instrument for teaching Hebrew letters and syllables. Cf Allen Ep 784:47.

he added to his Hebrew vocabulary; for I very greatly wish to know what authority lies behind it, and at the same time how it can be that, although according to the *Breviarium* of Philo the line of Solomon died out entirely, she is there said none the less to be descended from him. Pray try, dear Erasmus, to see that Reuchlin is so good as to enlighten me on these two points.' Again at the end: 'Farewell, good Erasmus, and give my most cordial greetings to Reuchlin whom, but for my episcopal trappings, I should undoubtedly visit myself.' This, my dear Reuchlin, the great man wrote to me with his own hand, and I have copied the exact words for you, to show how high an opinion he has of you. He deserves that you should kindly do what he asks, if only because of his very great regard for you.

As I write this, I am all packed up, and indeed extremely busy, for I am just off to Rome. As regards the publication of Jerome's works, so far am I from wishing to claim the least scrap of your work or your credit for myself, that I would rather transfer to you something of my own. When I took that work in hand, I did not know that you were engaged on the same task, although we have not really the same objective. To Hebrew I make no claim, for I barely set my lips to it. In short, each of us shall have the credit he deserves, and that in the fairest possible way. Farewell, and pray add the name of Erasmus to the list of your most true and sincere well-wishers.

1 March

325 / To Thomas Ruthall Basel, 7 March 1515

This is the preface to the edition of Seneca's *Lucubrationes* (Basel: Froben August 1515) upon which Erasmus had worked in England. Ruthall, the recipient of this dedication, was a powerful man who had been bishop of Durham since 1509 and was secretary to the king from 1500 to 1516. Erasmus had earlier sought his patronage both before and after his journey to Italy in 1509; cf Epp 192, 236:39n, 243:46. In his letter to Johann von Botzheim of 30 January 1523 (Allen I 13 lines 10–24) Erasmus described the carelessness of friends whom he had left in charge of the work in Basel, where he intended

* * * * *

17 Philo] The *Breviarium de temporibus*, falsely attributed to Philo of Alexandria, and printed at Rome and Venice in 1498, and at Paris in 1510 and 1512

27 off to Rome] Cf Ep 323:22.

28 work] Reuchlin had been revising the Hebrew passages in Jerome, and had visited Basel in the summer of 1510 for this purpose.

31 Hebrew] Erasmus had received help with the Hebrew in his edition of Jerome from the Amerbachs; cf Epp 334:132–3; 396:295–6.Oecolampadius supplied help with the Hebrew for the New Testament; see Ep 373:81.

that Froben should print it after his departure; cf Epp 328, 329, 330. An emended edition was published by Froben and Herwagen with a new preface in March 1529. For Erasmus' work on the tragedies of Seneca see Ep 263.

TO THE RIGHT REVEREND THOMAS RUTHALL,
BISHOP OF DURHAM, PRINCIPAL SECRETARY OF STATE
TO HIS SERENE MAJESTY THE KING OF ENGLAND,
FROM ERASMUS OF ROTTERDAM

By a curious coincidence, my lord Bishop, both you and I have been engaged at the same time in warfare, not of the same sort, it is true, but yet there is a kind of resemblance between them. You, under the prospering banner of a truly invincible king, have first put the French to flight and then, returning from one warlike field to another, have found the king of Scots invading the boundaries of your palatinate with large forces, well equipped, and thrown him back, routed him, cut him to pieces; I have taken two authors, the best of all but the least well preserved, St Jerome and Seneca, and with great efforts have rescued them from the corruptions, those most savage enemies of good literature, by which they had been hitherto not so much defiled as completely destroyed. Like you I had two enemies to fight, and I doubt whether at any point in your campaign you had more difficulty and more toil to face than I had in this business of mine. But there is one point in which my record is even better than yours: all by myself I was both general and private soldier, and engaged those thousands of enemies single-handed. Nor was the carnage in my conflict any less than on your fields of battle. For when you fought the French, a bloody battle was ruled out by the courtesy (what else can I call it?) of your enemies, who yielded at the first brush to better men than themselves in a way that suggested they had only come in order to contribute to your haul of booty. Apart from them, the Scots did indeed provide you with a glorious victory, their king himself and countless nobles falling on the field – and such a king as in the spirit of a gladiator (so they call it) planned complete destruction

* * * * *

325:8 flight] A reference to the campaigns of 1513 against France and Scotland. Ruthall, who accompanied Henry VIII to France, returned to help organize resistance from his see at Durham against the Scottish invasion led by James IV; cf LP I 4460–2.

23 yielded] At the Battle of the Spurs, 16 August 1513; cf Epp 283:165–6n; 360:6n.

25 victory] The battle of Flodden, 9 September 1513. The Scottish dead included the king and his son, the archbishop of St Andrews, who had been a pupil of Erasmus (cf Ep 216 introduction), a bishop, two abbots, and many of the higher nobility; cf Mackie 282.

27 spirit of a gladiator] *Adagia* I iii 76

for the whole of Britain; but that victory cost you many lives. I however in a single engagement slew, cut in pieces, and destroyed over four thousand foemen (monsters, rather); for such, I suppose, was the total number of corruptions I removed from Seneca alone. One may add that the Scottish troops had scarcely crossed the English frontier, and had seized only one fortress, from which they were soon driven out. But the whole of Jerome and the whole of Seneca had been occupied for many centuries by an infinite army of corruptions, so that nothing was left anywhere that was not held by the enemy.

And in this business I had my pen for a sword, the Muses, not Mars, to inspire me, and my battalions were my brains. Nor had I any outside help in all these difficulties except two ancient manuscripts, one of which was provided from his own library by the chief patron of my researches, that incomparable glory of our generation, William, archbishop of Canterbury, and the other was sent to my assistance by King's College, Cambridge; but these were imperfect and even more full of error than the current copies, so that less confidence could be placed in one's auxiliary troops than in the enemy. One thing however helped me: they did not agree in error, as is bound to happen in printed texts set up from the same printer's copy; and thus, just as it sometimes happens that an experienced and attentive judge pieces together what really took place from the statements of many witnesses, none of whom is telling the truth, so I conjectured the true reading on the basis of their differing mistakes. Besides which, I tracked down many things as it were by scent, following the trail of actual letters and strokes of the pen. In some places I had to guess; although I did that sparingly, knowing that the surviving works of such great men are a sacred heritage, in which one should move not merely with caution but with proper reverence.

And so I have left much for other men to unravel. The pieces which had wrongly acquired the name of Seneca I have not thrown out, for fear the reader might need something and not find it, but I have relegated them to

* * * * *

33 fortress] Norham Castle, which Ruthall prized; cf Mackie 280; LP I 4457.

39 two ancient manuscripts] There is no Seneca among the many books known to have belonged to Archbishop Warham. At King's College the library catalogue of 1452 lists two copies of the tragedies and one of the epistles; but if Erasmus was allowed to borrow the volume, it must have been in the circulating collection and not in the library. It was on parchment, with initials in gold and colour (cf Ep 2132). When at Christmas 1525 he asked Robert Aldridge, who had helped him before, to re-collate it, Aldridge failed to find it, and collated instead the library copy of the epistles, which Erasmus already knew to be worthless (cf Epp 1656, 1766, 1797). None of the books is now known to exist.

the end; the rest I have arranged in a more convenient order. I have added that very entertaining and very accomplished little work on the death of Claudius, recently discovered in my native Germany and expounded in very scholarly notes by Beatus Rhenanus. How I wish the book on earthquakes, which he mentions in his *Natural Questions*, were still extant, and likewise another on marriage cited in evidence by Jerome in his attack on Jovinian, and a third on superstition from which Augustine quotes some of the original words in his *De civitate Dei*! It did not escape my notice that no kind of literary work brings an author more tedium and less reputation; for while the reader gets all the benefit, he does not realise what he owes to the textual critic. And while nothing is more completely thrown away than a kindness done to an ungrateful person, even more truly wasted is the service rendered to a man who is unaware of it.

Although I was well aware of this, I thought these two authors both deserved a tribute of the kind. Jerome is the one author in sacred literature whom we can match even against the Greeks; without him I simply do not see whom we could put into the field who really deserves the name of theologian, if we are allowed to speak the truth. And Seneca was so highly valued by St Jerome that alone among Gentiles he was recorded in the *Catalogue of Illustrious Authors*, not so much on account of the letters exchanged between Seneca and Paul (which, being a critic of keen discernment, Jerome well knew were written by neither of them, though he wrongly uses them as a pretext for praising Seneca), as because he thought him the one writer who, while not a Christian, deserved to be read by Christians. Nothing sets a higher tone than his pronouncements, and he preaches the path of honour with such fervour that it is quite clear he practised what he preached. Seneca alone calls the mind away to heavenly things, exalts it until it despises the world of everyday, implants a loathing of all that is mean, and kindles with a love of honour; in a word, sends his reader away a better man, if he opened the book with the purpose of becoming better. For I am not much moved by the attacks of some ancient critics, none of whom dared criticize his life, though they find something

* * * * *

60–1 on the death of Claudius] The edition by Beatus was printed by Froben in March 1515, as part of the first Basel edition of the *Moria*.

62–3 on earthquakes] Seneca *Natural Questions* 6.4.2

64 on marriage] Jerome *Adversus Jovinianum* 1.49; PL 23:293

65 on superstition] Augustine *De civitate Dei* 6.11

69 thrown away] A sentiment frequently repeated; for example, Ep 277:21–2.

79–80 keen discernment] Literally, with a well-blown (we should say 'sharp') nose; *Adagia* II viii 59

wanting in his style. Caligula called his writing 'sand without lime'; but then he had such a low opinion of Virgil and Livy that he came near to turning their portraits out of all the libraries. Quintilian does not approve the way he writes, but criticizes him in such a way as to leave him almost in the highest class. A more severe attack is made on him by Aulus Gellius, but his immoderate passion for Cicero makes him more critical of Seneca than was quite fair.

Not but what there are some things in him which I would gladly change myself. Mean words sometimes offend one, and here and there a certain loquacity, like that of an old man, is somewhat tiresome; sometimes his humour is too unrestrained, his rhetorical appeals are artificial, and the vehemence of his style is too precipitate. Furthermore, while making large claims for himself, he is sometimes an unfair judge of other men's talents; in the *Controversiae*, for instance, it is surprising how rarely he approves of anyone, and how many men he makes fun of as though he were a superior being himself. And, as so often happens, his example recoils, I think, upon himself. But what author was ever so perfect that no fault could be found in him at all? There is such a high standard of morality in this man that, even if he could not write at all, he ought still to be read by all who aspire to a virtuous life; and yet there is so much eloquence that, even in that age of eloquent men, he was considered among the greatest, and Quintilian ran the risk of being thought jealous of Seneca. Not that I have failed to notice that many errors still remain; but they are of a kind that without the aid of ancient codices could hardly be removed by Seneca himself.

This then is the author, so capable of doing good, whom my efforts have restored as best I could, and who will now come before the public under the protection of your name, my lord Bishop. I remember when you had returned to England from your campaign overseas, you happened to meet me, and generously gave me a share in your French spoils, so that I, who had taken no part in the contest, should yet have my part of the prize. In my turn I dedicate and consecrate to you the trophies of my kind of warfare, for fear that after all the kindness and generosity I have experi-

* * * * *

91 Caligula] Suetonius *Caligula* 53; *Adagia* II iii 57. The rejection of Virgil and Livy is in *Caligula* 34.

93 Quintilian] 10.1.125–31

95 Aulus Gellius] 12.2

104 *Controversiae*] The *Controversiae* of the elder Seneca were at this date still attributed to his better-known son, the philosopher.

119 meet me] The chronology of Erasmus' visits to London at this time is conjectural; see Epp 278:7n; 280:37n.

enced at your hands I should be thought either to conceal altogether or not to recognize the greatness of my debt to you, and thus should show myself either an ingrate or an imbecile. Farewell, most distinguished of prelates.

Basel, 7 March 1515

326 / To the Reader — Basel, March 1515

The following are two passages selected by Allen for the sake of brevity from the third preface ('To the reader') for the second volume of Erasmus' edition of Jerome, *Hieronymi opera* (Basel 1516); cf Ep 396, 'To William Warham,' a preface to the whole edition. The autograph original in the Öffentliche Bibliothek of the university of Basel is Erasmuslade A IX 56, 381^{r}–390^{v} (Allen's α text for lines 1–71) and 391^{r}–403^{v} (Allen's β' text for the same passage). The former text is Erasmus' autograph for this third preface, the latter a manuscript copy by Konrad Brunner (Ep 331:6n), evidently made for use by the press. The second extract (lines 72–148) is not found in either α or β', and it is taken from the printed version. Clearly it was written after the receipt of Ep 304 (cf Ep 337), and hence after the visit to England during which Erasmus decided to dedicate the New Testament to Leo x instead of to Warham.

ERASMUS OF ROTTERDAM TO ALL WHO HAVE A LOVE OF SACRED LITERATURE

[f 189] ... There are others again who are not altogether lacking in judgment, but it is scarcely credible how great the force of imagination and previous conviction is, if they have already taken possession of the mind, and this we see not only in common folk but in highly educated men whose judgment is excellent. In the same way our eyes are deceived every day, and once upon a time the ears of the whole population could only be satisfied with Parmeno's pig, which later became proverbial. It will not be a waste of time to tell a few stories at this point to make my meaning clear. In my young days I had a friend in the household of that great man Hendrik, commonly called van Bergen, bishop of Cambrai, whose name was Pietro Santeramo, a Sicilian and a very amusing and well-read person. He used to tell how, when he was living in Paris, he had once written a couplet for fun which reproduced the effect of an echo:

* * * * *

326:9 Parmeno's pig] Parmeno was a Greek mimic (in one account a painter) whose imitation of the squealing of a pig was commonly regarded as more lifelike than the real thing (Plutarch *Moralia* 18C and 674B).

12 Santeramo] Nothing more seems to be known of this man; cf Allen I 589; III xxv.

Tempora fatalis quoniam sic limitis itis,
Tristia concentu funera solor olor.

As time's swift lapse thus brings death's era nearer,
Sad swans find comfort in enchanting chanting.

He gave it the title 'The dying swan before its cave.' Then he employed a skilled calligrapher to copy out this couplet, imitating an antique effect as closely as he possibly could, and deliberately leaving some letters imperfect, as though they had already been obliterated by lapse of time. The verses, thus got up, he showed to Fausto Andrelini, who has for many years now lectured there on the art of poetry; and he added that he had found the leaf among some very ancient relics of antiquity, knowing that the man would think it worthless if he said he had produced it himself a few days before. Fausto read it over and over again, and it is hard to describe how deeply he was impressed, how he was ravished by it, and almost revered such an accomplished, such an inimitable, piece of antiquity. Admiration for the venerable relic was unceasing and unlimited until Santeramo himself gave away his secret, and dissolved the whole affair in merriment.

A similar trick was played some time ago by Guillaume Cop, that immortal ornament of the city of Basel, where this hero first saw the light; in fact, the undying glory of my native Germany as a whole, and a great blessing to France, which has enjoyed the presence of that great man for many years now (and long may she do so!), adding distinction to the royal court, where he serves as physician-in-chief a king who is undoubtedly chief above all other kings. Although, if I were really to do him justice, I should call him a tower of defence to the whole world, which benefits from the way in which his most learned publications defend and refresh the most health-giving thing there is – by which I mean the art of medicine – now almost extinguished by the incompetence of those who practise it. Now he is not only a man of singular integrity and learning, but also has a very agreeable gaiety and humour, although never such as might not suit a man of high character. It happened once at supper that a dish was placed on the table full of vegetables of different kinds, and by chance a number of physicians were at supper; so he chose out a sprig of something very familiar even to the laity, which is called in Greek *petroselinon*, a kind of

* * * * *

24 Andrelini] Publio Fausto Andrelini of Forlì (1462–1518) taught at the university of Paris and was a prominent member of the humanist community there; cf Ep 323 introduction and Ep 84 introduction.

33 Cop] Cf Ep 305:208n.

38 king] Cop was court physician to Francis I.

parsley. 'It is the physician's business,' he said, 'to know the appearance and the virtues of herbs. Well, there are plenty of physicians present. Let him who can tell us the name of this herb.' No one dared to commit himself; all were convinced that this must be some rare outlandish kind of green-stuff, if the great man enquired about it so expressly. In the end he solved the problem with a laugh by sending for the cook-maid and telling her to answer where the doctors had failed; and she produced the name without hesitation.

Here is a third story for you, but this time it shall be nameless. One of the leading scholars in Italy was handed by someone a page torn from a manuscript in such a way that there was no heading to reveal the author. The man who gave it him observed that it looked like the work of some quite recent writer. Now the learned man was one of those whose passion for antiquity makes them despise everything modern. Immediately he protested against the filthy style, as he then thought it, heaping abuse upon the barbarian author who had spoilt good parchment with such uneducated rubbish. His scorn was unlimited and unceasing, until the other man showed him that what he had condemned so heartily was a bit of Cicero. The learned man accepted the correction and laughed to see how badly his fancy had misled him. So great is the force, even in good scholars, of a pre-existing conviction, and nothing is so likely when one forms a judgment to distort or cloud one's vision.

[f 191] In a previous preface I have already made it, I think, sufficiently clear that there is no class of author not disfigured in places with spurious works of this kind. Will you regard it as pious and fair-minded to allow any ignoramus to smuggle in what he pleases and corrupt as he pleases, and yet not allow learning and zeal to throw out what has been foisted in and correct what has been disfigured? You make your conditions perhaps: this requires the authority of the bishops. What nonsense! They are not indignant when some impostor has disfigured these sacred books without any authority at all, and they are furious with anyone who puts right what has been corrupted, unless he has the authority of the whole church behind him. It is not as though I am trying to go one better than the princes of the church; they are busy men, and I am doing what little I can to help. I put them on notice that I make no decisions; I indicate, not adjudicate. Nor have I the shadow of a doubt that they will be the first to accept my opinion. But it is bound to cause trouble, say they, to undermine what has been accepted for so many centuries. Yet was anything in the old days of more general acceptance than the Septuagint? And Jerome was not afraid, though certain bishops, and Augustine with them, disapproved in vain, to correct it in his translation. Is

any tale more familiar than those seventy separate cells? Yet Jerome did not hesitate to say that a story which everyone believed in , not only Augustine, was a fabrication. Has anything a wider circulation than his version of the New Testament? And did the truth of the Gospel lose any of its authority when Lorenzo, who was a specialist in rhetoric rather than theology, condemned certain passages as mistranslations? Do we now read the Pauline Epistles with any less confidence because Jacques Lefèvre d'Etaples, a man admirable no less for character than for learning, has denied that the version of them in common use can be by Jerome, and because he has followed Lorenzo in altering many passages that were corrupt or wrongly translated? In this field I too was working at the same time, and by a strange coincidence, neither of us knowing about the other's work, we were both engaged simultaneously on the same enterprise, though his edition came out first. I only wish it were of a quality that would render the edition I am preparing quite superfluous. I have the highest opinion of Lefèvre as a scholar of uncommon erudition, I respect him as a man of high character, and I wish him well as a close friend. But if in the secular field Aristotle decided that he must regard the truth as of more account than his friendship for Plato, much more should we take that line when we are concerned with sacred literature in what I may call its most sacred form. This I say, not because I do not much approve of his edition, but to secure forgiveness if I seem at any point to disagree with such a man.

But to return to my subject: what has happened to the church in these latter days? Is Christendom in peril because Paulus van Middelburg, bishop of Fossombrone, has published several books to show that we are all wrong about the date of Easter? Suppose it were true that innovation on

* * * * *

90 separate cells] Tradition had it that the Greek version of the Old Testament was made independently by seventy scholars, each in his own cell, who arrived at the same result.

90 Jerome] Cf *Praefatio in pentateuchum*, and also *Adversus Rufinum* 2. 25; PL 23:470; cf Allen Ep 843:337.

94 Lorenzo] Valla; Cf Ep 182.

96 Lefèvre d'Etaples] Cf Ep 304:100n.

100 I too] Cf Ep 337:879ff and the *Apologia ad I. Fabrum Stapulensem* LB IX 19BC.

107 Aristotle] *Nicomachean Ethics* 1.6.1(1096a.16)

113 Paulus van Middelburg] A graduate of Louvain, the bishop of Fossombrone (1446–1534) had held the chair of astronomy at Padua, and the see of Fossombrone since 1494. He was involved in controversy with doctors at Louvain about the precise date of the crucifixion, and the work here alluded to, *Paulina, de recta Paschae celebratione*, was published with a treatise on that subject at Fossombrone in 1513.

these important points not only fails to weaken ecclesiastical authority but actually strengthens it: why do they fear that the skies may fall if I have done my best to sift out illiterate and worthless stuff from the works of that great scholar Jerome? And I only wish it had been possible to extend to his other writings what I have achieved in his letters. In any case, if any authorization is required, I work under the favour, encouragement, and inspiration of many and great prelates who themselves are men of learning; and they not merely approve my industry but support it with the most liberal generosity. First and chief among them is my Maecenas, the one great patron of my researches, William Warham, archbishop of Canterbury, primate of all England, a man so accomplished in every kind of culture and virtue that the qualities which one scarcely finds separate in other people are united in him for all to admire, and he fully suffices by himself to serve as a picture of all the endowments of the perfect prelate. Nor shall the others be deprived of their due praise; but for the moment I must not burden the reader with a longer preface. One thing only I will add. Some time ago, Leo, the supreme pontiff (supreme indeed in every way), was told about this work of mine in letters from many excellent men apart from me; and I expect that so good a scholar and so good a man will not only confirm my labours with his authority but crown them with generous rewards.

More words have been expended on this argument, I admit, than the limits of a prologue would allow. But I have done all I could, I have left no stone unturned, to satisfy everybody, knowing that people are offended or pacified, some by one thing, some by another. If anyone can still be found so stupid, so unaware of his own best interests, so steeped in old familiar error that he prefers to waste precious time on this worthless prating, he in his turn shall have no cause to complain of me; for I put at his disposal everything that was included in earlier editions, much more correctly than before, with some additions not to be found in them. So careful have I been to avoid offending anyone that learned and unlearned alike, fair-minded and prejudiced, dullards past hope and men of the highest promise, all will find that I have done my best to give them what they want.

Farewell, friendly reader. Basel, March 1515

326A / From Willibald Pirckheimer [Nürnberg? April 1515]

The text of this letter is taken from a rough draft in Pirckheimer's hand in the Stadtbibliothek of Nürnberg, MS PP 131. Epp 362 and 375 show that the letter

* * * * *

137–8 no stone unturned] *Adagia* I iv 30

did not reach Erasmus, so that there is no scribal copy in the Deventer Letter-book as there is of Ep 375. Pirckheimer's references to this letter in Ep 375, however, indicate additions that were made to it in the final copy. The date is determined by the reference to Sir Robert Wingfield's presence in Augsburg (LP II 1 294, 377); I accept the view of E. Reicke (WPB Ep 355), however, that Nürnberg is the more likely place of writing. Wingfield's expectation that he would soon return to England was disappointed, and at the end of May he was sent further south to Innsbruck. It was likely this circumstance that prevented delivery of the letter, since by May Erasmus was back in England; cf Epp 326B introduction, 327 introduction.

If any man can be allowed to boast of his distinguished friends, I cannot think that I should be quite last in this respect, seeing that I am blessed with the friendship not only of private persons, but of great and famous princes in France and Italy as well as Germany. But, as I hope for Fortune's favours, among all those friends of mine you, Erasmus, most learned and delightful of men, are second to none but first and most eminent. I have read your letter, which gave me far more pleasure and satisfaction than if it had been written to me by some great monarch, not that I accept the praise you give me in it, but because I perceive that I have won your friendship, which I so much desired. I am grateful therefore to my dear Beatus, to whom I owe my introduction to so great a man, and grateful not less to you for showing yourself so kind and so approachable. So I reckon myself especially fortunate on this account, and with good reason set a special mark against the hour which brought me such a lucky letter; which I would have answered promptly had it not been so slow in coming. For although it was written on 24 January, it was not delivered to me until 1 April, when the Frankfurt fair,

* * * * *

326A:10 Beatus] Cf Ep 318.

13 special mark] Literally, a white pebble; *Adagia* I v 54

16 Frankfurt fair] One of the chief book fairs in northern Europe, that at Frankfurt developed from the established importance of the town's fair long before the appearance of printing nearby, at Mainz. The town was the chief trading centre of the Rhine region, where merchants met from all over Europe, and already in the fifteenth century it attracted booksellers from Italy and Switzerland as well as Germany. See H. Estienne [H. Stephano] *Francofordiense emporium* (Geneva 1574), ed and trans James Westfall Thompson as *The Frankfort Book Fair* (Chicago: Caxton Club 1910); L. Febvre and H.-J. Martin *L'Apparition du livre* (Paris 1958) 348–54.

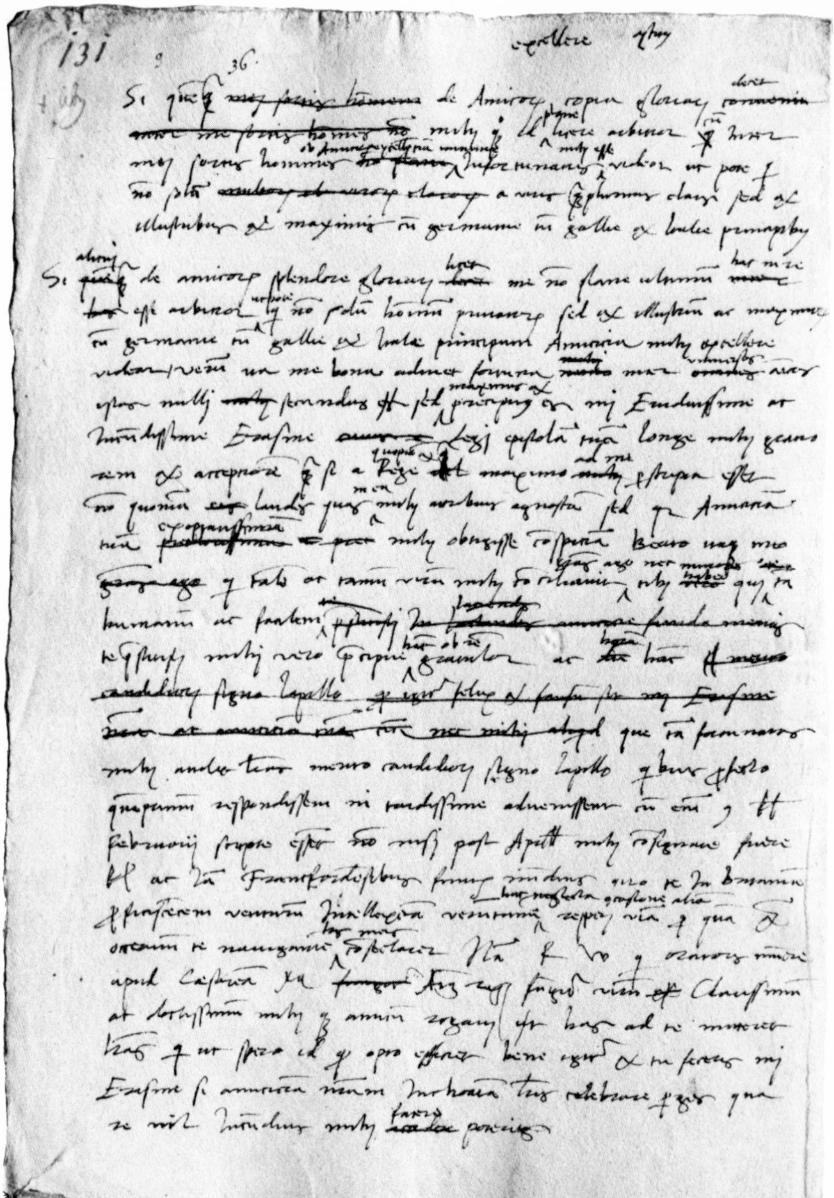

Autograph letter, rough draft
Willibald Pirckheimer to Erasmus, Epistle 326A
Stadtbibliothek Nürnberg, MS PP 131

which I had understood you would visit on your way to England, was already over. However, although I lost that opportunity, I have found another way by which I can overtake you with a letter, even though you sail upon the ocean. I have asked Robert Wingfield, who is the English king's envoy at the imperial court, a distinguished and well-read man and my good friend, to forward this letter to you; and this I hope he will succeed in doing. You for your part, my dear Erasmus, will do the right thing, if you continue to keep our new friendship green with a reply. You could do nothing that would give me greater pleasure.

326B / To Jakob Wimpfeling [Frankfurt, March/April 1515]

This letter, from the archives of the chapter of St Thomas in Strasbourg, was not included in Allen's edition. It was first published by A.W. Strobel in *Das Narrenschiff von Dr. Sebastian Brant* (Quedlinburg and Leipzig 1839) and more recently by P.O. Kristeller in *Florilegium Historiale: Essays presented to Wallace K. Ferguson* ed J.G. Rose and W.H. Stockdale (Toronto 1971) 52–8. The manuscript is not an autograph, but the work of a German scribe. It is addressed to Wimpfeling and the literary society of Strasbourg. The place and date of its composition are taken from Kristeller. Erasmus was on his way to England, having left Basel sometime in March, when he had also contemplated going to Rome (Epp 322:37 and 324:27n). He evidently visited the Frankfurt book fair, travelling from Strasbourg with the publishers: Matthias Schürer of Strasbourg and Wolfgang Lachner of Basel. He also visited Saint-Omer (Ep 327), Antwerp, where his host was probably Pieter Gillis (Ep 337), and Tournai, where he stayed with his old English patron Mountjoy, then governor of Tournai. The letter records Erasmus' first meeting with Reuchlin, an event hitherto known only from later reports (eg, letter to Wolsey, 18 May 1519, Allen Ep 967:72).

TO MASTER JAKOB WIMPFELING AND ALL THE LITERARY SOCIETY IN STRASBOURG

Cordial greetings. On one and the same day some evil genius dealt me a double wound. In Mainz I had counted up my small stock of money so that I could know if anything had gone astray, for I was so frightened by reports that a ship had been ransacked that I had concealed it in my leggings. I

* * * * *

20 Wingfield] Sir Robert (c 1464–1539) had served on diplomatic missions since 1508; see DNB and Wegg.

found sixty-six gold coins, among them two nobles, some écus de soleil, and ducats, the smallest of all a gold florin, if you except a single St Philip florin. There was a parlour with a stove in it attached to my bedroom of which I had sole use, in which we talked far into the night, Schürer and I and several other friends. When they had all gone I left my purse there and went to bed. In the morning, not suspecting trouble, I thought I would count the money again, to make sure how much I could afford to take out for buying books. I soon saw that I was two nobles short. My heart sank; I counted again, and found that twenty-two gold florins were missing as well. The thief had left me forty-eight gold pieces, being a civilized fellow and content with less than half. This mishap had not so pierced me to the heart, I do assure you , that I was immune from some superficial prickings of dismay! I hoped that this misfortune might let me off any other bad luck throughout my journey. But worse was at hand. Towards nightfall I felt very tired and knew this meant I was sickening. I dined most sparingly. I went to bed. Soon I was seized by the most violent fever I ever felt in my life. It lasted till the eighth hour next day. I sweated excessively. My breath and my water were just like fire. I think if the sweating had not supervened, the attack would have been fatal. But I am now in such a state that I have good hopes. Yet I do not regret this journey. It gave me the chance of an affectionate meeting with Reuchlin, a man whom I not only respect as a scholar of

* * * * *

326B:7 nobles] English gold coins, possibly ryals (rose-nobles), but more likely angel-nobles, then officially worth 6s 8d sterling = 9s 8d groot Flemish = 56s 11d tournois each. Cf CWE 2 146 (Ep 214:4n), 340 (plate); and CWE 1 312, 319 (plate), 325–6, 329, 336–7, 342–4.

7 écus de soleil] French gold coins, then officially worth 36s 3d tournois = 6s 2d groot Flemish = 4s 3d sterling each. In November 1516 the French government raised its official value to 40s 8d tournois. Cf CWE 2 145 (Ep 212:7n), 298 (Ep 296: 131–2n); and CWE 1 316–17, 336–7, 342–4.

8 ducats] Venetian gold coins, then officially worth 4s 7d sterling = 38s 9d tournois = 6s 7d groot Flemish each. Cf CWE 1 314, 338–9, 342–4.

8 gold florin] Possibly a Florentine florin, but, in view of Erasmus' itinerary, more likely a Rhenish florin of the Four Electors, then officially worth 3s 5d sterling = 4s 10d groot Flemish = 28s 9d tournois. Cf CWE 1 316–17, 336–7, 342–4.

8–9 St Philip florin] A Burgundian-Hapsburg gold coin, originally an imitation of the Rhenish florin, then officially worth 4s 2d groot Flemish = 3s 0d sterling= 24s 6d tournois. Cf CWE 1 318, 321 (plate), 336–9, 342–4; CWE 2 327–45.

15 twenty-two gold florins] If these were in fact Rhenish florins, the loss would have amounted to, in official values, £5 6s 4d groot Flemish = £31 12s 9d tournois = £3 15s 2d sterling. Cf CWE 1 338–9, 342–4; CWE 2 327–45.

27 Reuchlin] See introduction to this letter.

distinction but like quite particularly for a rare kind of courtesy and personal charm. I also met our friend Gerbel, or rather I enjoyed his company for several hours; his powers of conversation and character and learning are so much to my taste that for some years no man's society has given me the same pleasure. Of nothing have I greater hopes than of Beatus Rhenanus and Gerbel. Lachner was reluctant to sell the new *Proverbia* here, so as to clear off the old one first; you must get a copy from Basel. I am writing this in a great hurry, being all packed up ready to start. The rest of my news you shall have from England. I am grateful for your generosity, thanks to which I came away from my inn without having anything to pay. In this I find nothing new, but all the same your kindness towards me is a great delight. My best wishes to you all; I write to you as I would to a single person, and may you long continue bound by the unbreakable ties of this association.

Erasmus Rotterdam

327 / To Beatus Rhenanus — Saint-Omer, 13 April 1515

This is the preface to *Enarratio allegorica in primum Psalmum*, the psalm 'Beatus vir,' first printed in Erasmus' *Lucubrationes* by Schürer in Strasbourg, September 1515; he printed it again in June 1516, November 1517, and January 1519. Froben published the *Lucubrationes* in July 1518 and October 1519; Martens at Louvain printed the *Enarratio* separately in October 1515 (NK 814).

Erasmus was now on his way to England, probably to see manuscripts connected with his work on Jerome and the New Testament, and perhaps to obtain a copy of his complete Latin translation of the latter; cf Ep 384 introduction. His host in Saint-Omer was Antoon van Bergen, abbot of the monastery of St Bertin.

Beat Bild of Sélestat (1485–1547) took his humanist name Beatus Rhenanus from his father's place of origin at Rheinau in Alsace. His father, a butcher, had removed to Sélestat before his son was born, and seems there to have received the surname of 'Rinower.' Beatus was educated at the famous Latin school in Sélestat under Crato Hofman (cf Ep 323:13n), and in due course he was sent by his father to the university of Paris, where his great master was Lefèvre d'Etaples. He was at Paris from 1503 to 1507, and subsequently

* * * * *

29 Gerbel] Cf Ep 342 introduction.

32 Beatus Rhenanus] Cf Ep 327 introduction.

33 Lachner] Cf Ep 305:198n.

33 *Proverbia*] Erasmus must be referring to the first revision of his *Adagiorum chiliades*; this bears no date, but Froben's address to the reader is dated 1515, and our letter puts it in the first three months of that year.

worked with the printers Henri Estienne, Matthias Schürer, and, after 1511, Amerbach and Froben in Basel. There he also studied Greek with Johannes Conon; cf Ep 318:22n. After 1526 he returned to Sélestat where he died, and where his library is still preserved. He was responsible for a vast editorial achievement, including the supervision of much of Erasmus' own publications. See Adam 51–67.

ERASMUS OF ROTTERDAM TO BEATUS RHENANUS OF SÉLESTAT

When I see, my dear Beatus, how ordinary and uneducated people keep their friendships in repair by sending and receiving small presents from time to time, it has seemed to me wrong that those who pursue the humanities should be found wanting in this form of friendly attention, and we especially who are linked by our devotion to common studies in the closest possible relationship. And so the other day, when my horses were weary from a tiring journey and I was obliged to halt for a few days at Saint-Omer, I began, in order that the working-time might not be wholly wasted, to consider whether I could not get ready some modest gift for you. At that moment there came into my head a very sound precept of our favourite Seneca: one should take special pains to see that a present is appropriate to the recipient as well as worthy of the giver, for thus things of small value in themselves become most precious, simply because they have been aptly chosen. And what could a theologian more properly send than a choice nosegay plucked in the flower-garden of the Scriptures? What present could be more fit for a Beatus than an actual working-plan for true beatitude, sketched by the pencil of the Holy Spirit? A heavenly name indeed it is, for it transcends the nature of mere man, so that the Greek poets used to ascribe this quality to the gods as their especial attribute, and call them *Makares*, the blessed ones, *Beati*. Not of course that the honour of such a distinguished name belongs to any mortal, unless he is so engrafted in Christ that he is already as it were transfigured and made one with him, and so deserves to be given a share in his immortality and in that splendid name. For nothing less deserves the name of true blessedness than those whom the foolish multitude calls blessed. It calls them blessed with as much warrant as it calls them divine; if in error, to its discredit, and if in flattery, to something worse. This name *Beatus*, blessed, recurs so often in the mysteries of Scripture, and never do we find it given to a rich man, never to monarchs, never to Sardanapalus and his like. '*Beati*, blessed,' I find, 'are all

* * * * *

327:12 Seneca] *De beneficiis* 1.12

30 Sardanapalus] An Assyrian king, proverbial for wealth and effeminacy; *Adagia* III vii 27

30–3 'Blessed'] Psalms 127 (128):1, 31 (32):2, 40 (41):1, 118 (119):1

they that fear the Lord, and walk in his ways.' 'Blessed,' I find, 'is the man unto whom the Lord imputeth no sin.' 'Blessed,' I find, 'is he that considereth the poor and needy.' 'Blessed,' I find, 'are those that are undefiled in the way, and walk in the law of the Lord.' So many ranks of beatitude, of blessedness are there, and yet of those I name no more account is taken than of the Megarians in the old Greek proverb. The first *Beatus* is he whom the fear of God restrains from doing wrong. Blessed again is he who has fallen into sin, but washes away the wrong with tears of repentance so that the merciful Lord does not impute to him what he has done. Blessed too is he who makes up the errors of his earlier life with works of piety and charity, for in the day of judgment the Lord will deliver him from evil. But more blessed he who is kept free from all taint of sin by respect for the divine law; and most blessed of all the man whom it describes in this psalm, who not only is in the happy state of being untainted by sin, but lives continually according to the divine commandment in such a way that he himself always wears the flower of a blameless life, while contributing to others the lovely fruit of a high example and teaching that leads to salvation.

And so I send you yourself, a *Beatus* for a Beatus. What else could be more fitting – especially as you are blessed with a nature not prone to faults, and try hard to keep both life and reputation free from the stain of any fault? So hard indeed do you work at the best literature that, with Christ to prosper your admirable endeavours, you add not a little lustre and distinction to your native town, which, small as it is, is already famous as the mother of so many able men. There is good hope therefore that one day you will set the whole of Germany such an example as will show them all that your name Beatus was given you not by accident but by divine providence. And so this small present will not merely remind you of your Erasmus, but will set before you an example for yourself. If it please almighty God, as we have hitherto been linked in the sweet companionship of common studies, so may we hereafter be thought worthy to enjoy together the true beatitude that lasts for ever. Farewell, best of friends.

Saint-Omer, 13 April 1515

328 / From Beatus Rhenanus — Basel, 17 April 1515

BEATUS RHENANUS TO ERASMUS OF ROTTERDAM

Seneca makes capital progress, O cleverest of men, for we have two presses

* * * * *

36 Greek proverb] The people of Megara were thought to be negligible by the rest of Greece; *Adagia* II i 79.

328:2 Seneca] The *Lucubrationes*; cf Ep 325 introduction.

working on him. Nesen is most careful in reading proof, and I wish I were as successful in emending the text as he is 'right keen of scent' in sniffing out errors. In any case, as the copy is still disfigured by many mistakes (as you well know), you are the one person whose help it would still need. I happened lately on that chapter in the *De beneficiis*, book 4, which begins 'Non ideo per se non est expetendum, cui aliquid extra quoque emolumenti adhaeret. Eero enim pulcherrima quaeque multis et aduentitiis comitata sunt dolis, sed illas trahunt, ipsa praecedunt. Num dubium est quin hoc humani generis domicilium circuitus solis ac lunae vicibus suis temperet? quin alterius calore alantur corpora, terrae relaxentur, immodici humores comprimantur, alligatis omnia hyemis tristitia frangantur, alterius tempore efficaci ac penetrabili rigatur maturitas frugum? quin ad huius cursum foecunditas humana respondeat, quin ille animum obseruabilem fecerit circumactu suo?'

On the spur of the moment, when that sheet had already begun to be printed, I emended it like this; whether I was as clever as I was brave, I do not know: 'Fere enim pulcherrima quaeque multis et aduentitiis comitata sunt dotibus, sed illas trahunt, ipsa praecedunt. Num dubium est quin hoc humani generis domicilium circuitus solis ac lunae vicibus suis temperet? quin alterius calore alantur corpora, terrae relaxentur, immodici humores comprimantur, alligantis omnia hyemis tristicia frangatur, alterius tepore efficaci et penetrabili rigetur maturitas frugum? quin ad huius cursum foecunditas humana respondeat, quin ille annum obseruabilem fecerit circumactu suo?' There that passage ends; but I have done the same in many places, restoring, for instance, 'dementissime' for 'clementisse,' 'peierat' for 'perierat,' 'detestabili via' for 'de stabili via,' 'vota' for 'nota,' and much else of the same sort. But I do not like always relying on my own judgment, especially extempore, and under pressure from men who cannot stand delay. If only we had an ancient copy, there is nothing I should enjoy more than to emend this text in the places that are still left uncorrected, for by so doing I should be of use to scholars and advance your reputation, although you do say in your preface that you have removed most of the mistakes but not all.

Froben is asking if he may have your New Testament, and says he will

* * * * *

3 Nesen] See Ep 329.

4 keen of scent] An echo of Horace; *Adagia* I vi 81

7 *De beneficiis*] 4.22.4 to 4.23.1; Beatus arrived at the correct text, except that his *rigetur* should be *regatur*.

36 New Testament] Apparently Erasmus had not yet arranged for the printing; cf Epp 330; 324:27n.

give you as much for it as you could get anywhere else. He says Dunckel gave him no commissions about sending clothes, although I understood the contrary from both of you. I am sorry that you did not give the letter you wrote me (so Nesen says) to Lachner. If you gave it to Schürer, I don't know when I shall get it; you know what an astonishingly careless man he is. I might perhaps now be answering some of it. I would tell you how our friend Glareanus, when the hall was full of sophisters assembled for a disputation on the value of the *Parva logicalia*, came in on horseback, if I did not think the tale too foolish to be put in a letter to you, a wise man if ever there was one.

The *Moria* has only 600 copies left out of 1800, so it will be reprinted straight away, and it will be possible to add, if you like, the *Scarabaeus* and *Sileni*, Plutarch's *Gryllus*, and the *Parasitica* and *Praise of the Fly* by Lucian. Besides that, Froben will print your *Lucubrationes* forthwith (that is the name which stands on the title-page of the book), as soon as he is sure that it is no longer open to you to add or remove anything. Nesen sends you his greetings, and wishes he were as near the finish as he is the starting-line, which is still not far. If you have spent anything on buying clothes for Dunckel or anything else, Froben has solemnly promised that he will pay for all of it, and sends you his sincere good wishes. Our friend Glareanus

* * * * *

37 Dunckel] Also mentioned in Ep 330:21; a servant or secretary whom Erasmus may have taken with him to Cambridge; cf Allen IV xxiv.

39 letter] Cf Ep 330:15, 16.

40 Lachner] Cf Ep 305:198n.

43 Glareanus] Heinrich Loriti was born in 1488 in Mollis, canton Glarus, and died in 1563; cf Ep 440. At this time he was teaching at Basel, although he had only an MA, and had not yet been allotted a seat among the doctors at university gatherings. Rhenanus describes a theatrical attempt to force the issue of his status; see E. Hilgert 'Johann Froben and the Basel university scholars 1513–1523' *The Library Quarterly* 41 (April 1971) 146.

44 *Parva logicalia*] A textbook in logic composed by Marsilius of Inghen (d 1396), the first rector of the university of Heidelberg.

47 *Moria*] The first Froben edition was published in 1515. His second edition was undertaken in 1516; cf Ep 419:14n.

48–9 *Scarabaeus* ... Lucian] The 'Scarabaeus' and 'Sileni Alcibiadis' are two of the *Adagia* (III vii 1, III iii 1) added in the 1515 edition and printed separately by Froben with the *Bellum* in April/May 1517; the *Gryllus* and the works that follow were not printed by Froben with any of Erasmus' writings, although Beatus Rhenanus finished his translation of the *Gryllus*; cf Allen Ep 473:21.

50 *Lucubrationes*] Cf Epp 327 introduction; 342:30.

53 near the finish] *Adagia* III vi 46

has gone to Italy. We are looking forward with joy to your return in September. Farewell, cleverest of men, and do not forget your friend Beatus. Basel, 17 April 1515

329 / From Wilhelm Nesen — Basel, [c 17 April 1515]

Nesen (of Nastätten, near Koblenz) was of peasant origin and had completed his MA at Basel in 1515. He taught there and also worked among the printers, and in 1515 was employed by Froben as corrector for Erasmus' Seneca (Ep 325). This note may have been written to accompany Ep 328. See de Vocht CTL I 390ff and passim.

TO MASTER ERASMUS OF ROTTERDAM FROM NESEN

Greetings, most learned Erasmus. In the works of Seneca, which you have restored by great exertions for the benefit of all aspirants to a liberal education, I find in the margin that some things have been marked in your hand as though they were spurious and inserted, with the words 'added by some foolish fellow.' Please let me know, although I am too unscholarly myself to have the right to expect an answer from a great scholar, whether these are to be cut out, or printed with the rest. Farewell, most learned Erasmus, and count me too as one of your humble servants. In haste, at the boatside, in Basel

330 / From Beatus Rhenanus — Basel, 30 April 1515

BEATUS RHENANUS TO ERASMUS OF ROTTERDAM

Froben wants to get your New Testament from you, and says will you please also correct and send him your *Lucubrations*, the *Enchiridion of a Christian Knight*, that is. We shall put Plutarch's *Gryllus* with the *Moria*, also Lucian's *Parasitica* and *Fly*, and your *Scarabaeus* and *Sileni Alcibiadis*. Seneca is printing on two presses. I could wish the copy were cleaner and the reader a little more careful. But he does not detect all the mistakes, nor am I the man, if he sometimes does detect them, to set them all to rights, both because my knowledge is so very limited and because to be over-clever in someone else's book has something foolish about it. This kinsman of yours has accepted two gold pieces from Froben, and he was all the more welcome because he looks so like our dear Erasmus, so that even if he said nothing

* * * * *

330:6 reader] Apparently Wilhelm Nesen is meant.

10 kinsman] Nothing is known of Erasmus' kinsmen. His father had many brothers, as well as a son Pieter, older than Erasmus; cf Ep 3.

about it, the resemblance in feature at once proclaims him a relative of yours.

The other day I sent you a very long letter by Conrad the Paris bookseller about your affairs; but your letter which you wrote me from Frankfurt I have not yet had, and not a word yet from Schürer. Why is he plunged in this lethargy? We are hoping you will come back to us in August. Meanwhile please give some thought to finishing your art of letter-writing, and to emending Quintilian. I have sent you Seneca's Claudius. Greetings from Froben and his wife Gertrude, and from the Amerbachs, and from Nesen, who are all longing to welcome your return. My regards to Dunckel. Farewell, cleverest of men, and keep a warm corner in your heart for Beatus, as I know you do.

Basel, 30 April 1515

331 / From Bruno Amerbach — Basel, 1 May 1515

Bruno (1484–1519) was the eldest son of Johannes Amerbach and his wife Barbara Ortenberg. With his brother Basilius (1488–1535) Bruno matriculated at Basel in 1500, but the next year, with Lukas Klett and Sebastian Brant's son Onuphrius, the brothers removed to Paris, where they proceeded to the MA in 1506. Basilius returned home to study law under Zasius in 1507, and Bruno returned the year following to work in the press. He studied Greek with Johannes Conon (Ep 318:22) and Hebrew as well. Cf AK II Ep 518.

BRUNO AMERBACH TO ERASMUS

Greetings, dear Erasmus, most learned of men. I can think of nothing to say, except to ask you, if a request from me is in order, to come back to us soon. Believe me, your arrival will be looked forward to, not only by your friends (by us, that is), but by absolutely everybody. Farewell. My brother Basilius

* * * * *

15 very long letter] Ep 328

15 Conrad] Resch, a native of Kirchheim on the Neckar, who had family links with the book industry of Basel. In 1508–9 he was in Paris and Lyon representing Wolfgang Lachner, and by 1518 he was naturalized. He took over direction of the shop, Écu de Bâle, from his uncle Johann Schabler (Wattenschnee) and in 1526 sold it to Chrétien Wechel, when he joined Schabler in Basel. He was also active in and out of France, and was well connected among the well educated and influential. See P.G. Bietenholz *Basle and France in the Sixteenth Century* (Geneva 1971).

19–20 art of letter-writing] The *De conscribendis epistolis*; cf Ep 71.

21 Claudius] Cf Ep 325:60n.

23 Dunckel] Cf Ep 328:37n.

and our friend Konrad send their greetings. In haste, from our treadmill at Basel. 1 May 1515

Yours, for what he is worth, Bruno Amerbach

332 / To Pieter Gillis London, 7 May [1515]

Erasmus continued his journey to England, partly for work connected with the Jerome and the New Testament, partly no doubt, for renewed contact with his friends and prospective patrons. This letter was first printed in the *Farrago* (1519).

ERASMUS TO HIS FRIEND PIETER GILLIS

If you are well, I have good reason for great rejoicing. I spent longer on the journey than I had expected, for at Ghent the chancellor of our most illustrious prince detained me for three days; at Tournai my old friend Mountjoy, who now governs the city as viceroy; and at Saint-Omer the abbot of St Bertin's. The crossing was expensive and dangerous but rapid. My box which I had entrusted to Franz's brother has not arrived yet, which

* * * * *

331:6 Konrad] Brunner, known as Fonteius, of Wesen, who died in 1519 cf Ep 313:26n.

332:3 chancellor] Jean Le Sauvage; cf Epp 301:35n; 410.

3–4 our ... prince] On the death of Philip the Handsome on 25 September 1506 the rule of the Burgundian Netherlands was resumed by his father Maximilian, now styled emperor, for Philip's infant (aged 6) son Charles, duke of Brabant, the future Charles V. The government was headed by Margaret of Austria, widow of the duke of Savoy and daughter of Maximilian, who in March 1509 elicited from Maximilian the powers of regent. She was not able to dominate the local estates, and Jean Le Sauvage rose to the position of *chef et président du conseil privé* against her opposition. In April 1512 she established an independent household for the archduke Charles as a concession to local interest and patriotism, and by a new household ordinance of October 1513 divided the official guardianship of the prince between Maximilian, Henry VIII, and Ferdinand of Aragon, a consortium that represented firm resistance to French claims over the territory. At the end of 1514 the Estates General offered to purchase Charles' independence with a large subsidy, and as a consequence Maximilian declared Charles to be of age on 6 January 1515. It is therefore to Charles in his new authority as a native prince of the Netherlands that Erasmus here refers.

5 Mountjoy] Arrived in Tournai 5 February; LP II i 126, 147

6 abbot] Antoon van Bergen; see Ep 327 introduction; Ep 143 introduction.

7 Franz] Franz Birckmann of Cologne, bookseller and agent in Antwerp, who died in 1529; cf Ep 258:14n. Erasmus seems to have brought the manuscript of his edition of Jerome for further work in England, along with copies of the new edition of the *Adagia* just printed by Froben in Basel; cf Ep 269 introduction.

is the most unfortunate thing that could happen to me. All my materials for Jerome are in it, and unless I recover them soon, the men who are printing it in Basel will run out of work, not without great loss. If this has happened by accident, it was a most unfortunate one; if deliberately and on purpose, that they might unload their old *Proverbia* first, it was a most hostile act, for there is no way in which they could have done me more harm. I intended to present the bishops with their copies; as it is, I pay my respects empty-handed, and they send me away empty-handed in return. If they had sent the box as they promised, I should already be with you by now. Two of the best scholars in the whole of England, Cuthbert Tunstall, the chancellor of the archbishop of Canterbury, and Thomas More, to whom I dedicated my *Moria*, both great friends of mine, are in Bruges. If anything should emerge in which you can do them a service, your civility will prove to have been very well invested. Tell Franz about all this. I hope to revisit you before July. Look after yourself meanwhile, my incomparable friend.

London, 7 May [1514]

333 / To Raffaele Riario, Cardinal of San Giorgio

Riario (1461–1521) of Savona had been created cardinal in 1477 through the influence of his uncle Girolamo Riario, nephew of Sixtus IV, and was a candidate for the papacy in the elections both of 1503 and 1513, when he was the nearest rival of Leo X. He was the highest placed patron of Erasmus during his visit to Italy, and had introduced him to the papal entourage; cf Ep 296: 109; Renaudet *Italie* 93–5.

This letter was first published in the *Damiani elegeia* in August 1515 with the date 31 March 1515. The present date, which places the letter at the end of Erasmus' stay in England, is derived from manuscript evidence in Basel discovered by Allen, who concluded that the misleading date was fixed by the printer, perhaps under instruction from Erasmus, to lead Warham and Erasmus' friends in England to believe that in the earliest days of his visit he was already committed to dedicate the edition of Jerome to the pope; but see line

* * * * *

12 *Proverbia*] Cf Ep 326B:33n.

14 bishops] Warham at Canterbury and Fisher at Rochester, certainly; possibly Thomas Ruthall of Durham and Wolsey as well; cf Ep 333:20–30.

19 Bruges] This is the embassy described by More in the opening of book I of *Utopia*; for the royal commission see Rogers 10; it was issued to Cuthbert Tunstall, Richard Sampson, Sir Thomas Spinelly, Sir Thomas More, and John Clifford, the governor of the English merchants in Flanders. In point of fact the ambassadors had not yet left London and would not arrive in Bruges for another ten days. Cf Ep 362:12n; and E. Surtz 'St Thomas More and His Utopian Embassy of 1515' *Catholic Historical Review* 39 (1953) 272–97.

98n, and Allen Ep 835:14n. Allen's manuscript, which is not an autograph, contains the concluding portion of this letter, and, following on immediately on the same leaf, the whole of Ep 335; Öffentliche Bibliothek, university of Basel, Erasmuslade B II b 1. The text of the printed version, which is greatly amplified, is the one adopted by Allen and translated here. These two letters – Epp 333 and 335, with Epp 334 and 337 – were thus the first of Erasmus' letters proper to be published by himself; cf preface.

TO THE MOST REVEREND FATHER IN CHRIST RAFFAELE, CARDINAL OF SAN GIORGIO, FROM ERASMUS OF ROTTERDAM

If there has been silence on my part for some years now, most reverend Father, it is not that I have forgotten what I owe you, for I have never ceased to remember and to speak of that, and never shall. In part, a certain diffidence has restrained me, for it seemed selfish to interrupt with trifles of my own a man already harassed with so much important business – there are times when not to pay one's respects shows more respect; in part, it was the severity of that worse than iron age we live in. For if the law is silent in the clash of arms, how much more must the maiden Muses then be silent, when all is storm and uproar and confusion! But now that under the happy guidance of Leo, most supreme of pontiffs, peace is at last restored to the earth, that the discords among princes have been settled, and that that most perilous gulf that cleft the world has been done away with, not only is my letter eager to go to Rome, but I myself am fired with a kind of passion to revisit my benefactors of long ago. I have in England a position of the middle sort, less than I could wish and than my friends had promised, but more than I deserve. The king himself, Henry the Eighth, as good and as gifted by nature, believe me, as one can imagine, in his references to me and in his attitude could not be kinder or pay me more attention. The bishops think well of me almost without exception, and especially my lords of Durham, who is the king's secretary of state, and of Rochester, a man of

* * * * *

333:9 law is silent] Cicero *Pro Milone* 4.11

12 Leo] On 11 March 1513 Giovanni de' Medici, son of Lorenzo the Magnificent, was elected pope to succeed Julius II and took the name of Leo X. He was thirty-seven years old. He was ordained priest four days later, made a bishop on 17 March, and crowned on 19 March. He died in December 1521.

22 secretary] Thomas Ruthall, who was appointed king's secretary by Henry VII in 1499 and was kept in that post by Henry VIII until Ruthall's death in 1523; cf Ep 192 introduction.

22 Rochester] John Fisher; cf Ep 229.

singular piety and learning. Besides, there is the archbishop of York, who is now a great favourite with the king's majesty and wields incredible influence, for he is so attentive to the business of the realm that the greater part of public affairs rests upon his shoulders. Then the most revered archbishop of Canterbury, primate of all England, in whom what is best in human life is found in perfection: he watches over me, supports me, and encourages me with such perpetual generosity and, I could truly say, affection that, were he a brother or a father, he could hardly show more warmth.

And yet I cannot but be tormented by a longing for the city of Rome, whenever I recall the freedom, the noble setting, the light, the porticos, the libraries, the delightful conversations with eminent scholars, so many of the world's great men who took an interest in me, all that I left behind me when I left Rome. Indeed I sometimes think I may deserve any misfortune that may come my way by having exchanged for any situation elsewhere such a patron as yourself, who had done so much for me and were so ready and willing to do me honour and advance me in every way. But what else could I do? Mountains of gold, and more than gold, were promised in their letters by my friends. William Mountjoy was making a definite offer and a very large one, coupled with complete leisure and the freedom to choose my way of life which I regard as so necessary that, if deprived of that, I should think life not worth living. On the king's death he had been succeeded by a young man divinely gifted and initiated to some degree of elegance in humane studies, who moreover had shown such interest in me long ago that shortly before his father's death, when I was living in Italy, he had sent me a letter composed by himself and penned with his own hand; and such a letter that in it one could already discern singular gifts worthy of a crowned head. From all this, you may suppose, I had visions of Midas all over again

* * * * *

23 York] Thomas Wolsey (c 1474–1530) received his first significant promotion from Henry Deane, archbishop of Canterbury, and in 1507 became chaplain to Henry VII. In 1511 he was made a privy councillor to Henry VIII, in 1514 bishop of Lincoln and archbishop of York, and in 1515 he was promoted to cardinal and lord chancellor. His rapid rise to power was a tribute in part to his energy and ability, in part to the willing patronage of Richard Foxe, bishop of Winchester, and to the reluctance of both Foxe and Warham, archbishop of Canterbury, to assume secular administrative duties in these years; cf Ep 314:10n.

30 were he a brother] Cf Ep 253:14–15.

40 Mountains of gold] *Adagia* I ix 15

45 divinely gifted] Cf Ep 215:6. Henry VII died in 1509.

48 letter] Ep 206

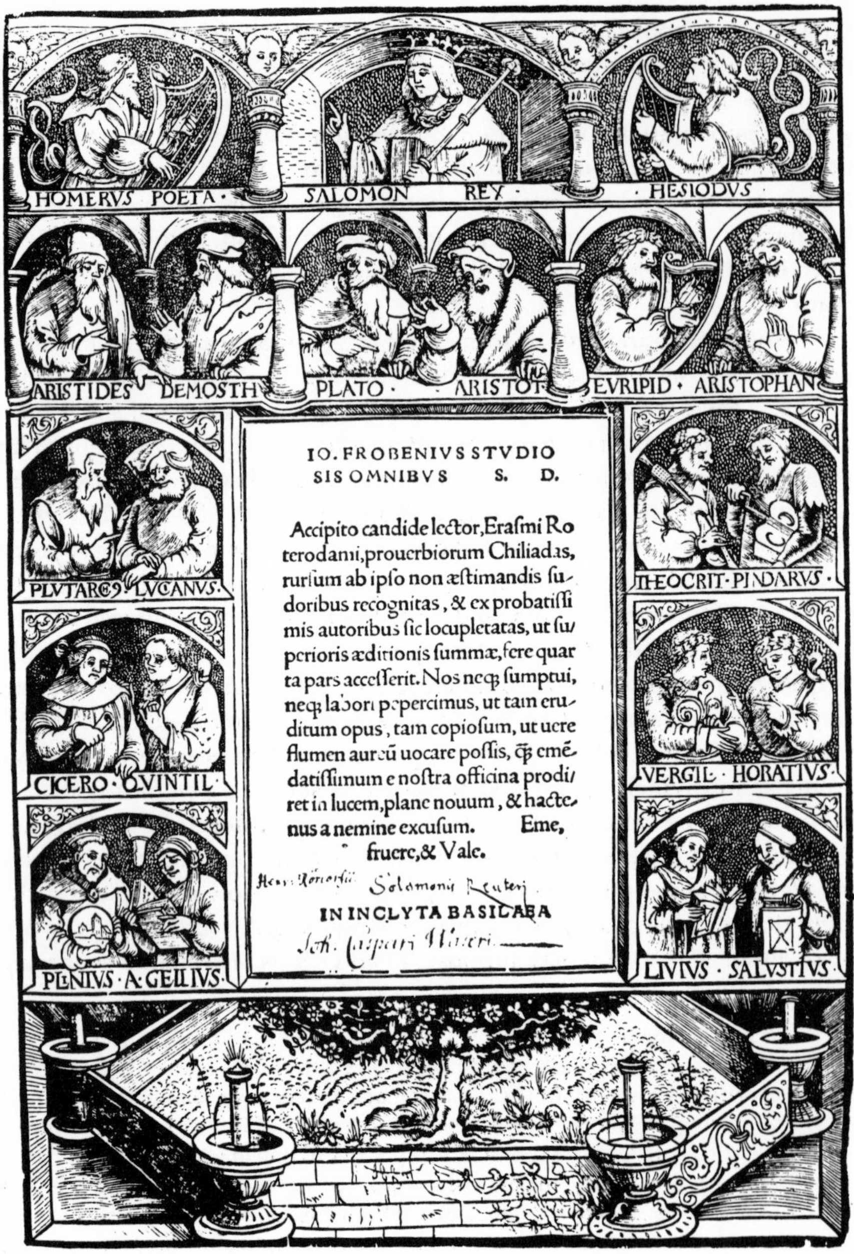
HOMERVS POETA · SALOMON REX · HESIODVS ·
ARISTIDES DEMOSTH PLATO · ARISTOT EVRIPID · ARISTOPHAN
PLVTARC9 LVCANVS · CICERO · QVINTIL · PLINIVS · A · GELLIVS
THEOCRIT · PINDARVS · VERGIL · HORATIVS · LIVIVS · SALVSTIVS

IO. FROBENIVS STVDIO
SIS OMNIBVS S. D.

Accipito candide lector, Erasmi Ro
terodami, prouerbiorum Chiliadas,
rursum ab ipso non æstimandis su-
doribus recognitas, & ex probatissi
mis autoribus sic locupletatas, ut su/
perioris æditionis summæ, fere quar
ta pars accesserit. Nos neq; sumptui,
neq; labori pepercimus, ut tam eru-
ditum opus, tam copiosum, ut uere
flumen aureū uocare possis, q̃ emē
datissimum e nostra officina prodi/
ret in lucem, plane nouum, & hacte-
nus a nemine excusum. Eme,
fruere, & Vale.

IN INCLYTA BASILAEA

Erasmus *Adagiorum chiliades* title page
Basel: Froben 1515
Houghton Library, Harvard University

and gold such as Pactolus and Tagus never knew. I dreamt of an age truly golden and fortunate isles – and then, to quote Aristophanes, 'up I woke.' Not but what, if truth be told, it was not so much that no position came my way as that I would not live up to any position; such is my abhorrence of ordinary business, and so far am I from ambition, so lazy if you like, that I need a position such as Timotheus enjoyed, and success caught in my nets while I sleep.

And so I have no call to accuse my friends, who were imposed upon by the same smiling hopes as I was. My other friends, and even the king himself, the parent of the golden age, were soon overtaken by the storms of war and torn from commerce with the Muses; with such a blast had Julius' famous trumpet roused the whole world to a passion for Mars. All the same, now that peace has been restored by your wisdom, I am girding myself as though for the first time for my literary duties. Not that I was ever idle, even when the tumult of that war was at its height. I have published, among many other things, a new edition of my *Adagia*, carefully revised and so much enriched that a quarter of the volume is new. St Jerome has been at press for some time now in his entirety, or rather he is being born again; for before this he was so much corrupted and mutilated that one might think he was now not so much revised as published for the first time. The text has been emended with incalculable labour and the comparison of many copies, and those of great antiquity; notes have been added in their places to make him easier to read without stumbling. You know that there are inserted here and there in Jerome passages so obscure that they bring the reader to a stop. Greek and Hebrew words I have either restored or corrected. Spurious works, and those falsely ascribed, some mixed in by chance and others by some impostor, I have not cut out, but have banished to a volume on their own, that a reader whose appetite is stronger than his standards of taste might find nothing wanting, and yet the worthless productions of some witless nonentity might no longer flaunt the name of such an admirable author. This great work is now at press, and will run, I think, to ten volumes; and so much expense and care have been lavished on the printing that I am prepared to swear that for these twenty years no work has issued from any printing-house that has had so much money and so much effort spent on it. I doubt if Jerome himself expended so much effort

* * * * *

51 Pactolus and Tagus] Rivers that once carried gold dust; *Adagia* I vi 75

52 Aristophanes] *Frogs* 51

56 Timotheus] An Athenian general famous for his good luck; *Adagia* I v 82

66 *Adagia*] Cf Ep 313 introduction.

on the writing of his works as they will cost me in the correction. At least I have thrown myself into this task so zealously that one could almost say that I had worked myself to death that Jerome might live again.

But I do it with a will, and am content if death finds me engaged on a work so pious and so rewarding. See how devoted I am to the task! Last year I spent eight whole months for this purpose in Basel, not without great expense, to say nothing of the hard work and the extreme peril of the journey. And next autumn I am resolved to visit Italy in order, of course, to search the treasures of your libraries. I shall never be found to have shirked any labour, if only I feel that your good will and the good will of others like you support my efforts. Besides which, I have not yet made up my mind, but shall take your advice in deciding to whom to dedicate this work. To the archbishop of Canterbury I owe everything; he richly deserves that every page I write should bear his name. Otherwise I saw clearly enough how appropriate it would be to dedicate the greatest of all theologians to the greatest of all pontiffs, or rather that all good literature as it blossoms once again should bear his name by whom peace, the nurse of literary studies, has been restored to the world of men. I perceive a mutual advantage: Jerome will benefit from a dedication to Leo; Leo will gain great honour from the dedication of the works of Jerome. But we will talk of all this at greater length in detail when we meet. In the meantime I beg that, should need arise, you will show yourself the same patron to your Erasmus that I always found you when I was in Rome. Should there be anything in which your Eminence would not be unwilling to use the services of a very humble dependant, especially in relation to the archbishop of Canterbury, I shall demonstrate that with all my failings I do not lack loyalty and zeal.

One thing I had almost forgotten. I beg and beseech you earnestly, in the name of those humane studies of which your Eminence has always been an outstanding patron, that that excellent man Doctor Johann Reuchlin should find you fair-minded and friendly in his business. At one stroke you

* * * * *

97 dedicate] It was dedicated in the end to Warham; cf Ep 396.

114–15 Reuchlin ... business] Cf Ep 300 introduction; the university of Paris condemned Reuchlin in August 1514. Prince Charles, Francis I, and the emperor all became interested in the question, and Jacob van Hoogstraten, the Dominican inquisitor from Cologne (cf Ep 290:11n; Allen Ep 1006), appealed Reuchlin's case directly to Rome. The pope then appointed a commission under Cardinal Grimani to investigate; cf J.H. Overfield 'A new look at the Reuchlin affair' in *Studies in Medieval and Renaissance History* VIII ed H.L. Adelson (Lincoln, Nebraska 1971) 167–207 for a discussion of the attitudes of individual humanists to the Reuchlin affair.

will render a great service to literature and all literary men, for the greater their learning the greater their enthusiasm for him. He has all Germany in his debt, where he was the first to awake the study of Greek and Hebrew. He is a man with an exceptional knowledge of the languages, accomplished in many subjects, eminent and well-known throughout Christendom for his published works, in high favour with the emperor Maximilian of whose council he is a member, honoured and respected among his own people where he holds the office of a magistrate, and of a reputation hitherto always unblemished; besides which, he is now old and deserves respect for his gray hairs. The time had come when for his part he deserved to enjoy at his time of life a pleasant harvest from his honourable exertions, and we on our part looked to see him bring out the results of so many years' work for the common good. And so it seems outrageous to all men of good feeling, not Germans only but English and French as well, to whom he is well known through his letters, that a man of such distinction and such outstanding gifts should be persecuted with such unpleasant litigation, and that too on a point which in my opinion goes beyond even the ass's shadow of the proverbial jest.The armies of princes have been restrained by your wise counsel; let it restore likewise to those who cultivate good literature the peace that should be theirs. Banished be everything that smacks of rancour and aggression! Now that the princes, thanks to you, are at peace once more, it is absurd for scholars to fight among themselves with volumes and with mutual abuse, and, while princes keep their weapons where they can do no harm, for them to pierce one another with pens dipped in poison. How much better it would have been for the effort and expense and time this man has lost on this foolish prosecution to have been devoted to honourable studies! Many men have happier memories of Julius II just because, when Jakob Wimpfeling, a man not only learned and saintly but of venerable age as well, was involved in legal process of this kind, he freed him by his personal *fiat* and silenced his traducers. Believe me, whoever restores Johann Reuchlin to the arts and letters will win countless men's grateful devotion. Respectful best wishes to your Eminence, to whom, such as I am, I present my humble duty.

London, 15 May 1515
Your Eminence's devoted servant Erasmus

* * * * *

132 the ass's shadow] *Adagia* I iii 52

143 Wimpfeling] In his controversy with the Augustinians in 1506; see J. Knappen *Jakob Wimpfeling (1450–1528)* (Freiburg 1902; repr Nieuwkoop 1965) 192–3.

Cardinal Domenico Grimani
Portrait medal, with the figures of Theology and Philosophy on the reverse
Roman School under Innocent VIII, Alexander VI, and Julius II
National Gallery of Art, Washington
Samuel H. Kress Collection A974–236A

334 / To Domenico Grimani London, [15 May] 1515

Grimani (1461–1523) was a member of a distinguished Venetian family and son of the exiled general Antonio, who became doge in 1521. Domenico was created cardinal in 1493 and patriarch of Aquileia in 1498, after which he became cardinal-bishop of Porto. He was a friend of Julius II and a munificent patron of arts and letters. With Cardinal Riario he was one of Erasmus' most influential patrons in Rome, and his personal interest in letters was recorded by the rich manuscript collections of his library. Erasmus addressed to him his paraphrase on the Epistle to the Romans (Louvain: Thierry Martens November 1517; NK 846). Cf Renaudet *Italie* passim. The letter was first published in *Damiani elegeia* (1515).

TO THE MOST REVEREND CARDINAL GRIMANI
FROM ERASMUS OF ROTTERDAM

After that first meeting, which proved to be our last, I never revisited your Eminence, as you had told me to do and I had promised; and the reason for this was not so much my own negligence as your unusual and quite special courtesy and kindness. What happened, in fact, was quite unprecedented: the very thing that ought most to have encouraged me to return was the one thing that deterred me from returning. And what pray, you will ask, was this unprecedented thing? I will answer frankly, artlessly, as a good German should. At that time my mind was entirely made up to go back to England. It was to England that the ties of old and dear acquaintance, the very generous promises of influential friends, and the very favourable attitude of a most successful king all summoned me. I had adopted this island to replace my native land, I had chosen it as the retreat for my old age. I was invited repeatedly, I was imperatively summoned, in letters that promised me mountains of gold; and from all this, although normally I have a vigorous contempt for money, I had formed the idea of so much gold as the Pactolus ten times over would scarcely suffice to carry. And now I was afraid that if I paid a return visit to your Eminence, I might change my mind. From the moment of our first meeting you had so weakened my resolution, so kindled my imagination: what was the likely effect, had my meetings with

* * * * *

334:3 first meeting] In 1531 Erasmus recalled this visit to Grimani's palace on the eve of his return to England, perhaps in July 1509. See Pierre de Nolhac *Erasme en Italie* 2nd ed (1898) 87–9; Renaudet *Italie* 100; Allen Ep 2465.

9–10 German] Cf Ep 321:16n.

16 mountains of gold] Cf Ep 333:40n.

18 Pactolus] Cf Ep 333:51n.

you been longer and more intimate? What adamantine purpose would not be turned by your charming courtesy, your honeyed eloquence, your recondite learning, your equally friendly and practical advice, and not least by the evident readiness of so eminent a prelate to earn my gratitude? Already I felt my resolution gradually failing, and had begun to have some misgivings about my plans; and yet I was ashamed to show myself a man of no strength of mind. I felt that my affection for the eternal city, which I had barely shaken off, was silently increasing once again, and that if I had not torn myself quickly away from Rome, I should never have left Rome thereafter. I hurried away, that I might not catch the infection a second time, and took wing, rather than set out, for England.

And now how goes it, you will ask. Do you repent of your design? Are you sorry you did not take the advice of one who offered you friendly counsel? Falsehood is not my way. My feelings on this topic are by no means simple. A deep regret for Rome is inescapable, when I think of its great store of great advantages available together. First of all, the bright light, the noble setting of the most famous city in the world, the delightful freedom, the many richly furnished libraries, the sweet society of all those great scholars, all the literary conversations, all the monuments of antiquity, and not least so many leading lights of the world gathered together in one place. In particular, whenever I bethink me of the remarkable favour shown me by other cardinals, and especially by his eminence of Nantes, the most cordial encouragement of the cardinal of Bologna, and from the cardinal of San Giorgio not merely encouragement but generosity quite out of the common; above all, that most promising conversation with your Eminence – all this makes me feel that no fortune could possibly fall to my lot generous enough to wean my heart from its longing for the Rome which I once tasted. Again, although I enjoy in England a position that need cause one few regrets, and certainly somewhat better than I deserve, yet to tell the truth it does not entirely correspond either to my wishes or to the promises of my friends. This is due not to any failure to keep faith on their part but to the unfavourable climate of affairs. The king himself, normally the most generous of monarchs, and one moreover who both thinks highly and speaks kindly of his Erasmus (as I know for a fact, partly from a letter which he wrote me and partly from many informants), was snatched from me almost completely by the storms of war that blew up all of a sudden; such is

* * * * *

43 Nantes] Robert Guibé, by this time bishop-administrator of Vannes; cf Ep 253.

44 Bologna] Francesco Alidosi; cf Ep 296: 109n.

45 San Giorgio] Riario; cf Ep 333.

the whole-hearted zeal with which that pious and high-spirited young man was preparing for a war which he thought necessary to maintain the dignity of the Roman church. And William Mountjoy, who after my lord Hendrik van Bergen, bishop of Cambrai, is the oldest patron of my studies, has been so overwhelmed by the burdens of the war that his help fell short of his affection, although he is a man of ancient nobility and incredibly generous towards students of the humanities; but as compared with the other barons of this realm he is more richly endowed with spirit than with worldly goods. I cast no blame for the moment on my own lack of initiative, for I really need such fortune as Timotheus enjoyed, to fill my net while I sleep.

But if I have less reason to regret my coming to England, the prime cause for this is William, archbishop of Canterbury, primate of all England not in style alone but in every form of distinction; a man beyond comparison in every way, chief and sole ornament and mainstay of this realm, in wisdom, judgment, learning, and authority greater than all the rest, yet in this way greater than himself, that with singular modesty he alone does not realize how great he is. His way of life is modest, his intellect wonderfully subtle, his spirit active and intolerant of doing nothing. He has great experience of affairs, having long ago seen much service on most important missions and in essential business both of kings and kingdom. As a result he not only is equal by himself to a mass of business for which several other men could barely suffice; he has time to spare for reading the best authors and for sharing in the private concerns of his friends; although apart from his duties as archbishop he holds the position of lord chancellor, that is, the supreme judicial authority of the realm. This man enfolds me with so much affection, gives me such standing by his support, and encourages me with such generosity, in short shows himself such a wonderful Maecenas in every way, that no father could be more indulgent and no brother more warm-hearted. As a result, all that I had left behind in Rome – so many distinguished cardinals, so many gifted bishops, so many learned scholars – I seemed to have made good in this one man.

Now however that the efforts of Leo, our truly supreme pontiff, have restored peace to the world, my position in England is much more agreeable. Even so, my mind is even more keenly tempted by the longing for Rome, for report commonly has it – and highly probable it is – that the accession of such a prince gave as it were a signal to whatever there may be anywhere of distinguished learning or outstanding excellence to gather at

* * * * *

60–1 Hendrik van Bergen] Cf Ep 49.

67 Timotheus] Cf Ep 333:56n.

this time in Rome as the supreme setting for its exercise. And so over two years ago I had made my preparations for the journey, expecting to accompany the right reverend John, bishop of Rochester, a man rich in every sort of excellence becoming to a bishop and, to set out his praises in brief, much like his grace of Canterbury whose suffragan he is; but he was recalled suddenly from his journey. Last year, again, I had got on my own initiative as far as Basel; but there too I was held fast by one particular business which, whatever others may think, I regard as of the highest importance – and important it must truly have been to keep me away from Rome.

I had long been working, and with no ordinary exertions, to be sure, towards this one purpose, that we might see the whole of St Jerome virtually reborn. He is so much the greatest theologian of our Latin world that we may almost call him the only one we have; and yet we possess him in so corrupt a form, so confused and adulterated, that, although no other author is so much worth reading, he more than any other cannot be read, let alone understood. So I took all his writings, especially those in the form of letters, which needed a great deal of work and, to begin with, set them in order; then removed, with the aid of old manuscripts and my own wits, the errors which more truly buried than disfigured him. I have added summaries, and also convenient notes in the right places, so that he can now be read without stumbling even by moderate scholars, although before (I speak boldly but it is the truth) even the most learned could not understand him. For as Romulus of old was said to be as great a showman of his exploits as he was a performer, so in St Jerome one can see original and wide-ranging learning allied with a kind of virtuous desire to exhibit it. The Greek and Hebrew quoted, which were either lacking altogether or added in such a form that it would have been better to have added nothing, I have restored with the greatest care. Works spurious and falsely ascribed, which form a considerable section, I have removed to a volume on their own, that the reader whose appetite exceeds his learning might find nothing wanting, and yet such ignorant rubbish no longer circulate under the name of so incomparable a man.

Left to myself, I saw clearly enough that Italy, with the resources of its libraries and its commanding position, would be invaluable for the publication of my work; but in the nick of time I found in Basel several people who were all set for this task and had in fact already started, especially

* * * * *

95–6 two years ago] Actually it was three years; cf Epp 252–4.

117 Romulus] Livy 1.10.5

129 nick of time] It is likely that Erasmus knew about the edition of Jerome in progress at Basel before he left England; cf Epp 263:31n and 283:182–9.

Johann Froben, whose skill and outlay are a mainstay of the enterprise, and with him three very learned young men, the brothers Amerbach, who have also a good knowledge of Hebrew. Jerome uses Hebrew in many places, and in this department I needed someone, as they say in Greek, to be my Theseus, for I had only sipped the cup of that language, as the saying goes. So I recruited them to share my labours, and set to work with the spirit of a proverbial Hercules. A great printing shop is now in full activity; St Jerome is printing (or rather, being reborn) in most elegant type, at such an expense of money and of effort that it cost Jerome less to write his works than it has me to restore them. I at least have expended so much effort on this task that I came near to death myself while trying to give him new life. The whole work, if I mistake not, will run to ten volumes.

But, you will ask, why tell all this to me? First, because I know that with your perpetual zeal for the advancement of learning you would equally be glad for Jerome's sake and well disposed towards my efforts, or rather towards Christian piety, which has much to gain, I hope, from what Jerome has written. Yet this task cannot be accomplished as it ought to be without the help of many well-furnished libraries. And so, if there is anything in your own well-furnished library, which is so rich and so well stocked with books of all kinds in all languages, or the papal library, or any others, it will be like your charitable self to let me have the use of it for the public benefit. And then again, it seemed to me highly suitable that a supreme theologian should issue forth into the hands of men, so much restored that he might seem never to have been published before, under the favourable auspices of a supreme pontiff, and that the most learned writer of them all should be commended to the world by one whose own family has given us so many great names in the literary way. Thus, I thought, we shall see the authority of so eminent a pope confer increased honour and dignity on Jerome, and in return Leo's glory will receive no small increase from the fame of an outstanding doctor of the church. Nor do I see that any other monument could be more suitable to secure immortality for his achievements. To him therefore I propose to dedicate Jerome reborn, particularly if my plan has your approval. Otherwise I had almost decided to offer it to the archbishop of Canterbury, to whom I owe everything. But if there is any glory to be had from this, he will gladly and willingly, I know full well, retire from it in

* * * * *

135 Theseus] He had a great reputation for helping other heroes in their exploits; *Adagia* I v 27. Cf Ep 324:31n.

135 sipped the cup] *Adagia* I ix 92

163 your approval] Literally, your voting-pebble; *Adagia* I v 53

164 everything] And to whom ultimately it was dedicated; cf Ep 333:97n.

favour of the Holy Father; such are his feelings for the Roman see. I too will link his memory with my praises of Leo, one great man with another, a primate with him who holds the primacy of Peter, in such a way that this course will prove to do still more for Jerome and also for the reputation of my patron.

I have published, besides many other things, a corrected edition of my *Chiliades*, so much enriched that a fourth part of the volume is new. Next summer I intend to issue various not unprofitable annotations of mine (or so I think them) on the New Testament, together with my version of the apostolic Epistles, designed to make them intelligible; a task which I have performed in such a way that, even after Lorenzo Valla and that learned and industrious man Jacques Lefèvre, I hope I may be thought to have had good reason to undertake it. I have in hand at the moment a small book on the education of a prince, which I intend for the most illustrious archduke Charles of Burgundy, grandson of Maximilian. When these tasks are done, I mean to take up again the work I once started on St Paul; for I have made up my mind to dedicate all the time that remains to me to Holy Scripture. Nor shall any exertion turn me from my purpose, if I have the support of your approval and that of others like you; for you know it is an experience of very long standing that ill will, more noxious than any viper, will direct its serpent hisses against every noble undertaking.

Of this I have lately been watching a very painful example in that great man Johann Reuchlin. It was already right and proper, and the time had come, that a man of his venerable age should enjoy his noble studies, and reap a pleasant harvest from the seed sown in the honest toil of his earlier years. It was only right that a man with such knowledge of so many tongues and so many subjects should in this autumn of his days pour out the rich produce of his brain for the whole world to enjoy. To this end he should have been stimulated with praise, lured by rewards, fired with enthusiasm by our support. Yet I hear that some nobodies have arisen who, being

* * * * *

175 intelligible] See Ep 384 introduction concerning Erasmus' approach to his edition of the New Testament.

176 Valla] Allen suggests that this sentence was added at the time of publication, as an answer to Dorp's hint (Ep 304:99–100) that the work of Valla and Lefèvre d'Etaples on the New Testament was sufficient. At the opening of Ep 337 Erasmus claims not to have seen the letter from Dorp with its cautionary warnings until he arrived in Antwerp the following May.

178 small book] Cf Ep 393.

181 work] Cf Ep 164:41–2; Allen Ep 495:43n.

188 Reuchlin] Cf Ep 333:114–15n.

incapable of anything distinguished themselves, have chosen a most perverse way to acquire a reputation. In heaven's name, the turmoil they have aroused on the most frivolous of pretexts! That one pamphlet, one letter even, and written in German too, which he never published himself nor thought worth publication, should be the starting-point of such an uproar! Who would ever have known that the thing had been even written, had that crew not spread it abroad? How much more conducive to peace it would have been, if any error had been found in it (and all men err), to suppress it or put an innocent interpretation on it, or at least to overlook it in view of the man's outstanding merits! I would not wish to say this because I see any error in it; on that others must pronounce. But this I will say: if anyone were to go through St Jerome's works in that hostile spirit of theirs – what Greek calls ἀποτόμως, relentlessly – he will find many things which differ far and wide from the decrees of the theologians. What then was the object of dragging a man who is entitled to respect for both his learning and his years into troubles of this kind for a matter of no importance, in which he is now wasting, I believe, his seventh year? If only he had been allowed to spend that energy and that time on helping to forward honourable studies! As it is, one who deserves a reward on every count is involved in the most damaging prosecutions, to the great grief and indignation of every educated man, and indeed of the whole of Germany. Not but what they all have great hopes that with your assistance this excellent man may be restored to the world in general and literature in particular.

Next winter will see me in Rome, if only Christ almighty so please, and the king's majesty together with the archbishop of Canterbury give me renewed permission to depart; and if I do not get this myself, St Jerome will secure it for me. May your Eminence be preserved in health and wealth for very many years, for our benefit and the benefit of sound learning, by Christ, the best of good Samaritans. With my entirely devoted service.

London, [31 March] 1515

335 / To Leo X London, 21 May 1515

This is a petition for permission to dedicate his editorial work on Jerome to the pope; cf Ep 396. For Leo X's reception of this letter see Ep 389:36–43. Like Ep 333, this was first printed in the *Damiani elegeia*, from which Allen's text was taken substantially. For the manuscript background see Ep 333 introduction; Öffentliche Bibliothek, university of Basel, Erasmuslade B II b 1.

* * * * *

198 pamphlet] Cf Ep 290:3n.

TO THE MOST HOLY FATHER LEO THE TENTH,
A PONTIFF TRULY SUPREME, FROM ERASMUS OF ROTTERDAM

If one were to take account of your exalted position, most holy Father, no one would be found even among the greatest princes who would not be afraid to write a letter to your Highness. Who would not fear to direct a letter to a personage who stands in majesty as far above all mortals as other mortals stand above the beasts, and plays the part among men of some heavenly power? And yet the singular goodness of your nature and the incredible kindness in which you transcend that very grandeur which transcends the grandest of us are not only matter of public report the whole world over but are to be seen at first glance (as they say) and shine forth in your whole demeanour. And so I, who had a taste of them from personal acquaintance with you when I was living in Rome, have gained thereby such confidence that, although I am a man almost of the lowest sort, I do not hesitate to interrupt your Holiness with a letter. I only wish I might kneel and kiss those most holy feet. Everywhere I see and hear, all over Christendom, high and low alike congratulating themselves on such a prince. And very good reason they have to do so; none better than those who are filled with zeal for true piety and the study of the humanities, in the first place because that noble family of undying fame, the Medici, to whom the world owes its Leo, was always one to encourage and to honour men who excelled in integrity and learning. Out of that family, as out of some Trojan horse, have sprung in these last few years so many leaders distinguished in every branch of knowledge, so many followers of Cicero and Virgil, of Plato and Jerome, that if ever there were a prognostic fit to rouse high hopes in all studious men, it is this: the providence of Heaven has given the world a Leo, that under him all noble virtues and all liberal arts may flourish once again.

Indeed, so far are you from falling short of your high lineage, that your own merits have outstripped the glory of your house, although in other ways it led the rest, and make it more illustrious by the very fact that your own splendid record almost puts its brilliance in the shade. And why? Because capital gifts were allied with a capital education, and that very fertile garden of your mind found by far the most elegant of men to cultivate it, that most polished scholar Poliziano. By his care you were initiated, not into the prickly and quarrelsome subjects of the schools, but into those

* * * * *

335:11 at first glance] Cf Ep 305:74n.

12–13 personal acquaintance] This meeting is referred to again in Ep 339:15–16 by Leo x.

22 Trojan horse] An echo of Cicero *De oratore* 294

genuine studies rightly called humane, the province of what they call the gentler Muses, who make even an untamed intellect into something mild and peaceful; and not only were you initiated, you were made an adept. Thus the two things which Plato calls for in a head of state, good natural gifts and correct education, are there before us in the head of the whole world so fully that even in our prayers we could imagine nothing better. Nor, after this splendid start, was there any cause to complain either of your own exertions or of the favour of heaven. Hence it was that, although it is not uncommon for the outspoken citizens of Rome to criticize even men of unblemished reputation, you brought to your exalted position a record and a name that were spotless in every way, and in reaching it you relied so little on the support of wealth or faction that, without either desiring or expecting election, you were not so much elected by the votes of men as selected and appointed by the will of Heaven.

And not a little lustre was added to your glorious record by the cruel injustice of Fortune, which (one supposes) must have descended on you by divine permission in order that your authentic greatness of spirit, like gold tried in the fire, might be displayed to mortals in a brighter light. Marius owes much of his fame to his changes of fortune, and some people think that Alexander deserves less celebrity because he enjoyed almost unbroken good luck; Timotheus' good fortune became the subject of popular cartoons. The skill of a ship's captain is proved in dirty weather; a great sculptor produces even greater marvels of skill, the harder and more intractable his material. Whatever the circumstances, true force of character makes itself felt, but never is it more evident than when some stepmother Juno puts her Hercules to the test in troubles of every kind. Ulysses won more fame from the hardships he endured than from the successful destruction of Troy. I know that we often see men who have bravely endured adversity corrupted afterwards by the smiles of indulgent Fortune. But you, after maintaining your integrity when things went wrong, have main-

* * * * *

40 Plato] For example, *Republic* 2.375ff

51–2 cruel injustice] Perhaps the expulsion of the Medici from Florence in 1494. Cardinal Giovanni de' Medici, the future Pope Leo X, had been captured after the battle of Ravenna, 11 April 1512.

53–4 gold tried in the fire] *Adagia* IV i 58

54 Marius] The Roman general, who oscillated between distinction and obscurity. He was six times consul in his prime, then exiled with a price put on his head, only to return at the head of an enemy force and be elected (under duress) to his seventh consulship, during which he died (in 86 BC).

57 Timotheus] Cf Ep 333:56n.

tained it still when elevated to the highest position in the world. The only difference is that we now feel your goodness more powerfully, when we see you more clearly as the image of Christ whose vice-gerent you unquestionably are, now that supreme goodness and supreme wisdom are matched by equal power: your goodness makes you wish to be of service, your singular wisdom shows you how to aid humanity, and your supreme position as pontiff makes this possible. For as nothing could happen more fraught with disaster than for wickedness and folly to be armed with the authority of the highest civil power, so heaven can confer on mortals nothing more conducive to felicity than a union of those three qualities in the prince, as they are united in God the ruler of all. In fact, the greater the power the greater the mischief, if it light on a fool or a wicked man.

As soon as the world perceived that Leo had been put at the helm of affairs, at once that age of worse than iron turned into an age of gold; so great, so fundamental, was the sudden change in everything that it was clear to all men that this was God's doing. The billows of war sank to rest; the mutual threats of princes were restrained; the greatest monarchs in bitter disagreement felt their spirits moved towards Christian harmony; that most pestilential schism was done away with, and so done away with, great peril that it was, that not even a scar remains behind. To say nothing for the moment of several princes of Italy restored to their citizens, and many citizens who had been driven into exile brought home; of the restoration of your own family, which had long suffered from the injustice of Fortune; of Florence, your native city, which so long flourished under the wise rule of your forbears, rendered more flourishing still. This was indeed to live up to your family name of Medici – to find a medicine on a sudden for so many and such incurable distempers which affected almost the whole world, and to do this without violence or cruelty, as it might be without amputation and cautery and painful treatment of other kinds, but by wisdom and prudence, by gentleness and moderation.

Let others exalt the wars aroused by the energy of Julius II or fought by him to a successful finish; let them tell of the victories won by his armies, and recount the triumphs that he celebrated in such kingly style. Great as the glory may be that they will adjudge him, they must confess all the same

* * * * *

85 schism] The schismatic cardinals of the Council of Pisa submitted to the Lateran Council in June 1513; cf Epp 236, 239, 247.

89 family] After the withdrawal of the French forces in 1512 a Spanish army, acting for the Holy League, crushed the republican régime of Piero Soderini. A new government formed by Medici sympathizers was essentially controlled by the family, and especially by Cardinal Giovanni, now Leo X; cf Ep 333:12n.

that it meant misery for many people; to say nothing for the moment of the fact that of glory won in war a large share is claimed by the princes under whose command wars are actually waged; a greater share perhaps by the soldiers who run the risks and bear the burden of the day; the greatest of all by Fortune, who is nowhere so much mistress as in war. But the glory of a Leo means no groans, no grumbles; no risk that, as so often happens, posterity may condemn the man whom his contemporaries thought wonderful. And again, your glory was not only a universal blessing and a cause of universal rejoicing; it is entirely due to you and to the powers of heaven, for it was won, to the great advantage of us all, by your wonderful wisdom under the fostering hand of God, and it belongs to you all the more because it comes by the gift of him who does not prosper the undeserving.

Julius was a very great man – the fact that he embroiled almost the whole world in war shows that, I grant you; but to have restored peace to the world proves Leo greater still. If the greatness of Julius was shown by his defeating in war, or at least harassing, Louis the redoubtable king of France, yours is more evident from the way in which he has submitted himself and all that is his to your discretion. The most serene king of England, Henry, eighth of that name, showed more respect for your authority when at your prompting he laid down his arms, than he did for Julius when inspired by him to enter the fray. Anyone may easily be moved to enter on a war by the hope of victory, the insidious appeal of which is felt by everyone, and perhaps most of all by those for whom Fortune is laying her snares; but to contrive that such a king, say rather a young man of high and invincible spirit, and moreover exulting as it were in his great success, should let a victory which is already certain slip through his fingers and pass from active hostility to complete concord – this does seem like the result of something more than human. Finally, while the severity of a Julius may have been necessary to match that time, the mildness of a Leo has done much more good, and approaches much more closely to the example of him

* * * * *

114 war] Julius II (Giuliano Della Rovere 1443–1513), elected to the papacy in 1503 in succession to Pius III, devoted his pontificate to the restoration and enhancement of the papacy's temporal power as a safeguard to independence. The vigorous diplomatic and military policy in which this involved him attracted the criticism of the humanists; cf Ep 502 introduction.

116–17 king of France] December 1513

120 at your prompting] It is likely that Henry was moved to conclude peace with Louis XII (in August 1514) as much through desire to seek revenge for Ferdinand's treacherous desertion of the anti-French alliance as by pressure from Rome.

whose place among mortal men is held by the Roman pontiff, I mean that Solomon the peacemaker, who by the alliance that he offers joins heaven to earth and holds them together, who won his victories by patience and not by battalions, who earned his triumph by dying, and so far from winning an empire for himself with others' blood, gave his own blood to buy for us a kingdom in Heaven.

And so Christendom has every reason to think itself much blessed in such a Leo, this lion in whose mouth the world finds something sweeter than honey. For what is sweeter than peace, especially after the severe and long drawn out tumult of the wars, in which we met each other headlong with immense loss of Christian blood, to the intense grief of all men of good will and the great joy of the Turks? Even to think of those days makes one's blood run cold. But whoever may be regarded by history as responsible for so much evil, it is to the Medici without a doubt that we owe the remedy. For the future I feel confident that, just as we have now read the depths of Samson's riddle, so, with Christ to bring your undertaking to fulfilment, we shall soon see the words of the Apocalypse equally apply to you: 'The Lion of the tribe of Juda hath prevailed.' Your wisdom and your moderation in their sweetness we have all experienced already, and the victorious lion of that promise we shall soon see fulfilled.

This is the promise held out to us by your incomparable qualities; this is the inner meaning of both your names, that which you brought with you to the papal throne and that which you adopted as pope. When we hear the names John and Leo, what are we to understand, if not a union of exceptional goodness and invincible courage? And another thing seems to augur well: we not only have a Leo, a name never yet borne by any Roman pontiff not of outstanding distinction, but Leo the Tenth. Things of exceptional magnitude were called in antiquity tenth of their kind. And so every good quality eminent in each previous Leo may be expected, all together, in the tenth of that name: the authority wielded with such success by the first Leo, the learned piety and the zeal for sacred music of the second, the missionary eloquence of the third and his spirit unshaken by fortune good or bad, the simple wisdom of the fourth such as Christ approves, the long-suffering sanctity of the fifth, the zeal for the restoration of universal peace which

* * * * *

138–9 sweeter than honey] In Judges 14:8–18 Samson finds bees hiving in a lion's carcass, and makes a riddle of it (What is sweeter than honey? are Samson's words).

147 Apocalypse] Rev 5:5

155 goodness] Jerome in his *Interpretation of Hebrew Names* says that John means 'the grace of the Lord': PL 23:892.

marked the sixth, the holiness worthy of Heaven of the seventh, the high character of the eighth, the ninth's wide-ranging benevolence. All these, I repeat, are promised us not only by the inner meaning of the names themselves, although this is by no means to be despised, but still more by what we have already watched you do and see you getting ready. Things happily begun promise a happy outcome. Furthermore, what makes our hopes of victory more sure is this: you see clearly in your wisdom that there must be a twofold victory, and therefore two campaigns, one against wickedness, the most pestilential and perhaps the only enemy of our Christian profession, and the other against enemies on a narrower front, the impious and barbarian opponents of Christianity and of the Roman see. The first war is the more necessary and by far the more difficult; it depends largely on ourselves, and must therefore be waged with the greater attention. Once we have duly won that, the winning of the second campaign will with Christ's help be easy.

Not to mention in passing that these two wars are of very different kinds, one of them such that some excellent men disapprove of it, the other meeting with unanimous approval. For to the war against wickedness we are summoned beyond a doubt by Christ and spurred on by Paul; but to fight the Turks we get no instructions from Christ and no encouragement from the apostles. Suppose we grant that both campaigns must be fought; greater effort at least must be devoted to the war which was declared by that Spirit from Heaven than to the one set on foot by man. Who knows? Christ himself with his apostles and martyrs subdued the whole earth by doing good, by long-suffering, by the teaching of holiness; shall we not be better advised to overcome the Turks by the piety of our lives rather than by arms, so that Christian dominance may be defended in the same way in which it was acquired? If however we must approve both wars – and we must beyond doubt accept whatever has the approval of the Roman senate – in neither direction is there any weakening of the unheard-of paternal affection, most holy Father, with which you buttress and rebuild the religion of Christ's ordinary people, which has long been in decay in various ways and tends daily more and more towards collapse, with (as they tell me) most salutary synodical constitutions; and at the same time with constitutions of such a kind as have no taint of profit or of the lust of power or despotic rule, but breathe a truly apostolic spirit – such constitutions as anyone could recognize for the work of fathers and not masters, in which religious minds can reverence the voice, as it were of Christ himself.

In this way, then, your Holiness is concerned to enrich the church of Christ with that real wealth which is truly hers, that she may be crowned with her proper glory and rule with her proper jurisdiction; in a word, that she may be filled full with those heavenly gifts which sometimes are most plentiful just when we are most ill-supplied with gifts of every other kind. Not but what you show no signs of neglecting virtue's other field of action, for by bringing all the princes into mutual concord and spreading peace in Christendom you are building both the fairest and the safest highway towards the subjugation or destruction of the Turkish infidel. One day our lion's roar will be too much for them, those monstrous brutes; it comes, it surely comes, the time when even the most ferocious of wild beasts will feel the invincible might of our Leo, mild as he is, and will find themselves unequal to a pontiff whose strength lies in piety rather than armies, who brings immortal powers into battle on his side. I saw long ago, most holy Father, how vast is the field of your glories that opens before me, but my modest intellectual powers are quite unequal to the exposition of such a mighty subject; to such more than human achievements my eloquence, or rather my want of it, cannot aspire. If only all scholars had the proper enthusiasm and the proper skill! Only then both would they and could they do justice by their powers of utterance to the virtues of Leo the Tenth, which deserve to live for all generations. Personally I am greatly deterred by your exalted position; who would not be? And yet somehow or other my spirit feels very strongly the urge to exert all its intellectual force to the best of its ability, to the end that Leo's great services to the people of Christendom should be seen in their true magnitude and renowned by posterity, undying for all time to come.

Long did I ponder this problem, for it was quite clear that it could never be solved by my own unaided wit; and it seemed almost possible that there was one way by which I might achieve my objective after a fashion, if I invoked the assistance of some other name which has its own immortality. I saw clearly that St Jerome is chief among the theologians of the Latin world, and is in fact almost the only writer we have who deserves the name of theologian (not that I condemn the rest, but men who seem distinguished on their own are thrown into the shade by his brilliance when they are compared with him); indeed he has such splendid gifts that Greece itself with all its learning can scarcely produce a man to be matched with him. What Roman eloquence, what mastery of the tongues, what a range of knowledge in all antiquity and all history! And then his retentive memory, his happy knack of combining unexpected things, his perfect command of Holy Scripture! Above all, with his burning energy and the divine inspira-

* * * * *

229 Long did I] Most of this and the following paragraph is absent from what appears to be the original form of the letter preserved in the Basel manuscript, and was added by Erasmus before its first printing in August 1515; cf Ep 333 introduction.

tion in that amazing heart, he can at the same moment delight us with his eloquence, instruct us with his learning, and sweep us away with his religious force. And yet the one man we possess who richly deserves to be read by all is the one author so much corrupted, so mixed with dirt and filth, that even scholars cannot understand him!

I saw that it would be a splendid achievement if by my efforts such a distinguished doctor could be given back to the world; but I foresaw so much difficulty in the enterprise that even Hercules single-handed would not suffice; so far was I from any confidence that I could be equal to it by myself, who am so far short of Hercules that I am only just a man. And yet scholars outdid each other in encouragement, bishops were impatient for it, and especially that unique patron not merely of myself but of all sound learning and virtue anywhere in England, William, archbishop of Canterbury, a man than whom that island has no one to show more completely furnished with scholarship and integrity and all the qualities that befit a bishop, nor at the same time anyone more devoted to the advancement of learning in the noblest subjects; a man, furthermore, who in all business that may contribute to the dignity, splendour, and majesty of the see of Rome is as dutiful and as loyal as a man could be. And then, when I was still hesitant and, faced with the enormous labour of the task I was undertaking, half regretting my decision, I was kindled afresh to my work by the words of the right reverend father in Christ Gianpietro Carafa, bishop of Chieti, who is now your Holiness' representative in England, who revived my spirits by his comments and his approval, and recalled me to the post of duty. A man with such a gift of speech might persuade one to do anything; who would not be moved by the authority of such an upright and authoritative prelate, or inspired by the rare holiness of that excellent man? For to an unusual familiarity with the three tongues and a knowledge of all subjects, but especially of theology, he adds, though still a young man, such integrity, such holiness of life, such modesty, such friendliness seasoned with an admirable dignity, that he does great credit to the see of Rome and offers every Englishman a finished model, whence all may draw their pattern for every virtue. This great man attached such great importance to these labours of mine that, were I the most conceited of men, I still could not accept his opinion. And yet somehow or other that praise of his applied the spur to my weariness, supported my exhaustion, and refreshed my flagging energy.

Spurred on therefore by the encouragement of these men and others

* * * * *

264 Carafa] Cf Ep 287:9n. He was bishop of Chieti and a founder of the Theatines.

277–8 applied the spur] *Adagia* I ii 47

like them, and relying above all on His assistance whose way is never to fail any pious undertaking, I now return like a new man to my interrupted task. The books of his letters, which I have taken as my special province, I have now purged of the errors by which they were not so much disfigured as destroyed, partly by comparison with ancient manuscripts and partly by my own ingenuity; the Greek, which was either missing entirely or supplied wrongly, I have replaced with the greatest care. I have done the same for the Hebrew, but not without my Theseus, as the Greek proverb has it, for I myself had only sipped the cup of that language. And then again St Jerome, as a past-master of the craft of letters, is a master also of the art of displaying his resources, for he loves to work in here and there anything rare and recondite that is to be found in writers of any language; which brings even the erudite reader to a stop in many passages like a rough place in the road. I have therefore added suitable notes in the appropriate places, whenever anything comes up which seems likely to delay the reader. Besides which, I have as far as possible put everything in proper order. The spurious and suppositious pieces which have been added to Jerome's authentic works, some by accident, some by the cupidity or ignorance of scribes, and some by the audacity of a certain shameless impostor, I have not expelled, but I have separated them from the rest, deprived them of their titles, and relegated them to a volume on their own, that the reader whose appetite is stronger than his critical sense might find nothing wanting, and yet on the other hand that such worthless productions might no longer flaunt the name of such an incomparable man. And to show that in this I was guided by judgment and not caprice, I have added prefaces and critical essays to tell the reader the principles which I have followed. Need I say more? I have borne in this such a burden of toil that one could almost say I had killed myself in my efforts to give Jerome a new lease of life. One thing I could even swear without hesitation: it cost Jerome less to write his works than it has cost me to restore and explain them.

So the great work is, and has been for some time, in full activity, and in the noble German city of Basel the whole of Jerome is being born again; in the printinghouse, moreover, of Froben, than whom none takes more pains, none publishes more excellent books, particularly in Christian literature. Nor is this one man's work or one man's expenditure; for on Jerome's other works, which I have not taken up myself, although as time serves I

* * * * *

285 manuscripts] See Ep 396 introduction.

288 Theseus] Cf Ep 334:135nn.

311 So the great work] This paragraph also first appears in the text as printed (see note to line 229).

lend a hand, several distinguished scholars have been toiling for some time now. Among them is that outstanding man Johann Reuchlin of Pforzheim, who is almost equally at home in the three tongues, Greek, Latin, and Hebrew, and such a master in every field of learning besides that he can challenge the leaders. It is quite right that the whole of Germany should admire and venerate this man as its true phoenix and especial glory. No little weight was added by Conon of Nürnberg, a theologian of the order commonly known as Preachers, who had a great knowledge of Greek and was indefatigable in the advancement of sound learning; and besides them by Beatus Rhenanus of Sélestat, a young man of rare erudition and very keen critical sense. But the greatest contribution of all has been that of the Amerbach brothers, who have shared the expense and the labour with Froben and who are the principals in the whole enterprise. In fact the entire Amerbach family seems to have been designed by the Fates themselves expressly so that by their agency Jerome might rise from the dead. The father, a most excellent man, had taken care to have his three sons taught Greek, Hebrew, and Latin. On his deathbed he commended this objective to his children as though part of their inheritance, and dedicated to it such resources as he had. Those excellent young men pursue with energy the splendid purpose entrusted to them by their worthy father, and have shared Jerome with me, on the understanding that everything outside the letters should be their responsibility.

But why tell me all this? your Holiness will ask. I was just coming to that, most holy Father. No name is better known than Jerome's, no person more universally acceptable; and yet I see a way to add to his renown, to give more weight to his authority. Pope Leo's fame is as glorious as it could be; and yet, if I mistake not, it might be not a little increased. How so? If that great, precious, famous body of work were to emerge as though reborn into the sunlight, into the hands of men, under the most favourable auspices of a dedication to your Holiness. And why not? All sound learning is the child of peace, and it is right and proper that it should blossom anew under the patronage of a pontiff who has restored leisure and peace, the nurse of literature, to the whole world. It will suit well enough if the first doctor of the Christian religion is dedicated to the supreme head of that religion, and the best of all theologians is commended by the name of the best of all pontiffs. I know well enough how carefully one should feel one's way before dedicating anything to your Holiness; what is to be offered to a higher being must be worthy of that being. Yet if I once feel that in this matter I

* * * * *

323 Conon] Cf Ep 318:22n.

have the approval of no less than your Holiness, I shall desire to consecrate to Pope Leo not this work only but the entire outcome of my researches. I myself expect no profit from all my labours except that, thanks to my industry, such as it is, the Christian life should receive reinforcement from the works of Jerome. He will reward me generously for whose sake I bear the burden of this toil. More people will read Jerome if more people understand him, and all will read him more readily if he is approved by the vote of so great a pontiff.

May your Holiness long be preserved in health and wealth for our benefit and the benefit of the whole Christian polity, and ever be blessed with favourable increase, by Christ the Almighty who gave you to the world.

My most revered lord the archbishop of Canterbury, a man rich in every sort of virtue and singularly devoted to the see of Rome and to your Holiness, has instructed me to add greetings in his name. He is my Maecenas, he shows himself such that I could not even wish for a more affectionate or more generous patron.

London, 21 May 1515

336 / From John Fisher — Halling, [May 1515]

Halling is a small parish on the Medway above Rochester, where the bishops of Rochester had a manor.

JOHN, BISHOP OF ROCHESTER, TO ERASMUS

My dear Erasmus, I have been reading in the last few days the dialectic of Rodolphus Agricola, which I found on sale in the bookshops. I was induced to buy it by the praise which you give him in your *Adagia*. For I never could persuade myself that a man could be other than very well worth reading, who was so much praised at the same time by you and by Ermolao. To put it briefly, I never read anything, as far as that art is concerned, more enjoyable or better informed; he seems to have put every point so clearly. How I wish I had had him for a teacher! I would rather that – and I am speaking the truth – than be made an archbishop.

* * * * *

367 Canterbury] The archbishop's greetings are in the manuscript text of this letter but were removed when it was printed.

336:2 dialectic] *De inventione dialectica* (Louvain: Martens 12 January 1515; NK 45)

4 *Adagia*] I iv 39

6 Ermolao] Ermolao Barbaro; cf Ep 126:150n.

But we will speak of this when we meet. When you are ready to set out on your journey to Basel, mind you come this way, for I shall need your advice. So please do this without fail, and may you live long and happy. From Halling.

Your sincere †John Roffen

337 / To Maarten van Dorp — Antwerp, [end of May] 1515

This letter, a defence by Erasmus of the *Moriae encomium*, replies to Dorp's Ep 304. It was evidently written in Antwerp while Erasmus was making his way from England back to Basel, travelling through Bruges (where Thomas More was in residence on a diplomatic mission), Antwerp, Mechelen, Cologne, Mainz, Speyer, and Strasbourg. He appears to have spent some time in the last place, and may not have reached Basel until July; cf Epp 342:1; 343:5,6; 344:1.

It seems from Ep 347 and More's letter to Dorp (Rogers Ep 15) of 21 October 1515 that this letter was sent to Dorp in a shorter form than that later printed in the *Damiani elegeia* and translated here. Dorp in Ep 347 refers to Erasmus' original version of the letter which has not survived. In the *Opera* of 1540 the present text, reprinted there for the first time, was included among the Apologiae, a name that More gave to it at once (Ep 388). From 1516 onwards it appeared with the *Moriae encomium* in all the early editions of that work. A good account of the controversy is given in de Vocht MHL 139–65; see also Sister M. Scholastica Cooper OSB 'More and the Letter to Martin Dorp' *Moreana* 2 (1965) 37–44; and Pierre Mesnard 'Humanisme et théologie dans la controverse entre Erasme et Dorpius' *Filosofia* 14 (1963) 885–900.

ERASMUS OF ROTTERDAM TO MAARTEN VAN DORP, THE DISTINGUISHED THEOLOGIAN

Your letter never reached me, but a copy of it – secured I know not how – was shown me by a friend in Antwerp. You say you regret the somewhat unfortunate publication of my *Folly*, you heartily approve my zeal in restoring the text of Jerome, and you discourage me from publishing the New Testament. This letter of yours, my dear Dorp, gave me no offence – far from it. It has made you much more dear to me, though you were dear enough before; your advice is so sincere, your counsel so friendly, your rebuke so

* * * * *

15 John Roffen] 'Roffensis,' the form of signature still used by the bishops of Rochester

337:3 letter] Cf Ep 334:176. Nichols' suggestion (II 182) that the letter was written in London in March rests upon an unnecessarily restricted interpretation of 'Antwerpiae' at the conclusion of this sentence.

affectionate. This is, to be sure, the mark of Christian charity that, even when it gives rein to its indignation, it retains its natural sweetness none the less. Every day I receive many letters from learned men which set me up as the glory of Germany and call me its sun and moon and suchlike grand descriptions as are more onerous than honorific. My life upon it, none ever gave me so much pleasure as my dear Dorp's letter, written to reproach me. How right St Paul was! Charity is never wrong; if she flatters, she flatters in order to do good, and if she is indignant, it is with the same end in view. I wish I could reply at leisure to your letter, and give satisfaction to so dear a friend. For I am truly anxious that whatever I do should be done with your approval, for I have so high an opinion of your almost divine intelligence, your exceptional knowledge, and your keen judgment, that I should value Dorp's single vote in my favour more than a thousand votes of other men. But I still feel the upset of my sea-voyage and the weariness of the riding that followed, and am, besides that, very busy packing; and so I thought it better to write what I could than to leave a friend thinking as you do, whether these thoughts are your own or were slipped into your head by others, who put you up to write that letter that they might use you as a stalking-horse for their own designs.

First then, to be perfectly frank, I am almost sorry myself that I published my *Folly*. That small book has earned me not a little reputation, or notoriety if you prefer; but I have no use for reputation coupled with ill will. Although, in heaven's name, what is all this that men call reputation, except a perfectly empty name left over from paganism? Not a few things of the kind have survived entrenched among Christians, when for instance they use 'immortality' for leaving a name to posterity, or call a man interested in any form of literature a 'virtuoso.' In all the books I have published my sole object has always been to do something useful by my exertions or, if that should not be possible, at least to do no harm. We see even great writers misusing their gifts to discharge their own personal feelings – one singing of his foolish loves, another flattering those he has set his cap at, another using his pen as a weapon to avenge some injury, another blowing his own trumpet and in the art of singing his own praises outdoing any Thraso or Pyrgopolinices. So be it; for myself, in spite of my small wit and most exiguous learning, I have always had one end in view, to

* * * * *

13 sun] Cf Epp 315:11; 323:31.

16 St Paul] 1 Corinthians 13:4–5

42 blowing his own trumpet] *Adagia* II v 86

43 Thraso or Pyrgopolinices] Two boastful soldiers, Thraso in Terence's *Eunuchus* and Pyrgopolinices in Plautus' *Miles gloriosus*

do good if I can; but if not, to hurt no one. Homer purged his dislike of Thersites by giving an unpleasant picture of him in his poem; Plato criticized many men by name in his dialogues; did Aristotle spare anyone, who spared neither Plato nor Socrates? Demosthenes had his Aeschines as a target for vituperation, Cicero his Piso and Vatinius and Sallust and Antony. How many men Seneca cites by name as objects for his mockery or his censure! Among the moderns, Petrarch used his pen as an offensive weapon against a certain physician; so did Lorenzo against Poggio and Poliziano against Scala. Who can you show me in the whole range of authors so modest that he never wrote with acrimony of anyone? Jerome himself, pious and serious as he was, sometimes cannot refrain from an outburst of indignation against Vigilantius, from levelling insults against Jovinian and bitter invective against Rufinus. It is a long-standing habit of

* * * * *

46 Thersites] Ugly, misshapen, and voluble, the very antithesis of a Homeric hero, Thersites is immortalized as a demagogue in the second book of the *Iliad*.

48 Aeschines] The celebrated Athenian orator against whom Demosthenes directed his speech *On the Crown* (330 BC)

49 Cicero] The invective against Sallust preserved with attribution to him is spurious; for his other enemies see the speeches *In Pisonem, In Vatinium interrogatio, Philippics*.

51 Petrarch] *Invectivae in medicum quendam*, an attack on one of the physicians at the court of Pope Clement VI; see *Opera omnia* (Basel 1554; repr 1965) II 1199–1233.

52 Lorenzo] On this controversy see Ep 24:34n.

53 Poliziano] A controversy on Latin usage with the chancellor of Florence, Bartolomeo Scala (1424–97), who was the target of certain members of the humanist circle around Lorenzo; cf Rossi 357. Antipathy between Scala and Poliziano degenerated into a violent literary quarrel in 1493–4; cf Ida Maïer *Ange Politien* (Geneva 1966) 377 n24.

56 Vigilantius] A theological writer from Gaul, known from his controversy with Jerome over the cult of relics, which he declared to be an idolatrous adoration. Jerome's reply was the *Contra Vigilantium* of 406 AD (PL 23:353–68).

57 Jovinian] A monk who was a critic of celibacy and asceticism and to whom in 393 AD Jerome addressed his *Adversus Jovinianum* (PL 23:221–352). He is mentioned also by St Augustine in his *De haeresibus* (PL 42:45), *De bono coniugali*, and *De sancta virginitate* (CSEL 41 187–231, 235–302).

57 Rufinus] A fourth-century monk of Aquileia and sometime associate of Jerome at school and in the practice of asceticism. He became involved in a celebrated controversy with Jerome, chiefly over the doctrines of Origen; cf *Apologia adversus libros Rufini* (PL 23:415–514) written in 401–2 AD. Rufinus' own writings are collected in PL 21.

learned men to confide their griefs or their joys to paper as though to a bosom friend, and to pour out all their emotions into that sympathetic ear. Indeed, you will find that some men have taken to authorship with no other purpose in mind than to stuff their books full of their own current feelings and in this way to transmit them to posterity.

But I, who in all the volumes I have published have spoken very sincerely of so many men, whose fair name have I ever blackened? On whose reputation have I cast the smallest slur? What people, class, or individual have I criticized by name? If you only knew, my dear Dorp, how often I have been provoked to do so by falsehoods no man could endure! But I have always fought down my resentment, moved more by the thought of what posterity will make of me than by the wish to treat their malignity as it deserves. If the facts had been as well known to others as they were to me, I should have been thought not satirical but fair-minded and even humble and moderate. No, I said to myself, my private feelings are no other man's concern. How can these affairs of mine be within the knowledge either of people at a distance or of posterity? I will maintain my own standard and not sink to theirs. Besides which, no man is so much my enemy that I would not rather, if I could, be on friendly terms with him again. Why should I bar the way to this, why should I now use language of an enemy which I may wish in vain that I had never used when he has become my friend? Why should I award a black mark to a man from whose record it can never be erased, however much he may deserve that it should be? If I must make a mistake, let me praise those who have done little to earn it rather than criticize those who deserve criticism; for if you praise the undeserving, this is ascribed to your open and generous character, while if you paint in his true colours a man who richly deserves to be exposed, this is sometimes thought to be due not to his deserts but to your vicious disposition. I need not mention in passing that the reciprocal exchange of injuries is not seldom the source of some dangerous conflagration, no less surely than reprisals for wrongs suffered on either side sometimes give rise to some enormous war; or that, just as it is unworthy of a Christian to return evil for evil, so it is unworthy of a generous heart to void its resentment in slander as women do.

Reasons like these have convinced me that whatever I write should hurt no one and draw no blood, and that I should never deface it by mentioning any wrongdoer by name. Nor was the end I had in view in my *Folly* different in any way from the purpose of my other works, though the means differed. In the *Enchiridion* I laid down quite simply the pattern of a Christian life. In my book on the education of a prince I openly expound the

* * * * *

59 friend] Horace *Satires* 2.1.30–1

96 prince] *Institutio principis christiani*; cf Ep 393.

subjects in which a prince should be brought up. In my *Panegyricus*, though under cover of praising a prince, I pursue indirectly the same subject that I pursued openly in the earlier work. And the *Folly* is concerned in a playful spirit with the same subject as the *Enchiridion*. My purpose was guidance and not satire; to help, not to hurt; to show men how to become better and not to stand in their way. Plato, serious sage that he was, approves the habit of taking wine with a man at drinking-parties on a generous scale, because he thinks some faults can be dissolved under the cheerful influence of wine which severity could not correct. Horace too thinks good advice even when given in jest no less effective than when serious. 'To tell truth with a smile,' he asks, 'does aught forbid?' And long ago some very wise men perceived this, and thought fit to set out the principles of a good life in fables which are humorous and at first sight childish, because truth by itself is a trifle astringent, and when thus made palatable finds an easier entrance into the minds of mortal men. This surely is the honey which physicians in Lucretius, when they have to give medicine to children, smear on the cup of wormwood. And the purpose for which those princes of old brought fools into their courts was simply this, that their freedom of speech might point out some lighter faults and put them right without offending anyone. Perhaps it may seem inappropriate to mention Christ in such a context. But if it is ever permissible to compare things heavenly and earthly, surely his parables have something in common with the fables of antiquity? The Gospel truth slips into our minds more agreeably, and takes root there more decisively, when it has charms of this kind to commend it than if it were produced naked – a theme pursued at length by St Augustine in his *De doctrina christiana*. I saw how the common throng of mortals was corrupted by the most foolish opinions, and that too in every department of life, and it was easier to pray than to hope for a cure. And so I thought I had found a way to insinuate myself in this fashion into minds which are hard to please, and not only cure them but amuse them too. I had often observed that this cheerful and humorous style of putting people right is with many of them most successful.

If you reply that my assumed character is too trivial to provide an excuse for the discussion of serious subjects, this is a criticism I shall perhaps admit. Ill-judged I do not much object to its being called; ill-

* * * * *

97 *Panegyricus*] *Panegyricus ad Philippum Austriae ducem*; cf Epp 179 introduction; 304:165n.

102 Plato] Cf Macrobius *Saturnalia* 2.8.5–6.

105 Horace] *Satires* 1.1.24–5

111–12 Lucretius] 1.936–8

natured I do object to. Though the first of these charges I could successfully rebut, if in no other way, at least by the precedents of all the eminent authors whom I have listed in my modest preface. What was I to do? I was staying at the time with More on returning from Italy, and was detained indoors for several days by pain in the kidneys. My books had not yet arrived, and if they had, my illness prevented anything more ambitious in the way of serious study. I began to amuse my idle moments with an encomium on Folly, with no thought of publishing it, but to take my mind off my physical discomfort. I showed a specimen of what I had begun to several ordinary friends, in order to enjoy the joke all the more by sharing it. They were highly delighted, and urged me to continue. I did as they said, and spent a week on it more or less which, considering how trivial the subject was, already seemed to me too much. After that the same people who had encouraged me to write it carried it off to France where it was printed, but from an imperfect as well as corrupt copy. What a poor reception it met with is shown, if by nothing else, by the fact that over seven editions were printed in a few months, and those too in different places. I wondered very much myself what anyone could see in it. So if all this, my dear Dorp, is ill-judged, your culprit owns up, or at least puts up no defence. Within these limits and in an idle moment and to please my friends I judged ill, and only once in my whole life. Who can be wise all the time? You yourself admit that my other things are of a kind that all religious and educated people highly approve of. Who are these stern critics, these grave and reverend Areopagites, who will not forgive a man for doing something ill-judged even once? What peevish pedantry is this, to take offence at one single humorous piece and instantly deprive the author of the credit won by nightly toil on his earlier works? What ill-judged things far worse than this I could produce by other men, even by eminent theologians, who think up the most frigid and contentious questions and do battle among themselves over the most worthless trifles as though they fought for hearth and altar! And they act their absurd parts, more farcical than the original Atellanes, without a mask. I was at least more modest, for when I wanted to show how ill-judged I could be, I wore the mask of Folly

* * * * *

135 More] Cf Ep 222 introduction.

152–3 wise all the time] *Adagia* II iv 29

163 Atellanes] A farcical form of Latin comedy, played in masks, which is supposed to have originated at Atella in Campania and became a literary form in the last century before Christ. Erasmus would know of it from references in Livy and other authors.

and, like Socrates in Plato, who covers his face before reciting an encomium on love, I myself acted my part in disguise.

You say that the self-same people who disapprove of my subject think well of the wit, the wide reading, and style, but are offended by the freedom of my satire. These critics actually think more highly of me than I could wish. Not that I care a ha'penny for their kind words, especially as I believe them to have no wit, wide reading, or style themselves; and if they were well supplied with these, believe me, my dear Dorp, they would not be so ready to take offence at humour which aspires to be useful rather than either witty or well read. I ask you: in the name of all the Muses, what can they have in the way of eyes and ears and taste who take offence at the biting satire in that small book? To begin with, what satire can there be in something which criticizes no one by name except myself? Why do they not remember what Jerome so often maintains, that the discussion of faults in general carries no criticism of any individual in particular? If anyone does take offence, he has no cause of action against the author; he may, if he pleases, bring an action for slander against himself as his own betrayer, for having made it plain that that criticism applies to him in particular, which was levelled against everyone in such a way that it was levelled at no individual except such as deliberately made the cap fit. Do you not see how all through the work I have refrained from mentioning people's names so carefully that I have been reluctant even to name a whole country in any critical spirit? For where I list the form of self-love peculiar to each nation, I call the Spaniards proud of their military prowess, the Italians of their literary culture, the English of their good dinners and good looks, and allot to each of the rest in the same way faults of such a kind as anyone, hearing them laid at his door, might not be reluctant to accept them, or at least would greet them with a laugh. Besides which, though the subject I had chosen takes me through every class of men and I spend my time criticizing the faults of individuals, where have I ever said anything scurrilous or bitter? Do I ever uncover a sink of iniquity or stir the mud of Camarina that lurks, as we know, beneath the life of man? Everyone knows how much may be said against evil popes, selfish bishops and priests, vicious princes, and, in a word, against any rank of society, if, like Juvenal, I had not been

* * * * *

165 Plato] *Phaedrus* 237a; cf 243b.

167 You say] Ep 304:60–2

178 Jerome] Jerome Ep 125:5; CSEL 56 122

187 self-love] LB IV 448B–E

195 Camarina] *Adagia* I i 64; cf line 690 below.

ashamed to record in writing what many men practise without shame. I have merely surveyed the humorous and comic, rather than the scurrilous, aspect of things, but have done this in such a way as sometimes to touch on major topics, and point out things in passing which it is very important they should know.

I know you have no time to spare for the descent into these details, but yet if you ever have the leisure, do look rather more carefully into the ridiculous jests that Folly makes; and you will find them a good deal closer to the teaching of the evangelists and apostles than some men's disputations which their authors think so splendid, so worthy of their professorial eminence. You yourself in your letter do not deny that much of what is there reported is the truth; only you think it inexpedient to 'let rough truths grate on tender ears.' If you think one should on no account speak one's mind and never tell the truth except when it does not hurt, why do physicians use bitter drugs, and reckon their *hiera picra* among their most highly recommended remedies? If they do so when treating the ailments of the body, how much more reasonable for me to do the same when seeking to cure distempers of the mind? 'Rebuke, reprove, exhort,' says St Paul, 'in season, out of season.' The apostle thinks faults should be attacked in every possible way;and do you think no sore place should be touched, and that, too, when this is so gently done that no one could even feel hurt unless he deliberately hurts himself? Why, if there does exist a way of curing men's faults without giving offence to anyone, that is, if I mistake not, the most appropriate way of all: to name no one by name, to refrain from things which good people cannot bear even to hear mentioned (for as some things in tragedy are too terrible to be displayed before the spectators and it is enough to tell the story, so in human behaviour some things are too disgusting to be described without embarrassment), and to recount what can be described in a lively and humorous fashion through the mouth of some ridiculous character, so that any grounds for offence are excluded by the light-hearted treatment. We all know what an effect a well-judged and well-timed pleasantry sometimes has even on the grimmest of tyrants. Could any supplication or any serious argument have mollified the heart of the king in the story so easily as the soldier's jest? 'Not at all' says he; 'if the

* * * * *

209 your letter] Ep 304:24–6

210–11 let rough truths ... ears] Persius 1.107–8

216 St Paul] 2 Tim 4:2

224 tragedy] Cf Horace *Ars poetica* 179–88.

232 king] Pyrrhus, king of Epirus; the story is told in Plutarch *Moralia* 184D and elsewhere.

flagon had not gone dry on us, we should have said far worse things about you.' The king laughed, and forgave them. There was good reason for the careful discussions on wit and humour in those two great masters of rhetoric, Cicero and Quintilian. Such is the power of wit and liveliness that we can take pleasure in a witty remark even when it is aimed at us, as is reported of Julius Caesar. And so, if you admit that what I said is true, and if it is humorous rather than indecent, what better means can be devised for curing the defects that are common to all men? For a start, pleasure alone is enough to attract the reader and hold his attention. For in every other department men's objectives differ; but pleasure attracts all alike, except those who are too stupid to feel any sense of pleasure from what they read.

Further, those who take offence where no names are mentioned seem to me to be swayed by the same sort of emotions as women who, if they hear anything said against loose members of their sex, are as indignant as if the criticism applied to them all individually; and conversely, if anyone praises virtuous women, they are as pleased with themselves as if what applies to two or three stood to the credit of the sex as a whole. Men should be above these ill-judged reactions, scholars still more, theologians most of all. If I find some accusation here of which I am not guilty, I take no offence, but think myself lucky to be free from failings which I see many people suffer from. If it touched on some sore place, and I see myself in the mirror, here too there is no call for me to be offended. If I have any sense, I shall conceal my feelings and not come forward to give myself away. If I am a virtuous man, I shall take the hint, and see to it that in the future no fault can be laid by name at my door like the one I see before me pilloried anonymously. Can we not allow this book at least the freedom conceded to those popular comedies even by the uneducated? Think of all the jibes discharged with such freedom against monarchs, priests, monks, wives, husbands, everybody! And yet, because nobody is attacked by name, everybody laughs; everyone either openly confesses his own fault or carefully covers it up. The most savage tyrants tolerate their zanies and court fools, though they are often criticized by them in public. The emperor Vespasian took no steps against the person who said he had a face like a man straining at stool. Who then are these friends of yours whose ears are so delicate that they cannot endure to hear Folly herself cracking jests against the way men live in general without giving anyone a black mark by name? The Old Comedy

* * * * *

235 discussions] Cicero *De oratore* 2.54.216 to 2.71.290; Quintilian 6.3

238 Julius Caesar] Cf Suetonius *Divus Julius* 73.

264 Vespasian] Suetonius *Divus Vespasianus* 20

268 Old Comedy] Cf Horace *Ars poetica* 281–4.

would never have been driven off the stage if it had refrained from mentioning leading citizens by name.

But you, my excellent Dorp, almost write as though my *Folly* had made the whole theology faculty my enemies. 'Why need you make such a bitter attack,' you say, 'on the faculty of theology?' and you lament the position I find myself in. 'In the old days,' you say, 'what you write was read with enthusiasm by everybody and they all longed to see you here in person. Now your Folly, like Davus, has upset everything.' I know you write nothing merely to find fault, and I shall not beat about the bush with you. I ask you, do you call it an attack on the faculty of theology if foolish and badly behaved theologians quite unworthy of the name come in for some criticism? If you think those ought to be the rules of the game, a man would make enemies of the whole human race who said anything against criminals. Was there ever a king so brazen as not to admit that there are a few wicked kings unworthy of a throne? Is any bishop too proud to admit the same about his own order? Is the faculty of theology the only one out of so many which offers us no stupid, uneducated, quarrelsome person, nothing but Paul and Basil and Jerome over again? Quite the contrary: the more distinguished a profession is, the fewer men in it who are good enough. You will find more good ship's captains than good princes, more good physicians than good bishops. In any case this casts no aspersions on the faculty; it tends to the credit of the few who in a most noble faculty have behaved nobly. Tell me, why are theologians more offended (if some have really taken offence) than kings, primates, magistrates, bishops, cardinals, popes? Or than merchants, husbands, wives, lawyers, poets – for no kind of mortal man has been spared by Folly, except that they are not so stupid as to think everything a direct attack on themselves which is said in general about bad men? Saint Jerome wrote to Eustochium on the subject of virginity, and in the process painted such a picture of the behaviour of lascivious women as Apelles himself could not have made more vivid. Was Eustochium hurt? Was she indignant with Jerome for casting aspersions on the good estate of virginity? Not in the slightest. And why so? Because, being a sensible woman, she did not think that, if any criticism was made of the bad members of her sex, it applied to her; on the contrary, she was glad to see virtuous women reminded that they must not sink to that level and equally

* * * * *

273 you say] Ep 304:28–30

274 you say] Ep 304:51–3

296 Eustochium] St Eustochium (c 368–c 418) was the third of four daughters of St Paula of Rome. She led a life of consecrated virginity and was one of the noble Roman ladies who received spiritual direction from St Jerome. The letter here referred to (Epistle 22) – one of several addressed to her – is perhaps his most famous letter; CSEL 54 143–211.

glad to see bad women told to be different in future. He wrote to Nepotianus about the lives led by the clergy and to Rusticus on the monastic life, painting the faults of both classes in lively colours and taking them to task brilliantly. His correspondents took no offence, because they knew that none of it applied to them. Why was there no estrangement between me and William Mountjoy, who is by no means least among noblemen at court, when Folly made all those humorous comments on eminent courtiers? Because, being himself a most excellent and most sensible man, he supposed (what is in fact true) that attacks on wicked and foolish grandees are nothing to do with him. Think of all the jests Folly aimed at wicked and worldly bishops! Why did the archbishop of Canterbury take no offence at all this? Because, being abundantly endowed with every virtue, he knows that none of this is meant for him.

Why need I go on to recount to you by name the eminent princes, the other bishops and abbots and cardinals and famous scholars, none of whom I have yet found estranged from me by one hair's breadth as a result of my *Folly*? Nor can I bring myself to believe that any theologians were irritated by it, except a few maybe who either do not understand it, or are jealous of it, or are so cantankerous by nature that they approve of nothing at all. Mixed in with that class of men, as everyone would agree, are certain persons so ill endowed with talents and with judgment that they have never been set to learn any subject, let alone theology. They get by heart a few rules from Alexander Gallus, and strike up an acquaintance with a little idiotic formal logic, and then get hold of ten propositions out of Aristotle, and even those they do not understand; after that they learn the same number of *quaestiones* from Scotus or Occam, intending to resort for anything else to the *Catholicon*, the *Mammotrectus*, and similar wordbooks, as

* * * * *

304–5 Nepotianus] St Nepotianus was nephew to the bishop Heliodorus of Altinum. Like his uncle, he had abandoned a military career for the clerical state. The letter is Ep 52, written in 394 AD (CSEL 54 413–41). Nepotianus died of a fever shortly afterwards; cf Ep 60 to Heliodorus.

305 Rusticus] A young monk of Toulouse to whom Ep 125 was written in 411 AD; CSEL 56 118–42.

326 Gallus] Alexandre de Ville-Dieu (fl c 1200), whose *Doctrinale*, a versified grammar for advanced students, was one of the most successful schoolbooks of the Middle Ages

330 *Catholicon*] Cf Ep 26:100n.

330 *Mammotrectus*] A glossary to the Vulgate, the *Legenda sanctorum*, and other writings, compiled about 1300 by the Franciscan Johannes Marchesinus of Reggio, first printed at Mainz and at Lucerne in 1470, and often reprinted. The title is a corruption of the Greek *mammothreptos*, understood to mean 'a baby at the breast,' since when armed with this book even babes and sucklings could face difficult Latin.

though they were a sort of horn of plenty. Whereupon it is astonishing the airs they give themselves, for nothing is so arrogant as ignorance. These are the men who condemn St Jerome as a schoolmaster, because he is over their heads; who poke fun at Greek and Hebrew and even Latin, and, though as stupid as pigs and not equipped even with the common feelings of humanity, they suppose themselves to hold the citadel of all wisdom. They sit in judgment, they issue condemnations and pronouncements, they know no hesitations, are never at a loss – there is nothing they do not know. And yet these men, often only two or three of them, often rouse the greatest commotions. Nothing is so brazen, so pig-headed, as ignorance. These are the men who conspire with such zeal against the humanities. Their aim is to count for something in the councils of the theologians, and they fear that if there is a renaissance of the humanities, and if the world sees the error of its ways, it may become clear that they know nothing, although in the old days they were commonly supposed to know everything. These are the men who raise all this clamour and tumult; it is they who run this conspiracy against the devotees of liberal subjects. They do not like my *Folly*, because they have no understanding either in Greek or Latin. If these gentry – not theologians, but men dressed up to look like them – receive one or two shrewd hits, what has this to do with the infinitely respectable body of theologians who are real scholars? If it is zeal for religion that animates them, why do they object to my *Folly* in particular? See what filthy pestilent godless stuff was written by Poggio! Yet he is a Christian author; he is in everybody's pocket and has been translated into almost every language. See how Pontanus pursues the clergy with slander and abuse! But he is read as a wit and a merry fellow. See how much filth there is in Juvenal! But some think that even preachers may find him useful. Look at the malice against the Christians shown by Cornelius Tacitus, the hostility of Suetonius, the impious mockery reserved for the immortality of souls by Pliny and Lucian. But these authors are read by everybody as part of their education, and rightly so. Only Folly, because she discharged a few shafts of wit, not against scholarly theologians who deserve the name, but against the frivo-

* * * * *

353 Poggio] Presumably in his *Liber facetiarum*, a collection of witty and often improper stories frequently directed against the clergy

355 Pontanus] Giovanni Pontano (c 1424–1503) of Naples, one of the most celebrated Latin poets in Renaissance literature. He was a prolific writer; this reference may be to his Lucianic dialogue *Charon*.

358 Tacitus] *Annals* 15.44.3ff

358 Suetonius] Nero 16

lous quibbling of ignorant dolts, and the absurd title of *magister noster*, they find quite intolerable.

And it is two or three worthless fellows dressed up to look like theologians who are trying to arouse feeling against me like this, as though I had attacked and antagonized the whole faculty. For my part I have such high regard for theological learning that it is the only learning to which I normally allow the name. For that faculty I have such respect and veneration that it is the only one in which I have entered my name and sought to be enrolled, though I am ashamed to claim so distinguished a title for myself, knowing as I do the gifts both of scholarship and of life required by one who would write himself theologian. The man who claims to be a theologian somehow claims something more than ordinary men. This is the proper dignity for bishops, not for men like me. Enough for me to have learnt with Socrates that I know nothing at all and, where I can, to lend a helping hand to the studies of other people. For my part I do not know where they lurk, those two or three gods among the theologians who you say in your letter are not propitious towards me. Personally I have been in many places since I published my *Folly*, and have lived in so many universities and great cities; and never have I felt that any theologian was annoyed at me, except one or two of the class that are enemies of all sound learning, and even they have never said a word of protest to me. What they may murmur behind my back I pay little attention to, relying on the verdict of so many men of good will. If I were not afraid, my dear Dorp, that someone might think I was boasting rather than speaking the truth, how many theologians I could list for you, renowned for holiness of life, eminent for scholarship, and of the highest station, some of them even bishops, who have never given me such a warm welcome as since the publication of my *Folly*, and who think more highly of that small book than I do myself. I could give you them one by one here and now, by name and title, did I not fear that for Folly's sake even such eminent persons might incur the displeasure of your three theologians. One of them at any rate I suppose to be the author of all this commotion in your midst, for I can guess pretty well what has happened. And if I were prepared to paint him in his true colours, no one would be surprised that such a man should disapprove of my *Folly*; in fact I would not approve it myself unless such people did disapprove. Not that I really like

* * * * *

363 *magister noster*] An allusion to Erasmus' characterization of the vanity of theologians in the *Praise of Folly*; cf LB IV 470D–471A

370 entered my name] Cf Ep 200:9.

378 letter] Not Ep 304

393 One of them] Possibly Jan Briaert; cf Ep 670 introduction.

it; but it is a good reason for misliking it much less, that it is not liked by these great wits. The judgment of wise and learned theologians carries more weight with me; and they are so far from accusing me of bitterness that they even praise my moderation and fairness of mind for dealing with a naturally licentious subject without licence and, given a humorous theme, for having poked fun without hurting. For to answer only the theologians who are, I hear, the only men to have taken offence, everyone knows how much is said even in public against theologians who are immoral. Folly touches on nothing of the kind. She confines her jests to their useless discussions on minute points, and even these she does not disapprove of indiscriminately: she condemns the men who see in them alone the stem and stern, as they say, of theological science, and who are so fully occupied with battles of words, as St Paul called them, that they have no time to read what was written by evangelists, prophets, and apostles.

I only wish, my dear Dorp, that fewer of them were exposed to this charge. I could produce for you men over eighty who have devoted their long lives to nonsense of this kind, and have never read the Gospels right through; I detected this, and at length they had to confess it themselves. Even under the mask of Folly I did not dare say what I have often heard deplored by many men who are themselves theologians, real theologians I mean, upright serious scholarly men who have drunk deep of Christ's teaching from the true springs. Whenever they are in company where it is permissible to say freely what they think, they regret the arrival in the world of this newer kind of theology and long for the return of the old sort. Never was anything so sacred, so noble, giving so much the true flavour and image of Christ's heavenly teaching. But the modern kind (to say nothing of the portentous filth of its barbarous and artificial style, its ignorance of all sound learning, and its lack of any knowledge of the tongues) is so much adulterated with Aristotle, with trivial human fantasies, and even with the laws of the Gentiles, that I doubt whether any trace remains, genuine and unmixed, of Christ. What happens is that it diverts its attention over much to consider the traditions of men, and is less faithful to its pattern. Hence the more intelligent theologians are often obliged to express before the public something different from what they feel in their own hearts or say when among friends. And sometimes they would be gravelled for an answer to any earnest enquirer, for they see that what Christ taught and what mere human traditions ordain are not the same. What can Christ have in common with Aristotle? What have these quibbling sophistries to do with the mysteries of eternal wisdom? What is

* * * * *

410 St Paul] 1 Tim 6:4

the purpose of these labyrinthine *quaestiones*, of which so many are pointless, so many really harmful, if for no other reason, as a source of strife and contention? But, you will say, there are things we must enquire into; on some points we must even have a decision. I do not dissent. But on the other hand there are a great many better let go than pursued (and it is part of knowledge to recognize that certain things are not for our knowing), a great many things on which to doubt is a more healthy state than to lay down the law. Finally, if laws must be laid down, let it be done reverently and not in arrogance and in accordance with Scripture, not with the so-called reasoning thought up by ordinary men. As it is, of these petty arguments there is no end; yet even in them what disagreements arise between parties and factions! And every day one pronouncement gives rise to another. In short, things have come to such a pass that the sum of the matter depends not so much upon what Christ laid down as upon the definitions of professors and the power of bishops, capable or otherwise; and in all this everything is now so much involved that there is no hope even of recalling the world to the old true Christianity.

All this, and a great deal else, is perceived and regretted by men of great piety and at the same time great learning, and they regard as the principal cause of it all this bold irreverent tribe of modern theologians. If only it were possible, my dear Dorp, for you to look silently into my thoughts – you would understand how much I deliberately leave unsaid at this point. But all this my *Folly* left untouched, or at least touched on very lightly, in order to hurt no one's feelings. And I took care to observe the same restraint throughout, to write nothing improper or corrupting or revolutionary, nothing that might seem to involve criticisms of any class of person. If anything is said there about the cult of the saints, you will always find something added to make it quite clear that criticism is confined to the superstition of those who do not venerate saints in the way they should. If any reflection is cast on princes or bishops or monks, I always go on to explain that no insult is intended to persons of that class, only to its corrupt and unworthy members, for I would not hurt a good man while pursuing the faults of bad ones. In so doing, furthermore, I have done what I could by suppressing names to give no offence even to bad men. Lastly, by conducting all the action in terms of wit and humour through an imaginary comic character, I have tried to arrange that even peevish folk who are hard to please may take it in good part.

One passage, you say, is criticized as not oversatirical but impious. How can the ears of a good Christian, you ask, endure to hear me call the

* * * * *

475 you ask] Ep 304:32–4

felicity of the future life a form of lunacy? I ask you, my worthy Dorp, who taught an honest man like you this kind of innuendo, or (which I think more likely) what clever man took advantage of your simple heart to traduce me like this? This is just how those pestilent experts in calumny take a couple of words out of their context, sometimes a little altered in the process, leaving out everything that softens and explains what sounds harsh otherwise. Quintilian picks up this trick in his *Institutio* and shows us how to play it: we recount our own story in the most flattering light, with supporting evidence and anything else that can mitigate or extenuate or help our case in any way; we should recite our opponent's case, on the other hand, shorn of all this assistance in the most invidious language it allows of. This art they have learnt, not from the teaching of Quintilian, but from their own malevolence; and its outcome often is that things which would have been most acceptable if reported as they were written, give great offence when recounted differently. Pray reread the passage, and observe with care the stages, the gradual progress of the argument, which led me to describe that felicity as a species of lunacy, and then observe the language in which I unfold all this. So far from giving offence to really pious ears, you will find plenty there which might actually delight them. It is in the way you read it that a slight cause of offence arises, and not in what I wrote.

For, since the purpose of my *Folly* is to embrace the whole world of things under the name of foolishness and to show that the whole sum of human felicity depends on Folly, she ranged over the entire human race as high as kings and supreme pontiffs; thence she arrived at the apostles themselves and even Christ, all of whom we find credited in the Scriptures with some kind of foolishness. Nor is there any risk that someone at this point may suppose that the apostles or Christ were foolish in the ordinary sense, but that in them too there was an element of weakness, something attributable to our natural affections, which when compared with that pure and eternal wisdom might seem less than wise. But this same folly of theirs overcomes all the wisdom of the world; just as the prophet compares all the righteousness of mortals to rags defiled with a woman's monthly discharge, not that the righteousness of good men is something foul, but because the things that are most pure among men are somehow impure when set against the inexpressible purity of God. Now I have set forth a kind of wise folly, and in the same way I produce a lunacy which is a sane and intelligent stupidity. And to soften what followed about the fruition of the saints, I

* * * * *

482 Quintilian] 5.13.23 and following

506 prophet] Isa 64:6

512–13 I begin] LB IV 439B

begin by recalling the three kinds of madness in Plato, of which the most blessed is the madness of lovers, which is nothing but a kind of ecstasy. But the ecstasy of godly men is nothing else than a foretaste of future blessedness, by which we are totally absorbed into God and shall live in future more in him than in ourselves. But this is what Plato calls madness, when a man, being rapt out of himself, exists in the object of his love and has the enjoyment of it. Do you not see how carefully I distinguish a little further on between the kinds of folly and insanity, so that no ingenuous reader could be misled by the words I used?

But I have no quarrel with the meaning, you say; it is the words themselves that revolt pious ears. But why are not those same ears offended when they hear Paul speak of the foolishness of God and the folly of the cross? Why do they not pick a quarrel with St Thomas for using about Peter's ecstasy words like 'In his pious delusion he begins to speak of tabernacles.' That sacred and blessed rapture he describes as delusions! And yet all this is recited in church. Why did they not bring me to court long ago for describing Christ in a certain prayer as a magician and enchanter? St Jerome calls Christ a Samaritan, although he was a Jew. Paul even calls him sin, as though that were more than to say a sinner; he calls him an accursed thing. What outrageous impiety, if one chose a malevolent interpretation! And what a pious tribute, if one accepts it as Paul meant it! In the same way, if one were to call Christ a robber, an adulterer, a drunkard, a heretic, would not all men of good will put their fingers in their ears? But suppose one expressed this in appropriate language; suppose one worked up to it, as though one were leading the reader by the hand up to this point gradually, until he saw how in his triumph through the cross he robbed Hell of its plunder which he restored to the Father; how he took unto himself the synagogue, like the wife of Moses (the wife of Uriah over again), that a peace-loving people might be born from her; how he was intoxicated with the new wine of charity when he gave himself for us; how he brought in a new kind of teaching, very different from all the current convictions of wise and foolish alike. Who could be offended then, especially as now and again we find some of these words used in Scripture in a good sense? I myself in

* * * * *

513 Plato] *Phaedrus* 244a–5c; cf *Moriae encomium* LB IV 439B–440A.

524 Paul] 1 Cor 1:23–5

525 St Thomas] Cf *Comm in Matt* 17:5.

529 prayer] *Precatio ad Virginis filium Iesum;* LB V 1213A: 'Nam tu, dulcissime Jesu, pius ille es incantator et magus.'

530 Jerome] *Translatio homeliarum Origenis in Lucam* 34; PL 26:316C.

530 Paul] Gal 2:17, 3:13

my *Chiliades* (it occurs to me in passing) have called the apostles Silenus figures and even Christ himself a sort of Silenus. Give me a prejudiced interpreter to put a brief and invidious explanation on this, and what could sound more intolerable? Let a pious and fair-minded man read what I wrote, and he will find the allegory acceptable.

It surprises me greatly that those friends of yours have never noticed another thing – how cautiously I put these things forward, and the care I take to soften them by adaptation. What I say is this: 'But now that I have donned the lion's skin, let me tell you another thing. The happiness which Christians seek with so many labours is nothing other than a certain kind of madness and folly. Do not be put off by the words, but consider the reality.' Do you see? To begin with, the fact that Folly holds forth on such a solemn subject is softened by a proverb, where I speak of her having donned the lion's skin. Nor do I speak just of folly or madness, but of 'a kind of folly and madness,' so that you have to understand a pious folly and a blessed madness, in accordance with a distinction which I go on to make. Not content with that, I say 'a certain kind' to make it clear that this is meant figuratively and is not literal. Still not content, I urge people not to take offence at the mere sound of my words, and tell them to watch more what is said than how I say it; and this I do right at the very beginning. Then in the actual treatment of the question, is there anything not said in a pious and thoughtful fashion – more reverently in fact than really suits Folly? But on that point I thought it better to forget consistency for a moment than not to do justice to the importance of the theme; better to lose sight of the rules of composition than to offend against piety. And finally, when my demonstration is finished, that no one may be upset by my having allowed a comic character like Folly to speak on such a sacred subject, I meet this objection too by saying: 'But I have been long forgetting who I am, and I have overshot the mark. If anything I have said seems rather impudent or garrulous, you must remember it is Folly and a woman who has been speaking.'

You see that I have never failed to cut short all excuse for the slightest offence. But this means nothing to men whose ears are closed to all but propositions and conclusions and corollaries. Should I mention that I provided my book with a preface in which I try to stop malicious criticism at the

* * * * *

546 *Chiliades*] *Adagia* III iii 1

553 'But now] LB IV 500B

558 proverb] *Adagia* I iii 66

573 'But I] LB IV 504C

outset? Nor have I the slightest doubt that it is found satisfactory by all fair-minded readers. But what can you do for men who are too obstinate to accept satisfaction or too stupid to know when they are satisfied? Simonides said that the Thessalians were too slow-witted to be deceived by him; and you can find some people like them too stupid to be placated. Nor is it surprising that a man should find matter for complaint who looks for nothing else. Anyone who should read St Jerome in that spirit will find a hundred places open to objection, and your friends will find no lack, in that most Christian of all the Fathers, of grounds for labelling him a heretic; to say nothing for the moment of Cyprian and Lactantius and others like them. Finally, who ever heard of a humorous subject being submitted for examination by theologians? If this is a good idea, why not by the same token apply these principles of examination to any frivolous stuff written by our modern poets? What a lot of impropriety they will find there, of things that reek of ancient paganism! But since no one regards these as serious works, none of the theologians supposes them to be any business of his.

Not that I would ask to be allowed to shelter behind the example set by your friends. I should not like to have written even in jest anything that in any way could weaken a Christian's faith; but I must be allowed a reader who understands what I have written and a fair and upright critic; one who is keen to learn the truth and not interested in making mischief. But suppose a man were to take into account the people you speak of, who in the first place have no brains and even less judgment; second, have never been in touch with liberal studies but are infected rather than educated by that mean and muddled schooling of theirs; and lastly, hate everyone who knows what they themselves do not know, bringing with them no object except to distort whatever it may be that perhaps they have half understood – such a man, if he wished to be free from calumny, would never put pen to paper. Need I add that some of them are led to make mischief by a desire for glory? Nothing is so vainglorious as ignorance combined with a delusion of knowledge. And so, if they have this thirst for fame and cannot satisfy it by honourable means, they would rather imitate that Ephesian youth who made himself notorious by setting fire to the most famous temple in the whole world rather than live obscure. And since they themselves cannot produce anything worth reading, they devote themselves to picking to pieces the works of famous men.

* * * * *

584 Simonides] Plutarch *Moralia* 15D

612 Ephesian youth] One Herostratus, who in 356 BC successfully sought posthumous fame by burning down the great temple of Diana at Ephesus

Other men's works, I mean, not my own, for I am nobody. My *Folly* I myself think not worth a straw, so let no one suppose me concerned about that. Is it surprising if men of the sort I have described choose out a few statements from a long work and make some of them out to be scandalous, some irreverent, some wrongly expressed, some impious and smacking of heresy, not because they find these faults there, but because they bring them in themselves? How much more conducive to peace and suitable to a Christian's fairness of mind to be well disposed to scholars and promote their work; and then, if anything ill thought out should escape them, either to overlook it or to give it a friendly interpretation, instead of looking for holes to pick in a hostile spirit and behaving like an informer rather than a theologian. How much more promising to work together in order either to instruct or to be instructed and, to use Jerome's words, to take our exercise in the field of the Scriptures without hurting one another! But it is astonishing how those men know no middle course! Some authors they read in a spirit of being ready to defend the most blatant errors on any pretext however frivolous, and towards some they are so unjust that nothing is too carefully phrased for them to pick holes in it somehow. How much better it had been instead, while they rend in pieces and are rent in turn, wasting their own time and other people's, to learn Greek, or Hebrew, or Latin at least! A knowledge of these is so important for our understanding of Scripture that it really seems to me monstrous impudence for one who knows none of them to expect to be called a theologian.

And so, my excellent Maarten, devoted as I am to your welfare, I shall not cease to urge you, as I have often done before, to add to your equipment at least a knowledge of Greek. You are exceptionally gifted. You can write – solid, vigorous, easy, abundant stuff, evidence of a spirit as productive as it is wholesome. Your energy is not merely untouched by years but still fresh and green, and you have successfully completed the conventional course of study. Take my word for it, if you crown such a promising start with a knowledge of Greek, I dare promise myself and everyone else that you will do great things, such as none of our modern theologians has ever done before. If your view is that for love of true religion we should despise all human learning, and if you think that the shortest way to such wisdom is to be somehow transfigured through Christ, and that everything else worth knowing is perceived more fully by the light of faith than in the books of men, I shall subscribe without difficulty to your opinion. But if, in the present state of human affairs, you promise yourself a true understanding

* * * * *

629–30 to take … one another] Jerome Ep 115; CSEL 55 397

of the science of theology without a knowledge of the tongues, particularly of the language in which most of Scripture has been handed down, you are wholly at sea.

And I only wish I were as able to persuade you of this as I am desirous to do; for my desire is in proportion to my fondness for you and my interest in your work, and the fondness is very great and the interest very sincere. If I cannot convince you, do at least listen to the prayers of a friend to the extent of making the experiment. There is no forfeit I will not gladly pay if you do not admit that my advice was friendly and reliable. If my affection for you carries any weight, if there is anything in our being fellow-countrymen, if you attach any weight I will not say to my learning but to my prolonged labours in the humanities, if my age has any influence with you (for as far as years go, I am old enough to be your father), let me persuade you to agree to this out of affection or respect, if not for my arguments. You habitually call me eloquent; I shall never agree with you, unless on this point I can win you over. If I do succeed, the result will be great satisfaction for us both, for me in having given you this advice and for you in having taken it; and you, who are now the dearest of all my friends, will on this account be not a little dearer to me, because I shall have made you dearer to yourself. Otherwise I fear that when you are older and have learnt from experience, you will approve my advice and regret your decision and, as so often happens, will not understand your mistake until it is too late to remedy it. I could recount a long list to you by name of men who have become children again to learn Greek, because they had observed after all that without Greek liberal studies are lame and blind.

But on this topic I have already said too much. To return to your letter. Thinking that the one way to reduce my unpopularity with the theologians and recover the good standing I once enjoyed would be to compose an encomium on Wisdom as a sort of recantation of my *Praise of Folly*, you beg and beseech me urgently to do so. For my part, my dear Dorp, as a man who despises no one except myself and who would be glad, if it were possible, to live at peace with the whole human race, I would not refuse to undergo this labour, did I not foresee that any small share of ill will I may have incurred from a few prejudiced and ignorant critics, so far from being extinguished, would be made much worse. And so I think it better not to stir up trouble that is not badly placed and to let this Camarina alone. This hydra, if I mistake not, will be better left to weaken with time.

* * * * *

683–4 you beg and beseech] Ep 304:81–3

690 Camarina] Cf note to line 195.

I now come to the second part of your letter. My work on the restoration of Jerome meets with your high approval, and you encourage me to take up other labours of the same sort. You spur a willing horse; though what I need is not so much people to spur me on to this task as helpers, such is its difficulty. But I hope you will never again believe anything I say if you do not find me speaking the truth in this: those friends of yours who take so much offence at my Folly will not approve my edition of Jerome either. Nor are they much better disposed towards Basil, Chrysostom, and Nazianzen than they are to me, except that their assaults on me are more outspoken; though sometimes in moments of irritation they are not afraid to say some very foolish and improper things about those great luminaries. They are afraid of the humanities; they fear for their own dictatorship. I can show you that I am not making this up. When I had begun work and the news had already got around, up came certain reputedly influential men and distinguished theologians, by their own valuation, and adjured the printer by all that is holy not to allow any admixture of Greek or Hebrew; these two languages, they said, are fraught with peril and there is no good to be got out of them; they were designed solely to satisfy idle curiosity. Even before that, when I was in England, I happened to find myself drinking wine with a certain Franciscan, a Scotist of the first rank, who in public estimation is a very clever man and in his own knows all there is to know. When I had explained to this man what I was trying to do in Jerome, he expressed astonishment that there should be anything in his works that theologians did not understand – and he such an ignorant man that I should be surprised if there are three lines in all the works of Jerome which he rightly understands. He added kindly that, if I had any problems in Jerome's prefaces, they had all been clearly expounded by LeBreton.

I ask you, my dear Dorp, what can one do for these theologians of yours other than pray for them, except perhaps find a reliable physician to cure their brains? And yet it is sometimes men of this kidney who talk loudest in any gathering of theologians, and these are the men who issue pronouncements about the Christian faith. They are terrified, as though it

* * * * *

692 second part] Ep 304:90ff.

694 willing horse] *Adagia* I ii 46

711 Franciscan] Evidently Henry Standish, later bishop of St Asaph; cf Allen Ep 608:14n; Knowles 53–5.

718 LeBreton] Guillaume LeBreton, the famous thirteenth-century Franciscan, wrote a work on St Jerome's biblical prologues, of which 45 mss are recorded by F. Stegmüller in *Repertorium Biblicum Medii aevi* II (Madrid 1950) nos 2824–72.

were something perilous and pestilential, of the very thing that St Jerome, and Origen too even in his old age, tried so hard to secure for themselves, that they might truly be theologians. Moreover Augustine, when he was already a bishop and an old man, deplores in his *Confessions* that in his youth he had been disgusted by the study which might have been of such value to him in his exposition of Scripture. If there is any peril here, I shall not take fright at a risk which men of such wisdom have gone out to look for. If this is idle curiosity, I have no wish to be holier than Jerome – and how ill these men served Jerome in calling what he did idle curiosity is their own lookout. There exists a very ancient decree of a pontifical synod providing for the appointment of professors to give public instruction in several tongues, while for the learning by heart of sophistics and Aristotle's philosophy no such steps have ever been taken, except that a question is raised in the *Decreta* whether it is permitted to study these subjects or no. And the study of them is disapproved of by many eminent authorities. So what the authority of popes has instructed us to do we neglect, and what has been called in question and even disapproved of is the only thing we accept. Why? Not but what they are as badly off in Aristotle as they are in Scripture. They are dogged everywhere by the nemesis that waits for those who despise Greek; here too they are subject to delusions, half asleep, blear-eyed, blundering, producing more monstrosities. To these eminent divines we owe the loss of so many of the authors listed by Jerome in his catalogue; so few survive because they wrote over the heads of our *magistri nostri*. We owe it to them that we possess St Jerome so corrupt and mutilated that it costs others almost more labour to restore his text than it did him to write it.

Then again what you write in the third part about the New Testament makes me wonder what has happened to you, or what has beguiled for the moment your very clear-sighted mind. You would rather I made no changes, unless the Greek gives the meaning more fully, and you say there are no faults in the version we commonly use. You think it wrong to weaken in any way the hold of something accepted by the agreement of so many centuries and so many synods. I ask you, if what you say is true, my most learned Dorp, why do Jerome and Augustine and Ambrose so often cite a

* * * * *

726 Augustine] *Confessions* 1.12.19 to 1.14.23

733 decree] A reference to the Constitution of Clement v, promulgated after the Council of Vienne

737 *Decreta*] Cf Ep 182:194n.

746 *magistri nostri*] Cf note to line 363.

750 third part] Ep 304:101ff

different text from the one we use? Why does Jerome find fault with many things, and correct them explicitly, which corrections are still found in our text? What will you do when there is so much agreement, when the Greek copies are different and Jerome cites the same text as theirs, when the very oldest Latin copies concur, and the sense itself runs much better? Do you intend to overlook all this and follow your own copy, though it was perhaps corrupted by a scribe? For no one asserts that there is any falsehood in Holy Scripture (which you also suggested), nor has the whole question on which Jerome came to grips with Augustine anything at all to do with the matter. But one thing the facts cry out, and it can be clear, as they say, even to a blind man, that often through the translator's clumsiness or inattention the Greek has been wrongly rendered; often the true and genuine reading has been corrupted by ignorant scribes, which we see happen every day, or altered by scribes who are half-taught and half-asleep. Which man encourages falsehood more, he who corrects and restores these passages, or he who would rather see an error added than removed? For it is of the nature of textual corruption that one error should generate another. And the changes I make are usually such as affect the overtones rather than the sense itself; though often the overtones convey a great part of the meaning. But not seldom the text has gone astray entirely. And whenever this happens, where, I ask you, do Augustine and Ambrose and Hilary and Jerome take refuge if not in the Greek original? This is approved also by decrees of the church; and yet you shuffle and try to reject it or rather to worm your way out of it by splitting hairs.

You say that in their day the Greek copies were more correct than the Latin ones, but that now it is the opposite, and we cannot trust the texts of men who have separated from the Roman church. I can hardly persuade myself to believe that you meant this seriously. What? We are not to read the books of renegades from the Christian faith; and how pray do they think Aristotle such an authority, who was a pagan and never had any contact with the faith? The whole Jewish nation turned away from Christ; are we to give no weight to the Psalms and the Prophets, which were written in their language? Now make me a list of all the heads under which the Greeks differ from the orthodox Latins; you will find nothing that arises from the words of the New Testament or has anything to do with this question. The whole controversy relates to the word *hypostasis*, to the procession of the Holy Spirit, to the ceremonies of consecration, to the poverty of the priesthood, to the powers of the Roman pontiff. For none of these questions do they lean

* * * * *

768 blind man] *Adagia* I viii 93

782 You say] Ep 304:122ff

on falsified texts. But what will you say when you see their interpretation followed by Origen, Chrysostom, Basil, Jerome? Had somebody falsified the Greek texts as long ago as that? Who has ever detected falsification in the Greek texts even in one passage? And finally, what could be the motive, since they do not defend their particular tenets from this source? Besides which, that in every department of learning the Greek copies have always been more accurate than ours is admitted by no less than Cicero, who is elsewhere so unfair to the Greeks. For the difference between the letters, the accents, and the actual difficulty of writing all mean that they are less easily corrupted and that any corruption is more easily mended.

Again, when you say that one should not depart from a text that enjoys the approval of so many councils, you write like one of our ordinary divines, who habitually attribute anything that has slipped somehow into current usage to the authority of the church. Pray produce me one synod in which this version has been approved. How could it approve a text whose author is unknown? That it is not Jerome's is shown by Jerome's own prefaces. But suppose that some synod has approved it? Was it approved in such terms that it is absolutely forbidden to correct it by the Greek original? Were all the mistakes approved as well, which in various ways may have crept in? Was a decree drawn up by the fathers of the council in some such terms as this? 'This version is of unknown authorship, but none the less we approve it, nor do we wish it to be an objection that the Greek copies have something different, however accurate they may be, or if a different reading is found in Chrysostom or Basil or Athanasius or Jerome, even though it may better suit the meaning of the Gospel, notwithstanding our high approval of these same authorities in other respects. Moreover, whatsoever in future may in any way, whether by men with a little education and rather more self-confidence or by scribes unskilled, drunken, or half-asleep, be corrupted, distorted, added, or omitted, we in virtue of the same authority approve, nor are we willing that any man should have licence to alter what has once been written.' A very comical decree, you say. But it must have been something like this, if you are to frighten me from this kind of work by the authority of a synod.

Finally, what are we to say when we see that even copies of our Vulgate version do not agree? Surely these discrepancies were not approved by a synod, which of course foresaw each change that would be made? I only wish, my dear Dorp, that the Roman pontiffs had sufficient leisure to issue salutary constitutions on these points, which would take

* * * * *

802 Cicero] *Ad Quintum fratrem* 3.5.6

806 when you say] Ep 304:111ff

care for the restoration of the works of good authors and the preparation and substitution of corrected copies. Yet I would not give any seats on that commission to those most falsely so-called theologians whose one idea is that what they learnt themselves should be the only thing of current value. And what have they learnt that is not utter nonsense and utter confusion? If they once become dictators, farewell to all the best authors! The world will be compelled to accept their brainless rubbish as oracles; and so little sound learning is there in it, that I would rather be a humble cobbler than the best of their tribe, if they can acquire nothing in the way of a liberal education. These are the men who do not like to see a text corrected, for it may look as though there were something they did not know. It is they who try to stop me with the authority of imaginary synods; they who build up this great threat to the Christian faith; they who cry 'the Church is in danger' (and no doubt support her with their own shoulders, which would be better employed in propping a dung-cart) and spread suchlike rumours among the ignorant and superstitious mob; for the said mob takes them for great divines, and they wish to lose none of this reputation. They are afraid that when they misquote Scripture, as they often do, the authority of the Greek or Hebrew text may be cast in their teeth, and it may soon become clear that what used to be quoted as an oracle is all a dream. St Augustine, that very great man and a bishop as well, had no objection to learning from a year-old child. But the kind of people we are dealing with would rather produce utter confusion than risk appearing to be ignorant of any detail that forms part of perfect knowledge, though I see nothing here that much affects the genuineness of our Christian faith. If it were essential to the faith, that would be all the more reason for working hard at it.

Nor can there be any danger that everybody will forthwith abandon Christ if the news happens to get out that some passage has been found in Scripture which an ignorant or sleepy scribe has miscopied or some unknown translator has rendered inadequately. There are other reasons to fear this, of which I prudently say nothing here. How much more truly Christian it would be to have done with quarreling and for each man cheerfully to offer what he can to the common stock and to accept with good will what is offered, so that at the same time you learn in humility what you do not know and teach others ungrudgingly what you do know! If some are so ignorant that they cannot rightly teach anything or so conceited that they are unwilling to learn, let us think no more of them (for they are very few) and concentrate on those who are intelligent or at any rate promising. I once

* * * * *

854–5 year-old child] *Confessions* 8.12.29

showed my annotations, when they were still raw, still fire-new from the mint, as they say, to men of the highest integrity, eminent theologians and most scholarly bishops; and all admitted that those rudimentary pieces, such as they were, had shed a flood of light for them on the understanding of Holy Scripture.

Furthermore, you tell me, but I knew already, that Lorenzo Valla had been active in this field before me, for I was the first to publish his annotations; and Jacques Lefèvre's notes on the Pauline Epistles I have seen. I only wish they had finished off their work, so that my efforts might not have been needed. Personally I think Valla most praiseworthy, as a man more concerned with literature than with theology, for having shown enough energy in the study of Scripture to compare the Greek with the Latin, while there are not a few theologians who have never read the whole Testament right through; although in some places I differ from him, especially in those that relate to theological science. And Jacques Lefèvre had his notes in hand already when I was getting this work under way, and it happened, a trifle unfortunately, that even in our most friendly conversations neither of us thought of mentioning his plans, nor did I learn what he had been at until his work appeared in print. His attempt also I heartily approve, although from him too I dissent in some places, reluctantly, for I should be happy to agree with such a good friend in everything, were it not necessary to consider truth more than friendship, especially where Scripture is concerned.

But it is not yet quite clear to me why you confront me with these two names. Is it to deter me from the project as though I were already anticipated? But it will be clear that even after such good men I had good reason to attack it. Or do you suggest that their efforts, like my own, were unpopular in theological circles? Personally I cannot see that Lorenzo added to his existing unpopularity; and Lefèvre I hear is universally approved. I might add that we do not attempt an exactly similar task. Lorenzo only annotated selected passages, and those, it is clear, in passing and with what they call a light touch. Lefèvre published notes on the Pauline Epistles only, and translated them in his own way; then added notes in passing if there was any disagreement. But I have translated the whole New Testament after

* * * * *

877 you tell me] Ep 304:99–100

878 publish] Ep 182 introduction

886 Lefèvre] Cf Ep 326:95ff.

888 conversations] Perhaps during Erasmus' visit to Paris in 1511; cf Epp 218–22.

903 light touch] *Adagia* I iv 27

comparison with the Greek copies, and have added the Greek on the facing pages, so that anyone may easily compare it. I have appended separate annotations in which, partly by argument and partly by the authority of the early Fathers, I show that my emendations are not haphazard alterations, for fear that my changes might not carry conviction and in the hope of preserving the corrected text from further damage. I only wish I had been man enough to perform what I so laboriously undertook! As far as the business of the church is concerned, I shall have no hesitation in presenting my labours, such as they are, to any bishop, any cardinal, any Roman pontiff even, provided it is such a one as we have at the moment. In the end I have no doubt that you too will be delighted with the book when it is published, although you now dissuade me from publishing it, once you have had even a brief taste of the studies without which no man can form a right judgment on these questions.

Observe, my dear Dorp, how by one kind deed you have made two parties grateful to you: one is your theologian friends, on whose behalf you have so diligently accomplished your mission, and other is me, for your friendly advice is fresh evidence of your affection for me. You in your turn will take in good part the equally outspoken return I have made you, and if you are wise you will adopt my advice (for I have no one's interests at heart but yours) rather than theirs, whose sole object in trying to bring over to their party a gifted nature like yours that was meant for great things is to strengthen their own forces by the acquisition of such a leader as you. Let them follow better courses if they can; if not, you at least must follow only the best. If you cannot make them better men, as I hope you will try to do, at least mind that they do not make you a worse one. What is more, you must present my case to them with the same frankness with which you have put theirs to me. Make my peace with them as far as you can, and make them see that I follow this course not in order to discredit those who know nothing of these languages, but for the general good, which will be available to anyone who cares to use it and will not be a burden on the man who prefers to do without; also that my attitude is that, if anyone arises who can or will teach us something better, I shall be the first to tear up and abandon what I have written and subscribe to his opinion.

Give my most cordial greetings to Jean Desmarez, and show him our discussion on the *Folly* on account of the notes on it which my friend Lyster dedicated to him. Commend me warmly to the learned de Nève and to that

* * * * *

940 Desmarez] Cf Ep 180 introduction.

941 Lyster] Cf Ep 495 introduction.

942 de Nève] Cf Ep 298 introduction.

very kind Nicolaas van Beveren, the provost of St Peter's. Abbot Meynard, whom you praise so highly (and, knowing your sincerity, I am sure he deserves it), I love and respect already for your sake, and shall not fail, when I have the opportunity, to mention him with honour in what I write. Farewell, Dorp, dearest of men.

Antwerp, 1515

337A / From Bruno Amerbach [Basel], [c June 1515]

This letter was formerly Ep 420. The text is taken from an autograph copy in the Öffentliche Bibliothek of the university of Basel, MS G II 13a 11. A rough draft of the letter is on the verso of Ep 464, itself a rough draft, and Allen conjectured that the two were close in date of composition. Alfred Hartmann however, has advanced convincing arguments for re-dating the letter to 1515; see AK II Ep 524.

Greetings, most learned Erasmus. Rustic am I, and call a spade a spade, so you must take my very foolish letter in good part. The volume of spurious works is going on even better than it deserves, though the manuscripts are so full of mistakes that it would be less trouble to clean out an Augean cowbyre. We shall finish, so far as I can guess, about the first of August. Unless you are content for Jerome to run dreadful risks, you will do well to come back to us soon. As for me, if I have made any mistake from my native ignorance, I will do my best to correct it.

In haste, from Messrs Froben's treadmill in Basel

Froben and my brother Basilius send greetings.

338 / From Leo X Rome, 10 July 1515

This letter and the next were first published in *Epistolae ad Erasmum* in October 1516, and later in the same year published separately as *Breve sanctissimi*

* * * * *

943 van Beveren] Nicholas of Burgundy; cf Ep 144 introduction.

943 abbot Meynard] Cf Ep 304:178n.

337A:1 call a spade a spade] A line from an unidentified Greek comedy (fragment 227 Kock), cited, eg, by Plutarch *Moralia* 178B and Lucian *Juppiter tragoedus* 32, *Quomodo historia conscribenda sit* 41. Bruno cites the original Greek.

5 cowbyre] To muck out the stables of Augeas was one of the labours of Hercules. For Bruno's language in the rough draft see Allen II 257 4n.

7 native] Reading *germana*; but *Germana* (Germanic) would come to the same thing.

Leo x, with his first cousins, the cardinals Giulio de' Medici
(who later became Pope Clement vii) and Luigi de' Rossi
Raphael, 1518–19
Uffizi Gallery, Florence

domini nostri Leonis X *ad Desyderium Erasmum Roterodamum* (Basel: Froben nd) by Beatus Rhenanus in response to a request from Ottmar Nachtigall (cf Ep 302:16n). The letters were sent to Erasmus in England, whence he had written (Ep 335), and were retained by Andrea Ammonio (LP II i 823; August 1515), along with Ep 340 from Cardinal Riario. On 2 October 1515 Erasmus still knew nothing of these letters (Ep 360:13), presumably because Ammonio himself was uncertain of Erasmus' whereabouts. In the event Ammonio sent Erasmus copies of Epp 338 and 339 together with 340 in February 1516, through Pace (Epp 427, 429). These travelled with Pace through Italy and did not reach Basel until Erasmus himself had left. They were sent after him (Epp 419, 460), but Erasmus first saw Ep 338 in Antwerp in July 1516 in the hands of Pieter Meghen (cf Ep 446 introduction) and Ep 339 in London shortly afterwards (Ep 429:7–8; Allen Ep 457:37–8). The letters sent through Pace, except Ep 340, finally reached Erasmus at Antwerp in September (Allen Ep 457:36–7; LP II i 2299). This letter and the one following were composed by Jacopo Sadoleto, who with Pietro Bembo had been appointed secretary to Leo X at his accession.

There are two manuscripts of the letter in the Öffentliche Bibliothek of the university of Basel; one (Erasmuslade MS B II b 2) is in the hand of Bonifacius Amerbach and was evidently taken from the documents sent to Basel by Ammonio. From the agreement between the texts it would appear that Rhenanus' printed version may have been printed from this MS. A second copy (Erasmuslade MS II b 3) in the hand of Konrad Brunner (cf Ep 313:26n) is independent but shows only negligible variants.

POPE LEO X

To our beloved son, greeting and apostolic benediction. We received great pleasure from your letter sent to us from London, for it conveyed both your affection for us and the honourable opinion which you entertain of us; and both these things give us much satisfaction. Both moreover acquired an added lustre, in that this approval came to us from no ordinary man, but from one of great learning, for whom we have a high regard, a man whom we have learnt to know in a lower station of life, so that it was recommended by the great integrity and great eloquence of the writer. We would therefore have you know for a certainty that, of two things, one we will accomplish: that is, given the opportunity we will requite your virtue and your good will towards us by some special exercise on your behalf of our paternal affection; in respect of the other, we will do our best to make our efforts match your excellent opinion of us. Would that the supreme author of all good actions and all good intentions, who solely by his liberality and his providence raised us for no distinguished merit of our own to this most lofty state of dignity and splendour, even as it was his will that we should desire those things that are apt and conducive to the welfare of the Christian polity, might now prepare before us a highway by which we could advance unhindered towards the restoration of true piety and virtue among men. We have indeed some enterprises still no more than begun, upon which you touch kindly in your letter. But far greater and far more difficult remain, for which we shall sorely need divine assistance; and if this is forthcoming, we will do our best to ensure that those who think well of us and our disposition shall be seen to have been right.

But this must be left to the mercy of God. For our part, we shall look forward with a sort of agreeable impatience to the volumes of St Jerome edited by you. You affirm that you will send us the fruits of all your labours, and this promise we shall reckon as a generous gift and be grateful to you for it. We feel great affection towards our venerable brother the archbishop of Canterbury on this account, since by lending his zealous encouragement to your virtue he confirms his own virtue and merit. Since moreover you are far away, and in an island ruled by a famous monarch who is in every way a most devoted son to us and to the apostolic see, we are writing to him a letter of recommendation on your behalf; and we have given orders for the letter and a copy of it to be sent to you, that you may deliver it if you think expedient. For our part, such is our general devotion and love towards sound learning and such our particular belief in your virtue and scholarship, we greatly desire that on some suitable occasion our liberality may find a way to serve your honour and your advantage, as our good will towards you demands and as your worth deserves.

Given at Rome at Saint Peter's under the ring of the fisherman on the tenth day of July in the year 1515, being the third year of our pontificate.

Ja. Sadoletus

To our beloved son Erasmus Rotterdam

339 / From Leo X to Henry VIII

See Ep 338 introduction; the earliest source is Vatican MS AA Arm 44, vol 5, f 71, a rough draft in Sadoleto's hand.

POPE LEO X TO OUR DEAREST SON IN CHRIST, HENRY, MOST ILLUSTRIOUS KING OF ENGLAND

To our dearest son in Christ, greeting and apostolic benediction. Towards

* * * * *

338:27 Jerome] In the printed version in *Epistolae ad Erasmum* 'and the New Testament' was added at this point to allow for the change in dedications.

learned men, and that which both truly is and is rightly called sound learning, we feel a certain warm interest and a more than common inclination, which was born in us from childhood, strengthened by the principles of our upbringing, and increased by the maturer judgment of advancing years; and this, not only because we have now learnt by repeated experience that these men who devote themselves to good letters and the arts are of excellent character and unimpeachable integrity, but also because we know that such knowledge, and the literary gifts of the doctors of Holy Church, have been the source of very great advantage and adornment to our Christian polity. For these reasons we have a high regard in the Lord for our beloved son Erasmus Rotterdam, whom we consider to be among the leaders of such learning and such arts, a man known to us aforetime from personal acquaintance in a lower station of life, and since then far better known and most highly esteemed for the works of genius which he has published. This man has sent us from England, where he now resides, a letter full of dutiful sentiments, which is all the more welcome in that it brings with it evidence from him of your royal excellence and kingly spirit, a reminder than which nothing could give us greater pleasure in view of the high place which your Majesty holds in our good will.

We have therefore thought fit to recommend him to your Majesty, not that at this time we have any definite request to make of you on his behalf, nor does he himself ask us for anything of the kind; but this is something we do of our own free will, to solicit on behalf of those who enjoy our sincere good wishes the same good will and favour from others who are in a position to comply. It will therefore give us great satisfaction, should he ask anything of your Majesty's grace, favour, and benevolence, if over and above the generosity which you may show him of your own mere motion, you should let it be known that this recommendation from us has added further weight. This will not only give us pleasure; it will, in our opinion, do honour to your Majesty.

Given at Rome at Saint Peter's under the ring of the fisherman on the tenth day of July in the year 1515, being the third year of our pontificate.

Ja. Sadoletus

* * * * *

339:16 personal acquaintance] The same phrase, *domestico congressu*, is used in Ep 335:12–13; cf the allusion in Ep 338:8, where the phrase *'in minoribus'* occurs, as here also. As a cardinal, the pope had travelled to the north of France at the turn of the century, and the meeting might conceivably have occurred then.

340 / From Cardinal Raffaele Riario Rome, 18 July 1515

This letter apparently did not reach Erasmus in 1516 along with the others sent through Pace, and in 1518 it had not yet reached Erasmus; cf Ep 338 introduction. It is a reply of course to Ep 333, and was first published in the *Opus epistolarum* (1529).

RAFFAELE, CARDINAL OF SAN GIORGIO, TO ERASMUS OF ROTTERDAM

Honoured sir, and my right good friend, I greet you well. Two things in your letter were especially welcome. One was the traditional and truly Roman eloquence, which had of course long been familiar and well known to me, in good measure from your scholarly conversation but much more fully from the distinguished products of your genius, which you have published with all the elegance of style both in Greek and Latin, both in prose and verse; these will secure for your name an imperishable memory in time to come, just as England, with so many other distinctions of her own, will gain no small increase in glory from having Erasmus as her adopted son. The other was as new as it was welcome, for you suggest that you are considering another visit to Rome. Warmly as I wish for this, I dare not count upon it for fear of giving way to groundless rejoicing. Would that you had determined once and for all to carry out your plan! For I am afraid, men's thoughts being so changeable, and so various the conjunctures of times and events, that something will arise to turn your mind in another direction, so that you will not visit us on the day you have determined. And further, just as I let you go reluctantly, and my affection would not give you your congé on any pleas, except that you had been invited to visit Britain in a series of letters from the king, from the archbishop of Canterbury, and from William Mountjoy, so this time I dare not seek to tear you away from such distinguished patrons by my selfish importunity.

I think my feelings are not unknown to you. I would only add this warning, knowing your sound sense: the opportunities in Rome are not to be overlooked, whether you seek pecuniary advantage or have an eye to your position, neither of which do I think you should despise. For you must procure in good time some provision for the old age that will surely come, and a secure position will defend you from the tooth of envy, the constant companion of outstanding merit. All men who have any gifts in the literary way flock to this city from every quarter as though it were a theatre, where not only do the greatest men – men like yourself – find generous rewards for excellence in store for them, but even persons of more common mould do not lack the honour that is their due, so that they are encouraged to pursue a higher standard. Nay more, has not Rome the right to demand your return as her own property? and though she shares this in common with many other cities, just as seven rival cities claimed property in Homer, yet in this contest it seems unlikely that this city will give way before the ambition of any other. Every man has his own mother country; Rome is the common mother of all men of letters, and nurtures and develops their gifts. You made us sad by your departure; gladden us now by your return.

That you have purged St Jerome and recalled him to the light of day touches me nearly, who share with him my priesthood in the Roman church. You have indeed raised in his honour a noble monument, and it will preserve your name eternally as well as his. I shall take steps to acquire him forthwith in his new guise, that as I read his pages I may be at once delighted by the elegance of the style, and taught the path to goodness by his sound instruction. And would that someday I might do this in your company, for when you were here before, you shed such light for me upon the art of writing as no one had ever shown me before.

Farewell, 18 July 1515

341 / To the Reader — Basel, 30 July 1515

This is Erasmus' preface to a revised edition of the *De octo orationis partium constructione libellus* (Basel: Froben August 1515). This was a brief work on Latin syntax written by William Lily for Colet's new school of St Paul's, as Erasmus here explains (line 21 and n). On the genesis of the work and Erasmus' alterations to it see ADS I 4 107–8; and Vincent J. Flynn 'The Grammatical Writings of William Lily, ?1468–1523' in *The Papers of the Bibliographical Society of America* 37 (1943) 98–101. A corrected edition of September 1517 was dedicated to Erasmus' godson Erasmius Froben, the younger son of Johann Froben.

ERASMUS OF ROTTERDAM TO FAIR-MINDED READERS

Experience teaches me the truth of the old Greek proverb: 'Good will untimely differs not from hate.' I observe the appearance in different places of men even more devoted to my reputation than I could wish, who claim as mine books which I never wrote, or at least did not write with a view to publication. It is a long-standing habit of academic people to commit all the thoughts of their hearts to paper as to a bosom friend (so Horace puts it); but we should not wish to see immediate publication of every word we ex-

* * * * *

341:2 Greek proverb] *Adagia* I vii 69

7 Horace] *Satires* 2.1.30–1

change, it may be in bad temper or in an idle moment, with some old crony. They have published epigrams which I wrote (I will not deny), but did not write with that in view. Some servant, I suspect, filched them, and sold them to the printers. Someone else, from a few poor pages full of mistakes in the copying, quotes and teaches, as though from something I had published, it is wonderful to say how many things about the art of letter-writing. And to say nothing of all the lesser pieces, here is this small book on syntax, which they have lately claimed as mine in retrospect, although it was published originally with no author's name.

John Colet, a leading theologian in England, was looking for a new book on syntax for his new school, which must be both short enough and clear enough to be suitable for his boys. At his request such a book had been written by William Lily, a man unusually well-versed in Latin and Greek and an expert in the education of the young. When he had finished it, Colet handed it to me, or rather forced me to take it for correction. What else could I do, when endlessly assailed with requests by such a close friend that I thought it wrong to deny him anything he might ask, and a man so highly thought of and so generous to me that he has the right not merely to ask his friend Erasmus for anything he pleases, but to give him orders? When however my corrections had taken the form of altering most of it (for that

* * * * *

10 epigrams] First published by Bade with the *Adagiorum collectanea* in December 1506/January 1507, and reprinted in Paris two or three times down to 1512; cf Reedijk 361.

11 servant] Erasmus had had more than one difficulty with manuscripts going astray; cf Ep 30:17n concerning the history of the *Antibarbari*, and also his experience with the manuscript of the dialogue *Julius exclusus* (cf J.A. Gee *The Life and Works of Thomas Lupset* (New Haven 1928) 53 and ff).

14–15 letter-writing] Cf Ep 71 introduction.

21 Lily] William Lily (1468?–1522) had studied with Grocyn while at Oxford, and was a companion of Thomas More in the Charterhouse. He subsequently made a pilgrimage to Jerusalem and followed this by intensive study of Greek and Latin at Rhodes and in Rome. After returning to England about 1500 he settled in London as a member of the More circle. In 1512 Colet appointed him first high master of St Paul's School, and he held the office until his death. This syntax was combined with two other grammatical treatises by Lily to form 'Lily's Grammar,' an authorized Royal grammar used for more than a century in England. The first known edition of this text appeared in 1542–3 as *An Introduction of the Eyght Partes of Speche* (STC 15605); see Flynn (see introduction) 104–13, and his edition in facsimile of the 1567 printing of the grammar (New York 1945). Lily was grandfather of the euphuist, John Lily; see A. Feuillerat *John Lyly* (Cambridge 1910) and McConica 49–51, 203–4, and passim.

seemed the easier course), Lily, who is modest almost to a fault, would not allow the book to be published under his name, nor did I think I could honourably claim as my own a book in which anything belonged to someone else. And so I told them firmly that they could put on it the name of anyone they pleased as long as it was not mine; and thus, since we both rejected it, the book appeared without an author, recommended only by Colet in a short preface.

So this is the book, and at this stage I shall neither praise it for fear of being thought conceited, nor speak ill of it lest I seem insincere. But it seemed worth writing these preliminary lines to stop people hereafter accepting as mine what I myself in the preface expressly disclaim. There are errors enough even in the things I publish myself; let no one else put out as mine what I have either not written or not corrected. Farewell, dear reader.

Basel, 30 July 1515

342 / From Nikolaus Gerbel Strasbourg, [beginning of August] 1515

Nikolaus Gerbel of Pforzheim (1485–1560) was a pupil in the Latin school at Pforzheim along with Wolfgang Capito and other future humanists. He studied at the university of Vienna under Conrad Celtis, and then in 1506 went to Cologne. In 1508 his interests led him to Tübingen, and after further studies, including a year at Bologna where he became a Doctor of Laws, he went in 1515 to Strasbourg, where he became secretary to the cathedral chapter. He also assisted Matthias Schürer and spent the rest of his life in that city as a member of its humanist and reforming community. He was an ardent supporter of Reuchlin and was mentioned in the *Epistolae obscurorum virorum*. In Strasbourg Erasmus had arranged with Schürer to publish a volume of *Lucubrationes* containing the *Enchiridion*, along with some shorter pieces; cf Epp 164 introduction, 349. See Bopp 1625; Ritter 166–7.

NIKOLAUS GERBEL TO ERASMUS GREETINGS IN CHRIST JESUS

How much I have regretted your departure I would hardly dare tell you either directly or in writing, for fear that you will accuse me once again of wishing to practise my powers of expression; and what a starveling I am in that department I discovered long since, so clearly that I need no one to tell

* * * * *

34 book] Printed by Richard Pynson (STC 5544) in 1513. According to Flynn it was printed in some 200 editions all over Europe from 1513–95 (99 n33). See also C.G. Allen 'The sources of "Lily's Latin Grammar": A Review of the Facts and Some Further Suggestions' *The Library* 5th series 9 (1954) 85–100, 14 (1959) 49–53.

me so. However, take it how you please, there is one thing I neither can nor will keep secret, that I never took more pleasure in the friendship of anyone, or more enjoyed his company, or got more real enjoyment from his conversation – such learned grace, so charming, so unspeakably delightful! – as I get from my beloved Erasmus. Were there but one or two things in my humble self as acceptable to you as everything about you is to me, I should publicly proclaim that my felicity was complete, and that no single thing however great could make me more perfectly happy than the knowledge that our friendship, in its humble way, was not wholly displeasing to the great Erasmus.

I know what you are doing now – smiling, I know. I know just what you think – that it is my tongue that speaks and not my heart. You have no idea, my learned friend, how wrong you are, I would rather not write a word than write a lie or – if anyone thinks that more creditable – use my fancy on such a subject. This is only pen-practice, you say? Even that can be done without flattery and fraud, and this side dishonesty. Tongue-practice, is it? Schoolboys do the same, and often on real subjects as much as invented ones. But this, you say, has nothing to do with friendship, friendship true and single-minded, whose only dwelling is the heart. As God loves me, that is just how I feel and act myself; and if you could only see into my heart, there would be no need, so far as this is concerned, of letter-writing.

But enough of this. I do not think Erasmus so heartless as to turn good into evil, and think a man who sincerely loves him a flatterer rather than a friend. Your *Lucubrationes* is being printed just now with more than common diligence, and I work at it as best I can with all my powers. You will, I think, like what we have done, and you will not be sorry that you fell in with our wishes. Please let us have the other things with speed, for about four quires are already finished; and if you have ready anything of the same sort, to make the book a proper size, and more saleable, give us a taste of your generosity, and let your devoted readers appreciate your devotion to Christ. I have written notes on a few passages in your *Enchiridion* which were somewhat above the heads of schoolboys; and in hopes that this work of mine at any rate might be of some service to them, I decided to add some comments of a kind at the end of the book. If you do not disapprove, I will continue; otherwise your opinion shall be decisive.

* * * * *

342:30 *Lucubrationes*] Published by Schürer in September 1515 with a preface by Gerbel. For its contents see Epp 93, 108, 164, 327.

40 disapprove] Apparently Erasmus did not take up this proposal.

Farewell, with my very best wishes, and do write back if you have any affection for your friend Gerbel. Johannes Rudolfinger, who is much devoted to you, sends you a thousand greetings, and so does Matthias Schürer, who begs Beatus Rhenanus to take Rodolphus in hand some time; for if Rodolphus were once corrected, he would publish him without further delay. Farewell once more.

Strasbourg, 1515

343 / From Nikolaus Gerbel

Strasbourg, 8 August 1515

NIKOLAUS GERBEL TO MASTER ERASMUS

I wrote to you a few days ago to tell you how we all are and about the publication of your *Lucubrationes*. Besides which, I asked you to send us the rest of the book, so that the work can be printed off quickly and well, as you wished. And now you can send it easily and safely, for you have a carrier, the man who is bringing you the bundle that was left with us by your servant. I have carefully reread your work, and put right a few things in it, wherever this could conveniently be done; in such a way, however, as not to go too far from your own corrections, only now and again there was something that might offend a careful reader. I have found a few crosses in the margin, the meaning of which I cannot guess. Please let me have a full reply about these, and the other points. I have written this in a great hurry, so please forgive its lack of polish.

Strasbourg, 8 August 1515

344 / From Udalricus Zasius

Freiburg im Breisgau, 9 August 1515

I have heard the most happy news of your return, my dear Erasmus, glory of the learned world, and they were such cheerful tidings and so much longed-for that, if my old bones had not kept me at a distance, I should by now have come flying to greet you and welcome your noble self. But this heavy old body of mine on puny pillar propped, with neither legs nor feet really equal to their task, has difficulty in standing where it is; and so, as a kindly and fair-minded man, you must take it in good part if I send you a letter to replace my attendance in person. Welcome then, Desiderius Eras-

* * * * *

43 Rudolfinger] Cf Ep 302:15n.

45 Rodolphus] Agricola; Cf Ep 311:27n.

343:7 work] Presumably a copy of the 1509 edition published by Martens (NK 836) and corrected by Erasmus

344:5 puny pillar] Juvenal 3.193

mus, our great inspiration, easily first among all the leaders in Germany of scholarship in Greek and Latin; and may that day of good omen long endure and be entered in a happier chapter of our annals that brings you among us once again. Basel surely owes you a debt on many counts for the lustre you so often shed on her. If only the golden radiance of your more than human gifts could have been shed on some lodging in our town as well, how happy we should be; what long-continued glory would await us! For this is something I can affirm with perfect confidence, that for six hundred years and more the whole of Germany has never been blessed with a better scholar than yourself. Your admirable learning is witness to the truth of this, and so are those teeming rivers of eloquence, to say nothing for the moment of your rich store of ideas. Lucian, most famous of stylists and satirists, were he alive today, would not dare compete with you on level terms, so shrewdly do you challenge him with your brilliant declamations; every time I read them, every time I note those saps and tunnels of insinuation, the indirect approaches, the siege-engines of the mind creeping slowly forward, the sudden stroke of proof and argument, the thunderbolt of refutation, and all the other weapons brought out from the inmost armoury of rhetoric, I am swept away, and gaze astonished as at the sublime achievement of some more than human power.

And then your *Adages*, that work beyond price, those flowing streams of discourse, the richness of development with which you set a mere dunghill beetle above an eagle, and can compass the gloomy clouds of war and over against them the calm radiance of peace, and much else of the kind, in vigorous language and with marvellous vividness – if I tried to commend all these incomparable qualities as they deserve, the goddess Persuasion herself seated on my lips would not be equal to it. What can I say of those exquisite *Adages*, with all their wit and all their charm? Long ago, in the garden of Alcinous, pear made way for pear, apple for apple; and in the same way one adage succeeds another with all the plenty and fertility of summer, as one ripening fruit treads on another's heels, so that whichever way you look you find something noble, delightful, beautiful, forcible, rich, and fresh. Then again, if I run over your *Copia*, with its horn of plenty stuffed with words and things; if I recall your *Moria*, or your elegant

* * * * *

31 dunghill beetle] *Adagia* III vii 1

31–2 war ... peace] *Adagia* IV i 1

35 lips] Cicero *Brutus* 15.59

37 garden of Alcinous] Homer *Odyssey* 7.120

40 forcible] We should probably read *inlustria*, 'vivid.'

translations from the Greek, I shall be supplied with immense materials for panegyric, to which my poor gifts are quite unequal, nor can it be confined in one short letter. This much I will say, that you above all deserve the admiration of the learned everywhere, and on you they should heap recognition of every kind by the barnful, as the saying goes. For my own part, I feel myself so deeply indebted to you that I shall count it a privilege if I ever have the opportunity, I will not say to obey your orders, but even to forestall your slightest wish.

I would have talked with you at greater length, and also asked you about some things which are on my mind. But my friend Bonifacius, a gifted young man and a solid scholar, is at my elbow. I hope to be with you in person in a week, or ten days at most. Farewell, from Freiburg, 9 August 1515.

Your sincere friend Zasius

Give affectionate messages from me to Beatus Rhenanus, and if you conveniently can, greet Philipp of Engen for me. There is much more I could say, but I will unburden myself face to face.

345 / To Udalricus Zasius [Basel, beginning of August 1515]

The autograph original in the Öffentliche Bibliothek of the university of Basel is MS Frey-Grynaeus II 9 135; it was first published in the *Auctarium* (1518).

ERASMUS TO HIS FRIEND ZASIUS

I had made up my mind, dear Zasius, my accomplished friend, to visit Freiburg mainly for your sake. But the Rhine floods had done so much damage to the roads that it would have been more swimming than riding. I want to see you very much. But first of all, my dear Zasius, mind you consider the state of your health. I could not wish my pleasure to cost you so dear. For my part, when your letter reached me, I had been for some days

* * * * *

47 by the barnful] *Adagia* III vi 61

52 Bonifacius] Amerbach, evidently the bearer of the letter

58 Philipp of Engen] Philipp Engelbrecht (c 1499–1528) was brother to the suffragan bishop of Speyer. He had matriculated at Wittenberg with Luther, and in 1514 was incorporated at Freiburg with an MA from the former university. At Freiburg he became a friend of Zasius. In the summer of 1515 he went to Basel to see to the republication of a poem in praise of Freiburg, and worked with Froben.

345:3 floods] Cf Ep 348:10–12. These experiences evoked the verses entitled *Cum multos menses perpetuo pluisset* of the end of June 1515, published in the *Epigrammata* (Basel: Froben March 1518); cf Reedijk poem 102.

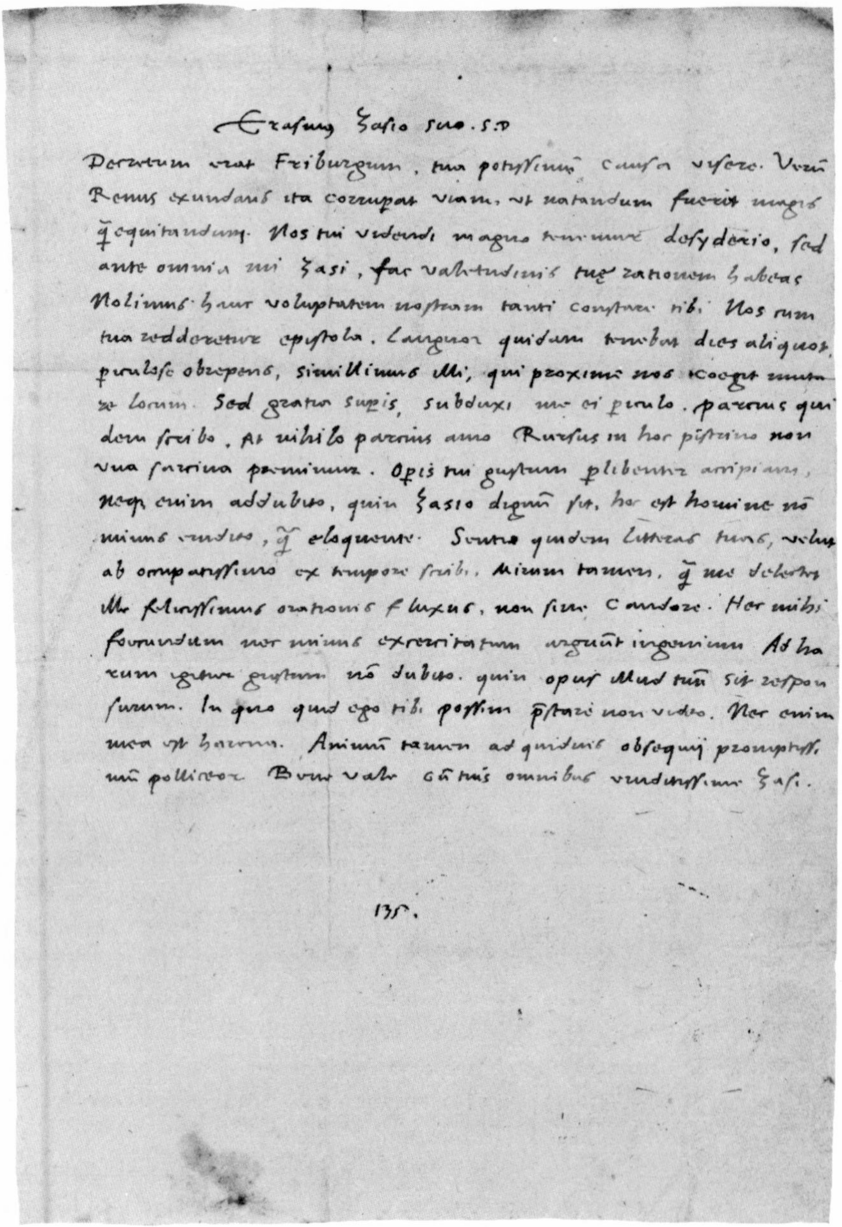

Erasmus Zasio suo S.D.

Decretum erat Friburgum, tua potissimum causa visere. Verum
Rhenus exundans ita corrupat viam, ut natandum fuerit magis
quam equitandum. Nos tui videndi magno tenemur desyderio, sed
ante omnia mi Zasi, fac valetudinis tuae rationem habeas.
Nolimus hanc voluptatem nostram tanti constare tibi. Nos cum
tua redderetur epistola, languor quidam tribus dies aliquos
periculose obrepens, simillimus illi, qui proxime nos coegit muta-
re locum. Sed gratia superis, subduxi me ei periculo. Parcius quidem scribo, at nihilo parcius amo. Rursus in hoc pistrino non
una sarcina premimur. Operis tui gustum plebeium arripiam,
neque enim addubito, quin Zasio dignum sit, hoc est homine non
minus erudito, quam eloquente. Sentio quidem litteras tuas, velut
ab occupatissimo ex tempore scribi. Miror tamen, quod nec deletus
ille felicissimus orationis fluxus, nec suus candore. Hoc mihi
foecundum nec minus exercitatum arguit ingenium. At harum genere gustum non dubito, quin opus illud tuum sit respon-
surum. In quo quid ego tibi possim praestare non video. Nec enim
mea est harum. Animum tamen ad quidvis obsequij promptissi-
mum polliceor. Bene vale cum tuis omnibus eruditissime Zasi.

135.

Autograph letter, Erasmus to Udalricus Zasius, Epistle 345
Öffentliche Bibliothek, University of Basel, MS Frey-Grynaeus II 9 f 135

kept down by a kind of weakness which crept over me in sinister fashion, very like the one which recently forced me to change my abode. But heaven be thanked, I have escaped that danger. I write a short letter, but there is no falling short in my affection.

Back in this treadmill I have more than one burden to bear. The sample of your work which you promise me I shall be very glad to see, for I have no doubt it will be worthy of its author, which means, a man who both is learned and can write. I feel that your letters are written on the spur of the moment, as by a very busy man; but I get remarkable pleasure from your felicitous and flowing style with its air of sincerity. These are signs to me of an original but no less a practised talent. So I do not doubt that your work will answer to the sample I find in your letters. In this respect, what I can contribute I do not see, for it is not my field at all. But my spirit shall, I promise, be most ready to do anything I can, not only in this business but wherever else a friend may be of service. Best wishes to you and yours, most learned Zasius. [1518]

To Zasius, the distinguished doctor of laws, his incomparable friend. In Freiburg

346 / From Josse Bade — Paris, 19 August 1515

Josse Bade, the Paris printer, was the most favoured publisher of Erasmus' works until Erasmus changed his preference to Froben: cf Ep 183 introduction. Among other things Bade had printed the revised edition of the *Adagiorum collectanea* in 1506 (Ep 126 introduction) and the *De copia* in 1512 (Ep 260). Erasmus however was dissatisfied with Bade's work and arranged, for example, to have his translations of Euripides reprinted by the Aldine press, Bade's edition of 1506 being so full of errors (Ep 207). Bade expected to publish the revised and enlarged version of the expanded *Adagia*, the *Adagiorum chiliades*, also printed by Aldus in 1508 (Ep 211), but Franz Birckmann, to whom Erasmus gave the manuscript for transmission to Paris, gave it instead to Froben in Basel (cf Ep 269 introduction). Whatever were Erasmus' true feelings in the matter (his account of it to Ammonio is sufficiently cheerful; cf Ep 283:182–96), he transferred his custom to Froben.

Bade's last letter to Erasmus before the present one was dated 19 May 1512 (Ep 263) and no letter from Erasmus to Bade survives before 1518 (Ep 764). Bade's letter of 1512 looks forward to publication both of the *Adagia* and of Erasmus' new edition of the letters of St Jerome (cf Ep 396 introduction); it may

* * * * *

12 sample] Not mentioned in Ep 344, but perhaps mentioned to Erasmus by Bonifacius Amerbach, who delivered the letter

contain an additional clue to Erasmus' change of printer, for, after acknowledging that his payment for these works would be no adequate recompense for Erasmus' 'ability, application, scholarship, and toil,' Bade urges Erasmus to consider that 'the most glorious rewards will be accorded in the first place by Heaven, and then by your own virtuous character' (Ep 263:47–9). See Ph. Renouard *Bibliographie des impressions et des œuvres de Josse Badius Ascensius imprimeur et humaniste 1462–1535* 3 volumes (Paris 1908).

JOSSE BADE TO MASTER ERASMUS

Dear Master Erasmus, my right good friend, I have received your letter, which bore every mark of your habitual kindness to me. God send that I may one day contribute to your honour and advantage as I would wish. My good will is engaged already, you may be sure, and will find an opportunity to make some provision, if you say the word. In the matter of your big *Adagia*, Franz has treated me fairly well. Your other things, printed in Germany with your new advertisement and apparatus, are doing harm to mine; but if this brings you profit and reputation, I shall put up with it, and indeed with a good grace. Cop and Lefèvre are well, and all the other friends whom you have not only made, but put under an obligation by your rare literary gifts and unusual learning. Budé is licking his *De Asse* into shape again. Ruel is getting Dioscorides ready for the press. I am redoing Quintilian as best I can, with the help of a fairly reliable copy, which belonged to Lorenzo Valla while he was alive. Farewell.

Paris, 19 August 1515

347 / From Maarten van Dorp — Louvain, 27 August 1515

For the background to this letter see Ep 337 introduction. For More's reply to it, 21 October [1515], from Bruges, see Rogers Ep 15. Erasmus suppressed his

* * * * *

346:7 Franz] Birckmann; cf Ep 259:14n.

7 other things] Schürer's edition of the *De copia*; cf Ep 311 introduction. The 'apparatus' is probably the index prefixed to that edition.

10 Cop] Cf Ep 305:208n.

12 *De Asse*] The first edition was published by Bade on 15 March 1515, the second on 14 October 1516.

13 Ruel] Jean Du Ruel of Soissons (1479–1537) was physician to Francis I and dean of the faculty of medicine at Paris in 1508–9. He published a translation of Dioscorides' *De medicinali materia* with Estienne at Paris on 24 April 1516.

13–14 Quintilian] The *Institutio oratoria*, with notes by Bade and others, was published by Bade and Jean Petit on 13 January 1516. Their edition made use of the celebrated manuscript annotated in 1444 by Lorenzo Valla, which is now Paris BN MS lat. 7723.

own response; cf Rogers Ep 75. The text of the letter is bound together with a number of other manuscript leaves at the end of a copy of the *Farrago* and the *Institutio christiani matrimonii* (Basel: Froben 1526) among Beatus Rhenanus' books at Sélestat (MS Cat Rhen 174).

DORP TO HIS FRIEND ERASMUS

The receipt of your letter, my dear Erasmus, gave me incredible satisfaction, first because I perceived that my own letter had been by no means unwelcome to you, which I for my part had written as to the chief of my friends and in a frank and friendly spirit; and also since you say that the reading of it increased your affection for me, and your affection is my dearest object. Only, if I may continue to speak freely to you (which you say you will never take amiss), I do not think you have at all done justice to the arguments I brought against your opinion; which does not surprise me, for you promise to answer more fully from Basel. That you should do so is a thing I want from you as much as I want anything in the world, and also that you should deal with all my arguments in good faith, turn them all inside out, leave none of their force unexplored, but rather, if they are weak in themselves, give them more strength by your own natural genius. But take care not to use any of those eloquent means of persuasion, by which I know you can make one believe anything; go for the facts, hit the nail on the head. You know there was a rule in the court of Areopagus that no speaker should attempt to arouse the emotions; he must content himself with an unvarnished recital of the facts.

Now for your letter. When you say that you have no use for fame coupled with ill feeling, my dear Erasmus, how right you are! That was just the point that I was trying so hard to make, if you look more closely, in the first part of my letter: it is sheer madness for a man to work really hard, and yet know that with all his efforts he will gain more odium than anything else. You express surprise that such disputes were aroused by your *Moria*, which enjoys wide popularity not only among theologians but bishops as well. And yet I am surprised at you, Erasmus, for thinking bishops better judges than theologians in a matter like this. You know the bishops of this generation, their lives, their characters, their learning (shall I say?) or ignorance. Some of them certainly deserve their high position, but there are

* * * * *

347:2 your letter] Ep 337 in its original, shorter form

10 from Basel] Cf Ep 337:23–5; Rogers Ep 15:51–4.

17 Areopagus] For the high standards of this Athenian court see *Adagia* I ix 41.

20 no use] Ep 337:30–2

25 surprise] Ep 337:271ff.

very few, especially such as satisfy the standard of what is needed in a bishop laid down by St Paul in his letter to Timothy. And then why should you wish to upset your old friends with something which you could have kept to yourself without great loss? Were you so short of subjects on which you could have won even greater reputation from the applause of the whole world? There is a maxim in Epictetus, that very wise man: do not think that everyone enjoys hearing what you enjoy saying. Suppose it were the other way round, and someone published an attack on the whole tribe of schoolmasters, poets, authors, and all the professed followers of the humanities. Suppose he said they produced worthless fables, poetic fancies, old wives' tales, or pure lies and ludicrous frauds and impostures: they memorize the wanderings of Aeneas, and do not stop to think how far off course they are themselves; they know how many children Niobe had and the whole family tree of Jupiter with all his cousins; and while they devote such effort to these enquiries, suppose someone were to declare that they were wasting the best years of their lives with enormous loss, and that nothing was more dangerous for the Christian religion. What then, Erasmus? Would none of this pierce your skin or even hurt? Would you still be satisfied at all points? I hardly think you would. And yet you have said things like this, and far more severely, against the theologians, whose authority it is really important to maintain, because they are the only people who can feed the Lord's flock on the pasture of the law of God. Unless of course you think that poets, or those exclusively who also know Greek, should be set at its head.

But to return to your letter. It does not mean that people regret the revival of good literature, if they do not sit bowed over those elegant authors of yours until they are gray-headed. Otherwise we should have to say that you regret the revival of painting and sculpture because you do not practise those arts yourself. As for Poggio, a most damnable and obscene writer fit only to be put on the fire, and Pontano likewise, do you think the theologians unfair to them? Why, what have these worthless fellows done except to write filthy books? They set before the young this poisonous stuff, sugared with all the charm and elegance of style, so that without knowing it they may swallow something whose effect may be worse than death.

And then again you call this a new school of theology, that has now

* * * * *

32 St Paul] 1 Tim 3:2–7

36 Epictetus] *Enchiridion* 33.14

51–2 feed … flock] cf 1 Pet 5:2

58 Poggio] Cf Ep 337:353.

59 Pontano] Cf Ep 337:355.

prevailed in our universities for many centuries, and say that if the world came to its senses we should see that many people who hitherto have wished to be thought to know everything in fact know nothing at all. So according to you, Erasmus, the whole world itself must now be very foolish. But what makes you say this? Is it because everyone, when he sees your pure, polite, cultivated, humane, literary literature, your Muses and your humanities and your liberal arts (they have plenty of other names), does not fall down and worship them? Has some oracle from one of the nymphs of Thespiae laid down that this is the only good literature? In what way are the two queens of language, Latin and Greek, any better than our good solid Dutch, except that it is in them that almost all knowledge has come down to us? No one questions the wisdom of the Greeks: but they knew no Latin. We know that the Hebrews were pursuing wisdom before the Greeks: but they knew no Greek. In so far therefore as either language has served as a channel of knowledge, to that extent it has priority. But who except a perfect fool would not rather be wise even if he were to be a shining example of barbarism, than write beautifully without wisdom? Very well, then, we ought to learn either Greek or Latin in pursuit of knowledge; I agree. But what prevents anything in Scripture that is written in Latin from being understood by a man whose elegance in composition would not suit Valla's taste? I understand people talking French as they go along; but I cannot put any of what I have heard into French myself. You must not think, my dear Erasmus, that our theologians do not understand what they read, and what belongs to their subject, even if they speak like barbarians. Although I am not sure whether your friends the grammarians have decided which is worse, to be called a barbarian or a Turk, I suspect they will prefer a Turk, and will have more good will towards a Jew, provided he is not wholly uneducated, than towards a fellow Christian infected with this malady of barbarism, which you could almost call the deepest heresy; so true is it that scarcely a man among them ever once uses a non-classical word. 'Behold, O Lord God,' says Augustine, 'behold with patience, as Thou ever dost, how these men observe the rules of grammar which they have received from their ancestors, and neglect the eternal rules of everlasting salvation which they have received from Thee; so that one who maintains and teaches those old conventions of euphony, if he breaks the rules of grammar and says

* * * * *

65 say] Ep 337:342–5

73 Thespiae] A town near the foot of Mount Helicon, the traditional home of the Muses

95 Augustine] *Confessions* 1.18.29

ominem without an aspirate in the first syllable, gives far more offence than if he breaks Thy rules and hates his fellow-man.'

In any case I do not see why this new school of Theologian has so pestilent an effect on our studies and our standards of behaviour. Did all those saintly men have a pestilent effect on the church: St Thomas, Bonaventura, William of Auxerre, Hugo, and all the rest? Were they too pestilent who wrote of holy things a thousand years ago? And yet the church has added these pestilent authors to the catalogue of saints, St Thomas indeed for the divine quality of his teaching. For when he and his miracles were under discussion in the conclave of cardinals, the Holy Father replied that he accepted as miracles the *Questions* he had left behind him, composed with such heavenly skill. And what cure can we find for this pest that has spread through the wide world? If the theologians are pestilent characters because they have not been initiated into the sacred rites of poesy, what about the lawyers? And the physicians? Can we suppose them fit to advise upon the law or to prescribe for their patients who may be even further removed from that sacred fire? And then the pope himself, the cardinals, the bishops, and the abbots, why do they not lay it down that no one shall be promoted to their order without a recommendation from the Muses? We should perhaps do better to summon from the heart of Turkey eloquent men of highest scholarship in the field of literature, to have them shed light within the church of God with public lectures on Ovid's fables, Apuleius' ass, and the dreams of Lucian; for the sacred Scriptures in Latin are barbarous stuff because the translator could not keep awake, and in the Greek I cannot think they are any match for Lucian. We should do better in our public schools to lecture on Virgil (the chief of poets, and I daresay prophets too) to those whose aim is an understanding of Holy Scripture. But what says Augustine in his *Confessions*, book I, chapter 16, where he

* * * * *

102 new school of Theologian] Ep 337:421ff

105 Bonaventura] Giovanni di Fidanza (1221–74), the Franciscan theologian of Paris, canonized as St Bonaventura in 1482 and known as 'doctor seraphicus'

105 William of Auxerre] A scholastic theologian (d 1231) and teacher at Paris, he was one of the first to use the doctrines of the newly translated Aristotle in his *Summa aurea*.

105 Hugo] Hugo of St Cher (cf Allen Ep 459:71n), or possibly Hugo of St Victor (c 1096–1141), the theologian and mystic

108 divine quality] Aquinas (1225–74), canonized in 1323, was known as the '*doctor angelicus*.'

125–6 chief ... of prophets] In the Middle Ages Virgil was thought to have prophesied the birth of Christ, *Eclogues* 4.5–7.

speaks of the inventions of Homer and the poets? 'O river of Hell, the sons of men are thrown into thee. Should we not know the words for rain and gold and bosom and trick and vault of heaven, unless Terence had invented a good-for-nothing young man taking Jove as a good precedent for fornication, as he looks at a picture painted on the wall: "There painted was how Jove / Did send on Danae's bosom a rain of gold / And tricked the lady ..." Now see how he plucks up courage for this lechery, as though heaven itself showed him the way: "But what a god!" he says, / "Who shakes the skies above with thunderous sound: / Shall I, mere man, not follow his example? / Follow I will, and have, and that right gladly." It is not at all true that those words are best learnt by way of this lascivious stuff; but words like these give them more confidence to be lascivious. I have no quarrel with the words – they are choice and precious vessels – but with the wine of error which we were given to drink in them by teachers who were already inebriate; and if we refused to drink it, we were whipped, nor was there any sober judge to whom we might appeal.'

Thus far Augustine, although in my copy there is a false reading, *Dianae* for *Danaae*: Danae is a word unfamiliar among theologians, while I suppose they have all heard of Diana somewhere; and so the corrector, whoever he was, put one in place of the other. But if one of our self-satisfied literary critics happens on the passage, he will at once cry out at the top of his voice: 'Away with these theologians who in their ignorance corrupt good manuscripts, because they have never had a taste of good literature, and have never even read Terence. Just see how ignorant they are! They think Diana was seduced by Jupiter, although she always remained a virgin.' And yet, Erasmus, what difference does it make whether a theologian reads *Dianae* or *Danaae*? Or whom he reads it to? A harlot, if he likes? Will he fail to understand the passage? Surely not, unless there is some immediate danger that through their ignorance all knowledge of the whole of Jove's genealogy will be lost, while they are devoting serious study to the genealogy of Christ. What can I say of Martial, of Ovid, even of Horace or Juvenal, when Terence, whom all suppose the most proper poet, is said by Augustine of all people to offer draughts of the wine of error? What do they offer except unmixed poison of the soul, and hellish drink contained in polished vessels of poetry?

But let us proceed, though slowly. 'Those who condemn the *Moria*,' you say, 'will not approve my edition of Jerome either.' This will be a new

* * * * *

130 Terence] *Eunuchus* 584–91

144 Augustine] *Confessions* 1.16.26

164 you say] Ep 337:697–8

distinction, if you publish something few approve. So the theologians will not approve? Who will, then? The lawyers? The physicians or the philosophers, putting their sickles into other men's corn? No, but you made it for people interested in grammar. Let the grammarians then sit on the throne and act as censors of all the other disciplines; let them bring forth our new theology, which will come to birth someday with the proverbial mouse. But there is some risk that serious scholars may refuse to bow beneath their sceptres. For their sceptres are the canes with which they hold sway in their flogging-ridden caverns, and, although more foolish than self-love and folly in person, they think that they know all subjects, because they understand the actual words and the structure of the sentences. So we need no universities; the school at Zwolle or Deventer will be quite enough; and indeed it is the opinion of that great man Jerome the Hussite that universities do no more good to the church of God than the Evil One himself. Nor does it move the schoolmasters in the slightest that his opinion was condemned at the Council of Constance, for it is notorious that the council did not contain a single educated man or one who knew Greek.

Now I turn to the remainder of your letter. I did not assert, my dear Erasmus, that there are no mistakes in the New Testament, for I knew perfectly well that it had been corrected by Jerome in a number of places; but I affirmed, and it is still my opinion, that it contains no error and no falsehood. You admit this in your letter, but you add that the true reading has been corrupted by the scribes. This is the point where we really disagree. Tell me, which are the copies by which you can judge that it was corrupted, after Jerome had corrected the text against the Greek sources? It was not surprising that they should have been the refuge of Jerome, Ambrose, Augustine, Hilary, the Fathers whom you cite, in their own day, for they were still pure and uncontaminated. But as it is, now that so many heresies have arisen in Greece, and that long schism, how can we be certain that their copies have not been corrupted? You say that what is at issue is

* * * * *

171 mouse] *Adagia* I ix 14

177 Jerome the Hussite] Jerome of Prague (c 1370–1416) was dispatched by John Huss to study the doctrines of Wycliffe at Oxford, and brought them back to Paris and Prague. After widespread activity on behalf of the movement in central and eastern Europe, he followed Huss to the Council of Constance. On 11 September 1415, after the death of Huss (6 July), he read a document condemning the teachings of Wycliffe and Huss, but a year later retracted this recantation and was himself condemned to the stake.

182 not assert] Ep 337:753–4

194 You say] Ep 337:803–5

the division between words, the accents, and that sort of difficulty; but I am surprised you should use an argument which you turn against yourself; for it is easier to make mistakes when there are many things one has to watch. How easily scribes may have omitted an accent! And this, if I rightly understand you, will make it a corrupted copy. And what is it that does not allow Latin books to be free from error? Is it not the combined carelessness and lack of skill of the printers? Now consider which is the rarer class – those who are equipped to print Greek books, or Latin – and you will know which copies you ought to consider the more correct.

But you do not see what effect this really has on the purity of the faith. This is the thing, my dear Erasmus, that I tried so hard to get from you: that if the translator had nodded anywhere, if his translation was clumsy or did not really give the meaning, you should write a note on this, provided you made no changes, if the Latin copies differed from the Greeks in meaning; for there we must follow the Latin texts. St Jerome admits that, when he was correcting the Gospels after emending them by comparison with the Greek copies, he adopted the principle that he would correct only things that seemed to alter the sense, and let everything else stay as it was. Here is Jerome, restoring whatever had lapsed from the true sense; and anything else, no matter how barbarous or foolish, he allows to stay as it is. If this sort of thing is corrected now, I have no complaints. But if in Jerome's time the Latin copies were corrupted, what reason is there, you will say, why the scribes should not have deviated again from his corrected text during so many centuries? I think the reason is the great care lavished by the holy Fathers on maintaining the integrity of the sacred texts which Jerome had corrected. If they can somehow be shown to be corrupt, I want, and I want badly, to be told why the same reasons have not affected the Greek copies; for the accents and other difficulties, as I said just now, present, rather than remove, the opportunity to make mistakes.

You ask in what council it was that the Vulgate edition, whose author is unknown, was officially approved. I did not say, Erasmus, that it was approved in any one council in particular, but that many councils, when confronted with some knotty problem concerning the faith, took refuge in this edition and no other; as you must know, if you have ever looked into the Decretals. And this, I think, is the reason why it is less elegant and less

* * * * *

204 you do not see] Ep 337:857–8

209 Jerome] *Praefatio Hieronymi in quatuor evangelia* PL 29:559

224 You ask] Ep 337:809–10

229 Decretals] Papal letters in response to a question, having the force of law

good Latin, that it answers the Greek more faithfully word for word. For the more you translate word for word, the drier you must become, because many things can be said conveniently in one language which cannot be rendered in another without using many more words or darkening the meaning or being unidiomatic. And so it is probable that of all the translations the church of God and the holy Fathers will have selected this one to be handed down to us, because it is the most faithful. Otherwise what chance would preserve this one out of so many? for Augustine says in the *De doctrina christiana* II 11: 'Those who turned the Scriptures from Hebrew into Greek can be counted, the Latin translators cannot. Any individual in the early days of the Faith who had a Greek codex in his hands and thought he had some skill in the two languages, took it upon himself to translate it.' Thus Augustine. Hence I am induced to believe that, in order that the faithful might not waver when they saw the variations in the texts, all were rejected, and this one alone, which had been corrected by St Jerome, accepted by the church. If you are willing to learn that things happened as I have said (unless you are going to start by saying that there is some reason other than their acceptance by the church of God why these Gospels which we accept are true), listen to Augustine: 'I would not believe the Gospel, unless the authority of the church compelled me to do so.' Tell me then, Erasmus, which edition is the church to approve: the Greek, which it does not use and has not used for centuries, any more than it is in communion with the Greeks themselves, who are schismatics; or the Latin, the only one cited when any definition has to be sought from Holy Scripture, passing over Jerome himself, if he happens to have a different reading, as not seldom happens?

You speak of 'your theologians,' meaning I suppose the faculty at Louvain, 'with their highly confused, and indeed highly foolish, teaching,' and would like to send them packing. But you must remember, Erasmus, that the heron finds all water muddy and says it is the water's fault, as it says in your own *Adages*; and in the same way in the logic of Aristotle (the only logic we teach here) a beginner finds everything confused the moment he enters the arena of dispute. If you call this doctrine foolish, by what spirit, pray, was it revealed, and in what passage of Scripture is it laid down, that

* * * * *

237 Augustine] *De doctrina christiana* book 2 c 11; PL 34:43

248 Augustine] *Contra epistolam Manichaei quam vocant fundamenti* 1.5; PL 42:176. Cf Allen Ep 1637:62–4.

258 send them packing] Ep 337:870

259 heron] This adage has not been identified.

frivolous poetry is to provide the salt to season the teaching of Christ? Personally I adopt the opinion of a great logician, St Augustine, in his *De doctrina christiana* II 13: 'Whether one says *inter hominibus* or *inter homines* makes no difference to the man who is interested in the meaning. Whether one says *ignoscēre* or *ignoscĕre*, with the third syllable long or short, is of little interest to the man who is asking God to forgive his sins. But people are more offended by things like this, the weaker they are, and what makes them weaker is the wish to appear more learned, not in the knowledge of things that lead to edification but of symbols, by which it is difficult not to be puffed up.' So far Augustine, and then below in chapter 31: 'The discipline of logical argument, of syllogism and definition and analysis, when applied to all sorts of questions that appear in Holy Writ, greatly helps the understanding.' And Jerome on Ezekiel chapter 25 (it is also included in our *Glossa ordinaria*): 'Whatever erroneous doctrine there is in the world, whatever pertains to terrestrial knowledge and is thought to be immovable, is undermined by the art of dialectic and dissolved as though by fire into dust and ashes, so as to prove that what seemed strongest is nothing worth.' Do you see, Erasmus, how this art of disputation is approved by Augustine and Jerome, and even thought to be part of the art of speaking grammatically, provided we do not deviate from the meaning?

Further, when you set up the hypothesis, Erasmus, that our theologians are interested in nothing but the practice of disputation, you are completely wrong. Tell me, they may know very little poetry, but what will prevent them from reading the Gospels, the Pauline Epistles, and the whole Bible? I can produce many men here who can leave their books behind and dispute with anyone on a text of Scripture simply on the strength of their memories. Do not make the mistake of thinking that the theologians are asleep like Endymion while you are awake and poring over your poets; or that no one can have any intelligence who does not write

* * * * *

265 Augustine] *De doctrina christiana* book 2 c 13; PL 34:44

273 Augustine] *De doctrina christiana* book 2 c 31; PL 34:58

276 Jerome on Ezekiel] PL 25:236D–237A

277 *Glossa ordinaria*] A term applied during the Middle Ages to commonly used compilations of glosses on any text, but most often used in canon law: see Ep 134:30–1n. The earliest *glossa ordinaria*, however, was that made on the Bible, and the best-known that made in the twelfth to thirteenth centuries, which is referred to here.

284 hypothesis] Ep 337:320, 412ff

291 Endymion] The handsome youth who received from Jove the privilege of perpetual sleep; *Adagia* I ix 63

poetry or elegant prose. Do we not see artisans of the lowest class and even the poorest servant endowed with the most remarkable intelligence? Then why all these epithets that are rained on the theologians – gross, rude, pestilent, mindless? It takes no skill to ladle out abuse, nor is it very creditable or the action of a virtuous man, if we consider the severe judgment of our Saviour: 'Whoso saith to his brother Racha, shall be in danger of the council; but whoso saith to his brother Thou fool, shall be in danger of hell-fire.' On which Jerome: 'If we have to give account of our lightest word, how much more of our contumely. He who says Thou fool to one who believes in God, has committed a blasphemy against religion.' Finally I do not really understand, being no doubt, my dear Erasmus, a little slow, why it is such a distinction, on which the grammar-mongers pride themselves so often in public, regarding it as their great pride and joy, to know absolutely nothing about sophistic logic. This is no distinction, my dear Erasmus; the real distinction is to know your subject, however humble it may be, provided it does not render you incapable of other and higher things. Suppose I produced an adept in sophistic logic who knows all that there is to know about the Scriptures? Must he in this case be excommunicated as a Gentile and a publican, that is, put beyond the pale of civilised society, because as a boy (horrible thought) he was trained in sophistic, or rather in dialectic? Suppose he did not repent of his sophistic interests until he reached the age when Augustine repented of his errors as a Manichaean, that is, at thirty, and then devoted himself with the greatest zeal and energy to Scripture? Is there to be no hope for him thereafter? Even less hope than if he had spent his days in the buying and selling of merchandise, or had lain asleep whole days snoring? You seem to have forgotten what your friend Plato says in the *Gorgias*, that he would not mind if he saw a youth engaged in sophistical disputation, provided he did not waste his whole life in it. And you must watch this too, my dear Erasmus: do not make the mistake of dismissing as sophists those who are the most sincere logicians of any alive today. You cannot rightly distinguish between a logician and a sophist if you are quite ignorant of either art. If you call every theologian in Louvain, and still more those in Paris, a sophist, the result is that there is no dialectic left in the world, and has not been these many centuries. Otherwise, pray tell me,

* * * * *

295 rude] Cf Ep 337:479, 638, 720

296 mindless] The passage is quoted by More although it is not in the printed version of Ep 337; cf Rogers 15:564–5.

298 Saviour] Matt 5:22

300 Jerome] Commentary on Matthew 5:22; PL 26:37C

318 Plato] *Gorgias* 485a

where in the world is what you call real logic publicly taught, granted that there may be two or three people of such intellectual gifts that without the assistance of teachers, that is, from the silent tuition of books, they can understand for themselves everything Aristotle lays down in his dialectic. He is already a second Augustine; for we must hope that he will not be called Aristotle. You should not therefore class as sophists those who tackle Scripture without knowing any Greek, or who have not learnt all the fables in Ovid and the rules of metre in Terence. Unless perhaps you regard as sophists all the men who are better at argument than you are, that is, all the logicians; as the grammarian Cresconius and his pupils, heretics all, refused to listen to Christian teachers, and most of all to Augustine, because he had the reputation of being the most powerful logician. But here Augustine himself can answer for me, showing that the apostle Paul constantly used logical argument, as can be seen in chapter 22 of the *Actus apostolorum* (excuse me if I use the usual form, when of course I know men of taste and disciples of Valla have to say *Acta*, and by our Lady Folly 'tis a nice point. This saint is now so popular, why should we not swear by her too?). If you have access to the works of Augustine, as I think you have, you will find his defence of logic in his book *Contra Cresconium grammaticum* I 12–20. Do not make the mistake of thinking, Erasmus, that your only perfect theologian is the man who has mastered the literal sense of the whole Bible, nor the one who knows how to work out the moral sense like a second Origen. Many other things remain to be learnt, more difficult to understand, and also more profitable to the flock for which Christ died. Otherwise how shall we know how the sacraments ought to be administered, what their proper forms are, when absolution should be given to a sinner, when he should be rejected, what according to the commandment ought to be given back and what may be retained, and countless points of the same kind? Unless I am much mistaken, it would need far less work to learn a large part of the Bible by heart, before you had learnt to solve one of these knotty problems. Yet many questions of this sort occur every day, where you may have to pore for hours over four words; unless you apply the name of theologians' nonsense even to things like this, which are concerned with the sacraments, without which God's holy catholic church maintains that man's salvation is in peril.

* * * * *

336 Cresconius] A schoolmaster who came to the defence of Petilianus, the Donatist bishop of Cirta, and to whom St Augustine addressed a letter in four books, *Contra Cresconium grammaticum*; PL 43:445–594

342 disciples of Valla] That is, students of the *Elegantiae*; cf Ep 23:108n.

345 defence of logic] *Contra Cresconium* book 1 chap 12–20; PL 43:454–60

358 nonsense] Ep 337:838

I know you think that a knowledge of Greek is necessary for my own studies, and therefore urge me to acquire it; and I know this proceeds from friendly feeling on your part; but on this point I disagree with you freely. If I knew Latin only and not Greek, shall I be unable to understand what is written in Latin? Suppose the thing is written in some barbarous language, and I know the language, why should I not understand it? Giovanni Campano was regarded as, and in fact was, a most eloquent man, and in elegance of Latin style yielded to none of the modern writers, and likewise Pomponio Leto; yet neither knew any Greek. Lorenzo Valla, the Hercules who slew the monsters of the Latin language, himself did not learn Greek until he was quite an old man. If they learnt what we now call the humanities without a word of Greek, and attained great distinction in them, what prevents me too from understanding the Scriptures without Greek, if God is good, except that I am so much inferior to those great men in capacity?

This is a long and long-winded answer to your letter, but it is written in a friendly spirit by one who is your very sincere friend. If I deliver a shrewd blow now and again, this does not mean that I am any more out of sympathy with you; I am always a devoted friend. But I have heard things from other people, partly from lawyers, partly from physicians and philosophers, not only from theologians (although of course from them too), and I have set them out as though I were playing a part. If any of what is said, not by me but by others, seems to you acceptable, adopt it; if not, this will at least rouse you to meet your readers' objections more fully, if you know in advance what they think. Nor could I have been led on, at any rate not to write so freely, unless I had read in several places in your books that criticism is often more profitable than praise, and that you would always prefer it because it can be of some use. The wounds of a friend are more faithful than the freely given kisses of an enemy. Remember therefore to live up to that most wise remark of your own, and do not be angry when a friend takes you to task. Master Jean de Nève, who is at the moment rector

* * * * *

361 you think] Ep 337:640–9

366–7 Giovanni Campano] Giovanni Antonio Campano (1429–77), a distinguished poet and scholar who was a pupil of Valla

369 Pomponio Leto] A pupil of Valla and founder of the Roman academy, Leto (1425–97) was a leading figure in an academy of poets in mid-fifteenth century Rome.

386 your books] Cf Epp 180:15–20; 182:62–9.

388 wounds] Proverbs 27:6

391 Jean de Nève] Cf Epp 298 introduction; 304:175

of the university, sends you his greetings, and says you are to rely on him for anything you could expect from a close friend; and you will feel the truth of this if you provide an opportunity of doing something for you or one of your friends. And Dirk van Aalst, our printer, who brings you this letter, has also asked me to recommend him to you, which I do, my dear Erasmus, most sincerely. He deserves your high regard and anything you can do for him on occasion, and you might well let him have something to print; I doubt if anywhere there is a man more attached to you. Your decision to mention abbot Meynard is a kindness well bestowed on a man who will not prove ungrateful. Finally I ought to say that I am reporting what some people say about you when you are not there; but in front of others they speak about you very differently. And so remember to think kindly of me; for you will be giving your friendship to one who is your true friend, and a supporter in public of your reputation, although there are these points in which I am of a different opinion from the greatest scholar of our time. Farewell.

Louvain, 27 August 1515

348 / To Thomas Wolsey Basel, 30 August [1515]

The reference to the flooded Rhine makes this letter contemporary with Ep 345. Wolsey became a cardinal shortly after it was written, on 10 September 1515. This letter was first published in the *Farrago* (1519), when presumably the title was adjusted.

ERASMUS TO THE MOST REVEREND THOMAS, CARDINAL AND ARCHBISHOP OF YORK

Respectful greetings, most reverend prelate. I regret that I could not enjoy a more intimate and longer conversation with your Eminence before I left England. I had fixed in you my last hope, the sheet-anchor (as they call it) of my felicity. But Jerome was pressing, an undertaking immense, distinguished, and (if I mistake not) destined for perpetual life, pious and fruitful too. This I have so much at heart that everything is subordinated to it. This journey was always at risk from robbers and never more so than now; besides which, the Rhine being swollen with snow and rain, everything

* * * * *

395 Dirk van Aalst] Dirk or Thierry Martens; cf Ep 304:165n. He was probably on his way to the Frankfurt book fair.

400 Meynard] Cf Ep 304:178n.

348:5 sheet-anchor] *Adagia* I i 24

was under water, especially around Strasbourg, so that there was more swimming than riding. I have made light of everything, if only Jerome can come out. In the press also is the New Testament in Greek, as it was written by the apostles, and in Latin, as translated by me, together with my notes. Other smaller works have also come out recently. These trifles keep me busier and more fully occupied than you with all your exalted business. Once these are all finished I shall hasten to return, especially if with your usual generosity you have in the meantime made some provision for the refreshment of mind and body after these exhausting labours. My best wishes to your Eminence, to whom I declare myself entirely devoted.

Basel, 30 August 151[6]

349 / From Nikolaus Gerbel Strasbourg, 31 August 1515

NIKOLAUS GERBEL TO MASTER ERASMUS

Thank you for your most elegant letter, in which you have cleared up for me some passages which I found rather obscure. That last note which you added on the word 'scatens' I will restore to its original clarity. Your book is now being printed, with special care from both of us; this is a hive of industry, 'the fragrant honey breathes the scent of thyme.' For what will your *Lucubrationes* be, if not pure honey and flowers and, in a word, a sea of good things? Unless my eye quite deceives me, you will be pleased with the book. There is only one thing I am really afraid of – that you will say I am a very poor diviner: in reading your writing I have so often been compelled to guess. It often happens that I have to torture this thick head of mine in all directions before I can discern what name to call some things by. But the thought of being some help to those who want to learn, the countless treasures lying hidden in this exposition, and my steady love and regard for you, my dear Erasmus, make everything easy for me. Above all, I shall never cease to urge you not to cease or go slow or relax your efforts, but to do all you can, that Christ may be magnified, that he may grow and flourish and be increased. For my part, if I can be any help to you in this, you cannot think how ready I am, how gladly I shall do whatever you tell me. As far as concerns myself, I beg you not to let my affection for you prove in vain; not that I am seeking an exact return for any service or any gift – only that you

* * * * *

13 New Testament] Cf Ep 384 introduction.

15 Other smaller works] The *De constructione* (cf Ep 341) and the *Damiani elegeia* (cf Ep 353:2n)

349:5 both of us] Gerbel and Schürer; cf Ep 342 introduction.

6 thyme] Virgil *Georgics* 4.169

should give me your friendship in return, and not forget me. Do you ask why does the man need to tell me this? I know that you do not need telling either to go on working for the benefit of all who want to learn, or to be a friend to someone like myself, since you can both discern and do all such things better than anyone, if you so wish. But since I had no better subject to write about, I decided to say these words in particular, to remind you of my humble self. Farewell and best wishes, and let me have news of the New Testament and of that book of yours that is printing at Basel, what is it? Farewell once more.

Strasbourg, 1515 August 31

In a few more days, if all goes well, we shall reach the end of the *Lucubrationes*. I wonder very much why I do not hear from Rhenanus. Perhaps he is ashamed of me, or there is some other reason why he does not answer. Mind you look after yourself. Very soon now you will hear news of our friend Reuchlin which will delight you particularly. A certain scholar very learned in Hebrew and Greek and Latin has written a work in sixteen books to support him against the Black and Whites. Take care of your health, and please write to me.

350 / To Richard Pace — Basel, 4 September [1515]

As Erasmus' annotation of Jerome is evidently still unfinished, only 1514 or 1515 are possible year dates for this letter. The latter is indicated, since the letter is clearly written to London, and Pace in September 1514 was in Italy. The letter presumably accompanied Ep 348; it was first published in the *Farrago*.

Pace was a priest who had made his career in the diplomatic service after an education at Oxford and in Italy. He first met Erasmus in Italy in 1508, and from 1509 to 1514 he was secretary to Cardinal Bainbridge in Rome. After the death of Bainbridge he returned to England in Wolsey's service, and thence to the service of the king, who sent him repeatedly on diplomatic missions. Cf

* * * * *

29 that book] Perhaps the *Damiani elegeia*; cf Ep 353:2n.

36 A certain scholar] Petrus Monggius (d 1539), known as Galatinus, Franciscan author of *Opus de arcanis catholicae veritatis* containing a defence of Reuchlin. The work was in hand and in circulation in the summer of 1515, although it was not completed for another year, and not published until 15 February 1518. See François Secret *Les kabbalistes chrétiens de la renaissance* (Paris 1964).

38 Black and Whites] The Dominicans, who in public wore a black cloak over their white robe and hood; cf Ep 290:11n.

Ep 211:53n; D.S. Chambers *Cardinal Bainbridge in the Court of Rome 1509 to 1514* (Oxford 1965); and the edition and translation of Pace's *De fructu qui ex doctrina percipitur* by Frank Manley and R.S. Sylvester (New York 1967).

ERASMUS TO HIS FRIEND PACE

I am quite confident, knowing your sincere and open character, my dear Pace, that you will be a lasting friend, nor will your friendship cool because you grow so much more successful. I wish indeed that much more success might come your way. If my notes have already arrived, as I suppose they have, please put them away carefully or, better still, deposit them with More until I ask for them back. Pray maintain my friendly relations with Linacre, and with Grocyn too if possible. I say this not because I fear anything untoward or hope to get anything out of them, but because I should wish men like that to be my friends always. They need no advertisement from me, but this I can truly say: even among the English there is no one with more generous feelings towards them or more ready to sing their praises than Erasmus. And I do not care to recall the moves that each of them made against me; who put them up to it, I do not know. This I learnt from the facts, it was not suspicion and guesswork; although I had scented something of the sort long before. But we are all human. For my part I shall be the man I always am, and balance all their other acts of friendship against this one injury. Linacre has been given an honourable mention in my notes on Jerome. It would be nothing out of the ordinary if I repaid contempt in kind and disliked those who have shown dislike for me. But educated men should vie with one another in mutual service, not resentment. With the archbishop of York, when you see an opportunity, be your own helpful self. Mind you look after your health.

Basel, 4 September [1519]

* * * * *

350:4 more successful] On Pace's return to England in 1515 he was recruited into Wolsey's service. By the end of October Pace was sent on an embassy to the Swiss to organize an attack on France.

5 my notes] The *Antibarbari*; cf Ep 30:17.

14 against me] Perhaps in relation with Erasmus' English patrons; cf Ep 388:174n.

18 Linacre] Mentioned in the first volume of the 1516 edition of Jerome, f 36 (scholia on the *Ep ad Furiam*)

23 health] This was probably not just a conventional injunction, since Pace's fragile health was ultimately to ruin his career.

351 / From Nikolaus Gerbel Strasbourg, 9 September 1515

NIKOLAUS GERBEL TO MASTER ERASMUS

In my last letter I told you what had passed between Lachner and myself and what I have undertaken to do, and the business is now held up by nothing but the shortage of carriers who have all gone off for the moment to the Frankfurt fair. But I will hurry over as soon as possible, although it would not be unwelcome if you would write me a line in the meantime to say in what state the business is that you wrote to me about. For if you did not need my help, seeing it is worth so little in such a case, or if you had changed your mind, or if there was someone else more suited to the task, I would save the expense. If you think otherwise, I will most gladly do whatever you say. I hope you will not find it troublesome to let me know.

I have had a most stylish letter from Rhenanus, full of sincerity and warmth, and I have read it and put it next my heart; it would have deserved an answer on many counts, had not the courier being in such an inordinate hurry deprived me of the opportunity. So if it is no trouble, I beg you most warmly to thank him on my behalf for all his kindness and friendship and the wonderful courtesy he has always shown me, and add that I send him a thousand greetings. Farewell and best wishes.

Strasbourg, 9 September 1515, in haste

352 / From Nikolaus Gerbel Strasbourg, 11 September 1515

The discussion of the form of the New Testament confirms the year date; in 1514 Gerbel was in Italy, where he visited Aldus and took a degree at Bologna; cf Ep 342 introduction.

NIKOLAUS GERBEL TO ERASMUS OF ROTTERDAM, GREETINGS IN CHRIST JESUS

I have not yet forgotten, most learned Erasmus, the promise by which I committed myself first to you and then to Lachner. Nothing holds me up except that so far I have quite failed to find a carrier to take me as far as Basel, so that once there I could try my hand at what you tell me to do, or discover

* * * * *

351:2 last letter] This letter is lost; Lachner (cf Ep 305:198n) had evidently suggested that Gerbel come to Basel to act as corrector for the edition of the New Testament.

12 letter] Also lost

352:4 to you] At Strasbourg, on Erasmus' return journey from England in the spring of 1515

what I might be capable of doing that could wholly meet your wishes. Your servant told me something about the production of your work, the arrangement of the page, the type faces, and the order in which you have thought best to print it, with columns corresponding to one another, so that everything is mingled together, Greek-Latin and Latin-Greek. I am very much afraid, dear Erasmus, that you yourself will dislike this arrangement as time goes on, and this for several reasons, which I thought I would write and tell you, as you are a dear friend. You know how intensely keen I have always been on this project of yours, and I cannot but rejoice that I have lived to see the day when this new sun is about to rise upon the world; and I am confident you will not take it in bad part, although I do write somewhat hastily and unwisely, for you well know the spirit in which I do so.

First, then, I think this will not be welcomed by those in particular who have made some progress in the study of Greek, seeing that they will for this purpose have no need of the Latin. Besides that, an arrangement in which the Greek is all together is both more pleasing to the eye and easier to use. Again, if you think you ought to put yourself to this trouble for the sake of ignorant readers and beginners, they too will find it something of a handicap, if the Latin version is always hanging over them in the right-hand column. For a man who has not really learnt his subject always turns his eyes to what he knows and has been taught and understands, in preference to what is difficult or quite unknown. And then we always find it happen that Greek when separate from Latin is easier to learn and sticks better in the memory, because the mind is occupied with one thing at a time. Nor is it very toilsome, if a man wishes to compare the Latin and the Greek, to turn over that number of leaves; for it often happens that a comparison which has succeeded after some expense of effort gives more satisfaction. Suppose it were printed in the arrangement used by Aldus for Gregory Nazianzen, is there a single educated man, setting out on a journey to Italy or France or Britain, who will not take a New Testament with him in Greek or, if it can be done or he can buy one, the Latin as well in the same volume? – and that is impossible, if the book is very big, an imperial folio.

* * * * *

11 mingled] This sentence conflicts with the evidence of Erasmus' letter to Wimpfeling of 21 September 1514 (Ep 305:228–9) suggesting that the method of setting up the new edition of the New Testament had been settled. The discussion that follows at least suggests that the printing had not yet advanced very far; cf Ep 356:12–13.

35 Gregory Nazianzen] *Carmina* (June 1504); Aldus printed the Greek and Latin on separate sheets; see A.-A. Renouard *Annales de l'imprimerie des Alde* (Paris 1803–12).

Nor will it have nearly such a pleasing appearance as each of them would if presented separately, resplendent in its own proper dignity, beautiful and noble in its own right. What could have a finer effect than that the assistance needed by beginners will not get in the way of scholars, and the beginners should have the gladdening prospect of some day being able to do without it? I could produce many objections; I perceive only one point that you could raise, that this makes it easier to compare the Latin and the Greek; and this I feel could be better and more reliably done if one were first to get a reliable knowledge of the Greek, which means the Greek by itself. After that he will compare them with more confidence, and understand them much better.

But please take this in good part, my dear Erasmus. I have no doubt that you have pondered this problem at length far more exactly, and have made your decision more wisely, and will carry it out far more successfully, than I could contrive to do, who know little or nothing. But we will discuss this fully when we are together, and the sooner the better. Farewell and best wishes, my most excellent Erasmus, and count me your friend.

Strasbourg, 1515, 11 September

Give my greeting to Beatus Rhenanus, that excellent and most learned man, and to Johann Froben. I will bring with me ten books by Erasmus, which are a present from Schürer to the author.

353 / From Johann Witz — Sélestat, 12 September [1515]

The date is inferred from books referred to.

JOHANN WITZ TO ERASMUS OF ROTTERDAM

Reading those pieces written partly by yourself and partly by other scholars of no common merit, which reached me not long ago as a present from Froben, I found my appetite quite insatiable; and the other men's pieces, being far inferior to yours, were the less able to satisfy me and seem to make me more hungry as the days go by. Yet I think them no less happy than yours, for they have the great advantage not only of being so closely related

* * * * *

58 ten books] Evidently the *Lucubrationes*; cf Ep 342:30n.

353:2 those pieces] *Lucubrationes*, although not the work of that title published by Schürer, but rather the *Jani Damiani Senensis ad Leonem X Pont. Max. De expeditione in Turcas elegeia* (Basel: Froben August 1515), containing four letters, all of May 1515. It was the only book in which Erasmus combined his writing with that of other authors. The letters by Erasmus are Epp 333, 334, 335, and 337; Ep 216 by Jacob Piso is another printed in the *Damiani elegeia*.

to yours, but of sharing their praise and glory and of living forever. Apart from that, the debt which my native place owes you for the praise you have lavished on it, and above all what I owe you myself – for you call me 'of Athens not unworthy' – to say nothing of other men, is more than my words could equal; for who would wish to compete in well-doing on level terms with a man who will be the admiration of posterity? It will be safer therefore to die with my debt unpaid than to torment myself with a burning desire to make it good, and risk some loss of reputation in the process.

Oh yes, my distinguished friend, there is another thing I would have you know, how satisfied and delighted my young people are now that they can abandon the tortuous stuff of other men, and reach a true knowledge of good Latin in safety under your guidance. I am ready to collect the money for Froben without fail in return for the books. Please greet him on my behalf, and my friend Beatus likewise; the courier's sudden departure meant that I could not write to him. I hope the Amerbachs are well, and John too, your English friend, a young man whose outstanding gifts make him worthy of your society. Farewell, great glory of the world, and spare a thought sometimes for your friend Sapidus.

In great haste, from Sélestat, 12 September

Greetings from Wimpfling with his good gray hair,
Greetings from Margery, my true love dear.

354 / From Johann Witz Sélestat, 15 September 1515

JOHANN WITZ TO MASTER ERASMUS

The man who brings you this letter from me, my honoured friend, deserves the privilege of your acquaintance, partly because of his endowments of character and learning, partly because there is nothing he so much desires to behold as the countenance of Erasmus, the prince of scholars. His name is Icolampadius, from which it is easily seen that he knows some Greek. How

* * * * *

9 praise] In *Encomium Selestadii* printed at the end of the *Damiani elegeia*, where Witz is said to be 'doctis quoque dignus Athenis.' The elegy is printed by Reedijk poem 98; cf line 23.

19 guidance] A reference to the *De constructione*; cf Ep 341.

22 John] John Smith; cf Ep 276 introduction; F. Bierlaire *La Familia d'Erasme* (Paris 1968) 49–51.

354:6 Icolampadius] Joannes Oecolampadius, as his name was more usually rendered; cf Ep 224:30n. He arrived in Basel on 21 September, as we know from Froben (cf citation at Ep 358:7), and spent the winter helping Erasmus with the *Novum instrumentum*: cf E. Hilgert 'Johann Froben and the Basel university scholars 1513–1523' *The Library Quarterly* 41 (April 1971) 158–9 for an appraisal of Oecolampadius' contribution.

great his knowledge of theology is, is evident, to say the least, from his habit of writing papers of great erudition, in which at the same time God is never far from his thought. Besides this, the man has a knowledge of Hebrew which is somewhat out of the ordinary. I beg you to give him such a welcome as will make him feel that an insipid letter from Sapidus carries some weight with you. Our friend Wimpfeling sends greetings. I hope you will not mind greeting Rhenanus and the Amerbachs and Froben on my behalf. If you admit greetings from the other sex, my Lucretia, the dearest thing I have, sends her good wishes. But I see this makes you laugh.

Farewell, from Sélestat, 15 September 1515.

355 / From Johann Kierher — Speyer, 16 September 1515

The writer of this letter (d 1519) was one of the lesser humanists of Alsace; he had received his MA from Paris in 1510 and had probably studied also at Freiburg under Zasius. He was a canon of the cathedral of Speyer, and may have met Erasmus either in August 1514 or in the spring of the next year when Erasmus returned from England; cf Ep 337 introduction. He is mentioned in Erasmus' *Encomium Selestadii*; Reedijk poem 317, 22n. See also Winterberg. This letter was first published in the *Farrago*, and has manuscript authority in the Deventer Letter-book.

JOHANN KIERHER OF SÉLESTAT TO MASTER ERASMUS

Your kindness and courtesy towards all lovers of learning, Erasmus, great scholar and brilliant writer though you are, were already well known to me from the various celebrated productions of your genius which as a matter of course display these and other virtues; but after the time that you passed so sociably with us in Speyer, I understood far more clearly how approachable you are to all men. So kind and charming were you to us all that you left behind a great desire to know and love you better, as anyone can see immediately from the way in which all speak of you, with praise and honour for your name, declaring you learned and modest and a delightful guest above all other men. They think themselves exceptionally fortunate not merely to have made your acquaintance, but (such is your affability) to have acquired you as a friend. This being so, I have some confidence that you will do what I ask without demur for the sake of a common acquaintance. My friend Maternus, whose hospitality you will particularly re-

* * * * *

14 Lucretia] His wife; cf Ep 353:28.

355:15 Maternus] Maternus Hatten, precentor of the cathedral of Speyer (fl 1517–46), who after the Reformation became canon of St Thomas' church in Strasbourg; see Bopp 1988.

member, came the other day upon a passage in St Jerome, in the prologue to the *Contra Jovinianum*, where he speaks of the numerical values of marriage, widowhood, and virginity; with considerable subtlety and the inevitable obscurity he works out these numbers on his fingers, explaining how by joining them together in different ways and twisting them in and out the ancients supposed the meaning to be in one place 30, in another 60, in another 100. As his digital computing was more obscure to us than the notorious Platonic ratios, Maternus proceeded to consult the theologians. Really, you cannot think how tedious and barren were their replies! One could easily suppose they had no wish to spend their time on the major Fathers of the church, so much as on futile questions, minute, knotty, and frivolous. Nor did this altogether surprise me; what can the ass do with the lyre? In his frustration, therefore, Maternus, who is an obstinate fellow in such matters, decided to refer the matter to you, as you with your universal learning must know it well, and all of us instantly approved his proposal with acclamation. And so Maternus wished (since you and I are old friends) that on this occasion I should perform the duty of writing to you on the point; I have done as he asked, and undertaken this office with a will.

And so he begs, or rather we all beg and beseech you, Erasmus, most delightful of talkers, that when leisure and your other occupations (which we know to be heavy) permit, you should untie this Jeromean, and to us Gordian, knot; for if you will, you can. And there are two things in particular which should spur you on to pursue this problem, lying as it does within your own special field. One is the very great gratitude we shall all feel for this considerable service. The other is that by explaining this passage you will deflate the arrogance of these useless theologians, and break the hissing heads of those who are always protesting against more liberal studies, as Hercules did the hydra's. If you comply with this very respectable request of ours, as your profession and our regard for you suggest you should, I hope that you will never regret the kindness you have done us: we shall always use our best endeavours to do whatever we think you might find useful, or even agreeable, if in any way we can. Farewell, sole light of liberal studies, and forgive your friend Kierher for his boldness.

Your keen supporter Thomas Truchsess, the man who invited you to

* * * * *

17 *Contra Jovinianum*] PL 23:223C–224A

27–8 ass ... lyre] *Adagia* I iv 35

50 Truchsess] A canon of Speyer, born in Wetzhausen, Bavaria, who died in 1523. He matriculated at Leipzig in 1484 and had been a pupil of Reuchlin as

dinner, and Maternus likewise, would be glad of an opportunity to be in your debt, and wish you health and long life in your literary labours.

Speyer, 16 September 1515

356 / To Pieter Gillis

[Basel, September 1515]

The date assigned to this letter is deduced from the books mentioned, and by inference from the arrival of Gerbel (Ep 358) and the resumption of the printing of the New Testament (cf Ep 360). See M.A. Nauwelaerts 'Un ami Anversois de More et d'Erasme: Petrus Aegidius' *Moreana* 4 (1967) 83–96. The text was first printed in the *Farrago*.

ERASMUS TO HIS FRIEND PIETER GILLIS

I wonder very much what that rascal of mine took into his head that made him leave your part of the world so suddenly, for that same day I had written from Mechelen to say what I wanted done. The worthless fellow had wandered about, from you to Mechelen, thence to Brussels and Louvain, and from there finally to Diest. After a month he arrived here, having lost his clothes and spent ten gold pieces; so I turned the monster off.

Please have delivered to the chancellor this letter which I have put with yours. I have published a few letters, among them the one in which I reply to Dorp, and I meant to add his letter to me, if you had given it to my servant as I had told you to. The bookseller will bring you the book. My *Enchiridium* is printed and some other pieces with it. The New Testament was started, but broken off again for want of a corrector; as soon as I can get

* * * * *

well as of Beroaldus the Younger at Bologna, where in 1504 he received a doctorate in canon law. In 1513 he became doctor of roman law also. When Reuchlin's case was submitted to the bishop of Speyer (cf Ep 290:15–16n), he was one of the delegates appointed to examine the *Augenspiegel*, and pronounced it free of heresy. He was dean of the cathedral from July 1517 until his death, and both Erasmus and Beatus Rhenanus drafted epitaphs for him.

356:2 rascal] Evidently a servant messenger

7 ten gold pieces] In all likelihood either Burgundian-Hapsburg florins of St Philip (still officially worth 4s 2d groot Flemish) or Rhenish florins (worth 4s 10d groot Flemish). Cf Ep 326B:8n above; CWE 1 317–18, 321 (plate), 336–9, 342–4; CWE 2 327–45.

8 chancellor] Jean Le Sauvage; cf Epp 410 introduction; 301:38n.

9 few letters] Cf Ep 353:2n.

9 the one] Ep 304

12 *Enchiridium*] That is, the *Enchiridion*, in the *Lucubrationes*; cf Ep 342:30n.

13 corrector] Cf Epp 351, 352.

even a little time to spare, I shall publish your epithalamium. I shall stay here until November. Best wishes to you and all yours, my best of friends.
[1518]

357 / From Udalricus Zasius Freiburg im Breisgau, 21 September [1515]

Is it not time you ceased, great man that you are, to load my humble self with these generous benefactions? Your kindness is indeed remarkable, that you should offer me gifts so elegant and so desirable, while I in turn respond with nothing, no, not the shadow of any recompense. But just as the range of your wonderful scholarship knows no bounds, so too the riches of your generosity towards me are to have no limits, so that the man who is without peer in the humanities throughout the German, and perhaps the Italian, world, takes also the first place for liberality. Then and then only can there be a truly liberal outlook, when it is nurtured by a true devotion to many fields of study. For my part, having no means of repaying your splendid and repeated gifts, I bind myself both in spirit and in mind to remain under your authority, always ready to carry out your instructions with instant obedience.

For the rest, as I am about to celebrate my daughter's wedding (with good omen, let us hope) on the second of October, I would urge you as strongly as I can to attend the ceremony if you can manage it. If you came, you would find a welcome from many excellent men who are your enthusiastic supporters, and would do me honour by adding a note of considerable distinction to the ceremony. My house would open wide its gates to so illustrious a visitor, and the whole school would gain lustre from your presence. But I dare not lay this burden on you as a social duty, while you know that I desire Desiderius whole-heartedly, if you are willing to come, and will see to it that you do not suffer from the expenses of the journey. My friend Philipp had given me to understand that he would not leave until he had my letter to take with him, but he has departed, under the pressure of some opportunity or compulsion. For he suffers in body (Heaven send nothing may come of it), although in other respects he is a worthy and educated man. And so I gave my letter to the man who brings it to you, my

* * * * *

14 epithalamium] Cf Ep 312:93n.

357:14 daughter] Clementia was Zasius' younger daughter by his first marriage; she married a Freiburg merchant; see R. Stintzing *Ulrich Zasius* (Basel 1857; repr 1961) 177.

24 Philipp] Engelbrecht; cf Ep 344:58n.

son-in-law. Farewell, O glory of literature and chief of literary men. Your devoted Zasius

From Freiburg, 21 September

Give Beatus Rhenanus, a man of rare integrity and learning, anything you can that is handsome and friendly and respectful in the way of greetings; I heartily wish he were to share in your journey, if you find you are able to undertake it, and in the distinction which will be shed upon my family.

358 / To Udalricus Zasius [Basel, end of September 1515]

The letter was carried by Engelbrecht (cf Ep 366:1n) who went to Basel from Freiburg about 21 September and returned there again soon afterward (cf Ep 357:23–6). The manuscript is a copy of the letter by Bonifacius Amerbach on the last leaf of a manuscript translation of Lucian made by him in the summer of 1515 and dedicated to Zasius: Öffentliche Bibliothek, university of Basel MS C VIa 73 339v. It was first published in the *Farrago* (1519).

ERASMUS TO HIS FRIEND ZASIUS

If there were any way in which I could take wing out of this treadmill, which I would do with the greatest pleasure, I would rather visit you outside the time of your wedding so as to enjoy your uninterrupted society. Just now there will be so many people about that I should be allowed very little of your time. I send you my *Enchiridion* very lately printed. Beatus returns your greeting with equal warmth; Gerbel and Oecolampadius are here too. Farewell, my learned friend. I pray that your daughter's wedding may be equally a pleasure and a blessing to you and yours.

To Zasius, incomparable doctor of laws. In Freiburg

359 / From Willibald Pirckheimer Nürnberg, 1 October [1515]

This letter is taken from the Deventer Letter-book and is WPB 370.

WILLIBALD PIRCKHEIMER TO ERASMUS OF ROTTERDAM

I cannot tell you, much as I would like to, what pleasure your earlier letter

* * * * *

358:6 *Enchiridion*] Cf Epp 342:30n and 356:12n.

7 Gerbel] Cf letter from J. Froben to Bonifacius Amerbach, Basel, 22 September 1515 (AK II Ep 535:10–13).

359:2 earlier letter] Ep 322; the later letter referred to is apparently lost.

gave me, and now this latest one; they were so much looked forward to, and more than welcome. And if I could tell you, I should still feel I was falling short of what your kindness and good will towards me demand. All the same I did answer your first letter some time ago, and made it clear with what joy I accepted your generous and open-hearted offer of friendship. Since you said in that letter that you were setting off for Britain, I sent my letter to Britain by the English envoy at the imperial court; only, now that you have stayed in Germany, I suppose that it did not succeed in reaching you. So I will now repeat briefly what I said then since it will always remain not only on my lips but in my inmost heart: I mean, that there is no one in the world of the living, not even kings, for whom I have the same devotion as I have for Erasmus, who was long ago designed by his great qualities to be a man after my own heart, and now, as he himself has generously confessed, is properly my friend. Do not cease therefore, my dear Erasmus, to keep our friendship alive by your delightful letters, now that it has so happily begun, for you can do nothing that can give me greater pleasure.

The lady whom you recommended to me in your last letter I have looked after as well as she could have expected and I could manage; for there is nothing I would not think worth doing for your sake. Give my greetings to our common friend Beatus, although I am not a little jealous of him, much as I love him; for he is given the chance of enjoying your society and your delightful conversation, which are denied to me. But my spirit, which is not altogether a false prophet, foresees that one day I shall have the opportunity to see you both and live with you in friendship. Amen, so be it.

Farewell, second founder of the Latin tongue, in whose hand are the keys to sound learning, sole glory of Germany.

Nürnberg, 1 October

* * * * *

3 latest] From Mechelen; cf line 19 and Ep 362:24.

8 letter] Ep 326A

9 envoy] Robert Wingfield; cf Ep 326A:20n.

10 have stayed] Erasmus evidently had not recounted his movements to Pirckheimer in his letter from Mechelen.

13 kings] Reading *reges* for *roges*

19 The lady] The sister of the man to whom Erasmus dedicated the *Enchiridion*, identified by Allen as Johann Poppenruyter; cf Ep 164 introduction. She was in court service at Mechelen; cf Ep 362:24.

360 / To Andrea Ammonio Basel, 2 October [1515]

The date is inferred from the reference to the New Testament and to publication of the *Damiani elegeia*. The letter was first published in the *Farrago* (1519).

ERASMUS OF ROTTERDAM TO ANDREA AMMONIO

All has gone nicely hitherto, until it came to the reek of the stoves, which have lately begun to be lit. Jerome goes forward. They have started on the New Testament at last. I can neither stay here to face the intolerable reek of their hothouses, nor go away with so much work on hand which cannot possibly be finished without me. My Swiss neighbours are highly indignant with the French because they did not yield the day to them politely as they did to the English some time ago, but scattered many of them with their artillery. Rather fewer returned home than went out, ragged, maimed, and wounded, with their flags in tatters; and so requiem rather than rejoicing is the order of the day.

I have had my letter to Leo and a few others printed, but have added to it; if there is any reaction which particularly concerns me, write and let me know, but with caution. If my health permits I shall stay here until Christmas; if not, I shall either return to Brabant or go straight on to Rome.

My lord of York has presented me with a prebend at Tournai, but it will prove one of those gifts that are no gifts if conditions change. His commissary has been excommunicated in Flanders, with notices nailed up everywhere; such is the respect they show there for his grace of York. That

* * * * *

360:4 New Testament] Resumed after the delay referred to in Ep 356:13

7 yield] At the battle of Marignano, 13–14 September 1515. The English had defeated the French at Guinegate on 16 August 1513 in the 'Battle of the Spurs,' so called because of the hasty flight of the French, cf Ep 325:17.

12 letter] Ep 335

16 prebend] Obtained by Mountjoy and offered first to Erasmus at Bruges; cf Ep 337 introduction; Ep 388:32. By the time Erasmus decided to accept it, Wolsey was promising provision for Erasmus in England; LP II i 889, 890.

17 gifts that are no gifts] Sophocles *Ajax* 665

17 conditions] The see of Tournai was contested between the French claimant, Louis Guillard, and Wolsey, to whom Henry VIII gave it after the English occupation. The rivalry continued until the English evacuation in 1518.

18 commissary] Wolsey's commissary was Richard Sampson; cf Ep 388:38n.

man is alive and well and master of the field, as bishop of that place, well-born, well-read, well-endowed. Still I have accepted it; nothing is easier than to give it up.

I should be glad of your epigrams, if possible; I have said so before. You would readily excuse this letter if you knew how I am overwhelmed with other things of the same kind. Farewell, Ammonio, my learned friend, and mind you remain the same to your Erasmus that you have always been.

Basel 2 October [1513]

361 / To Johann Kierher — Basel, [October 1515]

This letter was first published in *Epistolae ad diversos* (1521).

ERASMUS OF ROTTERDAM TO JOHANN KIERHER

Since you are a very well-read man yourself and have so many learned friends, I very much wonder, my excellent Kierher, why you thought of asking this question with so much circumstance of me. But there is nothing so difficult that a word from my old host Maternus will not get it out of me, provided it is the kind of thing I can do for him. But on this system of numbers which in the old days were represented by the position of the fingers, I shall publish a note derived from the fragments of Bede, which it would take too long to repeat now, as the volume will be coming out shortly. Not but what I do not really approve of this sort of minute curiosity in providing numbers with a meaning, nor is it sufficiently clear whether the same system that Jerome records was in use among the Hebrews.

The mass of labours and researches in which I am involved does not allow me at the moment to write a longer reply. Please give cordial greetings on my behalf to Thomas Truchsess, a man learned without ostentation and

* * * * *

20 bishop] Bishop Louis Guillard (d 1565) was the son of the president of the Parlement of Paris, and had been the pupil of Josse Clichtove at the Collège de Navarre in Paris. He occupied the see from 13 February 1519. He promoted learning and received the dedications of several scholarly works, including many of Clichtove's.

23 epigrams] Probably not a reference to any published work by Ammonio. P.S. Allen suggests that Erasmus might have been contemplating a joint venture like the volume he later published with More.

361:4 this question] Cf Ep 355:15 and ff.

8 note] See the 1516 edition of Jerome, vol iii, fols 25 and 31, the latter containing additional notes from a MS of Bede lent to Erasmus by Ludwig Baer (Allen).

friendly without artifice, and to Maternus, sincerest of friends. Farewell, my special friend Johann.

Basel [1516]

362 / To Willibald Pirckheimer

Basel, 16 October [1515]

The date assigned to this letter is inferred from the books mentioned in it, the *Enchiridion* (Ep 342:30n) and *Enarratio in primum psalmum* (Ep 327) of September 1515, and the Jerome and the New Testament, still in progress. The manuscript source is British Library MS Arundel 175 f 18; it was first published in *Pirckheimer*: WPB Ep 371.

TO THE HONOURABLE WILLIBALD PIRCKHEIMER, GLORY OF LETTERS AND OF GERMANY, FROM ERASMUS

I think it must be some fore-ordained inclination of my mind that makes me so specially fond of my Willibald. Beatus Rhenanus can bear me witness that when I had barely tasted your translation I felt at once the warmth of some new affection for you, and now both your letter to me and the learned achievements of your mind increase that affection every day. Surely you are a very rare bird in this age of ours, combining as you do such outstanding scholarship with so splendid a position in the world, and with that again such a courteous and friendly spirit; for you do not hesitate to include me and men of no importance like me in the number of your friends. A short work translated by you was shown me in Bruges by Thomas More on my return from England; for he was then serving as envoy in my country for his king and people. Of a letter he said nothing; he merely added in passing that it was sent to me, but did not say by whom. I suspect that you entrusted your letter to Sir Robert Wingfield who, although he often greeted me in

* * * * *

362:5 translation] His translation of Plutarch's *De his qui tarde a numine corripiuntur* (Nürnberg: F. Peyp 30 June 1513) which he had asked Erasmus to revise; cf Ep 375.

11–12 short work] Pirckheimer's translation either of Plutarch's *De vitanda usura* (Nürnberg: 26 January 1515) or of Lucian's *De ratione conscribendae historiae* (Nürnberg: March 1515)

12 More] More arrived in Bruges on the evening of 17 May 1515, and Erasmus evidently arrived a few days later; cf LP II 473, 474 (reporting that More arrived in Bruges about 18 May 1515).

16 Robert Wingfield] Erasmus has confused the two brothers, Sir Robert (who was at Maximilian's court in Augsburg) and Sir Richard, who had earlier been in France but returned to England on 2 May 1515.

England and on one particular day also had a longer conversation with me, never (I wonder why) said a single word to me on the subject.

By awarding me more praise than I could possibly accept, were I the most conceited of men, you have at least contrived to make me a little less dissatisfied with myself. I am overwhelmed here by two burdens, either of which would demand a Hercules rather than an Erasmus. Apart from lesser things, I support Jerome and the New Testament, which is now printing. The woman whom I recommended to you from Mechelen is the sister of the man to whom I dedicated my *Enchiridion*. That work is now printed in Strasbourg. I have added a commentary on the psalm 'Beatus vir,' dedicated to my dear Beatus Rhenanus; for he is the best friend a man could have. I would have sent you the book, had they not replied that it has already been despatched to your part of the world. I write this not only under incredible pressure of work, but also after supper, having been told suddenly of the courier's departure. One thing I will add, that, though I may be outstripped in learning and in position in the world, in affection and zeal I shall never yield to my Willibald, invincible though he may be. When I am given the chance (and I shall be given it, I hope, quite soon), I shall write you not letters but whole volumes. Beatus Rhenanus, who is a friend after Pythagoras' own heart, that is, one soul with me, thanks you for your good wishes, and returns them with interest. Farewell, great glory of the world of letters.

Basel, St Gall's day, late at night

363 / From Wolfgang Angst — Haguenau, 19 October [1515]

This letter was evidently written in 1515 since it accompanied the gift of a copy of the first part of the *Epistolae obscurorum virorum*, which appeared in print in the autumn of 1515. The writer himself had been involved in the production of the work of Crotus Rubeanus and Ulrich von Hutten. Angst was born about 1488 in Kaysersberg and made his first studies at Strasbourg, whence he went to the recently founded university of Frankfurt an der Oder, where he received his BA in 1507. He matriculated there with Ulrich von Hutten, with whom he was a lifelong friend. He was apprenticed to Schürer in 1510; in

* * * * *

24 woman] Cf Ep 359:19n.

26 Strasbourg] This is the edition printed by Schürer in the *Lucubrationes* of 1515; cf Ep 356:12n.

26 'Beatus vir'] Cf Ep 327.

36 Pythagoras] *Adagia* I i 2

1514–15 he worked with Gran at Haguenau, and in the summer of 1517 joined Froben at Basel, where he corrected the *Adagia* for Froben's edition of 1517. See Schmidt II 154–8; Ritter app no. 141.

WOLFGANG ANGST OF KAYSERSBERG TO MASTER ERASMUS

The Unfamous Men, that caterwauling chorus over whose birth I presided in our barren sandy desert, have now plucked up their courage and wish to pay you a state call. I do all I can to forbid such a thing, but they retaliate all the more forcibly, retorting that Erasmus will give them a very warm welcome. Did he not long ago repeat one of their more vigorous productions from memory at Strasbourg? Are they not close relatives of the gentry so brilliantly recorded in his *Moria*? Their pressure was too much for me; I had to run with the wind. For the rest, it is up to you not to refuse a day's hospitality to a party which, as you know, was so keen to make your acquaintance. I beg you not to despise their humour or take it amiss; it is not within the means of my humble self to offer anything to a prince of scholars like you, except good intentions. Farewell, and long life.

Haguenau, 19 October

364 / To Johann Witz

This letter has been assigned a different date and now appears as Ep 391A.

365 / From Ulrich von Hutten

Worms, 24 October [1515]

The writer (1488–1523) was one of the most turbulent personalities of the Reformation, a violent critic of the papacy, and an ardent promoter of the spirit of German nationalism. He came of a noble Franconian family and was forced by his father to enter the Benedictine monastery of Fulda. After he left in 1505, he studied in several universities, obtaining a BA at Frankfurt. In Italy he maintained himself as a student at Bologna by fighting in the imperial armies. Eventually he became a counsellor to Archbishop Albert of Mainz (1517), having been crowned poet laureate by Emperor Maximilian. He met Erasmus for the first time at Mainz in 1514 (cf Epp 300:14, 314:5) and at the time

* * * * *

363:2 caterwauling] Literally, singing myrtle-branch in hand; see *Adagia* II vi 21.

7 Strasbourg] During the visit of June 1515; cf Ep 337 introduction; *Spongia* LB X 1640EF.

of this letter was returning to Italy where he took up the study of Greek. In a letter of 9 August 1516 to Richard Croke, written from Bologna, Hutten explains that he had been nine months in Italy (HE 37:16); Böcking and Allen both dated the present letter 1515. See W. Kaegi 'Hutten und Erasmus. Ihre Freundschaft und ihr Streit' *Historische Vierteljahrschrift* 22 (1924/5) 200–78, 461–514.

ULRICH VON HUTTEN TO ERASMUS OF ROTTERDAM

I think all the gods must be angry with me; it is their will that prevents me from passing several years in your company, and they tear me from your side. Otherwise, had Fortune permitted, I should have clung to you more closely than ever Alcibiades did to Socrates. Why indeed should I not call you the German Socrates, Erasmus, for as regards literature you have done as much for us as he did for his fellow-Greeks? I am not perhaps the sort of man who can give you complete satisfaction, for to be capable of pleasing you requires a special kind of good fortune; but I might not have proved unworthy to sit at your feet and learn Greek, to have followed you zealously, guarded you watchfully, obeyed you dutifully, carried out all your orders, and leapt to my feet at the least hint from you. Nor would it have been to your discredit to have had a German knight like myself serving you with such wonderful devotion and loyalty. I would have preferred this, my dear Erasmus, not merely to the life at court, which I am summoned to take part in with so much tedium, but even, I do assure you, to my proposed wanderings in Italy.

And to tell you briefly the plans I had lately formed, I had decided to go and join you, and might perhaps have followed you as far as England. But this excellent plan was interrupted by the ill-timed liberality of my relations; they call it liberality, for they are paying my expenses to go and study the law, and for this purpose I am now being sent to Rome. I am on my journey as I write this, and surrounded by the noise of an inn full of guests. You must forgive my hasty scribble. There will be no opportunity to see you again. Against my will I am bound for a place where I cannot see you and enjoy your society. My travelling-companions are such as could not be persuaded to pass through Basel. This is not surprising, for not everyone realizes what a great man you are. I wish I might persuade you to believe how much I am attached to you.

You will see a poem I have published called *Nobody*, not perhaps entirely despicable, in the preface of which I have made honourable men-

* * * * *

365:30 *Nobody*] This evidently refers to Ulrich von Hutten's *Nemo*, the first edition of which appeared in Erfurt in 1510. The second version, containing a preface to Crotus Rubeanus in which Erasmus is mentioned, was not pub-

tion of you, as was right and proper. I am quite recovered from my ague, and also from the trouble in my foot. If you should come to Italy, nothing will stop me from coming to see you, and quitting the legal dungeon to which my relatives are consigning me. I would have asked you to give me an introduction to someone in Rome, had I come to Basel; with your usual generosity, you would not have refused me this kindness. If you have a spare moment, write to Rome and recommend me to someone in literary society; I don't want to curry his mules or rub down his horses, but to use his library. I have no time for more.

Farewell, from Worms, 24 October.

366 / To Udalricus Zasius [Basel, October 1515]

The date must be not long after Ep 358, but at an interval in which Erasmus might have expected an answer to that letter. This letter may not have been delivered to Zasius until some months afterwards; cf Ep 379:12–13n. The autograph original is in the Öffentliche Bibliothek of the university of Basel, MS C VIa 35 I 107.

ERASMUS TO HIS FRIEND ZASIUS

I wrote to you by Philipp and by the same hand sent you as a present a copy of my *Enchiridion*, nor do I doubt that both reached you. I am almost overwhelmed with work and so badly caught in the double pressure of Jerome and the New Testament that I think Hercules had less trouble with his hydra and his crab. But I could not have it on my conscience not to have sent a word of greeting to my incomparable friend Zasius. My labours leave me no chance to enjoy the society of my friends though I have so many in Germany; but 'even to this god will vouchsafe an end.' If you and yours are well, write and let me know, and I shall be all the more delighted. Farewell, my very learned Zasius. Give my greetings to Master Philipp.

Beatus returns your good wishes, and with him all our society of scholars here.

To the distinguished professor of laws Udalricus Zasius, his incomparable friend. In Freiburg

* * * * *

lished until August 1518 at Augsburg; see Josef Benzing *Ulrich von Hutten und seine Drucker* Beiträge zum Buch- und Bibliothekswesen Band 6 (Wiesbaden 1956) 22, 45, items 5, 62. The date of this letter and the nature of the reference to Erasmus in the 1518 preface led Allen to suggest that an edition and preface that did not then appear were envisaged by Hutten in 1515.

366:2 Philipp] Engelbrecht; cf Ep 344:58n.

9 'even to this ...'] Virgil *Aeneid* 1.199

367 / From Udalricus Zasius Freiburg im Breisgau, 30 October 1515

UDALRICUS ZASIUS TO MASTER ERASMUS
WITH RESPECTFUL GREETINGS

Acchatius, the bearer of this letter, my dear Erasmus, brought me a message of greetings from you, and it was very welcome, great man that you are, but I should have preferred one of your delightful letters. This however is only a respectful suggestion; let me not seem to abuse your kindness by asking too much. I know how honourable and how important the business is that prevents you – to give all the assistance in your power to the growth of sound learning in our native Germany; so that it is no surprise if you write seldom, and especially to a man like me of no importance, who ought to be satisfied if from time to time you mention him by name. Apart from that, the good wishes for my daughter's wedding which you sent in your last elegant letter, I took as an oracle rather than an omen, as though those blessings had issued from some divine being; for how should I not think you worthy of divine honours, when we see united in you every good quality divine or human that God or nature can confer upon a living man? Had you been present in person to grace our festival, I should count myself truly happy. But you have aroused hopes of a visit one day, and to this all of us who wish you well and so much depend upon you look forward with longing; for there are many good men here who long not only to see you and enjoy your society and your friendship, but also to enlist under your banner, the banner of the prince of humane studies. And unless you come soon, we shall descend upon you, your liege men, your faithful flock.

I should have come myself long ago, but I am assailed by ill-health, an enemy who never lets go, who attacks the citadel, my head and ears, and has almost taken it, unless the helping hand of God brings me relief. But although frail in other respects, I am absolutely resolute in research, and this is my own restorative and consolation. Gerbel, a man of learning lightly carried who richly deserves his doctorate, has given me a present I badly wanted, your brilliant books, the *Enchiridion* and several others for which I have been thirsting for so many years, and have sought to secure by

* * * * *

367:3 Acchatius] This reference has not been identified.

13 letter] Ep 358

30 *Enchiridion*] The copy of the *Enchiridion* sent with Ep 358 (cf Ep 366:3) seems not to have reached him, although the letter, with Erasmus' prayerful good wish for the daughter's wedding, is referred to in line 13.

collecting New Year's presents from every source. God send I may one day be able to do something for him in return. My life upon it, I will show myself a model of gratitude. Please give my greetings to him, and to my dear friend Rhenanus, and to Oecolampadius, the most upright man I know; I would have written to them, but I am absorbed by the second book of *De orig. iur.*, my commentary on which is nearly finished, and if I take so much as a moment's rest from my reading, I must not be distracted.

Farewell. From Freiburg, 30 October 1515

368 / From Paul Volz — Hügshofen (Honcourt), 30 October 1515

Volz was born at Offenburg (1480–1554) and matriculated at Tübingen in 1496. He entered the Benedictine order at a monastery near his home, and in 1512 was elected abbot of Hügshofen near Sélestat, as a measure to introduce the Bursfeld reform there. He was a member of the literary society of Sélestat, through which he must have made Erasmus' acquaintance. The 1518 re-edition of the *Enchiridion* carried an important new preface addressed to Volz (Ep 858), whom Erasmus also remembers with a legacy of one hundred florins in his will. See Bopp 5390; Adam.

PAUL, ABBOT OF HÜGSHOFEN, TO ERASMUS

Given this opportunity, I could not fail to send a greeting to one so distinguished as yourself, who are beyond a peradventure the most learned of men. Greetings, therefore, my very dear friend, you who have laid the whole world of learning under an obligation, not only by the many-sided scholarship which is so visible in everything you do, but especially by your well-mannered *Moria* and your *Folly* turned wise, who appears again better than ever in your reply to Dorp. Your friends and mine, Jakob Wimpfeling and Johann Witz, have been reading this with me at dinner, and we have been filled with laughter and admiration; indeed it has almost taken the place of meat and drink, and so forth. Farewell in Christ Jesus, and may he give you strength one day to finish successfully what you have begun.

In haste, from my monastery, 30 October 1515

Give my best wishes to B. Rhenanus.

* * * * *

36 second book] Reading l[ibro] ii° for l[ege] ii[a]

37 *De orig. iur.*] The *De origine iuris* which was published in Zasius' *Lucubrationes* of 1518; cf Epp 303 introduction, 390:9ff.

368:8 reply to Dorp] Ep 337; it had recently appeared in the *Damiani elegeia* (Basel: Froben August 1515).

369 / From Nikolaus Gerbel [Strasbourg, November? 1515]

This letter seems to have been written before Ep 383 and after the writer's return from Basel; cf Ep 364 introduction.

NIKOLAUS GERBEL TO MASTER ERASMUS

Our common friend Matthias Schürer complains that he is under great pressure from the men who carry books up and down the country for sale, and that demands for your *Parabolae* are accompanied by something like abuse. I told him that it was hardly possible for you to give them a second revision at this moment in view of your immense labours, which bear upon you from all sides and never allow you to draw breath. He replies that he is forced to it, unless he is prepared to have your works entirely taken out of his hands by the men who copy everything like monkeys. He says that the greatest service you could possibly do him at the moment would be for the book to appear in a revised edition with your corrections; but if this is impossible, he must at all events publish according to the copy you sent him some months ago. On this question please let me know if there is anything you can do, or what you would wish done. There is nothing we are more anxious to do than to follow your wishes. If you conveniently can, do fall in with the desires of the reading public, and also of a faithful friend. Any help I can give, such as it is, I place gladly at your service.

All good wishes, and please let me know how you are. Give my greetings to your companions, who are as friendly as they are learned. My friend Rudolfinger wishes to be remembered to you, and so do your other friends, who ask me continually for news of your health and what you are busy on now. I give them very high hopes of the New Testament, and also of the Jerome, which they are all eager to see. Once more farewell.

* * * * *

369:4 *Parabolae*] Reprinted by Schürer in February and November 1516.

16 and also] Some word seems to be missing in the Latin.

16 friend] There is no evidence that Erasmus, who was persuading Bade to print a new issue, undertook any of this suggested revision; cf Epp 383, 434, 472.

20 Rudolfinger] Cf Ep 302:15n.

370 / From Jan Becker van Borssele — Arlon, 22 November 1515

On the background to this letter see Ep 320 introduction.

JAN VAN BORSSELE TO ERASMUS OF ROTTERDAM, THEOLOGIAN

The letter you wrote me on the first of October reached me a few days ago as I write this, not delivered by the man to whom you had entrusted it when he was coming this way, but sent all the way from Louvain to which it had somehow been carried. So there was no chance to speak with anyone and ask what I wanted to ask about you, and time is so short that I fear it may prevent this from reaching you before you leave Basel. I have therefore written more shortly than I had intended, having so far secured no reliable messenger going in your direction.

I must first of all thank you most warmly for your great kindness in writing to me over such a great distance, and overwhelmed as you are with business, and in such kindly terms. Second, I would beg you, if a chance offers of writing to me again, let me know more fully how things are with you, all the books you have written or translated and corrected from the Greek, and where you will go next. For I hear from time to time in letters from friends in Brabant that an opportunity to lead an honourable existence in any part of that province has been offered you and is now available, in the form of an annual salary of a substantial amount from the prince's treasury, and that all educated men hope that you will accept the offer without misgiving. In fact, unless you accept, it will be clear, not that you have been neglected by the rulers of our country, as all of us have often complained, but that it is you who neglect and despise this land of ours,

* * * * *

370:2 letter] This letter is lost.

18 salary] The first mention of Erasmus' appointment as councillor to Prince Charles; cf Ep 392:17n. The annual value was 200 florins (cf Allen Epp 597:26n; 628:49), but payment was slow and infrequent. If these florins were the actual gold St Philip coins, this salary would have been worth £41 13s 4d groot Flemish = £245 tournois = £30 sterling; but if the florin or gulden money-of-account (livre de 40 gros) was meant, then only £33 6s 8d groot Flemish. Cf Ep 386:84 below for Duke Ernest of Bavaria's offer to Erasmus of an annual salary of 200 'gold pieces,' probably Rhenish florins in this instance, amounting to about £48 6s 8d groot Flemish.

20 it will be clear] These words are not in the only surviving copy of this letter in the Deventer Letter-book.

unless of course you reject this offer because one more lucrative and more honourable has been made elsewhere. But whatever there may be of this kind, if you have already made up your mind, I should dearly like to know. For you wrote that you would be where you are until December, and did not add where you would go then; and so I, like everyone else, am filled with one great hope, that you will accept the offer and come to our beautiful Brabant, where you will spend the rest of your life in great glory and peace. And may I live to see the day.

You ask about my own position, and do not approve, indeed strongly disapprove, that I grow old in this teaching post of mine. It shows your old liking for me and the feelings of an affectionate teacher, that you should wish to see me devote my time to greater and more distinguished affairs. I fully agree with you about one day giving up the job of teaching children, as not very suitable to my time of life; besides which, pressure has been put on me for more than a year now from my own country, with great force and most generous promises almost against my will, the prime mover being the provost of Aire, to whom I am so bound by ties of gratitude – a virtue I have always wished to possess, and to be seen to possess – that I thought I could not in honour say him nay. But the task itself, both because I am now of mature years, and from the boorishness of this region, which I find very unpleasant, and the lack of educated people – the task and the responsibility I find far more difficult than I expected. I should certainly do my work with much greater peace of mind, if I could exchange this place at an early date for some well-known school. But having once started, I am resolved not to abandon the responsibility except for some really suitable and extremely honourable opportunity; of which I see the time almost at hand, if it were not possible next summer to move to some place in Gaul or France. As far as concerns my health, I have always hitherto kept very fit, and I endure the climate and the food here without serious trouble.

Farewell, from the town of Arlon in the country of Luxembourg. 22 November 1515

* * * * *

26 wrote] Evidently a letter now lost; cf line 2 and Ep 360:14–15, written at the same time.

32 teaching post] Cf Ep 320:12–23. Erasmus was undoubtedly concerned at the waste of his abilities and wanted him appointed to the chair in Latin at Busleyden's college; cf Ep 291 intro; Allen Ep 794.

39 Aire] Jérôme de Busleyden; cf Ep 205 introduction. He was provost of the chapter of Aire, in Artois, and a member of Prince Charles' great council at Mechelen.

49 France] That is, the Ile-de-France

371 / From Jean Molinier

Tournai, 23 November 1515

Molinier, whose name is also found as Du Moulin, Molendinaris, a Molendino, and Molinus, was a student of Lefèvre d'Etaples and a colleague when he became a professor at the Collège du Cardinal Lemoine. He later became a canon of Tournai and was a close friend of Pierre Barbier, dean of Tournai (cf Ep 443 introduction). He became involved with Barbier in the matter of Erasmus' annuity from Courtrai (cf Ep 436:6n); see Renouard II index.

JEAN MOLINIER TO MASTER ERASMUS

His Grace of York has suffered a change of heart, a specially common complaint at court. The canonry he conferred on you a long time ago he has now given to someone else, a son of the king's surgeon-in-ordinary; although I do not think he will find it plain sailing if things in that quarter go the other way. However, the archbishop himself has promised to give you either another canonry here or something more important in England, as Mountjoy explained to me personally, although on promises like that any beggar may be rich. I cannot say what a satisfaction it would have been to me and to most of the other canons if the fickle goddess had brought you safely into port here after your various and exacting toils. Yet saw I never the righteous forsaken. Mountjoy also said he would soon be setting off for England, and wanted me to let you know. I will in any case hold your mandate or procuration, as they call it, in case I have a chance of using it to your advantage.

You say in your letter that your Jerome is getting on nicely. I can hardly say how much I long to see it, to read it and make it welcome, together with your other works, and the New Testament. Keep it up therefore, my dear Erasmus; press on with all your might to finish these famous studies, which are destined to win you an immortal name and everlasting glory. But press

* * * * *

371:2 change of heart] Literally, has sung a palinode; *Adagia* I ix 59

3 canonry] Cf Ep 360:16n.

4 surgeon-in-ordinary] Marcellus de la More, appointed on 6 August 1513; LP I 4390

8 promises] Ovid *Ars amatoria* 1.444

12 forsaken] Ps 36 (37):25

12 Mountjoy] Despite a long-standing desire to return to England, Mountjoy did not succeed in doing so until 1517; cf LP II appendix 10 1112; Allen Ep 508:17n.

16 letter] Probably one contemporary with Ep 360; cf Ep 370:2, 26n.

on in such a way as always to take account of your state of health; it is most important for the world of letters that you should live as long as possible. Farewell therefore, and may you live long as well as happy.

From Tournai, 23 November 1515

372 / From Paul Volz — Sélestat, 25 November 1515

PAUL, ABBOT OF HÜGSHOFEN, TO ERASMUS

When I read the letter which you sent on the eve of Martinmas to our common friend Jakob Wimpfeling, which was brought me by another friend Johann Witz, I discovered that, after expressing excessive thanks for the very small service I had rendered you, you wish to know what the passage is in the preface to Ezekiel which I said had so often puzzled me. It comes at the end of the preface that normally stands in all Bibles before Ezekiel, where it says (to within a few words at least, for I have no text by me) something like this: 'But if my rivals sneer at this too, I fear they will suffer the fate (as Greek more expressively puts it) of being called "phagolidori," which means "eaters of seneciae".'

What 'senecia' means I do not know, and after long search I have failed to find it, except in Lyra and the *Mammotrectus* and *Catholicon* and suchlike, who produce on this word the most arrant nonsense. 'Senecio' is a plant in Pliny's *Natural History* book 25, last chapter, which he says is called in Greek *erigeron*; but how this should come in here, I cannot say. Now this Greek proverbial expression φαγωλοίδοροι, which is much clearer if we write λοιδοροφάγοι, on the analogy of κρεωφάγοι and ἰχθυοφάγοι, could also be rendered in Latin by one newly coined word 'conuiciuori' or

* * * * *

372:2 Martinmas] 12 November; the letter is lost.

12 senecia] Cf Pliny *Natural History* 25.13.167. The abbot is puzzled by two things, the nonce-word *senecias*, for which modern texts read *sannas* 'sneers,' and the form of the Greek word. One who makes cheap abuse his meat and drink might be called a 'sneer-eater,' on the analogy, as he says, of 'meat-eater' and 'fish-eater,' but ought not to be an 'eat-sneerer.'

13 Lyra] Nicholas of Lyra (c 1270–1349), from Lyre in Normandy, was a Franciscan and a distinguished theologian and exegete. Among biblical scholars of the Middle Ages his scholarly training was outstanding; he had a command of Hebrew and familiarity with Jewish commentators on Scripture. His *Postillae perpetuae* set forth the literal sense of Scripture and were highly esteemed, becoming the first biblical commentary to be printed: cf Ep 182:128n.

13 *Mammotrectus*] Cf Ep 337:330n.

13 *Catholicon*] Cf Ep 26:100n.

'calumniuori,' which would mean gluttons for abuse, malice-mongers, men whose mouths are always full of abuse and quarrelling. That is the best my thick head can do, and you must make of it what you can. Have a care for your health, so that you may be a blessing to many people. Farewell, you and all my friends, and the sweet child Jesus have you in his keeping.

From Sélestat, St Catherine's day 1515

373 / To the Reader — Basel, [c December] 1515

This is the preface to Erasmus' annotations on the first edition of the New Testament, known as the *Novum instrumentum* (Basel: Froben 1516); cf Ep 384. The annotations were a product of his earlier Scripture study, and remind us that the edition of 1516 came into being as the climax to a series of scholarly undertakings that date at least from the turn of the century. In considering this background the development of Latin and Greek elements in his final text should be kept distinct.

Erasmus had no opportunity to devote himself seriously to the study of Greek until he arrived in Paris about 1495. He did not really come to grips with the language until after he left England in 1500, when he was more than thirty. His purpose then was twofold: to rectify a serious deficiency in his mastery of classical literature and to deepen his grasp of Scripture. As he later wrote to Colet about the connections between his study of Greek authors and sacred studies, 'experience teaches me this, at any rate, that we can do nothing in any field of literature without a knowledge of Greek, since it is one thing to guess, another to judge; one thing to trust your own eyes, and another to trust those of others' (Ep 181:101–4).

On his return to Paris Erasmus applied himself energetically to Greek, at first without even a tutor (Epp 123:25–7; 124:72–4; on the development of his Greek studies see Allen I 592). He worked both at the Epistles of St Paul (Ep 123:25) and at pagan authors, and by the summer of 1501 was perhaps starting at the task of translation (Ep 158:18n). Certainly part of his programme of study was the translation of Libanius, Lucian, Euripides, and Plutarch (Epp 177; 187; 188; 264:27–8; for the texts of Libanius, Lucian, and Euripides and editorial comment see *ASD* I 1); and in the forefront of his mind was the revision of the *Adagiorum collectanea* of 1500 (Ep 126), which seemed to him 'thin and poor' once he had read the Greek authors through (Ep 181:94–5).

The deepest influence that can be documented for his work in Greek Christian sources is his lifelong interest in his much-admired teacher and model St Jerome; his project to edit Jerome's letters with commentary, also begun at this time (1500), itself required an expert knowledge of Greek (cf Epp 139:166 and ff; 141:18 and ff). The influence of Colet, important beyond doubt

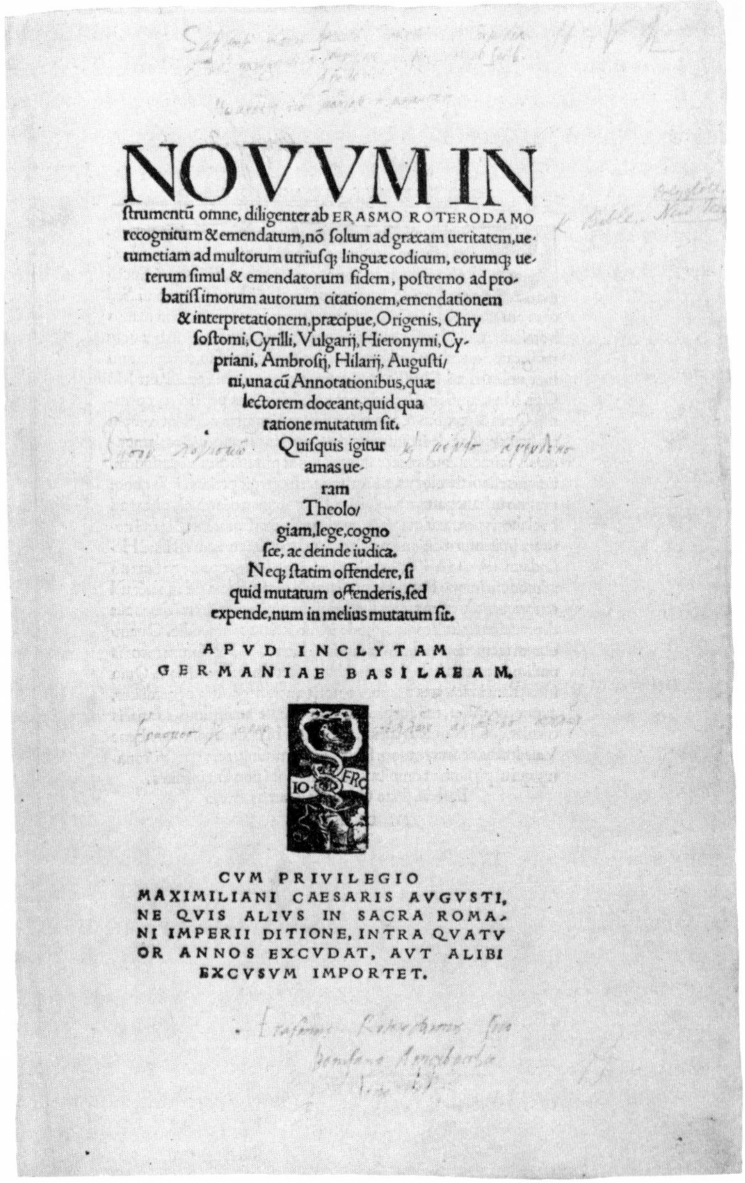

NOVVM INstrumentũ omne, diligenter ab ERASMO ROTERODAMO recognitum & emendatum, nõ solum ad græcam ueritatem, uerumetiam ad multorum utriusq; linguæ codicum, eorumq; ueterum simul & emendatorum fidem, postremo ad probatissimorum autorum citationem, emendationem & interpretationem, præcipue, Origenis, Chrysostomi, Cyrilli, Vulgarij, Hieronymi, Cypriani, Ambrosij, Hilarij, Augustini, una cũ Annotationibus, quæ lectorem doceant, quid qua ratione mutatum sit.

Quisquis igitur amas ueram Theologiam, lege, cognosce, ac deinde iudica. Neq; statim offendere, si quid mutatum offenderis, sed expende, num in melius mutatum sit.

APVD INCLYTAM GERMANIAE BASILAEAM.

IO FRO

CVM PRIVILEGIO MAXIMILIANI CAESARIS AVGVSTI, NE QVIS ALIVS IN SACRA ROMANI IMPERII DITIONE, INTRA QVATVOR ANNOS EXCVDAT, AVT ALIBI EXCVSVM IMPORTET.

Erasmus *Novum instrumentum* title page
Basel: Froben 1516
British Museum, C 24 F 14

in deepening Erasmus' general concern with biblical study, seems to have had to do more immediately with theological rather than philological exegesis: see W. Schwarz *Principles and Problems of Biblical Translation* (Cambridge 1955) 107–8. However in conjunction with his work on the text of Jerome in 1501 Erasmus compared the Septuagint Greek text of some Psalms with the Vulgate translation and concluded that the Latin text could only be understood by comparison with the Greek from which it had been taken (Ep 149:24ff). By the time he wrote Colet at the end of 1504, 'all agog to approach sacred literature "full sail, full gallop"' (Ep 181:29–30), he had also been through a good part of the works of Origen, whose allegorical exegesis, he found, 'demonstrates some of the basic principles of the science of theology' (Ep 181:47–8). At this time too – the very time he was composing the *Enchiridion* with its marked Pauline character – Erasmus was preparing a commentary on the Epistles of St Paul. The undertaking was no doubt connected also with his Greek studies in general, and although he later told Colet he gave up the attempt for lack of Greek, he had enough confidence in the enterprise to complete four volumes on Romans (Epp 181:37–8; 123:25; 164). For this work, which has been lost, he gathered as many commentaries as he could, including the homelies of Origen (Ep 165:9–12).

A final and decisive influence in these years was his discovery in the abbey of Parc near Louvain of a manuscript of Valla's annotations on the New Testament, a manuscript which he edited and published for the first time in 1505 (Ep 182 introduction). In Valla's work Erasmus found a clear statement of the principles of philological exegesis that he had developed for himself in his apprenticeship from 1500 to 1504. Erasmus returned to England in 1505 and made his translation of the New Testament, using two Latin manuscripts lent him by Colet, now dean of St Paul's. These Latin manuscripts seem subsequently to have perished, and of the Greek texts available to him at this time nothing is known except that they were inadequate for a truly critical edition. However the translation itself was copied by Pieter Meghen at Colet's direction: cf Allen's account in his introduction to Ep 384 (Allen II 182–3) and Schwarz's comment on the nature of Erasmus' approach (140–1).

It seems likely that Erasmus' own annotations date from the period when he worked on Valla's (cf the statement of Beatus Rhenanus, in Allen I p 64 lines 280–1). They were probably composed intermittently during his work on the text of the New Testament in subsequent years (Ep 305:14); conceivably they may include elements gathered during his early work of commentary on St Paul. In August 1514 he told Reuchlin that he had written annotations on the entire New Testament (Ep 300:33). By that time he was considering a Greek text too, having now in hand complete annotations and a complete Latin translation of his own. The annotations, however, were made upon the

Vulgate text, and many more were prepared while the first edition of the New Testament was actually in press. See Ep 384 introduction, and Basil Hall 'Erasmus: Biblical Scholar and Reformer' in T.A. Dorey ed *Erasmus* (London 1970) 94–5.

ERASMUS OF ROTTERDAM TO THE PIOUS READER GREETING

Although I did do so to the best of my ability at the very outset of this work, yet it may be worth while to warn the reader briefly once again both what he ought to expect from these brief notes and what demands I can reasonably make upon him in return. In the first place, what I have written are short annotations, not a commentary, and they are concerned solely with the integrity of the text; so let no one like a selfish guest demand supper in place of a light luncheon, and expect me to give him something different from what I undertook to produce. This for the moment is the play I have undertaken to perform; and thus, just as I have to keep to my programme, so it is reasonable that the courteous and fair-minded reader, like a friendly spectator, should do his best for the actors and attune himself to the scene before him.

I have taken what they call the New Testament and revised it, with all the diligence I could muster and all the accuracy that was appropriate, checking it in the first instance against the true Greek text. For that is, as it were, the fountain-head to which we are not only encouraged to have recourse in any difficulty by the example of eminent divines, but frequently advised to do so by Jerome and Augustine, and so instructed by the actual decrees of the Roman pontiffs. Second, I checked it against the tradition of very ancient copies of the Latin version, two of which were made available by that distinguished master of the divine philosophy John Colet, dean of St Paul's in London, in such ancient styles of writing that I had to learn to read them from the beginning, and in order to pick up the rudiments I had to become a schoolboy again. A third was provided by the illustrious lady

* * * * *

373:2 outset] In the preliminary *Apologia*

19 Augustine] The phrase 'frequently … Augustine and' was added in the second edition of 1519, and 'A third … important to name' (lines 25–35) in the third edition of 1522.

25 third] The reference is to the so-called Aureus Codex, an eleventh-century Latin manuscript of the Gospels which had belonged to Matthias Corvinus, king of Hungary, and had recently come to the Royal Library at Mechelen through the offices of the regent Margaret. Erasmus had the use of it for his second edition (Froben 1519); cf Ep 384 introduction, and the previous note.

Margaret, aunt of the emperor Charles; its evidence I have frequently cited in this third edition under the name of the Golden Gospels, because it is entirely clad in gold and finely written in gold letters. After that, I was provided with several manuscripts of remarkable antiquity by the equally ancient and celebrated collegiate church of St Donatian at Bruges. Previously the house of Korssendonk had supplied me with a manuscript very neatly corrected, not to mention some lent me by those excellent scholars the brothers Amerbach. It is not therefore that I have made a certain number of corrections dreamed up out of my own head; I have followed the manuscripts listed, and others like them which it is not so important to name. Finally I have checked by the quotations or corrections or explanations of authors who are fully and universally approved – Origen, Chrysostom, Cyril, Jerome, Ambrose, Hilary, Augustine, Theophylact, Basil, Bede – whose evidence I have adduced on many passages with this in mind, that when the intelligent reader has perceived that in certain definite places my correction and their opinion coincide, he may give me his confidence in other places too, in which probably by chance they have neither supplied a note nor supported me in any other way.

I knew however that it is human nature to object to novelty in everything, but especially in the field of learning, and that most people expect to find the old familiar taste and what they call the traditional flavour; and I also reflected how much easier it is, nowadays especially, to corrupt a sound text than to correct a corrupted one. Consequently, after revising the sacred books I added these pointers (so to call them), partly to explain to the reader's satisfaction why each change was made, or at least to pacify him if he has found something he does not like, for men's temperaments and judgments vary; partly in hopes of preserving my work intact, that it might not be so easy in future for anyone to spoil a second time what had once been restored with such great exertions. First then, if I found anything

* * * * *

30 St Donatian] In August 1521 during the meeting between the emperor and Wolsey Erasmus visited the library of this foundation and discovered four Latin manuscripts of the New Testament, some of which he dated from the eighth century. Cf *Annotationes in Matt.* 1.18, 3.16, and *Ioan.* 1.5.7.

31 Korssendonk] An Austin priory near Turnhout which supplied a twelfth-century Greek manuscript of the New Testament complete except for Revelation, and a ninth- or tenth-century Latin manuscript of the Gospels. Both were taken to Basel by Erasmus for the printing of the second edition (1519).

38 Theophylact, Basil, and Bede] Added in the third edition

46 traditional flavour] *Adagia* II iv 19

damaged by the carelessness or ignorance of scribes or by the injuries of time, I restored the true reading, not haphazardly but after pursuing every available scent. If anything struck me as obscurely expressed, I threw light on it; if as ambiguous or complicated, I explained it; if differences between the copies or alternative punctuations or simply the ambiguity of the language give rise to several meanings, I laid them open in such a way as to show which seemed to me more acceptable, leaving the final decision to the reader. And although I do not willingly disagree with the translator, whoever he was, because his version is traditional and commonly accepted, yet when the facts proclaim that he nodded or was under a delusion, I did not hesitate to make this also clear to the reader: I have championed the truth, but so as to criticize no man. Blunders that were obvious and unnatural I removed, and I followed the rules of correct writing everywhere so far as it was possible to do so, always provided that there was no loss of simplicity. Wherever the idiom of the Greek or its peculiar expression has something about it that helps towards the underlying meaning, I was always ready to demonstrate this and make it visible.

Finally I collected and weighed up the Old Testament evidences, not a few of which are cited either from the Septuagint version or from the Hebrew original, if the form in which they are current differs from their Hebrew source; although this I could not do single-handedly 'without my Theseus' as the Greek proverb puts it, for nothing is further from my character and temperament than like Aesop's crow to set myself off with others' plumage. So in this department, when I was first publishing this work, I secured no little help from a man eminent for his knowledge of the three tongues no less than for his piety, which is as much as to say a true theologian, Joannes Oecolampadius of Weinsberg; for I myself had not yet made enough progress in Hebrew to take upon myself the authority to decide.

For my part, I was well aware that these minutiae, these thorny details, promised far more work than reputation, and that this sort of labour does not usually earn its author much gratitude, while the reader gets more benefit than entertainment from it. But if I have gladly endured so much

* * * * *

66 Blunders] This sentence was added in the second edition (1519).

76 Theseus] He assisted Meleager against the Calydonian boar and Hercules against the Amazons (Zenobius 5.33); cf Ep 334:135n; Allen Ep 797:3ff.

78 when I was first publishing this work] Added to the second edition (1519)

81 Oecolampadius] He went to Basel at the invitation of the bishop, Christoph von Utenheim, and assisted Erasmus with the Hebrew of the *Novum instrumentum* (1515–18).

tedious labour in consideration of the general good, it is surely only right that the reader too, for his own good, if for no other reason, should digest a certain amount of what may irk him and contribute for himself and his own advantage the spirit that I have shown in helping others. The points of which I treat are very small, I agree, but their nature is such that almost less effort would be needed to deal with those great problems of which our grand theologians with their lordly manner make such heavy weather, whose swelling cheeks bulge until they crack with pride; what is more, such is their nature that for the sake of these minuscule minutiae one sometimes actually needs to explore those major problems. Minute they may be, but because of these minute points we see even the greatest theologians sometimes make discreditable mistakes and fall into delusions, as I shall indicate in a certain number of places, not for the pleasure of attacking anyone (a disease which ought to be kept poles apart from a Christian's work and indeed from his whole life), but in order to justify my good faith to the reader by a few examples produced without criticizing anyone, so that no one may despise these as worthless trifles; for in reality, as Horace puts it, 'to serious things these trifles lead the way.' Why are we so particular over the serving of our meals, offended by the smallest details of personal attire, ready to think nothing in money matters too small to be taken into account; and in Scripture alone disapprove of thus taking trouble, and prefer neglect? To say nothing for the moment of the majesty of the subject, of which no detail can be so unimportant that a religious man can think it beneath him, so mean that it does not require reverent and devoted treatment. It crawls along the ground, they say; it torments itself over pitiful words and syllables. Why do we regard as beneath our notice a single word uttered by him whom we worship and revere as the Word himself? – all the more so as he tells us himself that one jot or one tittle shall in no wise pass away. It is the least part of Scripture, what they call the letter; but this is the foundation on which rests the mystic meaning. This is only rubble; but rubble that carries the august weight of the whole marvellous edifice.

St Jerome calls some eminent Greek authors to account because they despise the historical sense and prefer to indulge in allegory as their fancy leads them, and deplores his own behaviour in producing with youthful confidence an allegorical interpretation of the prophet Obadiah of whose

* * * * *

105 Horace] *Ars poetica* 451

115 himself] Matt 5:18

119 Jerome] Jerome Ep 51:4; CSEL 54 400–3

121 deplores] In the Prologue to his commentary on Obadiah; PL 25:1097

history he says he knew nothing. The precious pearl lies hidden in a worthless shell, splendid grain is wrapped in flimsy chaff, within a dry and tiny envelope lurks the astonishing vitality of a seed; even so in words that seem ordinary enough and in syllables and in the very strokes of the letters lie hid great mysteries of divine wisdom. He who wonders why that divine Spirit chose to conceal his riches in wrappings such as these may wonder equally why the eternal Wisdom assumed the person of a man poor and lowly, despised and rejected. To learn these details St Jerome was not too proud to take lessons from a Jew, lessons at night, and spurned no drudgery. For their sake St Augustine, when already a bishop and old man, went back to the Greek studies he had rejected as a boy. For them Origen, old and gray-headed, became a child again and learnt the elements of Hebrew, outdoing even Roman Cato. To these details Ambrose alludes with pleasure; Hilary lingers over them. They are often discussed, and inner meanings found in them with pious persistence, by Chrysostom, golden author not in tongue alone. In his footsteps Cyril unfolds a great mystic meaning in the Greek definite article, in the one poor letter ὁ, from which he borrows an invincible weapon to launch against heretics. To say nothing for the moment of something else: that while these details are our ostensible subject, those wide views sometimes open as we proceed; for as those who expound the meaning are sometimes obliged to explain the precise wording, so I, whose business is to explain the wording, am obliged from time to time to open the meaning in its full force. Lastly, I had prepared for this by a more serious enterprise, by starting some time ago my commentaries on St Paul, from which it will perhaps appear whether it was wise judgment or mere chance that made me descend to these minutiae.

After all, let any man who so pleases imagine that I was incapable of doing more, and that either the slowness of my wits and the chill in the blood around my heart or lack of knowledge reduced me to this humble task: even so a Christian spirit should take in good part the humblest service that is performed in pious devotion. Christ praised the farthing dropped into the treasury by a poor woman, valuing something worthless

* * * * *

133 Greek studies] *Confessions* 1.14.23

138 Cyril] St Cyril of Jerusalem (c 315–86), who protested the Nicene term *Homoousios*

147 commentaries] Cf Ep 164:41ff.

151–2 chill in the blood] Virgil *Georgics* 2.484

154–5 farthing … treasury] Mk 12:38–40; Lk 21:1–4

in itself by the motive of the giver. In some really splendid enterprise the humblest duties have their own distinction. In kings' palaces sweepers and cooks are thought respectable; and in the house of God what service can seem contemptible? I have brought only a load of rubble, but it is for the building of God's temple; others out of their riches will add ivory and gold, marbles and precious stones. I have paved by my own efforts a road that was once beset with rough places and with bogs – a road on which in future great theologians can drive more easily with coach and horses. I have levelled the ground of an arena in which they can now display the splendid pageants of their wisdom with less risk of accident. I have hoed up the weeds in a fallow lately blocked with thorns and briars, to make it easier for them to work the fertile soil. By clearing obstacles away I have opened up a field in which those who wish hereafter to expound the Holy Scriptures can share their sport more readily or meet in conflict with less waste of time. Those who have a feeling for the old theology have a powerful support to help their efforts towards the goal. Again, he who says with the man in the parable 'The new wine is better,' and neglects the old through his interest in our more recent vintage of theology – he too has the means of indulging his preference with greater certainty and confidence. And even supposing he gains nothing from this, at least he will lose nothing from his own store if these advantages accrue to those who would rather draw their knowledge of Scripture from the purest springs than from such streams and pools as may be handy, so often poured from one of them into another, not to say fouled by the muddy feet of swine and asses. No: fruit tastes better that you have picked with your own hands from the mother tree; water is fresher that you draw as it bubbles up from the actual spring; wine drinks better which you have drawn off from the cask in which it was first laid down. In the same way the Scriptures have about them some sort of natural fragrance, they breathe something genuine and peculiarly their own, when read in the language in which they were first written by those, some of whom took them down from those divine and sacred lips, and some bequeathed them to us under the influence of the same Spirit. If Christ's sayings survived in Hebrew or Syriac, handed down, that is, in the same words in which he first uttered them, who would not love to think them out for himself and to weigh up the full force and proper sense of every word and even every

* * * * *

170 old theology] The *vetus theologia* of the Church Fathers and pre-scholastics

172 old wine] Luke 5:39

188 Syriac] Added to the 1535 edition

letter? At least we possess the next best thing to this – and we neglect it. If anyone shows us Christ's robe or his footprint, we fall down and worship it and kiss it. But even could you produce his every garment and all the furniture of his mother's home, there is nothing that can so exactly represent, so vividly express, so completely show forth Christ as the writings of the evangelists and apostles.

And so, if anyone either cannot or will not spend time on these pious pleasures, at least let there be no protests, no interruptions, no ill will, aimed at those who follow the better course. Let such men embrace what they love, let them have it for their own and enjoy it: no man says them nay. It was not for them that I wrote this. But there will be some on the other side who will think all this amounts to very little, who would rather see no agreement with the Vulgate version. But my object was to make the language more correct and lucid, not to polish it; this was no place to look for what is not there, like knots in a rush. What we all ought much more to hope for is that there should be no passage anywhere in Holy Writ that needs this treatment. In the Gospels, where the course of the story in itself is clear and almost self-explanatory, and flows on in a simple unaffected style, it was not really possible for either translator or scribe to do very much damage; although, if one counts them up, there are too many mistakes of this kind, in a text where there should have been no doubt at all. But in the apostolic Epistles, where both language and sense are obscure, more changes were needed. All the time I controlled the density of my annotation, so as to be neither tiresomely scrupulous nor so careless that I seemed to flag. And throughout I have indicated the point in as few words as possible instead of explaining it fully, for fear that a business naturally without much charm should be made more tedious by my loquacity.

This is a work of piety, and it is Christian work. And so, my excellent reader, I ask you in your turn to bring pious ears and a Christian heart to your reading of it. Let no man take up these pages in the spirit in which perhaps he opens the *Nights* of Gellius or Angelo Poliziano's *Miscellanies*, to test, I mean, as though against a kind of touchstone, their intellectual vigour, their eloquence, their recondite learning. The material on which I work is sacred, and it has won its way in the world by simplicity and purity above all. On such material it would be absurd to seek to display human

* * * * *

205 knots in a rush] *Adagia* II iv 76

221 *Miscellanies*] Cf Ep 126:166.

222 touchstone] Literally 'Lydian'; *Adagia* I v 87

learning and impious to make a show of human eloquence; even were the eloquence there, it would be proper to conceal it, for fear someone might object that it was perfume on lentils. It is with simple and pure zeal that I lay this before my Christian readers, in hope that hereafter this most sacred philosophy may find more men to follow it and with more enjoyment, in a word, that their labours may be less and their profit more. May Christ himself, who is the witness and support of these efforts of mine, show me little mercy, if this is not the truth: so far am I from seeking any advantage out of these labours, that I have knowingly and willingly accepted a great and definite pecuniary loss. As for the sweets of fame, so little am I tempted by them that I would not even have set my name to the work, had I not feared that this might reduce its power to do good; for all men suspect a book with no author's name. I am ready equally for both, either to defend myself if what I have said is right, or openly to confess my error wherever I can be proved wrong. 'I am a man; the common lot of men / Is my own business.'

This then is the spirit in which I offer you this, my excellent reader, and in the same spirit you must accept it. This will be to the advantage of us both: you will get more out of the book if you accept what it offers gladly and with an open mind, and I shall have less regret for all my nightly vigils if I know they have been useful to men of good will. If there is anyone so absolute and hard to please, or so bigoted and unfair, that no kind words will move him, this much at least I shall try to win from him, by prayers if need be, that he should allow to sacred study the same measure of equity as the courts give to those accused of murder and sacrilege: there it is thought disgraceful if sentence precedes evidence, and the verdict is not given before the case has been fully heard. Let him first read it and see what he finds, and then if he pleases he may damn it and throw it away. It is arrogant to pass judgment on a book you cannot understand; more so, to judge one you have not even opened.

And so farewell, reader, whoever you may be, and let me urgently request you, if you have gained any advantage from my labours, to remember your duty as a Christian, and commend me in return in your prayers to Christ, from whom alone I look for a lasting reward for this work.

Basel, 1515

* * * * *

228 perfume on the lentils] Proverbially the waste of something precious; *Adagia* I vii 23

240 'I am a man ...] Terence *Heautontimorumenos* 77

374 / From Johannes Caesarius — Cologne, 3 December [1515]

The writer was born in Jülich about 1468 and died in 1550. He was educated at Deventer, matriculated at Cologne in 1491, and became a pupil of Lefèvre d'Etaples at Paris where he received his MA in 1498. He subsequently taught at Deventer and began publishing. About 1508 he went to Bologna to study Greek, and returned to Cologne after a few years as an independent humanist teacher, editing Boethius, Horace, and Pliny's *Natural History*. He was a warm supporter of Reuchlin, and among his pupils were Heinrich Loriti, called Glareanus, Cornelius Agrippa, and Heinrich Bullinger. Erasmus dedicated to him his translation of Theodore of Gaza's *Grammatica institutio* (Ep 428).

JOHANNES CAESARIUS TO ERASMUS OF ROTTERDAM

Whenever I call to mind your consummate labours, and survey the publications of unquestioned eminence with which you strive continually and most successfully to restore and promote good literature, some of it of the very highest class, I can scarcely say, most excellent sir, how much I marvel at you. My recent opportunity to make your acquaintance, when you were with us in Cologne, I reckon (believe me) as no small portion of my felicity – such felicity, at least, as men can achieve in this stormy life. What greater good fortune could befall the age in which we live, especially for men who are fond of learning, than to possess already such great scholars, whose unceasing toil and incredible industry are now at last bringing humane studies back into the light? So long, to our shame, have they been neglected, while not only in profane and secular literature but, what is most to be regretted, even in sacred authors and indeed in our religion itself, in other respects so pure, during the last eight hundred years and more various monstrous absurdities have grown up. I do not doubt that by some destiny, or rather by the divine will, it will come to pass that you like a second Hercules, and certain other people with similar effort but less brilliant success, will drive out these monsters, exterminate them, and do them finally to death.

I would urge you in fact to press on as you have begun, did I not know for certain that of your own accord you mean to do just this. But one thing I must not forget to tell you, that your works are daily expected with remarkable enthusiasm, and all men think very highly of them with no trace of envy, even those who still produce monstrous works of the old school, being accustomed to produce almost nothing else. This, as anyone can see,

* * * * *

374:7 Cologne] Either on his journey to England or on his return

must be accounted a marvel. And so the fame that awaits you in the future and after your death, which tends to exaggerate everything, is more than you yourself can conjecture. The rest of us pray continually to almighty God that you may long be spared, and I trust that our prayers may be heard. Farewell.

Cologne, 3 December

I hear that Glareanus, a man of much learning, has returned from Italy and is now with you; in which respect he is certainly more fortunate than myself, although in other ways I am sorry for his unexpected misfortune. Please give him most courteous greetings from me; I would already have written to him myself, and done my best to give him pleasure in a letter, if time had permitted. For I have scarcely been able to write this to you, having heard belatedly that there was someone here who could take this letter, or rather these outpourings, to you. Heaven is my witness that I would not have dared, had I not been encouraged by previous experience of your kindness, which does not despise the likes of me. Farewell again and again, great glory of Germany, and do not forget your promise and my humble self.

375 / From Willibald Pirckheimer — Nürnberg, 13 December 1515

There is a rough version of this letter in Pirckheimer's hand in the Stadtbibliothek Nürnberg, MS PP 127b. The copy in the Deventer Letter-book (Deventer MS 91 f 169v) was accorded a higher authority by Allen since it represents the letter actually received. It was first published in LB; WPB Ep 376.

WILLIBALD PIRCKHEIMER TO MASTER ERASMUS

Another delightful and most welcome letter from you has arrived, and so I am greatly in your debt for not forgetting me when you are so busy. It was a disappointment that my letter did not reach you with the book, because in it I tried to express my joy at the acquisition of such a friend as yourself. I likewise asked you to point out the mistakes in my Plutarch, as my friend Beatus told me you had promised to do, and I still beg you to do so, for I am sure you will do it quite frankly. I had given that letter to Robert Wingfield,

* * * * *

33 Glareanus] His return from Italy indicates the year-date of this letter; cf Ep 328:56–7.

41 would not have dared] *Testor Deus quod ausus eram*; the Latin is perhaps corrupt.

375:4 my letter] Ep 326A

6 Plutarch] Cf Ep 362:5n.

but ever since then he has been in attendance on the court; you have perhaps had speech meanwhile with his brother, who has also sometimes served as his king's envoy to the emperor.

I rejoice that St Jerome has at last found someone to restore him to his original purity, and cannot think that this has happened without some special divine providence. You are indeed to be congratulated, for your labours will win you the favour of God and of his saints, and of the world. I on the other hand am obliged to follow the noise and bustle of the law and the squabbles of princes, in which even to please God is perhaps impossible; and how meanly Fortune treats those who immerse themselves in public business, history has many examples to show. Go on then as you have begun, my dear Erasmus, and do not hide the light the Creator has given you under a bushel. It was his will to produce a creature in whom eloquence could display all her ancient power; it is for you to continue by the path that you have entered on, and win yourself a name that will outlive riches and royalty.

But enough of this, lest I seem to flatter you. One thing I desire above all else, that I may one day see you face to face, and when you have finished your Jerome, you will easily be able to oblige me. I know you will not regret having seen a city-state unique in Germany, and a friend who loves and venerates you more than any. In the meantime, farewell.

Nürnberg, 13 December 1515

376 / From Udalricus Zasius — Freiburg im Breisgau, 16 December 1515

A manuscript copy of this letter in Basel, begun by Zasius and continued (after the end of the third sentence) by his pupil Bonifacius Amerbach, was used by Allen to correct the text in the Deventer Letter-book (Öffentliche Bibliothek, university of Basel, MS C VIa 35 II 13).

Just see, dear master, how far effrontery can go. I want your assistance, I rely on your help, and I am not afraid to appeal to you, although I have never done you the least shadow of any service. It is your kind heart that makes me so presumptuous, and your mildness that provokes my misbehaviour. Your serenity of mind and unruffled spirit and kind words have given me confidence. And so, if an outsider like myself breaks in upon your sanctum, you will ascribe this not so much to my own effrontery, although that is not

* * * * *

10 brother] Sir Richard Wingfield (c 1469–1525), educated at Cambridge and Ferrara, was a professional diplomat like his older brother Robert; cf Epp 326A:20n; 362:16n.

wholly absent, as to your own mildness and courtesy. What is it then, you will ask; a small thing to you, but to me a great one. I have, it seems to me, rolled away the darkness, if there is any, in the second book of the *De orig. iur.*; for there are many dark places there, not for learned men like you, but for those who pursue the law, who have nothing in common with sound learning; and I have explained the historical allusions and added a number of other *scholia*, as you call them. I am sending two quires, for I have not yet given it final revision, although only a little remains at the end, which I hope to finish over Christmas. What I want is your opinion, a severe opinion, and one that bespeaks the judge's frown. If you throw them overboard, they will get no further support from me; I am quite unmoved, whether they are voted down or retain their place, for your judgment, the judgment not only of the prince of scholars but of a really just man, will be as good as any oracle of Hammon. And your labour, if it is labour and not more truly occupation, will not fall to the ground; for whatever may be the value of these trifles of mine, I intend to recompense your efforts with a suitable reward. Farewell. Forgive me that I write so little and so badly phrased; I am so burdened actually even on a Sunday with secular business that I can hardly breathe. Farewell, glory and leading light of Germany.

From Freiburg, 16 December 1515

Our friend Bonifacius is entirely devoted to you without reserve; but even when he has screwed himself up to it, he does not dare write to you, for you are so much greater than your public, you frighten them. But he is just as much devoted to you as he is to legal studies, and that is to say, entirely, with every breath he breathes.

377 / To Gianpietro Carafa — Basel, 23 December [1515]

The year date is determined by the reference to the New Testament as almost finished. The letter was first published in the *Farrago*.

TO THE RIGHT REVEREND PIETRO CARAFA, BISHOP OF CHIETI, APOSTOLIC NUNCIO IN ENGLAND, FROM ERASMUS OF ROTTERDAM

Right reverend Father, I realised I had made a mistake about what I was

* * * * *

376:10–11 *De orig. iur.*] Cf Ep 367:37n.

18 overboard] Literally, off the bridge; *Adagia* I v 37

18 quite unmoved] Zasius uses a phrase from Plautus; *Adagia* I iii 83.

21 Hammon] A famous oracle of Jupiter in the Libyan desert

29 screwed himself up to it] Literally, put on a brazen face; *Adagia* I viii 47

asking from you; but too late, too late! I had put you on notice to give me assistance and not merely good will, and what I meant to mean literary and learned help, you thought I was saying about money. I cannot say how often I felt ashamed afterwards of what I had done. The New Testament is now almost finished, and has gone well enough, except that I am half dead with overwork. I have a man to give me some help with the Hebrew. The whole work will run to about eighty six-leaf quires. I have made up my mind to dedicate it to Leo the Tenth. I expect you have seen my letter to him, for it is already in print; I mention you in it too. Jerome goes on briskly, but is an enormous task. Farewell.

Basel, 23 December 151[4]

378 / To Andrea Ammonio — Basel, 23 December [1515]

For the year date see Ep 377 introduction. The letter was first published in the *Farrago*.

ERASMUS TO HIS FRIEND AMMONIO

This man Galeazzo, who is flying off to your part of the world as an envoy on behalf of the Milanese and carries this letter, is obliged to return this way within a month. I shall stay here until the first of March; do please write me a letter by him, if there is anything you think I ought to know. The archbishop of York had made me happy with a beautiful dream of a prebend at Tournai; to be let down like this hurts more than to lose the money. The New Testament is almost finished. It will run to about eighty gatherings. It will be dedicated to Leo. Pace is here, but I have only communicated with him by letter. Farewell, and do not fail to write.

Basel, 23 December 151[7]

* * * * *

377:9 a man] Oecolampadius; cf Ep 373:81.

11 my letter] Ep 335; the reference to Carafa is in lines 264ff.

378:2 Galeazzo] Visconti (b c 1456), of the Milanese noble family. At this time he was a confidential agent for Henry VIII.

7 prebend] Cf Epp 360:16n, 388:32–49.

9 Pace] Pace's missions had taken him to the Emperor's court at Innsbruck at the beginning of November; LP II i 1136, 1146. He left Innsbruck for Switzerland on 16 November (LP II i 1162); arrived at Constance on 22 November (LP II i 1188); and two days later arrived at Zürich, where he met up with Galeazzo Visconti, on the same business of enlisting Swiss support for Henry against France (LP II i 1193). Erasmus' use of 'here' implies no more than Pace's presence in the region of Basel.

379 / To Udalricus Zasius [Basel], [December 1515?]

This letter survives as an undated autograph, possibly in answer to Ep 376, judging from the mention of Zasius' book and the message to Bonifacius Amerbach. The manuscript was hastily written and folded up wet, evidently a copy by Erasmus of his own original draft. In his haste he omitted a passage ('I would rather ... yourself') which Allen reconstructed conjecturally. The letter was first published in the *Farrago*, and the manuscript is in the Öffentliche Bibliothek, university of Basel, C VIa 35 I 106.

ERASMUS TO HIS FRIEND ZASIUS

I could hardly read your letter, my dear Zasius; otherwise, nothing could give me greater pleasure. Why need I praise your book? I will be brief. It is pure Zasius, by which I mean very good indeed, and deserves a worldwide public. I will do my best, as soon as I have the leisure, which will be within a couple of months. Not but what by citing Thomas you have somewhat spoilt the brilliance of your style. But I know for whom you did it, and accept it; otherwise I should prefer the flow and colour of your own style to remain unbroken. And then you cite me with too much warmth, I mean far more than I deserve. Farewell.

Bonifacius I love particularly for more than one reason, and have great hopes of him. I send you a second letter which I wrote some time ago, but it was left behind here by mistake by the courier. Beatus too likes your book; mind you finish it; and if it can be done, [I would rather see the whole work, not only the parts you have written yourself,] but also what you cite from less polished authors, clothed in your charming Zasian style.

To the incomparable doctor of laws Udalricus Zasius. In Freiburg

380 / From Udalricus Zasius [Freiburg im Breisgau], 26 December 1515

This letter evidently follows Ep 376, but there is no suggestion in it that Zasius has received Ep 379 as yet.

Greetings, dear Erasmus, great luminary of the learned world. Our friend Froben arrived today, but not until far into the twilight, and has made plans

* * * * *

379:6 Thomas] Since Zasius scarcely mentions Aquinas in the *De origine iuris* it would seem that he acted on Erasmus' criticism in revising the manuscript, if this letter is correctly placed.

12 second letter] Perhaps Ep 366; if it had been received at once, some mention might have been expected of it in Ep 367:30.

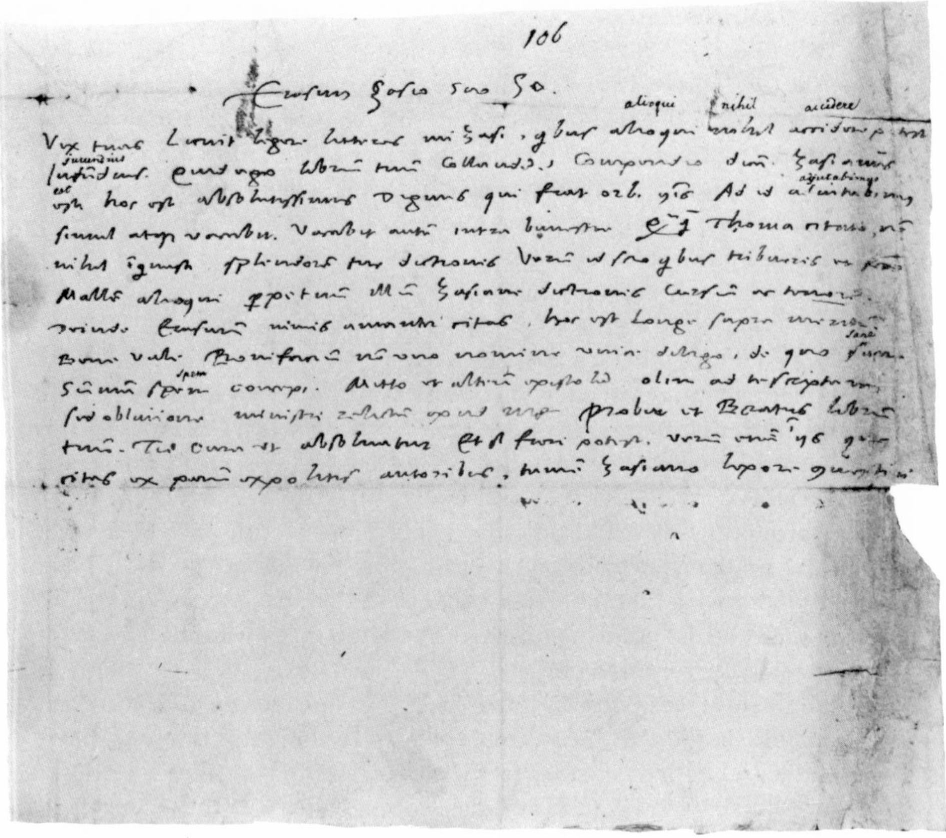

Autograph letter, Erasmus to Udalricus Zasius, Epistle 379
This brief letter was hastily written, and evidently folded up wet, so that the last line has blotted across the page.
Öffentliche Bibliothek, University of Basel, MS C VIA 35 I 106

to depart tomorrow morning; so I have had no chance of a more intimate talk with him, only just to say welcome and goodbye. Welcome to you therefore, most welcome of men, for if all is well with you, all is well – and in the highest degree – with scholarship. And goodbye, too, you from whose good health stems all the good of humane studies, for as long as you are flourishing, Germany can carry off the laurels of victory in the field of learning as she lately did in war. Who can furnish me with the equipment for such a theme? What style, what eloquence, what concentration, what force of mind, what exertion can raise my writing to a fervour and enthusiasm equal to a description however modest of Desiderius Erasmus, my friend, and the friend of scholars everywhere? Words, mind, tongue, spirit, energy, and application, all alike fail me when you are the subject. So what I desire with so much effort, in spite of all my efforts, eludes me, and in writing to the prince of scholars I am obliged to be what I should be ashamed to be before other and ordinary men, barbarous and tongue-tied. And yet I cannot keep silence: I am so much moved by your genius that I count it an honour to expose my incompetence, although in the home of genius incompetence has no place.

Friendship must answer the charges levelled by lack of skill; for even kings and princes whose outward raiment is gold and purple are seen by their friends in more modest apparel and familiar guise. The fact is that I cannot speak of you adequately, any more than any mortal man can admire you as you deserve. Our Saviour, the semblance of whose crib we carry round (and how unworthily!) at this season, be my witness, at the mention of your name I feel such awe that I am not merely benumbed as Meno was by Socrates, I am shaken to my foundations by the terrors of Medusa. Farewell.

May I ask you to run your eye over my poor piece? I know there are two reasons why you cannot think well of it: the historical parts have been familiar to you from boyhood, and the legal parts are not to your taste. But you can perhaps give a general opinion, which I shall value more highly than an oracle from Hammon. Farewell.

26 December 1515
Your devoted Zasius

* * * * *

380:28 Socrates] Plato *Meno* 80a; the sight of Medusa's severed head turned men to stone.

34 Hammon] Cf Ep 376:21n.

381 / From Andreas of Hoogstraten Liège, 10 January [1516]

The dating of this letter is provided by the allusion to Ep 299, and by Girolamo Aleandro's departure from Liège in March 1516 for Rome; cf Ep 299 introduction.

ANDREAS OF HOOGSTRATEN TO ERASMUS

I was much distressed when it became clear that a letter from you, which in other circumstances would have given me great pleasure, had been lying in my house for more than a year, from which I learnt that owing to my absence by some misfortune your plans had miscarried; and conversely, when I received your last letter, despatched from Basel on 5 October with a present which was as welcome as the giver was generous, I was highly delighted, especially because I hoped that on your return you would pass by Liège, as I beg you seriously to do, and urge you to stay in my house. I hope that the city itself, which in your earlier letter you say you like very little, will please you as much as any other, when you have friends to show you round, and the company of Girolamo Aleandro, who is here as canon of our famous cathedral church, chancellor of the bishop of Liège, and provost of St Peter's. Farewell, my right good friend.

From Liège, 10 January

382 / From Jakob Wimpfeling Sélestat, 15 January 1516

The year is 1516 since Oecolampadius is at Basel (see the letter cited in Ep 358:7n) and the Jerome is not finished (Ep 396).

JAKOB WIMPFELING TO MASTER ERASMUS

Are they still alive, or have they departed this life? Or has the society of men of war and ruffians infected them with some sort of inhumanity – Master Erasmus Rotterdam, I mean, and Joannes Oecolampadius and Beatus Rhenanus – so that all this time they send not a line to their devoted friends, not a scrap of news, not a hint about their welfare, their state of health, when they will be here again, whether the works of Jerome are finished? As for me, I am full of sores and have an attack of the gout; if only it had not

* * * * *

381:6 last letter] Apparently lost

382:3 war] Resumed by the combined efforts of England and the empire against France; Swiss troops were employed to invade Italy and by the end of March they had reached Milan; cf LP II i 1352.

made this mistake (for it has laid a poor man low, although it is supposed to be a disease of the well-to-do), I should have appeared in Basel long ago. The bishop of Basel sent a mule with a servant for me. But oh dear! I cannot mount, I cannot leave the house, such pain afflicts me day and night.

In a list of the archbishops of Mainz which I have been compiling, I have made very honourable mention of Dr Erasmus Rotterdam. I hope Oecolampadius will return to Sélestat, so that he can take with him what I wish to give him to be delivered to some great friends of mine in Heidelberg. Tell Beatus Rhenanus that his aged father expects him and is longing to see him. My very best wishes to the three of you.

From Sélestat, 15 January 1516

383 / From Nikolaus Gerbel Strasbourg, 21 January 1516

NIKOLAUS GERBEL TO MASTER ERASMUS, GREETING IN CHRIST JESUS

How very surprising, my most learned friend, that you have not sent us a copy of your *Parabolae*, for that courier of yours has never shown signs of losing anything – especially since you yourself have expressed the wish for some reliable messenger who could bring it to us. Not but what you have plenty of excuses in the shape of your indefatigable labours; but nothing would have given Schürer greater satisfaction, and nothing in my opinion would be more valuable to students, than if your work could have been published in revised form. Still, as there is nothing else to be done, we will do our best to see that the book when it appears is as accurate as is in his power. Someone wrote to me that you were willing to give our common friend Schürer the pleasure of some introductions to Cicero and also to Virgil's *Aeneid*; and if you can manage this, you cannot think how hard we shall try to prove Gerbel not ungrateful and Schürer not ungenerous.

I hope, best of friends, that you are well and prosperous. Write and send me news of your state of health and of the world of letters and of all your work. Give my greetings to that learned and modest man Beatus

* * * * *

13 list] In MS, perhaps autograph, at the Hofbibliothek, Aschaffenburg (Allen)

17 father] Antonius Bild of Rheinau, who died on 21 November 1520. He was a butcher by trade, and became burgomaster of Sélestat; cf Ep 327 introduction.

383:4 *Parabolae*] Cf Ep 369:4n.

13 Cicero] Schürer published works of Cicero in June and August of 1516, but without any known help from Erasmus.

Rhenanus and all our other common friends. All the leaders of learned society here send you their greetings, and especially Johannes Rudolfinger.

Strasbourg, 1516, 21 January

384 / To Leo X Basel, 1 February 1516

In this preface to the *Novum instrumentum* (Froben 1516) Erasmus sets forth his editorial procedures and principles, as in the preface to the annotations (Ep 373). He summarized them again while he was preparing the edition of 1519 (Ep 864 introduction).

The edition was prepared in great haste. Work with Froben must have begun in August 1515 (Ep 348:13–14); a month later Nikolaus Gerbel was still making suggestions as to the form of printing (Ep 352:7f), but by the end of September he and Oecolampadius were prepared to correct proofs; cf Ep 358 and a letter by Froben to Bonifacius Amerbach, 22 September 1515 (AK 535:9–12). Two presses were used to speed the printing. Erasmus enlarged his annotations while the work was still in the press (Ep 421:53–4), and he was assisted by the correctors Gerbel and Oecolampadius, who had to work under extreme pressure and proved unequal to the task. As Erasmus himself admitted, the work was edited and printed simultaneously, with a ternion (twelve pages) printed every day (Ep 421:63–4). The final colophon of the edition was dated February 1516, and that of the annotations 1 March 1516. On 7 March Erasmus announced that the work was published (Ep 394:38): a folio volume of some thousand pages had been printed and revised extensively in from five to six months. A copy reached Budé in Paris on 26 April (Ep 403:27–8), and a week later the work was for sale in the Paris market (Ep 403:28n). Reuchlin found it at the Frankfurt spring fair (Ep 418:1). Under the circumstances it is not surprising that Erasmus began correction for a new edition immediately after publication (Epp 402:1–2; 417; 421:76–7).

For the second edition (Froben 1519) Erasmus revised the Greek text with the aid of a new Greek manuscript (Allen II 165) and returned very nearly to his original translation, which had been considerably modified for the first edition in the direction of the Vulgate (Allen II 183). The 1519 text was again revised for the third edition (Froben 1522). In the fourth and definitive text (Froben 1527) the Vulgate version was printed alongside the Greek text and Erasmus' new Latin version. This edition had been extensively revised again and incorporated many readings from the critical text of the Complutensian Polyglot Bible (see below). Cf Allen II 164–6, 183–4, and his introduction to Ep

* * * * *

20 Rudolfinger] Cf Ep 302:15n.

864; Metzger 102; Basil Hall 'Erasmus: Biblical Scholar and Reformer,' in T.A. Dorey ed. *Erasmus* (London 1970) 104; J. Hadot 'La critique textuelle dans l'édition du Nouveau Testament d'Erasme' in *Colloquia Erasmiana Turonensia*, ed Jean-Claude Margolin II (Paris/Toronto 1972) 754–5. A fifth edition (Froben 1535), the last which appeared during Erasmus' lifetime, contained only minor alterations to the fourth.

As has been seen (Ep 373 introduction), Erasmus' study of the Latin texts of the New Testament began in 1505–6. In the years that followed he examined many manuscripts both Latin and Greek (cf lines 54–8 below; Ep 296:64–6; and C.C. Tarelli 'Erasmus's Manuscripts of the Gospels' *Journal of Theological Studies* 44 (1943) 155–62; 48 (1947) 207–8); and seems to have accumulated material so that in time he was prepared to attempt a recension of the Greek text itself. This recension was done in England, probably in 1512–13 (Epp 264:16; 270:67; LB IX 986EF). For this undertaking he had four Greek manuscripts, one of which was the Leicester Codex. This is a manuscript (Codex 69) of the entire New Testament, copied by a Greek from Constantinople who worked for Archbishop Neville of York about 1468, and it is now in the museum of Leicester, England. In the early sixteenth century it was available to Erasmus in Cambridge (see Allen II 164 and Metzger 62).

In July 1514 Erasmus wrote to Servatius Rogerus: 'I have also revised the whole of the New Testament from a collation of the old Greek manuscripts, and have annotated over a thousand places ...' (Ep 296:164–6). He must have negotiated with Froben during August 1514, since on 2 September Beatus Rhenanus rightly or wrongly announced an agreement between them: 'Novum Testamentum Graece hic imprimet Frobenius cum annotationibus illius' (BRE. 40). On 21 September 1514 Erasmus described to Wimpfeling a work combining his Latin version with a Greek text and annotations (Ep 305:228–9); the work he subsequently described to Cardinal Grimani in May 1515, however, was on a less ambitious scale (Ep 334:173–4). During his visit to England in April 1515 Erasmus probably obtained a copy of his complete Latin translation, and by the time he returned to Basel he had evidently decided to proceed with Froben (for evidence of hesitations and further negotiation see Epp 324:26–7; 328:36; 330:1; 389:11n; the death of Aldus on 6 February 1515 may have deterred Erasmus from taking the work to Venice, to take advantage of the experience of that press with setting Greek type); work then began in August.

Most of the manuscripts used by Erasmus in Basel were from the bequest of Cardinal Ivan Stojković of Ragusa to the Dominicans of Basel; cf Ep 300:35n. It appears that he had hoped to find a good Greek codex to serve as a base text for his edition, but he was disappointed (Ep 421:55–7). In the end five manuscripts chiefly were employed, including that borrowed by Reuchlin from the

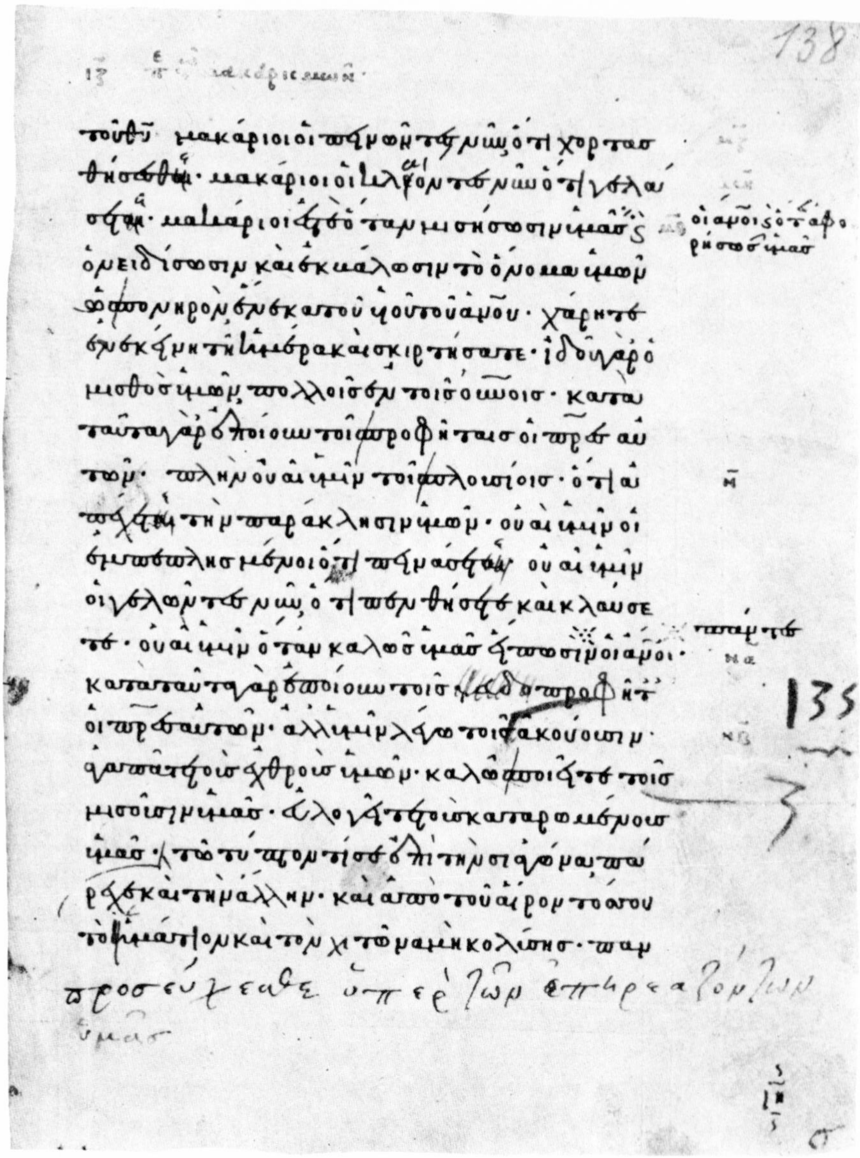

A page from Codex 2e, the Greek Gospel manuscript
prepared by Erasmus for the printer's use, and showing both
his corrections and the printer's marks.
The text is that of Luke 6:20–30.
Öffentliche Bibliothek, University of Basel, MS AN IV 1 f 138r

tion, of the New Testament in the Aldine Bible in Greek (1518), and, through the third edition of Robert Estienne's Greek Testament, for which it was the base text (Paris 1550; the first edition to have a critical apparatus), Erasmus' New Testament heavily influenced the Greek Testament of Théodore de Bèze (1519–1605). It is this text that underlies the King James version and the Elzevir Greek Testament in 1633, which proclaimed it the 'received text' ('Textum ergo habes, nunc ab omnibus receptum'). Thus was created the so-called 'Textus receptus,' the foundation of Protestant biblical scholarship for three centuries, until the nineteenth century ushered in a new era of biblical criticism.

TO LEO THE TENTH, PONTIFF SUPREME IN EVERY WAY, FROM ERASMUS OF ROTTERDAM, LEAST OF THEOLOGIANS, GREETING

Many and great were the distinctions, most holy Father, which made you universally renowned and respected before you ascended the pontifical throne as His Holiness Pope Leo the Tenth; on the one hand the uncounted glories of the house of Medici, no less celebrated for the legacy of its eminent scholars than for the glorious line of your ancestors, on the other the innumerable gifts of body and mind of which some were lavished on you by the bounty of Heaven and some achieved under Heaven's encouragement by your own efforts. Yet nothing distinguished you more truly or more amply than your bringing to an office which is the greatest that can fall to a mortal among mortal men an equally great integrity of character – a life far, far removed from everything discreditable and, what is more, a reputation unsullied by any shadow of suggestive rumour. Hard enough anywhere, this is particularly hard to achieve in Rome; for in that city the liberty (not to call it licence) of speech is such that integrity itself is not safe from slander and even those men who are entirely free from faults are not free from aspersions. We can truly say that to have deserved the papal dignity brought Leo far more true glory than to have received it.

And now, in the exercise of your most holy office, you in turn enhance the eminence conferred upon you by many glorious acts and many outstanding virtues; but nothing more effectively commends you alike to Heaven and to mortal men than the great zeal and wisdom with which you take as your particular aim the daily advancement of the Christian life, which through the fault of the times and especially the wars has hitherto been undermined and shown signs of collapse. Like all else in human affairs it naturally sinks back by degrees into something worse and seems to degenerate, unless we fight against this with all our might. But to restore great things is sometimes not only a harder but a nobler task than to have introduced them. And so, since you present yourself in the guise of a second Esdras, doing all you can to pacify the storms of war and vigorously pursuing your chosen purpose to rebuild religion, it is right that Christians of all lands and all peoples should support, each of them to the best of his power, one who follows this most noble and most profitable aim. Already I see men of outstanding gifts, like great and wealthy kings, sending our Solomon their marbles, their ivory, their gold, their precious stones for the building of his Temple. We petty chieftains, we mere mortals, gladly bring what we can, timber perhaps or goatskins at any rate, rather than contribute nothing – an offering worth very little if measured by the help we actually give, but (unless I am all astray) likely to be of not a little use though not much beauty in the temple of Christ, especially if it win the approval of him whose yea or nay alone governs the whole sum of human things.

For one thing I found crystal clear: our chiefest hope for the restoration and rebuilding of the Christian religion, our sheet-anchor as they call it, is that all those who profess the Christian philosophy the whole world over should above all absorb the principles laid down by their Founder from the writings of the evangelists and apostles, in which that heavenly Word which once came down to us from the heart of the Father still lives and breathes for us and acts and speaks with more immediate efficacy, in my opinion, than in any other way. Besides which I perceived that that teaching which is our salvation was to be had in a much purer and more lively form if sought at the fountain-head and drawn from the actual sources than from pools and runnels. And so I have revised the whole New Testament (as they call it) against the standard of the Greek original, not unadvisedly or with little effort, but calling in the assistance of a number of manuscripts in both languages, and those not the first comers but both very old and very

* * * * *

384:32 Esdras] The Greek and Latin form of Ezra, the name of the prophet involved in the rebuilding of the temple after the Babylonian exile; cf Ezra 7.

38 Temple] An allusion to the building of St Peter's

45 sheet-anchor] *Adagia* I i 24

48 Word] Here rendered by *verbum*. In the second edition of March 1519 the word used was *sermo*, following the change in his accompanying translation of John 1:1. The second version departed from a prudent adherence to the Vulgate text to return to Erasmus' original reading. The ensuing controversy resulted in his *Apologia de 'In principio erat sermo,'* printed by Froben in August 1520. See C.A.L. Jarrott 'Erasmus' *In principio erat sermo*: a controversial translation' *Studies in Philology* 61, 1 (1964) 35–40.

57 very old] On the merits of this claim see the introductions to Epp 373 and 384 and the works cited there.

correct. And well knowing that sacred subjects demand equally scrupulous treatment, I was not content with that degree of care, but passed rapidly over all the works of the classical theologians, and ran to earth from their quotations or their comments what each of them had found or altered in his text. I have added annotations of my own, in order in the first place to show the reader what changes I have made, and why; second, to disentangle and explain anything that may be complicated, ambiguous, or obscure; and lastly as a protection, that it might be less easy in future to corrupt what I have restored at the cost of scarcely credible exertions. Not but what, to speak frankly, this whole undertaking might be thought too lowly to be offered to one than whom the world can show nothing greater, were it not fitting that whatever contributes to the restoration of religion should be consecrated by choice to the supreme head of our religion who is its champion.

Nor is there any fear that you may reject this gift of mine, such as it is, for it is not in your high office alone that you represent him whose custom it is to value gifts by the intentions of the giver, who preferred the poor widow's two mites to the rich and splendid offerings of the wealthy. Do we not see every day, hung up in honour of the saints among the offerings of kings gleaming with gold and jewels, garlands of meadow flowers or garden greenery offered by humble folk who are poor in this world's goods but rich in piety? Otherwise, whatever be the produce, great or small, serious or playful, of this small-holding of my mind, it can be claimed entire with perfect right, even if I did not so dedicate it, by the supreme patron and champion of the virtues and of literature among his own people, William Warham, archbishop of Canterbury, true primate of all England in merit as well as title and 'legatus natus,' as they call it, of your Holiness, to whom I owe all that I am and not merely the entire produce of my labours. For, to say nothing for the moment of what he has meant for me in public and in private, he does for his native England what Leo does for the whole world, and what the house of Medici has so long been doing for Italy (making it, if for no other reason, the most fortunate country of them all); he is for his fellow-Englishmen a kind of favourable star, a gift of Fate itself, that under his leadership all that is good may germinate afresh and grow. For, just as though several great men were united in one body and more than one divine spirit dwelt in that single heart, he is in a wonderful way archbishop to the church, legate to the Roman see, privy councillor to the court, chancellor to the courts of justice, and Maecenas to the humanities. It is his doing more than any man's that an island long renowned for its men and arms and riches now shows such a high standard also in laws, religion, and public morality, and even in gifted minds cultivated in every branch of letters, that it can contend on equal terms with any other region of the world.

But to secure for this labour of mine a wider sphere of usefulness I have decided to borrow your name, as one which all men venerate, to bait the hook as it were, for the general advantage of the world, especially as this course is suggested by the facts: it was exquisitely appropriate that this Christian philosophy should be channeled to every mortal under the auspices of him who holds the citadel of the Christian religion, and that the heavenly teaching should set out on its mission to the human race through him, through whom it was Christ's will that we should receive all that raises man from earth to Heaven. Although for that matter why should not this book go forth into men's hands supported by a double commendation, that is, with even better prospect of success, by being dedicated in common to the whole world's two greatest men, just as we see altars and churches gain in sanctity and grandeur when they are dedicated to more than one saint? It does not matter how novel this may seem, provided it is for the public good. And Leo is so modest, so approachable, that this quality contributes to his greatness not less than the other quality in which he far surpasses all other great men; the archbishop is so outstanding in every kind of merit that, if Leo with his all-round supremacy is to have a colleague, one could not find a more suitable one. And one last word: if it is proper before so great a prince to show a touch of Thraso in the comedy, this work of mine may look at first sight as humble as you please, but I am confident that the attentive reader will find much more within than my work displays on the surface.

But your Highness must be continually attentive to the welfare of the whole world, and if I take up more of your time by writing at greater length I shall do the public a disservice; so I must from this point forward do business with the common reader. First let me say a prayer: May it be his will whose providence gave us our tenth Leo to make the world a better place, that he may live among us as long as possible in health and happiness.

Basel, 1 February in the year of our salvation 1516

385 / To Jakob Wimpfeling — Basel, 3 February [1516]

The year is deduced from mention of the New Testament and Jerome. The letter was printed in Battista Spagnuoli's *Fasti* (Strasbourg: Schürer August 1518), a book edited by Wimpfeling as a suitable work to be read in schools.

* * * * *

120 Thraso] The boastful soldier in Terence's *Eunuchus*

ERASMUS OF ROTTERDAM TO JAKOB WIMPFELING

We are alive and well and often think of you and are devoted to you, all of us, and if you can manage it conveniently, we look for a visit from you too. The New Testament is hastening to its finish. Jerome is coming along nicely. Witz's opinion surprises me. I must say, whoever it was who persuaded him to take that line, he was a perfect idiot. I would rather have half a line of Mantuanus than thirty thousand by Marullus. Mind you recover your health and throw off both your gout and your sore places. I had written to abbot Volz but the letter went astray; I don't know whose fault it was. I wrote so as to stop you complaining that I had not written. Farewell. Greetings from our whole society – all scholars excepting me, all devoted to you not excepting me.

Basel, morrow of the Purification, 151[7]

386 / From Urbanus Regius to Johannes Fabri

Ingolstadt, [c February 1516]

With this letter an offer of a post at the university of Ingolstadt was conveyed to Erasmus from Duke Ernest (1500–60), third son of Duke Albert IV of Bavaria. The prince had been educated in Italy by private tuition, and in 1515 matriculated at the university founded by his kinsman, Duke Louis, in 1472, on the model of Frederick II's university at Naples, to provide an educated nobility for the administration and church of Bavaria. The writer, whose real name was probably Urban Rieger, was born in 1489 in Langenargen on Lake Constance, and died in 1528. He had been a pupil of Zasius, and in about 1510 removed to Ingolstadt with Johann Eck, who eventually secured for him a lectureship in rhetoric and poetry. In 1517 he was crowned poet laureate by Maximilian. He writes to another pupil of Zasius, Johann Heigerlin (1478–1541), known as Johannes Fabri, the son of a smith of Leutkirch in the Allgäu, from whose occupation he took his adopted name. He had studied at Tübingen as well as Freiburg, and by this time was chancellor to the bishop of Basel. He later

* * * * *

385:5 Witz] Cf Ep 323 introduction.

7 Mantuanus] For Erasmus' high opinion of his poems see Ep 49:112–15.

7 Marullus] Michael Tarchaniota (c 1445–1500), the classical scholar, was born of Greek parents at Byzantium and brought to Italy after the Turkish conquest. He was in the service of Lorenzo de' Medici as soldier and humanist, and his *Epigrammata* were printed at Rome in 1490 and 1493 and in Florence in 1497, with his *Hymni naturales* addressed to the gods of Greece and Rome. Schürer had reprinted this last volume in 1509 with two prefaces by Beatus Rhenanus, one addressed to Witz.

became bishop of Vienna and a patron of scholarly support for the Catholic Reformation, in which role he founded the trilingual college of St Nicholas at the university of Vienna. He was a staunch supporter of Erasmus, and in 1528 tried to persuade him to settle in Vienna. The letter was first published in the *Epistolae ad Erasmum* (1516).

TO THE RIGHT WORTHY DR JOHANNES FABER, DOCTOR OF CANON LAW, EMINENT THEOLOGIAN, FROM URBANUS REGIUS

I wrote to you lately, eminent sir, describing the present state of my affairs, the studies on which I am engaged, and what hopes I now have after the many ups and downs through which I have had to pass. How gratefully I accepted the hospitality of yourself and Dr Wolfgang is easier imagined than described; but you have seen that, if I lack all else, it is not loyalty and gratitude. My brother, who has delivered this letter to you, has only one very small request to make of you, which is help in finding a post as a servant-pupil. He is a young man of mettle, which indulgence on my part might have encouraged, but exile and correction by strangers will bring this down without much trouble. In this matter if you can assist him – he is an inexperienced boy, but in other ways reliable – you will find you have secured another brother.

It is reported that the great scholar Rotterdam is with you, who has long been most closely associated with you, because your lives and interests have so much in common. I will therefore entrust to the kindness of yourself and Dr Wolfgang something which I much want to bring to his attention, for it would be improper if I had written to so great a man directly. You are, I think, aware of the more than paternal love and generosity with which the illustrious Duke Ernest of Bavaria encourages and enriches our university at Ingolstadt, adding the lustre of his own distinguished presence, so that it may risk comparison with the greatest academic institutions; and he has it in mind to offer employment to the best scholars to be found anywhere in Germany and endow them splendidly at his own expense, that under his auspices barbarism may be routed at last, and all liberal studies, which have been hard pressed on both flanks until now, may flourish once more and be restored to their original brilliance. Now Erasmus, the man of universal learning, with his wonderful gifts and

* * * * *

386:6 Wolfgang] Köpfel, also known as Faber or Capito; see Ep 459 introduction.

8 brother] He is not otherwise known.

21 Duke Ernest] See introduction.

exceptional range of knowledge, seems to our prince to deserve honour and encouragement of every kind; and therefore he has made careful enquiry whether there are any terms on which this great champion of humane studies could be induced to give regular courses among us on some subject, and water our desert with the manifold rivers of his eloquence and erudition: a proposal which has met with strong opposition in some quarters, while others maintain that his presence is much to be desired. The prince himself has adhered obstinately to his proposal, and means to spare no expense to secure Erasmus.

I want therefore to know from you what you think: should a lucrative offer be made to Erasmus? If you think he could be persuaded to say yes to so great a prince, who sets the highest value on him, write back to me as soon as possible. There are many reasons which should move him, as a German, to spend the rest of his life in Germany. First of all the enthusiastic support of a great prince and his genuine love of humane studies, for the prince has had a good education in these subjects from teachers who are by no means to be despised, and hence would have a very special affection for Erasmus, which to a man of exalted mind must seem a great advantage. And then he will be generously provided for and endowed with an honourable salary and benefices, if he accepts. If he excuses himself on the ground of age, when the labours of teaching are already burdensome, there is nothing here to deter him, for he will be ensured a peaceful and pleasant life; he is not invited in order to wear him out, but that this exceptional man may be seen among us, and by his presence add lustre to our university. Besides, there is the beauty of the place, and a wonderful healthy climate such as he will not easily find elsewhere, so that this home of seekers after knowledge well deserves its name of 'Angel-city.' To this one may add the honours which an upright mind gratefully accepts as the due reward of virtue; for there will be such competition to load him with distinctions that, with his exceptional modesty, he may well complain that what is done for him is onerous rather than honourable. To conclude, everything will smile upon Erasmus. If, before he accepts an offer of this kind, he would prefer to come and see our prince and to inspect the place, the prince gladly offers to pay his travelling expenses and a by no means despicable honorarium. Please therefore make it your business to go and see Erasmus and persuade him by every means in your power; apply exhortation and encouragement; show him with emphasis how much the prince admires him; and urge him, if you can, to live in Germany, under his native sky with his own people, and be of

* * * * *

43 German] Cf Ep 310:18.

use to them, instead of with strangers. Among them, perhaps, everything that makes for comfort or reputation may be available beyond his needs, but one's own country should command more affection and respect, especially when it longs with such ardent enthusiasm for the leader and the teacher of all knowledge, who is its own son.

Such is the subject on which at this moment I set out to write to you, my teacher and patron, and very much to the point; for such is your influence with Erasmus, that no one could persuade him better or more easily than you. Farewell, most excellent of teachers.

From Ingolstadt. Urbanus Regius

I wrote this on instructions from Prince Ernest and Master Leonard Eck, a man of good family and a doctor in arts and law, the head of our university, with whom I am on most friendly terms; he has seen and approved my letter. Moreover the prince is so anxious to get Erasmus that he has sent the courier whom you see to Basel for the sole purpose of inviting him. If he is unwilling to come with the intention of remaining with us, if he will not take two hundred gold pieces a year and very lucrative benefices, the prince makes one further request which he is sure will be granted, that Erasmus should come and pay a visit to the university. He should devote a month to the journey, that the prince may see him and make him welcome, for he is sincerely anxious to see him. He will provide generously for the expenses of the journey and will remunerate him liberally, to show him that the prince admires and respects nothing so much as literature and literary men. Farewell once more.

I have written this in the character of a secretary at the prince's dictation, so pray accept it and act upon it in confidence, as though the prince himself were speaking to you. I send you, my kind master, some speeches of my friend Eck the theologian, who has the highest opinion of you.

* * * * *

79 Eck] Leonhard von Eck of Kelheim (d 1550), of a noble Bavarian family, was a graduate of Ingolstadt who had studied law at Siena before being appointed tutor to Duke William IV. In 1519 he was chancellor to the duchy of Bavaria.

84 two hundred gold pieces] Probably Rhenish florins of the Four Electors. If so, this annual sum would have amounted, in official values, to about £48 6s 8d groot Flemish = £287 12s od tournois = £34 3s 4d sterling. Cf Epp 326B:8n, 15n; 370:18n; CWE 1 317, 336–9; CWE 2 327–45.

95 Eck] Johann Maier of Eck, known as Johann Eck or Johannes Eckius (d 1543), the theologian and famous opponent of Luther, who had been professor of theology at Ingolstadt since 1510. Two collections of his *Orationes* were published at this time, both in Augsburg: J. Otmar 24 December 1513; and J. Miller 5 December 1515.

387 / From Thomas Bedyll London, 10 February [1516]

Bedyll graduated BCL from New College, Oxford, on 5 November 1508, and died in 1537. At this time he was secretary to Archbishop Warham, Erasmus' patron, and later found active employment with Cromwell's many commissions; see Dom David Knowles *The Religious Orders in England* III (Cambridge 1959) 273–4.

THOMAS BEDYLL TO MASTER ERASMUS

Greetings, most learned Erasmus. I took care to raise your business about the stipend with his Grace, and he has written to Maruffo to send it to you without deduction; this he promised to do by courier, when both More and I were present. His Grace warmly approves your plan that the new version of the New Testament made by yourself should be dedicated to the Holy Father, and speaks most highly of you in every respect whenever your name is mentioned (which happens quite often on my initiative), because you lavish so much labour and all these midnight hours on good literature and the Holy Scriptures. This not only promises you an immortal name, but has secured it already. That is why my master has solemnly undertaken that he will never fail to assist you generously as you deserve. Your reverence will feel the effects of this more fully every day; and if there is anything I myself can do that can secure you long life and prosperity, you shall not want for it.

London, 10 February

388 / From Thomas More [London, c 17 February 1516]

This, the first surviving letter from More to Erasmus, is replying to three letters that More had received from Erasmus since June. Its dating centres on the reference (line 114n) to Tunstall's appointment. Allen has argued that the similarity to Ep 389 suggests that the two letters are contemporary, and that this one is slightly earlier since there is no allusion in it to the birth of Princess Mary. This demands the plausible supposition that Tunstall knew about his appointment before the actual commission was signed. The letter was first published in *Epistolae ad Erasmum*.

* * * * *

387:3 Maruffo] Raffaele (fl 1509–35), a merchant of Genoa in England, through whom Erasmus' English annuity was usually paid. The deduction was no doubt a commission for his services. There are regular references to him in the early correspondence, and in 1535 he is mentioned as the source of one report on the fate of More and Fisher (Ep 3042).

14 want for it] Reading 'potest, non desiderabit quo diu' etc

THOMAS MORE TO HIS FRIEND ERASMUS

Since you left us, dearest Erasmus, I have received three letters from you in all. If I were to say I had sent you three answers, you will perhaps not believe me, even if I lie in the most sanctimonious manner, especially as you know me so well for a very idle correspondent, and not so morbidly devoted to the truth that I would as soon commit parricide as utter a modest fib. Our friend Pace is on a mission in your part of the world, although not exactly where you are; he is lost to us, but this does you no good. He can converse with me by letter, but face to face neither with me nor with you; I only hope his business will go well and he will soon return home, so that I may enjoy the society of one-half of myself, at any rate. For when I am to expect you I do not see, if you have a mind to go to Italy, where you will fall into the hands of people who I fear will not allow you to be torn from them. In the meantime I feel as though I had lost one-half of myself in Pace, and the other half in you. I hope we shall see some outstanding piece of good fortune come his way, such as he deserves. I really think the king's intentions and the good will of the cardinal and the support of everyone worth having point towards his promotion to some really distinguished post.

For you, were not my hope so often disappointed, I should expect much greater things; though, even now, why should not one hope for the best? If we have not had much success hitherto, it does not follow that we lose hope for the future; in fact I am more confident now than I ever was. Fortune never continues always the same for anybody, and she cannot be ungenerous to you much longer, now that pope, kings, bishops, and almost all mortal men all over Christendom strongly support you and admire you so much. Among us here it is unnecessary to say what the attitude of the bishops is, and quite specially of his grace of Canterbury, and what a high opinion of you the king himself has. If so far no benefice adequate either to your wants or to the high opinion held of you by our great men has come your way, the reason lies partly in you, for neglecting the objects of other men's ambition, and partly in some sort of bad luck; as has happened just

* * * * *

388:2 three letters] These letters, which are lost, were perhaps written at the same time as those to Ammonio. Cf Ep 389 introduction and line 2.

7 Pace] He was involved in negotiations with the Swiss; cf Ep 382:3n; Ep 378:9; and also Ep 211:53n.

12 I do not see] Erasmus returned to England in July/August 1516.

16 deserves] Pace was employed continuously in diplomatic activity until 1525, and although he was well rewarded with lucrative preferments, his strenuous career ruined his health; see Wegg chap 13.

lately with that canonry, as they call it, at Tournai, which Lord Mountjoy had secured for you. You seem now not to be against the idea, for you say in your letter that you have sent Mountjoy all the documents which you thought relevant to your appointment to it. But I spoke with you about it, if you remember, when you were with me in Bruges, and you listed all the advantages and also the disadvantages of the benefice, and seemed to be against it; nor did you conceal this from Sampson, who is the bishop of York's vicar-general in Tournai. You were inclined to this opinion, not only because you feared your tenure would be short-lived, unless you could also secure the approval of the other bishop, whom you did not expect to find ready to ratify his rival's action, since he tries to undo everything the other does; but also since, besides nearly ten pounds of our money which you would have to pay in cash on your first entering on the benefice, you had to pay off a mortgage of two hundred nobles or more on the house. Such is the custom there, and unless you comply with it, you will get hardly six nobles

* * * * *

32 Tournai] Cf Ep 360:16n.

36 Bruges] In May or early June, during More's embassy to the prince Charles to restore the advantageous commercial relations interrupted on the accession of Francis I; cf Ep 362:12–14.

38 Sampson] Richard Sampson (c 1484–1554) was a chaplain to Wolsey, who made him vicar-general in September 1514, when Wolsey was bishop of Tournai. Sampson was a BCL from Trinity Hall, Cambridge (1506), and had studied further at Paris and Siena, receiving his DCL in 1513 at Cambridge. He entered Wolsey's service on condition that he be allowed to continue his legal studies, and was still in Tournai early in 1518 when Erasmus met him there, having known him earlier at Cambridge. He became a distinguished royal diplomat and apologist, and held the sees of both Chichester (1536–43) and Lichfield and Coventry (1543–54).

41 other bishop] Louis Guillard; cf Ep 360:20n.

43 ten pounds] £10 sterling, worth approximately, in equivalent silver values (the mint par), £14 10s 9d groot Flemish = £84 7s 5d tournois. Cf CWE 1 330, 347; CWE 2 327, 345.

44 in cash] Reading 'numerandae'

45 two hundred nobles] By 'noble' More probably meant the traditional money-of-account value of one-half a mark or 6s 8d sterling, the value of the current gold angel-noble, and not the gold ryal (rose-noble). If indeed the former, this mortgage would have been worth at least £66 13s 4d sterling = £96 13s 4d groot Flemish = £568 17s 9d tournois, by relative gold values. Cf CWE 1 312, 319 (plate), 325, 336–7; CWE 2 146 (Ep 214:4n), 327–45, 340 (plate); and below Epp 421:140, 425:12, 436:6.

46 six nobles] If half a mark is again meant, as above, then a sum of £2 0s 0d sterling = £2 18s 0d groot Flemish = £17 1s 4d tournois, by relative gold values.

a year – and even those you will not get, by what I have heard, unless you reside there permanently. These were the reasons why both Sampson and I thought you were not going to accept that canonry.

A little after you had left me I went to Tournai. There I heard from Lord Mountjoy and also from Sampson that the archbishop of York had written to both of them that the benefice should be given to someone else, to whom apparently he had promised it, not knowing it was destined for you. On hearing this I concealed the fact that I understood the benefice was not really what you wanted, and advised them to write back that it had been granted to you, and the position was that a change could not be made unless he provided you with something better. His grace of York replied that this place would not be at all suitable for you, since it was inadequately endowed if you were in residence and brought in nothing to an absentee; so they must take his word for it that you would be given something better. So, while I was there, and certainly with no discouragement from me, they had decided to give that benefice to the bishop's candidate. What happened after that I do not know. But this I do know, that unless you have this one, the cardinal owes you a richer one, and I hope he will soon redeem his promise. He often threw in a very friendly mention of you.

As for your annuity, it was quite unnecessary for me to ask the bishop for it. He remembered it of his own accord, and before he got my letter had taken up the question with Maruffo, whom as you know he always uses as his agent in such matters, and sometimes as his banker too, until they compare accounts at regular intervals and square up. But the moment he had my letter (for he was then at Otford), he wrote to the man to jog his memory: would he send you twenty pounds of our money without delay? promising that he would reimburse Maruffo as soon as he knew from your signed receipt that the money had reached you. I went to see Maruffo. He said he would write and ask you to send him with all speed the document that proves you have had the money, so that he can take it to the bishop; and when the money has been paid over to him in cash on that understanding,

* * * * *

62 bishop's] *Episcopus*, ie Wolsey, the archbishop of York. Cf Allen Epp 468:5; 481:82.

66 bishop] Warham, as at lines 76 and 81

68 Maruffo] Cf Ep 387:3n.

71 Otford] A residence of Archbishop Warham in Kent

72 twenty pounds of our money] £20 sterling, worth approximately, in equivalent silver values, £29 1s 6d groot Flemish = £168 14s 10d tournois; in equivalent gold values, at official rates, £29 0s 0d groot Flemish = £170 13s 4d tournois. Cf CWE 2 327–45; and Epp 421:140, 425:12, 436:6 below.

he will at last arrange for it to be remitted to you. When I heard this, I was afraid there might be a certain risk that, if the cash were not immediately paid to him, the delay might in turn be passed on to you. 'No,' I said, 'there is no need for this subterfuge. Either send the money at once in the bishop's name and trust him to refund it to you or, if you do not like to send it unless you have had it first, I will see that you get the cash forthwith.' 'It's all right' was his reply; 'you have nothing to be afraid of. I will arrange for Erasmus to get the money immediately, and in fact he has already got it now. He has a letter of credit from me, on which he can draw a thousand ducats whenever he likes; and any part of that that he may take up is due to be made good to me (that was the arrangement between us) out of this annuity.' Those are his words. Personally I hardly believe he would have given you any letter on which you could draw cash, unless he had previously seen the money deposited on his counter. So if things are different from what he says, mind you let me know soon.

The archbishop of Canterbury, after some years of strenuous effort to secure his liberty, has at last been allowed to resign the office of chancellor and, having secured the privacy he has so long desired, is now enjoying the delights of leisure among his books and the memories of a most successful administration. His Majesty has appointed the cardinal of York in his place, and he is doing so well that he goes far beyond universal expectation, although this was very great on account of his other virtues, and (a very difficult achievement) wins golden opinions even after such an admirable predecessor.

My mission, since you are so good as to ask after it, went pretty well, as do all my affairs, except that things were spun out to greater length than I hoped or wanted. When I left home, I expected to be away barely two months, and I wasted on that mission more than six. But the long delay issued at last in a fairly satisfactory result. So when I saw that the business for which I had come was now completed, and yet that one thing was

* * * * *

86 a thousand ducats] Venetian gold coins, or equivalent value. At official rates this sum would have been worth £229 3s 4d sterling = £1938 0s 0d tournois = £329 3s 4d groot Flemish. Cf CWE 1 314, 338–9, 342–4; CWE 2 327–45.

93 Canterbury] Warham resigned as chancellor in favour of Wolsey on 22 December 1515; LP II 1335.

97 York] Wolsey received the Great Seal on 24 December; LP II 1335.

102 mission] More's embassy, which began with the commission of 7 May 1515; cf Epp 332:19n, 362:12n. Wolsey allowed him to return to England by mid-October, and he left Bruges about 22 October. The meeting with Pace was on 24 October; cf LP II 1059, 1067.

leading to another, which might be the beginning of still more delay (there is never any lack of such things in the affairs of princes), I wrote to the cardinal and obtained permission for myself to return, using for this purpose the help of my friends and especially of Pace, for he had not yet left. But while I was on my way home, I suddenly fell in with him at Gravelines, travelling in such a hurry that he would hardly stop for an exchange of greetings. Tunstall has just returned to his post after a stay here of barely ten days, none of which he spent agreeably as his own master; but after devoting the whole of that time to an anxious and tedious exposition of the affairs which had been the object of his mission, lo and behold he is posted off again suddenly on another errand to the same place, and most reluctantly (as I know full well) if he had had the chance to refuse.

I never much liked the position of an envoy. Nor does it seem to me so suitable for us laymen as it is for you priests, who to begin with have no wives and children at home, or find them everywhere. We laymen, if we are away for a short time, are immediately haled back by longing for our wives and families. And then, when a priest is sent, he can carry his whole household with him wherever he likes, and feed for the time at the king's expense the mouths he would otherwise have to feed at home at his own. But when I am away, I have to support two households, one at home and the other abroad. The king made me quite a generous allowance for the party I took out with me; but no account was taken of those I had meanwhile to leave at home, and I failed completely (although I am, as you know, a kind husband, an indulgent father, and a reasonable master) to persuade my family for my sake to go without eating for a short time until my return. Lastly, priests can be very easily rewarded by monarchs for their labour and expense with ecclesiastical preferment, without any expenditure on their part; but we cannot be dealt with so generously or so easily; although on my return the king did award me an annuity, and one that was very much not to be despised, whether one considers the honour or the profit of it. Hitherto however I have refused it, and it looks to me as though I should maintain

* * * * *

112 Gravelines] The port just west of Dunkirk

114 Tunstall] He returned to England from Brussels on 29 January 1516, and on 19 February received a fresh commission to arrange a treaty between England and Castile; cf LP II 1458, 1459, 1574.

136 annuity] Of £100 sterling (= £145 7s 6d groot Flemish = £843 14s od tournois), granted to him on 21 June 1518, backdated to Michaelmas 1517; he then resigned as under-sheriff of London. See G.R. Elton 'Thomas More, Councillor' in *St. Thomas More: Action and Contemplation* ed R.S. Sylvester (New Haven 1972) 88–90.

my refusal. If I accepted it, I should have either to abandon my present position in London, which I prefer even to something better, or (which I should much regret) to incur some unpopularity among my fellow-citizens by retaining it; for if any question about their privileges arose between them and the king (as sometimes happens), they would think me less single-minded and less devoted to their interests, as being in receipt of an annual subvention from his Majesty.

All the same there were some things in that embassy of mine which I enjoyed very much. First of all, the prolonged and unbroken association with Tunstall, for not only is he as good a scholar in the humanities and as upright in character and life as anyone we have, but no one's company anywhere is more enjoyable. And then I struck up a friendship with Busleyden, whose reception of me was very splendid for he has a great fortune, and very courteous for he has a kind heart. He opened to me his house, with its exceptional decoration and remarkable contents; his great collection of antiquities, of which you know me to be very fond; and lastly his nobly furnished library, and his own mind better stored than any library could be, until there was no more spirit left in me. I hear that he is very shortly to undertake a mission to our king. But in all my travels I had no greater good fortune than the society of Pieter Gillis, your host in Antwerp, such a good scholar and so amusing and modest and such a good friend, that I swear I would cheerfully barter a good part of my fortune for the sole pleasure of his company. He sent me your *Defence* and your notes on the first psalm, the '*Beatus vir*,' dedicated to Beatus Rhenanus, who is truly blest (if for no other reason) in the receipt of so great and enduring a memorial from his friend. Dorp has arranged to have his letter printed, to be prefixed to your *Defence*. I had hoped to meet him, had an opportunity arisen. Since this was impossible, I paid my respects at least by letter, or rather by a truly Laconic missive, for there was no time for anything longer;

* * * * *

151 Busleyden] Cf Ep 205 introduction. He had a great mansion at Mechelen, now the town museum, which More describes here. The *Utopia* was printed with an introductory letter by Pieter Gillis to Busleyden, and More's *Epigrammata* contain verses on this house and his coin collection. He left the Netherlands in June 1517 to accompany Charles after his accession as king of Castile and died on the way, in Bordeaux, of pleurisy.

158 Gillis] Cf Ep 184 introduction.

161 *Defence*] Ep 337; see introduction.

161 notes] Cf Ep 327 introduction.

164 letter] Ep 304

167 missive] Rogers Ep 15

but I was unwilling to pass over without any greeting a man whom I approve of to a surprising degree, not only for his exceptional learning but on many other grounds, not least because by criticizing your *Moria* he gave me the opportunity of writing something in your defence.

I am delighted that Jerome and the New Testament make such good progress. It is remarkable how keenly they are awaited by everyone on all sides. Linacre, my dear Erasmus (take my word for it), both thinks of you and speaks of you everywhere in a most proper spirit, as I have lately heard from people who were present when he was speaking of you to the king at dinner in a most affectionate and warm-hearted way. And in the same conversation the king in his turn replied in such terms that my informants gained the clear impression that some piece of outstanding promotion would soon be conferred on you; which I pray Heaven it may see fit to ratify.

Farewell, dearest Erasmus, and give my greetings to Rhenanus and to Lyster; I feel I love them more and know them much better from what you have told me of them and from their writings than many of the people I meet every day. My wife sends her respects, and so does Clement, who makes such daily progress in Latin and Greek that I have formed no small hopes of his being one day an ornament to his country and to learning.

* * * * *

174 Linacre] Erasmus had long been unsure of Linacre's attitude towards him; cf Epp 237:62–7; 350:7ff; Allen Epp 502:18–19; 513:8–9.

183 Lyster] Gerard Lyster, a humanist member of the Froben circle, wrote an important commentary on the *Moria*; see Ep 495 introduction.

185 my wife] His second wife, Alice Middleton

185 Clement] John Clement (d 1572) married in 1530 Margaret Giggs, who had been brought up in More's household like a daughter of his own. Clement was educated at St Paul's School, where he was a pupil of Lily, and he became a servant-pupil of More himself. In 1515 he accompanied More on his embassy to Bruges, and by September 1516 he was able to assist Colet in his study of Greek. He also taught More's children, and in April 1518 entered the service of Wolsey, who sent him to his newly founded college at Oxford (1518) as reader of rhetoric and humanity. He left early in 1520 to study medicine at Louvain, and went on to Italy where he received an MD at Siena in 1525. He later assisted in the Aldine edition of Galen, and in 1544 became president of the College of Physicians in London. He was twice exiled for refusal to accept the royal supremacy. In the reign of Edward VI his household became the focus of English recusant migration to Louvain, and after the accession of Elizabeth he finally settled at Mechelen, where he died. Simon Grynaeus' edition of Proclus' *De motu* (Basel: Bebel August 1531) is dedicated to Clement, and he and his wife both received the tribute of one of Leland's *Epithalamia*. See A.W. Reed 'Jo. Clement and his Books' *The Library* 4th series 6 (1926) 329–39.

Farewell once more. You must make do with this one letter for many months, for I am like a miser: he rarely invites anyone to dinner, and if he ever does, he gives the man a prolonged meal, in order for the price of one dinner to escape the expense of having to invite him every day. Farewell for the third time.

The bishop of Durham much appreciated the dedication of your Seneca. You see I am your sincere admirer, for I now send you a letter in someone else's hand, just as you lately did to me – so much resolved to imitate you, in fact, that I should not have written even this with my own hand, except to leave you in no doubt that this letter comes from me.

389 / From Andrea Ammonio — London, [18] February [1516]

This letter, like the preceding letter from More, was evidently Ammonio's first to Erasmus since his departure from England the previous May. It was sent to Pace and failed to reach Erasmus, so that Ammonio sent another copy of it in June, by which time Erasmus had returned to the Netherlands (Epp 427, 429). On the uncertainty in England about Erasmus' whereabouts see Ep 338 introduction. This letter was first published in *Epistolae ad Erasmum*.

ANDREA AMMONIO TO ERASMUS

What peace-offerings can I make, after waiting to answer two of your letters until a third arrived? I would rather confess my offence than produce foolish reasons, although there are some reasons which seem to me not altogether foolish. I was afraid of wasting my time, which I have to economize very carefully just now under the pressure of tedious business, as I should be writing to an uncertain address; because when you had had more than enough of those stinking stoves, you said at first that you would be leaving Germany about the first of November, and later you said after Christmas, but you seemed not yet to have made up your mind whether you would go to Rome or come back here or set off for Venice. And so before I answered I expected to be told where you had settled down. Meanwhile, however, in case you had gone to Rome, I wrote to commend you warmly to my old patron the bishop of Worcester, our king's envoy to the holy see. From him

* * * * *

193 Durham] Erasmus dedicated his *Senecae lucubrationes* to Ruthall on 7 March 1515; cf Epp 325, 437.

389:11 Venice] Perhaps a Venetian publisher had been talked of as an alternative to Froben.

14 Worcester] Silvestro Gigli; cf Ep 521 introduction.

(and indeed the very columns of the palace echoed with it) you would at once have learnt of the exceptional interest which the pope takes in you, and you would have been caught up immediately into his entourage. If on the other hand you had preferred Britain to Italy, what need was there of a letter between neighbours? But now that you have postponed your departure from where you are until the first of March (as you say in your letter) or until the first of May (which is my own guess), I am willing to risk a little trouble on you. So let me tell you what I think you ought to know.

I have had from the pope three of those letters which they call briefs, two addressed to you in exactly the same wording, and another to the king, in which you are most warmly recommended to him, as you will learn from this copy of it. The letter addressed to you I took the liberty of opening, presuming on the rights of friendship, for I wanted very badly to know what grounds for hope it might contain; and I now send you one of the briefs, together with the copy of the letter of recommendation, but the letter itself and the other brief I am carefully keeping for you here. If you do not return here, let me know what you want done with the letter of recommendation. You will say that you ought to have thought about this before, and maybe you will think the letter too ancient to be delivered to the king. But take my word for it, it will be just the same as if it had been done lately. Hardly any attention is paid to such details, when it is not a question of demanding money on a bill of exchange. The bishop of Worcester also wrote to me that Leo was highly delighted with your letter, and made diligent enquiries about you, where you are, what you are engaged on, and whether he thought you would be willing to come to Rome, with many other signs of his being very well disposed towards you. He then turned to some who were with him, good scholars and very rich people, and gave them your letter, adding his own judgment on your rare genius and learning; and all vied with one another in singing your praises. For the old custom still holds good, 'at least admire and praise the learned man,' though our Leo does at least encourage and enrich them, and he is the great hope of liberal studies. To him I should advise you to hasten with all speed, if I thought of your own advantage; if of my own pleasure, I should say hurry back to us. Whichever you decide, may God bless the outcome.

As for Jerome, I do not doubt that your efforts have been well spent,

* * * * *

23 briefs] Cf Ep 338 introduction.

37 your letter] Ep 335

44 learned man] Juvenal 7.31

and I look forward greatly to its appearance. Your edition of Seneca is now on sale here. Do you ask my opinion? – I would say you have followed Apelles' method in painting his Venus. With your New Testament I am quite delighted, and I congratulate you on it; in my view it is a work of true religion, which richly deserves to be studied by everyone, full to the brim of genius and erudition, and signally worthy of you and of the pope to whom you have decided to dedicate it. Well done indeed! – this way to the stars. What is this about a dream, in which you say you were endowed by the archbishop of York and think he made a mockery of you? I wish you had written in more detail. In any case it cannot be right about the mockery; nothing could be less like him. In fact I know he has a very high opinion of you; but something happened that he neither wished nor expected, which perhaps could still be put right.

That is all I have to report about your affairs at the moment. I will add some English news. The queen has had a charming baby daughter. Your friend the archbishop of Canterbury has resigned his office with the king's leave, and his grace of York after urgent entreaty has succeeded him, and is doing very well. More has completed his mission among those Dutchmen of yours with distinction, and is now home again; he haunts those smoky palace fires in my company. None bids my lord of York good morrow earlier than he. Pace is getting on so well in your part of the world that I think he is much to be congratulated. My own affairs go forward slowly, but not badly, if only I can keep my health. And mind, my dear Erasmus, you keep yours.

London, 18 February [1517]

390 / From Udalricus Zasius Freiburg im Breisgau, 20 February 1516

UDALRICUS ZASIUS TO MASTER ERASMUS, WITH HUMBLE DUTY

Spare me a moment, greatest of men; let me send you my greetings, and also

* * * * *

50 Seneca] Cf Ep 325.

52 Apelles] In painting his Venus he put together the most elegant features of all the most beautiful women he knew; so the Seneca is an anthology of perfections.

56 Well done] Adapted from Virgil *Aeneid* 9.641

57 dream] Cf Epp 360, 388.

64 daughter] The princess Mary, born at 4 am on 18 February; LP II 1556, 1573.

69 good morrow] Cf Martial 1.55.6.

warn you briefly that these are my sons-in-law who come to call upon your illustrious self. One of them is a member of the best business circles in Augsburg, an educated man, especially in the law, and one whose character deserves respect; the other is also in business; both are young. If you would show them the kindness of a brief interview, when you have a spare moment, you will make me a happy man; for nothing that comes from you, even the smallest utterance, can fail to make a man happy.

Farewell, dear patron, from Freiburg, 20 February 1516.

In my work on the origin of law, I have been obliged sometimes to use very ill-written authorities, because I write for uneducated students, who do not know what good writing is. I am afraid that, barbarian as I am, my style will be more polished than my readers can swallow; so far have the admirable principles of the classical lawyers fallen out of use. I am not capable of a solo part, I cannot write for the learned; you must forgive me if I play my humble flute while others dance. I leave to you the great and splendid themes, the heights of Latinity and philosophy and ethics. You shall be the captain who navigates the three-decker; if I can steer my cockboat, I shall be content.

391 / From Nikolaus Basellius — Hirsau, [c February 1516]

The writer, from Dürkheim near Mannheim, became a Benedictine monk of Hirsau in Würtemberg. At some time he had been a pupil of Trithemius, as had Nikolaus Gerbel. Cf Ep 397 introduction.

NIKOLAUS BASELLIUS TO MASTER ERASMUS OF ROTTERDAM

That I forestalled your learned and delightful letter, most scholarly of all scholars, with my own nonsense, and was the first to break the ice by writing, you will not (I would gladly think) deny, nor suppose that I did it unadvisedly. I could hardly wait for a suitable moment or a certain messenger, but overcome by a sort of unwillingness to brook delay, I should have hastened to send a hireling courier of my own, had not my friend Thomas, who found the bringing of this letter actually a lightening of his burden, fixed a definite day for his departure. Such a love of your charming conversation overcame me long ago during our brief association in Speyer

* * * * *

390:3 sons-in-law] Cf Ep 357:14n for one; the second, Georg Funck, married the elder daughter Catherine about 1513. He came from a mercantile family in Augsburg; cf Winterberg 39–40.

391:3 break the ice] *Adagia* III v 95

10 Speyer] Erasmus was there in June 1515; cf Ep 337 introduction.

(the only time we ever met), and such a strong attachment left its mark upon me, that I could not really control it even if I wished to do so. So outstanding are the unique learning and universal knowledge which in such copious brilliance abound or rather overflow in you, the most learned man in all Germany, that I confess myself intoxicated with admiration and almost beside myself, so that just like Ulysses delayed on his journey home, nothing is so rooted in my mind, nothing has made so permanent an impression on my heart, as the unique and vivid idea of you.

For when my religious duties, and such spare time as I can find for reading, are finished, and I proceed to lay my weary limbs down to rest, I can scarcely tell the dreams that seem to disturb my mind and weary it with strange imaginings; such that I seem as it were to see you face to face and enjoy your conversation even while my senses are bound in sleep, in such a way that my very spirit seems to be exalted beyond itself by a kind of joy. But when I have laid down my religious duties and turn myself for a time to books and leisure (the busiest part of my day), there is nothing in my literary resources sweeter – sweeter than honey from Mount Hybla – or neater or more to be savoured than the works of Erasmus (and do not think that I whisper this in your ear alone); nothing so successful in refreshing my memory of the past and giving me a new understanding and fresh enjoyment of the present and of what goes on under my very eyes, as the learned, polished, and highly wrought productions of your workshop and your anvil. As for example your *Moria*, your *Adages*, your *Parallels*, your *Copia*, and all your translations, clear as daylight, from the Greek, in which you show yourself no maker of paraphrases but a just champion and critic, and equal, if you do not surpass, Gorgias, Demosthenes, Isocrates, Aeschines, and the other outstanding and imperial figures of Greek literature.

Happy indeed is the Germany of our time, which with you as the sole and only German leader now dares to drive out, wipe away, and delete the age-long barbarism of its Latinity and to challenge the Italians (whose thirst for petty fame is too great already); for there is no one who can tread the name of Erasmus under foot or undervalue his learning or make light of his universal knowledge, brilliantly sprinkled as it is with the salt of eloquence,

* * * * *

20 lay] Virgil *Georgics* 4.438

33 *Parallels*] The *Parabolae sive similia* (Strasbourg: Schürer 1514)

41–2 tread ... under foot] This is probably what Basellius meant, although the word means 'supply.' His grasp of Latin (unlike nearly all of Erasmus' other correspondents) seems to have been uncertain, although Allen with characteristic courtesy treats his errors as scribal mistakes.

unless he be Zoilus himself, or a man devoid of any tincture of education. For your continuing fame and glory remain and shall remain after your death; and with them the honour you will win with this one critical edition of St Jerome's works, which all men judge to be the fruit of exceptional labours; for all libraries in the whole round world will never suffer the famous name of Erasmus to die out, but will extol it to the stars. To this eternal memory you and you alone will lay claim as of right, for all that your rivals may burst like Codrus with envy. You, I repeat, you are the glory of Germany, its eye, its sun, its shining light, which cannot be hid even though it may chance to be placed under a bushel by the envy of wicked men, for you know not how to surrender to Italian pride or to yield the palm to curly-pated Gauls. Whether they will or no, then, these ignorant praters, these boorish brawling good-for-nothings, these Black and White theologizers will find themselves obliged to praise Erasmus, once they have seen the sacred scriptures of both covenants (of which with more falsehood than truth they profess themselves professors) restored to their integrity by your zealous efforts, your unsleeping labours, your intelligence, and your energy; or if they do not, I shall then judge them to be unworthy even to be a burden on the earth. Off then with them to Hell while they are still alive, these foes to literature of every kind! Let Cerberus tear them limb from limb, since that is what they deserve, and down with them into perdition!

But no more of that. For what remains, I shall never regret that I have exceeded the narrow limits of a letter. It must be your part, dear Erasmus, to put as kind and friendly an interpretation as you can upon my headlong utterance, such as it is; for there is nothing I more value than to write to you, although you are a great scholar and I an ignoramus and a man of straw. Now, at the end, I come to beg you, of your well-known kindness, to enrol me even in the lowest rank among your friends, that I may gain more courage for the future and write more freely as friend to friend and as a pupil to his lord and master. Farewell, and think well of me.

From Virgin Wisdom's home at Hirsau

* * * * *

44 Zoilus] The bitterest of ancient critics, often wrong; *Adagia* II v 8

51 Codrus] A jealous shepherd in Virgil *Eclogues* 7.26

52 sun] Cf Ep 337:13n.

53 bushel] Cf Matt 5:15; Mark 4:21.

54 surrender] *Adagia* I ix 78

56 Black and White] Cf Ep 349:38n.

391A / To Johann Witz Basel, [second half of February 1516]

This letter, which responds to a poem by Witz, *Ad sodales Erasmo Roterodamo consuetudine iunctissimos Ioannes Sapidus Sletstadiensis Germanus*, was printed in *Epistolae elegantes*, a collection dated April 1517. In the poem Witz lists Erasmus' many friends in Basel: Gerard Lyster, Bruno and Basilius Amerbach, Beatus Rhenanus, Johann Froben, Konrad Nesen, Heinrich Loriti (Glareanus), Oecolampadius, Nikolaus Gerbel, Hieronymus Artolf, and Konrad Brunner (Fonteius). Witz may have intended to reply to the compliment of the *Encomium Selestadii*: cf Ep 353:9n; his own poem was printed before this letter in the various editions of the *Epistolae*.

Allen re-dated the letter to c October 1515 on the ground that Witz's poem mentioned Gerbell, and that Gerbell had returned to Strasbourg by December 1515. The present editors have retained the date originally given, since it eliminates the supposition (see note to line 30) that Witz had advance notice of a reduction in salary, and since it seems entirely possible that Witz might still have included Gerbell among the familiar associates of Erasmus in Basel in his poem, even if he knew, by the time he wrote it, that Gerbell had returned to Strasbourg. Adoption of the present date also affirms the likelihood that Erasmus, in April 1517, would have had a fairly accurate idea of the year in which so recent a letter was written, and eliminates the anomaly of the collection in *Epistolae elegantes* including only one letter of 1515. It might be added that the tenor of the poem and the present letter harmonize well with Witz's tribute to 'all the Erasmians' in Basel in his letter of 11 April following (Ep 399:13).

ERASMUS TO JOHANN WITZ, TEACHER OF THE LIBERAL ARTS

Your poem, dear Witz, my learned friend, gave particular pleasure to our whole society, for are they not particularly devoted to you? For my part, of course I was grateful, but I could not really enjoy it. No man can be at the same moment both delighted and embarrassed – unless perhaps you suppose me to have so little modesty that I can read your tributes without a blush. But on one thing I must protest. You say how fortunate so many scholarly and warm-hearted friends are in my society, but you do not say how happy I am in my turn in seeing so much of them, as though the good fortune in this were less mine than theirs. I seem to myself to be living in

* * * * *

391A:2 poem] *Ad sodales Erasmo Roterodamo consuetudine iunctissimos Ioannes Sapidus Sletstadiensis Germanus*, printed preceding this letter in the *Epistolae elegantes* (Louvain: Martens April 1517; NK 819)

some delightful precinct of the Muses, to say nothing of so many good scholars, and scholars of no ordinary kind. They all know Latin, they all know Greek, most of them know Hebrew too; one is an expert historian, another an experienced theologian; one is skilled in the mathematics, one a keen antiquary, another a jurist. How rare this is, you know well. I certainly have never before had the luck to live in such a gifted company. And to say nothing of that, how open-hearted they are, how gay, how well they get on together! You would say they had only one soul.

Nor have you any reason to lament your absence from our table. To speak as a good Platonist, you are with us as much as anybody. We never dine or sup, we neither walk nor talk, without our Witz. In fact, your lot is, I agree, laborious; that it is tragic, as you call it, or pitiable, I absolutely deny. To be a schoolmaster is an office second in importance to a king. Do you think it a mean task to take your fellow-citizens in their earliest years, to instil into them from the beginning sound learning and Christ himself, and to return them to your country as so many honourable upright men? Fools may think this a humble office; in reality it is very splendid. For if even among the Gentiles it was always an excellent and noble thing to deserve well of one's country, I will not mince my words: no one does more for it than the man who shapes its unformed young people, provided he himself is learned and honourable – and you are both, so equally that I do not know in which of them you surpass yourself. As for the reduction in your salary, Christ himself will make it up to you abundantly in his own way, for virtue is its own sufficient reward. Nor should it move you at all that you see some really idle people assigned a substantial annual income from public funds, who live to please themselves or in the service of princes and not in the interests of the commonwealth, while the man who is shared by all the children as a parent and performs a public service with so much expenditure of effort in the most important field of all is paid such a pitiful salary. An upright man who is above all temptation is what that office needed, a man devoted to his duties even if he is paid nothing. A big salary and the prospect of high social standing might attract every criminal to the post. You yourself, my dear Witz, will add dignity by your own endowments to an office which may carry little glamour among men, but before Christ is high in honour.

Nor is there any reason why you should envy Basel this society. Sélestat too has its shrine of the Muses, although maybe there are fewer devotees; but how many men you can outweigh with the one name of Paul

* * * * *

32 salary] Witz's term was for four years from 12 February 1512.

Volz, the abbot of Hügshofen! In heaven's name, what a clear mind, what a frank open nature, what simple wisdom, what a passion for study, and with all these gifts absolutely no opinion of himself! Surely, surely, such were, I conceive, those spiritual leaders of the early church, the Antonies and Hilarions and Jeromes. And so if you count up your company, there are I admit very few of you; but if you weigh it, many, for that one man is a host in himself. I beg you seriously to make him understand that I have not forgotten him. To your delightful wife Margaret who is such a comfort in your labours, more precious than any pearl, please give my warmest greetings. Farewell.

From Basel, [1516]

392 / To Urbanus Regius

Basel, 24 February 1516

This reply to Regius' invitation to Ingolstadt (Ep 386) is mentioned in Ep 413 and must therefore belong to 1516. It was first published in *Epistolae ad diversos* (1521).

ERASMUS OF ROTTERDAM TO URBANUS REGIUS

Your letter was shown to me by my special friend and patron Johannes Fabri, the bishop's official, but at a moment which could hardly have been more ill-timed, for not only was I deeply involved in the finishing of a piece of work which was also the most important part of it, but I was half dead (tired is no word for it) after months of continuous labour. I owe it one thing at any rate: I have made the acquaintance of Urbanus, a man (as his letter shows) open-hearted, sensible, eloquent, well-read, gifted in short with all the endowments of the Graces and the Muses. Such a prince, a truly great prince, is a matter for congratulation to our native Germany, and would there were many like him, ready to devote themselves to the ends which have always been regarded as worthy of our greatest men. On many grounds already I owe him a very great debt, whether for his kindly over-estimation of my humble self or for his generous invitation and encouragement to take up a position which might well be the goal of all my endeavours, were I free to bind myself to anyone, now that I am bound to

* * * * *

49 Volz] Cf Ep 368 introduction.

56 Margaret] Cf Ep 353:28.

392:2 Your letter] Ep 386

9 Such a prince] Duke Ernest of Bavaria; cf Ep 386 introduction.

Prince Charles
Bernart van Orley, c 1516
Musée du Louvre
Cliché des Musées nationaux

the most illustrious prince Charles and my own prince, and that too with my freedom reserved or, more accurately, recovered by the votes of the prince's council – and if my freedom is endangered, I resign everything. Nor have I failed in loyalty, nor ever shall, to my eminent patron, the archbishop of Canterbury. But set as I am between the two, I am confident of fulfilling my obligations to both my countries, the land of my birth and the land of my adoption. Otherwise even old age should be no excuse, although I am senile rather than aged, for I am in my forty-ninth year and no more. But age must be reckoned by strength rather than years. If the plan of my journey permits, I shall expend two or three days without hesitation to purchase the sight of so excellent a prince. You invited me on his behalf; pray thank him in return on mine with the same expressive language.

If my letter is brief and unpolished, the press of business must be my excuse; and if you really knew how busy I am, so far from taking exception, you would wonder how I could write even these poor lines. Farewell.

Basel, 24 February 1516

393 / To Prince Charles [Basel], [about March 1516]

The preface to the *Institutio principis christiani* (Basel: Froben 1516), dedicated to Prince Charles, was later (in the summer of 1518) revised for dedication to Ferdinand. The work is first mentioned in a letter from London of 15 May 1515 (Ep 334:178–80), but in the letter to Botzheim Erasmus twice asserts that he did not write it until after he was appointed councillor (Allen I pp 19, 44; Ep 370:18n). Allen suggested that the passage in Ep 334 was inserted after the *Institutio* was printed. The most likely time of composition is the summer of 1515 after Erasmus returned to Basel; the printing was still unfinished when he left Basel the following May (Ep 407:7–8). The work was published by Froben along with the *Panegyricus* (Ep 179) and the translations from Plutarch

* * * * *

17 prince Charles] An appointment first mentioned in Ep 370:18, probably beginning in January 1516

19 resign] Erasmus echoes Horace's disclaimer to Maecenas his patron: *Epistles* 1.7.34.

23 adoption] England

24 forty-ninth year] This estimate points to the year 1467 as that of Erasmus' birth; cf CWE I xxii; Allen I app II. This figure was repeated in the 'Methodus' prefixed to the *Novum instrumentum* (February 1516), but in the edition of the 'Methodus' printed by Martens in November 1518 (reprinted by Froben in January 1519 and included in the New Testament of that year) it is changed to 53.

(Epp 272, 297). This volume was reprinted in its entirety by Martens (Louvain August 1516; NK 830 and 2952); Bade's edition of 1 March 1517 contained only the *Institutio* and the Isocrates. The revised edition for Ferdinand was published by Froben in July 1518 and June 1519. See ASD IV i 95–219.

TO THE MOST ILLUSTRIOUS PRINCE CHARLES,
GRANDSON OF THE INVINCIBLE EMPEROR MAXIMILIAN,
FROM DESIDERIUS ERASMUS OF ROTTERDAM

Wisdom in itself is a wonderful thing, Charles greatest of princes, and no kind of wisdom is rated more excellent by Aristotle than that which teaches how to be a beneficent prince; for Xenophon in his *Oeconomicus* rightly considers that there is something beyond human nature, something wholly divine, in absolute rule over free and willing subjects. This naturally is the wisdom so much to be desired by princes, the one gift which that most intelligent young Solomon prayed for, despising all else, and wished to have seated continually beside his royal throne. This is that virtuous and beautiful Shunamite, in whose embraces David, wise father of a wise son, took his sole delight. She it is who says in Proverbs: 'By me princes rule and nobles dispense justice.' Whenever kings invite her to their councils and cast out those evil counsellors – ambition, anger, greed, and flattery – the commonwealth flourishes in every way and, knowing that it owes its felicity to the wisdom of its prince, says with well-earned satisfaction: 'All good things together came to me with her.' And so Plato is nowhere more meticulous than in the education of the guardians of his republic, whom he would have surpass all the rest not in riches and jewels and dress and ancestry and retainers, but in wisdom only, maintaining that no commonwealth can be happy unless either philosophers are put at the helm, or those to whose lot the rule happens to have fallen embrace philosophy – not that philosophy, I mean, which argues about elements and primal matter and motion and the infinite, but that which frees the mind from the false opinions of the multitude and from wrong desires and demonstrates the principles of right government by reference to the example set by the eternal powers. Something of the sort must have been, I think, in Homer's mind, when Mercury arms Ulysses against Circe's witchcraft with the herb

* * * * *

393:6 Xenophon] *Oeconomicus* 21.12

12 Shunamite] 1 Kings 1:2–3

13 Proverbs] Prov 8:16

18 her] Wisd 7:11

28–9 Homer's mind] *Odyssey* 10.302–6

called moly. And Plutarch has good reason for thinking that no man does the state a greater service than he who equips a prince's mind, which must consider all men's interests, with the highest principles, worthy of a prince; and that no one, on the other hand, brings such appalling disaster upon the affairs of mortal men as he who corrupts the prince's heart with wrongful opinions or desires, just as a man might put deadly poison in the public spring from which all men draw water. A very famous remark of Alexander the Great points usefully in the same direction; he came away from talking with Diogenes the Cynic full of admiration for his lofty philosophic mind, unshakeable, invincible, and superior to all mortal things, and said: 'If I were not Alexander, I should desire to be Diogenes'; in fact, the more severe the storms that must be faced by great power, the more he well might wish for the mind of a Diogenes, which might be equal to the immense burden of events.

But you, noble Prince Charles, are more blessed than Alexander, and will, we hope, surpass him equally in wisdom too. He for his part had seized an immense empire, but not without bloodshed, nor was it destined to endure. You were born to a splendid empire and destined to inherit one still greater, so that, while he had to expend great efforts on invasion, you will have perhaps to work to ensure that you can voluntarily hand over part of your dominions rather than seize more. You owe it to Heaven that your empire came to you without the shedding of blood, and no one suffered for it; your wisdom must now ensure that you preserve it without bloodshed and at peace. And such is your good nature, your honesty of mind, and your ability, such the upbringing you have had under the most high-minded teachers, and above all you see around you so many examples among your ancestors, that we all expect with confidence to see Charles one day perform what the world lately looked for from your father Philip; nor would he have disappointed public expectation had not death carried him off before his time. And so, although I knew that your Highness had no need of any man's advice, least of all mine, I had the idea of setting forth the ideal of a perfect prince for the general good, but under your name, so that those who are brought up to rule great empires may learn the principles of government through you and take from you their example. This serves a double purpose: under your name this useful work will penetrate everywhere, and by

* * * * *

30 Plutarch] *Moralia* 778D

36 Alexander] Plutarch *Moralia* 782A; *Alexander* 14

57 Philip] He died on 25 September 1506; cf Ep 205:11.

these first fruits I, who am already your servant, can give some kind of witness to my devotion to you.

I have taken Isocrates' work on the principles of government and translated it into Latin, and in rivalry with him I have added my own, arranged as it were in aphorisms for the reader's convenience, but with considerable differences from what he laid down. For he was a sophist, instructing some petty king or rather tyrant, and both were pagans; I am a theologian addressing a renowned and upright prince, Christians both of us. Were I writing for an older prince, I might perhaps be suspected by some people of adulation or impertinence. As it is, this small book is dedicated to one who, great as are the hopes he inspires, is still very young and lately invested with the government, and so has not yet had the opportunity to do very much that in other princes is matter for praise or blame. Consequently, I am free of both suspicions, and cannot be thought to have had any purpose but the common good, which should be the sole aim both of kings and of their friends and servants. Among the countless distinctions which under God your merit will win for you, it will be no small part of your reputation that Charles was a prince to whom a man need not hesitate to offer the picture of a true and upright Christian prince without any flattery, knowing that he would either gladly accept it as an excellent prince already, or wisely imitate it as a young man always in search of self-improvement. Farewell.

394 / To Urbanus Regius — Basel, 7 March [1516]

We are indebted for the survival of the text of this letter to Osvaldus Myconius, owner of the copy of the *Moria* of March 1515 which was illustrated by Holbein for Erasmus' amusement; the letter is copied on a blank leaf bound up in the volume, which is in the Öffentliche Kunstsammlung, Kunstmuseum, Basel. It was first published in the *Opus epistolarum* (1529). See Ep 861.

* * * * *

65 servant] A reference to his appointment as councillor; cf Ep 370:18n.

67 Isocrates] The *De institutione principis ad Nicoclem regem*, which formed an introduction to the *Institutio* in Froben's edition. Issued in the same book were the *Panegyricus* (with separate colophon dated April 1516) and translations of four minor works of moral counsel by Plutarch. The colophon of the whole was dated May 1516.

69 aphorisms] Cf Ep 523.

76 lately invested] Charles was invested with the government of the Netherlands on 5 January 1515.

ERASMUS OF ROTTERDAM TO URBANUS REGIUS

My feeling is this, dear Urbanus my most learned friend, that at this moment I owe everything to the illustrious prince Ernest or to you for the support you have given me. And so I thought it would be a way of paying some part of the debt if, since much as I would like to I am not free to do it myself, I pointed out to you a man who can do what you wanted me to do far better than I can. There is among us here one Henricus Glareanus, who has been crowned with the poet's laurel by the emperor, although I for my part reckon that the least among the young man's distinctions. In all the subjects included under the name of mathematics he has had exceptional training and more than average experience. In all the Aristotelian philosophy, as it is now taught in the universities, he has advanced to a point at which he can take on the leaders. He has also covered a large part of theology, and is well qualified in geography and history. In a word there is no department of sound learning in which he is not perfectly at home, and he has also learnt Greek up to a middle standard; here too he will soon be perfect, he is so quick and so industrious. Besides which he is just the right age for the work. He is coming up to thirty, an age which is too old to be treated disrespectfully and far the most capable of all kinds of hard work.

Glareanus however, apart from his age, is especially gifted by nature with the desire and capacity for scholarly work. What he does not know, he is eager to learn; what he knows, he is ready and generous to teach. His personality is lively and cheerful; you could fairly call him a man for all seasons. I will add one last argument, which I think should count among the very first: integrity is his second nature. He has a great aversion to the intemperance of these fashionable drinking-parties, and to dicing, obscenity, and wenching; the mere mention of them disgusts him. He receives many offers, and on terms by no means to be despised, and I thought he was already promised. But in the course of conversation I felt that the man might be steered in your direction, granted that he were offered something not unworthy of his merits. He is still young, and has more learning than he has wealth or worldly standing, although already he gains not a little in standing every day. The majesty of your prince will bring him out into the light, and he in his turn will do honour to the lineage and high station of the prince; the distinction that he borrows from his Highness he will one day repay, maybe with interest. I thought you might be grateful if I wrote and told you this. And I know the man I am recommending.

* * * * *

394:7 Glareanus] Heinrich Loriti; see Ep 328:43n and Ep 440 introduction.

23–4 man for all seasons] *Adagia* I iii 86

The New Testament is published. Jerome is receiving the finishing touches. Farewell.

Basel, 7 March 1515

395 / From Nikolaus Ellenbog — Ottobeuren, 30 March 1516

Ellenbog (1480–1543), the son of a lecturer in medicine at Ingolstadt, studied both in Cracow and at Montpellier, where he intended to read medicine. He entered the Benedictine house of Ottobeuren near Memmingen, however, to fulfill a vow made during an attack of plague in 1503. He continued an extensive correspondence, and furthered his principal interests in astronomy, Greek, and Hebrew. Almost a thousand of his letters survive copied by himself into letter-books, some of which form an important source of information about the Peasants' Revolt. This letter is in the Württembergische Landesbibliothek, Cod. hist. quart 99 f 212; a copy of the text received by Erasmus is in the Deventer Letter-book.

BROTHER NIKOLAUS ELLENBOG TO MASTER ERASMUS OF ROTTERDAM

Most learned Sir, having heard that you are at Basel with the printers, I could not refrain from writing, to give you some idea at any rate of my feelings towards you. For some time now I have read your works as they were struck off with great skill by the press, and the reading of them has specially delighted me. From that time forward I have constituted myself an unofficial herald of your reputation, and count it my greatest pleasure to speak of your name with honour whenever time and place allow. I write this, not to curry favour, but to show you clearly how I feel towards learned men, and with no ulterior purpose except that you should henceforward add the name of Nikolaus Ellenbog to the list of your friends. For the rest, please let me know about the works of the great Jerome, which I have heard are now off your hands, where they can be bought and how much they cost. Besides which I would urge you, if the New Testament which I hear you have translated from Greek into Latin has appeared, to give a copy please to the man who brought you this letter, and he will pay you cash for it. Farewell and best wishes, and do not forget that I am a most faithful supporter of your name and reputation.

From Ottobeuren abbey, 30 March 1516

396 / To William Warham — Basel, 1 April 1516

This is the dedicatory letter to Erasmus' part of the great Froben edition of the works of St Jerome, completed in the summer of 1516 in nine volumes. The first four volumes contained the letters edited by Erasmus; the last five other works (cf Ep 326 introduction). This preface is printed at the end of volume I and forms the preface to the entire edition. It resembles Epp 334 and 335 and *Adagia* III i 1.

Erasmus' work on Jerome derived from one of the formative influences of his early life. We know little about this, but at Steyn he was already familiar with the letters of Jerome (Ep 22:22). His comment while there to Cornelis Gerard, that if men who oppose the study of poetry 'looked carefully at Jerome's letters, they would see at least that lack of culture is not holiness, nor cleverness impiety,' is perhaps a sound index to the affinity Erasmus felt for this author (Ep 22: 18–20). At Paris in 1498 he was certainly studying the letters of Jerome seriously (Ep 67) and by 1500 he declared his 'burning desire' to edit the letters (Ep 141:18 and ff; cf Ep 373 introduction).

To Batt, from Orléans, he had already announced his commentary (Ep 138:45; cf Epp 139:166–72; 149:67–75). The work was an accompaniment to his continuing work on the New Testament in these years, and the two great enterprises grew together. In a letter to Ammonio from Cambridge in November 1511 he speaks of his work on Jerome, on whom he also lectured in the university (Ep 245:5). The following May the Paris printer, Josse Bade, negotiated with Erasmus to print his edition (Ep 263:31–5). The task was by no means finished however (Epp 264, 270, 271, 273, 281), and by the time the edition was ready Erasmus had transferred his favour to Basel, no doubt partly because a great edition of the entire works of Jerome was already under way there (Ep 346). It might be noted that it is in the volumes edited by Erasmus that the great dogmatic treatises to which Erasmus so often refers in the letters of this period are found.

At Basel Erasmus' work joined that of scholars like Reuchlin and Conradus Pellicanus who had been at work for several years under the direction of Johannes Amerbach; cf Epp 324:28n; 308; 309; Allen II 211; cf J. Amerbach to Reuchlin, April 1507, AK 335. The undertaking was finally completed by Froben in the summer of 1516, as the prefaces to the volumes of works which followed Erasmus' volumes of letters indicate. These prefaces were all in the name of Bruno Amerbach, that of his brother Basilius being joined to his only in volume V. They are addressed to the reader and are dated as follows: VIII, 13 January; VII, 7 March; V, 7 May; VI, 1 June; IX, 26 June; a supplement to VIII, 25 August – all in 1516. These prefatory ascriptions to the Amerbachs should not however be understood as attribution of authorship.

Of the prefaces contributed by Erasmus to his own volumes, those to volume II have been mentioned already (Ep 326 introduction). Volumes III and IV each carried a preface to the reader announcing the contents of the volumes, and these are dated from Basel 5 January and 1 March 1516. There is also a brief preface to volume I with Erasmus' notes on the *Catalogus scrip-*

ERASMVS ROTERODAMVS SACRAE THEOLO
GIAE PROFESSOR REVERENDISSIMO PA
TRI AC DOMINO DOMINO GVLIELMO
VVARAMO ARCHIEPISCOPO CAN·
TVARIENSI TOTIVS ANGLIAE
PRIMATI ET EIVSDEM REGNI
CANCELLARIO SVMMO
S. D.

TAnta ſemper fuit litterarũ apud ethnicos quoq; ueneratio,
Gulielme præſulum decus, & uirtutum ac litterarũ antiſtes,
ut diſciplinarum omnium origines, haud aliꝭs q̃ diꝭs autho
ribus conſecrandas ducerent: eaq; cum primis cura ſummis
ac florentiſſimis regibus digna uideretur, ſi excellentium uirorũ libros,
quo pluribus uſui eſſe poſſent, in diuerſas linguas transferẽdos curarẽt:
hinc uidelicet & ſibi ueriſſimam certiſſimamq; laudem, & regno præci-
puum ornamentum acceſſurum rati, ſi bibliothecam, q̃ optimis ſimul
& emendatiſſimis codicibus poſteritati traderent. Nec ullam grauiorẽ
iacturam accidere poſſe iudicabant, q̃ ſi quid ex id genus opibus inter-
cidiſſet. Proinde ne qui ſuis ingeniꝭs, ſuiſq; uigiliꝭs, tantopere de morta-
libus uniuerſis meriti fuiſſent, horũ memoria, iniuria temporũ nihil nõ
oblitterantium intermoreret, authores ipſos ſtatuis ac picturis expreſ-
ſos, paſſim in porticibus ac bibliothecis ponebant, qua certe licuit, illos
ab interitu uindicantes. Tum eorundem apophthegmata, marmori,
ærïq; paſſim inſculpta, mortalium oculis ingerebant. Libros ingenti re-
demptos precio, magnaq; fide uel religione potius deſcriptos, cedrinis
incluſos capſulis, tum cedri ſucco oblitos, in templis reponebant, partim
ut rei tam ſacræ tamq; diuinæ cuſtodia, nõ aliꝭs q̃ ipſis numinibus con-
crederetur, partim ne quid ſitus aut caries illa monumenta uitiaret, quæ
ſola principum gloriam a ſitu carieq; queunt aſſerere, & impune inter-
morerentur, quæ præſtant omnibus immortalitatem. Fuerunt qui nec
hac contenti diligentia, codices ceu theſaurum incomparabilem, in altiſ-
ſimis terræ latebris reconderent, tanta cura, ut nec incendiꝭs, nec bellorũ
α 2 procellis,

Dedicatory letter, Erasmus to William Warham, Epistle 396
Hieronymi opera I (Basel: Froben 1516)
Öffentliche Bibliothek, University of Basel

torum ecclesiasticorum. The preface chosen by Allen for inclusion in the correspondence is the one that follows here. The edition was reprinted by Froben in 1524–6, and again by the firm in 1536–7, 1553, and 1565, and it was also reprinted by Chevallon in Paris in 1533–4 with a short preface by Erasmus: see P.S. Allen 'Erasmus' Relations with His Printers' *Transactions of the Bibliographical Society* 13 (1913–15) 316.

Of the manuscript sources for Erasmus' edition little is known, and the basis of his edition was early printed texts, especially those of Rome 1468 and Mainz 1470. Although he refers to MSS frequently in his notes (cf Ep 335:285), he gives no clue to their identity so that, as with the annotations on the New Testament, we are reminded that we are witnessing only the first developing awareness of modern critical methods. It is certain that English manuscripts played an important part in the development of his text (see above and Ep 332:8–9). Two manuscripts were borrowed from the monastery of Echternach, the Hieronymian Martyrology and the Pseudo-Jerome (now Paris lat. 10837 and 9525); see Allen IV xxiv and *Proceedings of the British Academy* VII (1915–16) 282–3. Another manuscript was borrowed for him from the monastery of Reichenau in November 1515 (cf AK Ep 540). For an account of the manuscript *scholia* of Erasmus on his edition of the letters see Fritz Husner 'Die Handschrift der Scholien des Erasmus von Rotterdam zu den Hieronymusbriefen,' *Festschrift Gustav Binz* (Basel 1935) 132–46. See also D. Gorce in *Festgabe Joseph Lortz* ed E. Iserloh and P. Mans I (Baden-Baden 1958) esp 260–76.

ERASMUS OF ROTTERDAM, DOCTOR OF DIVINITY, TO THE MOST REVEREND FATHER AND LORD, WILLIAM WARHAM, ARCHBISHOP OF CANTERBURY, PRIMATE OF ALL ENGLAND AND LORD HIGH CHANCELLOR OF THE SAID REALM, GREETING

So great was the veneration always accorded to literature even by pagans, William, paragon of prelates and champion of the virtues and of sound learning, that they supposed the origins of all the liberal arts should be ascribed to the gods alone as their inventors, and the most powerful and prosperous monarchs thought no concern more becoming to them than to arrange for the translation of works of outstanding authors into various tongues, that more men might enjoy them. This was, they thought, the way to secure the truest and most lasting renown for themselves and a special ornament for their kingdoms, if they bequeathed to posterity a library equipped with most accurate copies of the very best authors; nor did they think a more serious loss could befall them than the destruction of any of their riches in this kind. They were concerned therefore that the memory of those whose gifted natures and whose exertions had done so much for the whole human race should never succumb to the attacks of time that effaces all things; and so they placed statues and pictures of the authors themselves everywhere in cloister and library, to protect them from oblivion at least as far as in them lay. Further, they had the maxims of great authors inscribed everywhere in marble or bronze and set them up for all men to see; they bought their works at vast expense and had them faithfully and almost religiously copied, enclosed them in chests of cedar wood and rubbed them with cedar oil, then laid them up in their temples. For this there were two reasons: something so sacred, so divine, should not be entrusted for safekeeping to any but the gods themselves, and no neglect or decay must be allowed to spoil the only monuments which can keep neglect and decay from the glory of princes, nor should works be allowed to die defenceless which confer immortality on all men.

For some even this degree of care was not enough, and they laid up their books like some incomparable treasure in storehouses deep under ground, intending by these precautions to protect them from destruction by fire or by the storms of war, which so often confound everything sacred and profane, that they might survive at least for the benefit of posterity. They perceived of course, those princes distinguished no less for wisdom than for royal state, that it was barbarous for the corpses of the dead to be so carefully embalmed sometimes with unguents and spices and woad to preserve them from decay, when their preservation served no purpose since they could no longer reproduce the features or figure of the deceased, which even a statue of stone can do, and to take no such care to preserve the relics of the mind. And so they thought it far more appropriate to transfer that solicitude to the books of great men, in which they live on for the world at large even after death, and live on in such fashion that they speak to more people and more effectively dead than alive. They converse with us, instruct us, tell us what to do and what not to do, give us advice and encouragement and consolation as loyally and as readily as anyone can. In fact, they then most truly come alive for us when they themselves have ceased to live. For such is my opinion: if a man had lived in familiar converse with Cicero (to take him as an example) for several years, he will know less of Cicero than they do who by constant reading of what he wrote converse with his spirit every day.

Now if such honour was paid even to works of superstition like the books of Numa and the Sibyl, or to volumes of human history as was

* * * * *

396:55 Numa] In 181 BC a chest was found on the Janiculan hill in Rome alleged to contain twelve books written by Numa, the second king of Rome.

customary in Egypt, or to those that enshrined some part of human wisdom such as the works of Plato and Aristotle, how much more appropriate that Christian princes and bishops should do likewise by preserving the writings of men inspired by the Holy Spirit, who have left us not so much books as sacred oracles! And yet somehow it happened that in that field our ancestors did singularly little. We may not think much, I grant you, of the loss of pagan authors, the only result of which is that we are less well informed or less eloquent, but not less virtuous. But think of the admirable and really saintly authors bequeathed to us by Greece, that seat of learning, or its rival Italy, by Gaul, once such a flourishing home of culture, or Africa with all its originality, or Spain with its tradition of hard work. How impressive was their recondite learning, how brilliant their eloquence, how holy their lives! And yet, I ask you, how few of them survive, preserved more by accident than by any help from us! And those survivors, how foully mutilated, how badly adulterated, how full throughout of monstrous errors, so that to survive in that condition was no great privilege! For my part, far as I am from despising the simple piety of common folk, I cannot but wonder at the absurd judgment of the multitude. The slippers of the saints and their drivel-stained napkins we put to our lips, and the books they wrote, the most sacred and most powerful relics of those holy men, we leave to lie neglected. A scrap of a saint's tunic or shirt we place in a gilded and bejewelled reliquary, and the books into which they put so much work, and in which we have the best part of them still living and breathing, we abandon to be gnawed at will by bug, worm, and cockroach.

Nor is it hard to guess the reason for this. Once the character of princes had quite degenerated into a barbaric form of tyranny, and bishops had begun to love their lay lordships more than the duty of teaching bequeathed to them by the apostles, the whole business of instruction was soon abandoned to a certain class, who today claim charity and religion as their private trademark; sound learning began to be neglected, and a knowledge of Greek, still more of Hebrew, was looked down on; to study the art of expression was despised, and Latin itself so much contaminated with an ever-changing barbarism that Latin by now was the last thing it resembled. History, geography, antiquities, all were dropped. Literature was reduced to a few sophistic niceties, and the sum of human learning began to be found only in certain summary compilers and makers of excerpts, whose impudence stood in inverse proportion to their knowledge. And so they easily allowed those old classic authors to fall out of use or, what is more like the truth, they deliberately contrived their disappearance, for they now read them in vain, lacking all things necessary for their understanding. They did, however, make a few haphazard extracts from them which they mingled with their own notes; and this made it even more in their interest that the old authors should disappear, to save them from the charge of plagiarism or ignorance. It was worth their while for Clement, Irenaeus, Polycarp, Origen, Arnobius to fall out of use, that in their stead the world might read Occam, Durandus, Capreolus, Lyra, Burgensis, and even poorer stuff than that. So under their long and despotic rule such was the holocaust of humane literature and good authors that a man who had meddled even slightly with sound learning was expelled from the ranks of the doctors.

The result of this was the total loss of so many luminaries of the world, whose names alone survive and cannot be read without tears; and if by some chance any have escaped destruction, they are damaged in so many ways and so much mutilated and adulterated that those who perished outright might seem fortunate. Now this seems to me a perfectly monstrous fate for all learned authors, but far more monstrous in Jerome than anywhere else, whose many outstanding gifts deserved that he, even if no one

* * * * *

101 Durandus] Identified by Allen as the thirteenth-century canonist and bishop of Mende. The context however would seem rather to point to the Dominican scholastic philosopher Durand de Saint-Pourçain (c 1270–5 to 1334) who lectured on the Sentences at Paris and subsequently (1313) was lector in *sacra pagina* at the papal court at Avignon. He was promoted to be bishop of Limoux in 1317, of Le-Puy-en-Velay in 1318, and of Meaux in 1326. He was an early exponent of nominalism, and his widely read commentary on the Sentences was printed by Josse Bade in 1508, and reprinted in 1515, a circumstance that also recommends this identification. See Renaudet *Préréforme* 470; Ph. Renouard *Bibliographie des impressions et des œuvres de Josse Badius Ascensius* II (Paris 1908; repr New York 1963) 410–11; T. Kaeppeli OP *Scriptores ordinis praedicatorum medii aevi* I (Rome 1970) item 927; J. Quétif and J. Echard *Scriptores ordinis praedicatorum recensiti* I (Paris 1719) 586–7.

101 Capreolus] Johannes Capreolus (c 1380–1444) belonged to the Toulouse province of the Dominican order, and in 1407 was assigned to lecture on Peter Lombard at Paris. His only known work is his *Libri defensionum theologiae divi Thomae de Aquino*, composed between 1408 and 1433, an elaborate defence of Thomistic teaching in the form of a commentary on the *Sentences*. His work was printed at Venice in four folio volumes from 1483 to 1589.

101 Lyra] Cf Ep 372:13n.

101 Burgensis] Paul of Burgos (c 1351–1435) was born of a wealthy Jewish family in that city and was trained as a rabbi. He was led to accept Christianity partly by his study of Aquinas, and in 1390 was baptized as Paul of Santa Maria. After the death of his wife he was ordained priest, and became bishop of Cartagena (1405) and of Burgos (1415). He composed *Additiones* to the *Postilla* of Nicholas of Lyra and his *Scrutinium Scripturarum* was printed at Rome about 1470.

else, should be preserved complete and uncorrupted. Other authors have each a different claim upon us; Jerome alone possesses, united in one package, as the phrase goes, and to a remarkable degree, all the gifts that we admire separately in others. Distinction in one department is a great and rare achievement; but he combined overall excellence with being easily first in everything separately, if you compare him with other authors, while if you compare him with himself, nothing stands out, such is his balanced mingling of all the supreme qualities. If you assay his mental endowments, where else would you find such an enthusiastic student, such a keen critic, such prolific originality? What could be more ingenious or diverting, if the subject should call for something entertaining? If however you are looking for brilliance of expression, on that side at least Jerome leaves all Christian authors so far behind him that one cannot compare with him even those who spent their whole time on nothing but the art of writing; and so impossible is it to find any writer of our faith to compare with him that in my opinion Cicero himself, by universal consent the leading light of Roman eloquence, is surpassed by him in some of the qualities of a good style, as I shall show at greater length in his life. For my part, I have the same experience with Jerome that I used to have with Cicero: if I compare him with any other author, however brilliant, that man suddenly seems as it were to lose his voice, and he whose language has no rival in my admiration, when set alongside Jerome for comparison, seems to become tongue-tied and stammers. If you demand learning, I ask you, whom can Greece produce with all her erudition, so perfect in every department of knowledge, that he might be matched against Jerome? Who ever so successfully united every part of the sum of knowledge in such perfection? Was there ever an individual expert in so many languages? Who ever achieved such familiarity with history, geography, and antiquities? Who ever became so equally and completely at home in all literature, both sacred and profane? If you look to his memory, never was there an author, ancient or modern, who was not at his immediate disposal. Was there a corner of Holy Scripture or anything so recondite or diverse that he could not produce it, as it were, cash down? As for his industry, who ever either read or wrote so many volumes? Who had the whole of Scripture by heart, as he had, drinking it in, digesting it, turning it over and over, pondering upon it? Who expended so much effort in every branch of learning? And if you contemplate his lofty character, who breathes the spirit of Christ more vividly? Who has taught him with more enthusiasm? Who ever followed him more exactly in his way of life? This man, single-handed, could represent the Latin world, either for holiness of life or for mastery of theology, if only he survived complete and undamaged.

As it is, I doubt whether any author has had more outrageous treatment. A good part of all he wrote has perished. What survives was not so much corrupted as virtually destroyed and defaced, and this partly by the fault of illiterate scribes whose habit it is to copy an accurate text inaccurately and make a faulty text worse, to leave out what they cannot read and to corrupt what they do not understand – for instance, the Hebrew and Greek words which Jerome often brings in; but in a much more criminal fashion by sacrilegious men, I know not whom, who have deliberately cut down very many passages, added some, altered many, corrupted, adulterated, and muddled almost everything, so that there is hardly a paragraph which an educated man can read without stumbling. What is more (and this is the most pestilential way of ruining a text), as though it were not enough to have put together so many idiotic blunders, showing equally ignorance and inability to write, under the name of one who is equally a great scholar and a great stylist, they have mixed in their own rubbish into his expositions in such a way that no one can separate them. Ascribe a book to the wrong author, and there are many indications that this is wrong; but if scraps are intermingled, like darnel in wheat, where is the sieve that can screen them out? That all this has happened I shall shortly demonstrate in the catalogue of Jerome's works, and in the two prefaces and critical introductions of the second volume.

I was roused therefore, partly by this insufferable ill-treatment of so eminent a doctor of the church, on whose immortal works these worse than Calydonian boors have wreaked their fury unpunished, and partly by thoughts of the general advantage of all who wish to learn, whom I saw debarred by these outrages from enjoying such a feast – I was roused, I say, to restore to the best of my ability the volumes of his letters, which were the richest in learning and eloquence and proportionately the worst corrupted, although I well knew how difficult and arduous was the task I took in hand. To begin with, the labour of comparing together so many volumes is very tedious, as they know who have experience of working in this treadmill. Often too I had to work with volumes which it was no easy business to read, the forms of the script being either obscured by decay and neglect, or half eaten away and mutilated by worm and beetle, or written in the fashion of Goths or Lombards, so that even to learn the letter-forms I had to go back to school; not to mention for the moment that the actual task of detecting, of smelling out as it were, anything that does not sound like a true and genuine reading requires a man in my opinion who is well informed,

* * * * *

171 wheat] Cf Matt 13:24–30.

quick-witted, and alert. But on top of this far the most difficult thing is either to conjecture from corruptions of different kinds what the author wrote, or to guess the original reading on the basis of such fragments and vestiges of the shapes of the script as may survive. And further, while this is always extremely difficult, it is outstandingly so in the works of Jerome. There are several reasons for this. One is that his actual style is far from ordinary, starred with epigrams, highlighted with exclamations, rich in devious and cunning artifice, in pressing close-packed argument, in humorous allusions, sometimes seeming to use all the tricks of the rhetorical schools without restraint, and everywhere exhibiting the highly skilled craftsman. As a result, the further his style is from the understanding of ordinary people, the more blunders it is defiled with. One man copies not what he reads but what he thinks he understands; another supposes everything he does not understand to be corrupt, and changes the text as he thinks best, following no guide but his own imagination; a third detects perhaps that the text is corrupt, but while trying to emend it with an unambitious conjecture he introduces two mistakes in place of one, and while trying to cure a slight wound inflicts one that is incurable.

Besides all this, there is the astonishing way in which Jerome mixes material of the most varied kinds. He even went out of his way to do this, but with complete success. It was a kind of ambition and ostentation, if you like, but of a pious and holy kind: to display his own resources with the object of shocking us out of our lethargy and awaking his drowsy readers to study the inner meaning of the Scriptures. There is no class of author anywhere and no kind of literature which he does not use whenever he likes – sprinkling here and there, pressing harder, ramming it home: Hebrew, Greek, Latin, Chaldaean, sacred and profane, old and new, everything! Like a bee that flies from flower to flower, he collected the best of everything to make the honey stored in his works; he plucked different blossoms from every quarter to adorn his chaplet; he put together his mosaic out of tesserae of every colour. And of all these it was the most recondite material that he habitually wove in with the greatest readiness. There is nothing so obscure in the meaning-within-meaning of the Prophets, in the hidden senses of the whole Old Testament, in the Gospels or the Epistles, that he does not use as though it were familiar, sometimes with such a sidelong glance that only a well-instructed and attentive reader will catch the allusion. What is there in the literature of the Hebrews or Chaldaeans, in rhetorical or geographical textbooks, in poetry and medicine and philosophy, and even in books written by heretics, from which he does not draw thread to weave into his book? To understand all this, encyclopaedic learning is essential, even if the texts were faultless; and what happens, do you suppose, when everything is so damaged, so mutilated, so muddled that, if Jerome himself came to life again, he would neither recognize his own work nor understand it?

And then there was a further handicap. The greatest part of the authors upon whom Jerome drew as his sources have perished, and with their support it might have been possible to repair somehow the results of repeated damage or even loss: for this is, as it were, the sheet-anchor in which scholars normally take refuge in their greatest difficulties. For since I did not undertake this labour to secure either reputation or reward, I at least was not so much moved by something that might perhaps have deterred another man from setting his hand to any business of the kind. What is that? you will ask. I mean this: no other work brings a man more tedium and weariness, and equally no work brings its author less repute or gratitude, because, while the whole advantage of one's exertions is enjoyed by one's reader, he fails to appreciate not only how hard one has worked for his benefit but even how much he has gained, unless someone by chance were to compare my work with the texts in current use. The reader wanders at leisure over smiling fields; he plays and runs and never stumbles; and he never gives a thought to the time and tedium it has cost me to battle with the thorns and briars, while I was clearing that land for his benefit. He does not reckon how long a single brief word may sometimes have tormented the man trying to correct it, nor does he bring to mind how much I suffered in my efforts to remove anything that might hold him up, how great the discomforts that secured his comfort, how much tedium was the price of his finding nothing tedious.

But I shall be tedious myself if I recount all the tedium I have endured in this affair; so let me say just one thing, which is bold, but true. I believe that the writing of his books cost Jerome less effort than I spent in the restoring of them, and their birth meant fewer nightly vigils for him than their rebirth for me. The rest any man may conjecture for himself. Why need I mention here the ingratitude and ignorance of some men I could name, who would rather have no changes whatever in the text of the best authors? They do nothing themselves, and object noisily to the distinguished efforts of others; men whose judgment is so crass that they find errors in what is perfectly preserved and stylish elegance in the foulest corruptions, and (what is worse) of such perversity that, while they do not grant scholars the right to correct a faulty text by hard work, they allow some worthless fellow to befoul and stultify and ruin the works of the greatest authors at his own sweet will without a protest. And so it is inevitable that one should earn no gratitude from the majority and win the resentment of this last class of men even for the service one has done them. You may say that profit means nothing to the noble soul, and that honour and glory are easily despised by the good Christian. Yes: but even men of the highest character look for gratitude if they have deserved it. Who can tolerate scandal and abuse in return for doing good?

Of all this I was well aware; but I was moved by a great desire to rescue Jerome, by the thought of being useful to those who have the Scriptures at heart, and last but not least because your Highness approved and would have it so, and you above all others gave me the impulse and unflagging encouragement to undertake this. And so I despised all the difficulties, and like a modern Hercules I set out on my most laborious but most glorious campaign, taking the field almost unaided against all the monsters of error. I cannot think that Hercules consumed as much energy in taming a few monsters as I did in abolishing so many thousand blunders. And I conceive that not a little more advantage will accrue to the world from my work than from his labours which are on the lips of all men. To start with, by comparing many copies, early copies especially, and sometimes adding my conjectures as the traces of the script suggested, I have removed the blunders and restored the correct reading. The Greek words, which had been either omitted or wrongly supplied, I have replaced. I have done the same with the Hebrew also; but in this department what I was less able to manage for myself I have achieved with the assistance of others, and especially of the brothers Amerbach, Bruno, Basilius, and Bonifacius, whom their excellent father Johannes Amerbach equipped with the three tongues as though they were born expressly for the revival of ancient texts. And in this they have even outstripped their father's wishes and expectations, thinking nothing more important than the glory of Jerome and for his sake sparing neither expense nor health. For my part I was very grateful for their help, having only dipped into Hebrew rather than learnt it. And yet I saw to it that the keen reader should find nothing lacking even if I lacked it myself, and what fell short in my own capacity has been fully supplied out of the resources of others. Why should I be ashamed to do in the defence of such an author what the greatest monarchs do without shame in the recovery, and even the destruction, of paltry towns?

I have added a summary to each treatise or letter, opening the door, as it were, to those who wish to enter. And then, since not everyone is blessed with such wide linguistic and literary knowledge, I have thrown light on anything that might hold up a reader of modest attainments by adding notes, hoping to achieve a double purpose: first, to make such an eminent

* * * * *

293 Hebrew] Cf Ep 324:31n.

author, who hitherto could not be read even by men of great learning, accessible to those whose learning is but small, and second, that it may not be so easy in future for anyone to corrupt what other men have restored. Not content with this, the pieces wrongly circulating under Jerome's name, many of them such that their author is clearly not Jerome but some botcher as witless as he is impudent, I have not cut out, in order that a reader whose appetite is greater than his taste might run no risk of disappointment (to put it more bluntly, so that every donkey may find its thistle), but exiled to a suitable place, although in themselves they deserve no place at all. Next, I divided the whole corpus (I speak of the section which I took for my own province) into four volumes. In the first I have grouped together his pieces of moral instruction by exhortation and example, because what deals with the ordering of life deserves attention first. The second I have divided into three classes, into the first of which I have put certain things that show some degree of culture and are worth reading, but are falsely ascribed to Jerome; into the next, things which are not his, but carry an author's name in their headings; the third class is a kind of cesspool into which I have thrown the supremely worthless rubbish of some impostor, I know not whom, of whom it may fairly be doubted which is the greater, his inability to write, his ignorance, or his impudence. At least, whoever he was, he seems to me to deserve public execration for the rest of time; and he must have had a very low opinion of the intelligence of posterity if he hoped that there would never be anyone who could distinguish the ravings of a half-witted noisy fellow from the works of a man of the highest eloquence, learning, and sanctity. The third volume I have allotted to his works of controversy and apologetics, those, that is, which are devoted to refuting the errors of heretics and the calumnies of his opponents. The fourth I have kept for the expository works, I mean the explanations of Holy Scripture.

With something of the same zealous intentions I have lately produced a New Covenant equipped with my annotations, and I decided that the dedication of that work should be shared by Leo the supreme pontiff and your Highness, that my new undertaking might come before the public protected and recommended by the names of the whole world's two greatest men. But Jerome, recalled to the light from some sort of nether region, I prefer to dedicate to you alone, either because I owe you without

* * * * *

319 every donkey] *Adagia* I x 71

327–8 in their headings] These pieces, while not by Jerome, are closely related to his work and controversies, and carry attribution to their authors in their headings.

342 shared] Cf Epp 333 introduction and lines 97ff, 384:79ff.

exception everything I have, or because you always have a special concern for Jerome's reputation, perceiving with your usual wisdom that after the writings of the evangelists and apostles there is nothing more deserving of a Christian's attention. For my part I would gladly believe that Jerome himself takes some pleasure in the thought that his restoration to life in the world has the authority of your most favourable name, for he is no more the greatest of theologians than you are second to none among bishops whom all admire. He mastered to such good effect the whole cycle of knowledge in its completeness, and you likewise have blended in a wonderful harmony the full circle of a bishop's virtues.

In all other respects the agreement is admirable. I have one anxiety, that my limited powers may fail to do justice to Jerome's importance or to your eminent position; for nowhere do I feel more clearly how small my talent is than when I am striving to make some sort of response to your exalted virtues and your unbounded goodness to me. But what was I to do, bound to you as I am by so many and such great obligations that if I sold myself into slavery I should not be in a position to repay any part of my debt? I have done what bankrupts often do, making a token payment to bind themselves yet more irrecoverably, and thus proving that it is the means and not the will they lack; they are ill-starred rather than dishonest debtors, and for this very reason often secure the good will of a jury, because they are not so much ungrateful as unfortunate. In such cases the only means of showing gratitude is to be a frank and cheerful debtor, and to acknowledge one's debt is the first step towards paying it. Or rather, to compare a situation even more like mine, I have followed the example of those who would rather raise a fresh loan than go to prison for non-payment, and have borrowed from Jerome the wherewithal to repay you. Though why should it any longer look like something borrowed rather than my own? – real estate often passes from one ownership to another by occupation or prescriptive right. In any case, in this line of business Jerome himself has laid down a principle for me in his preface to the books of Kings, repeatedly calling that work his, because anything that we have made our own by correcting, reading, constant devotion, we can fairly claim is ours. On this principle why should not I myself claim a proprietary right in the works of Jerome? For centuries they had been treated as abandoned goods; I entered upon them as something ownerless, and by incalculable efforts reclaimed them for all devotees of the true theology.

It is a river of gold, a well stocked library, that a man acquires who

* * * * *

377 preface] That is to the books of Samuel; PL 28:603B

possesses Jerome and nothing else. He does not possess him, on the other hand, if his text is like what used to be in circulation, all confusion and impurity. Not that I would dare assert that none of the old corruptions, no traces of his previous ruined state, remain; I doubt if Jerome himself could achieve that without the aid of better manuscripts than I have yet had the chance to use. But this with all my zeal I have achieved, that not many now remain. And if I have done nothing else, at least my attempt will spur on some other men not to accept hereafter indiscriminately whatever they may find in their books, however badly corrupted by one impostor after another or masquerading under some false title, and read it and approve it and cite it as an oracle. I only wish that all good scholars would devote all their forces to the task of restoring as far as possible to its original purity whatever in the way of good authors has somehow survived after such numerous shipwrecks! But I should not like to see anyone enter this field who is not as well equipped with honesty, accuracy, judgment, and readiness to take pains as he is with erudition; for there is no more cruel enemy of good literature than the man who sets out to correct it half-instructed, half-asleep, hasty, and of unsound judgment.

If only all princes were of the same mind as you – if they would let go these wars with all their madness and their misery, and devote themselves to the task of adorning their generation with the arts of peace, firing the zeal of learned men to these most salutary labours by suitable rewards! Very soon we should see all the world over what has come to pass in these few years in your native England. For many years she has been strong in manhood and in wealth; and lately she has become so well endowed, has achieved such distinction, and so blossomed forth in religion, justice, gracious living, and last but not least in all the study of the classics (and all this your doing!), that this remote island can serve as a spur even to the most civilized regions in their pursuit of the highest things.

Farewell in Christ Jesus, most illustrious prelate, and may he preserve you in health and wealth as long as possible for the increase of religion and the advancement of humane studies.

Basel, 1 April 1516

397 / To Thomas Anshelm [Basel], 1 April 1516

This commendatory letter was written for the first edition of Nauclerus' *Memorabilium omnis aetatis et omnium gentium chronici commentarii* (Tübingen: T. Anshelm March 1516). The work consists of two folio volumes containing chronicles by Nikolaus Basellius for the years 1500 to 1514 (Ep 391). Anshelm matriculated at Basel in 1485, having been born in Baden-Baden. In 1500 he set up his own press at Pforzheim; in July 1511 he removed to Tübingen, drawn by the influence of Reuchlin. Although he was not a graduate, his press was supported by the humanists of Tübingen, even after his removal to Haguenau in 1516. He died in 1527; cf Ritter 377–88.

Johannes Verge, called 'Nauclerus,' was a Swabian scholar of noble family. He advanced in princely service, and in 1477 was appointed professor of canon law at the foundation of the university of Tübingen. The next year he became chancellor also, and he held both offices until his death in 1510.

D. ERASMUS OF ROTTERDAM TO THOMAS ANSHELM, MOST SKILFUL AND MOST RELIABLE OF PRINTERS

Your industry, my dear Thomas, and still more your accuracy have put all lovers and students of the humanities all the world over under a heavy debt, for they are supplied by your printing-house with the most approved authors printed in Latin, Greek, and Hebrew types of the greatest elegance. But our native Germany is particularly obliged to you for the light which you cast upon her from time to time by the publication of new tributes of the kind that can alone bring true and lasting glory. I only wish that everyone had it equally at heart to compete with the Italians in this field, which could do them no harm, would be a public benefit, and would bring us much more credit than to engage them in barbarous fashion with rocks and iron weapons; for in that contest the victor is the more barbarous and the vanquished is the more unfortunate, while in this the winner is the greater benefactor and the loser at least leaves the field a wiser man. And so a great reward in terms of real glory will be won both for you and for Germany as a whole, if I mistake not, by this history compiled by Nauclerus, a most industrious author and born for this task; for this department of learning would make an outstanding contribution to the leading of an honourable life, if discernment were always at hand to help the reader distinguish what to imitate and what to avoid. Elegance of style will not be greatly missed by anyone who remembers that in history nothing is as important as accuracy. I pray Heaven that your hard work may be as profitable to you as it is valuable to scholarly pursuits. Already all over Germany the study of liberal subjects is growing most prosperously, and I am confident that it will soon come to harvest with the energetic support of you and others like you. Farewell.

1 April 1516

* * * * *

397:17 Nauclerus] See introduction to this letter.

398 / From Georgius Precellius Ulm, 5 April 1516

Nothing is known of this priest of Ulm; a 'Jeorius Pratzel' matriculated at Heidelberg in 1496 and graduated with a BA the next year. The edition of the *Adagia* quoted is that of 1508, not 1515.

GEORGIUS PRECELLIUS OF ULM TO ERASMUS

Most eminent of men, some time ago when printing the larger edition of your *Adages*, you inserted, learned Sir, towards the end, near the paragraph beginning 'Scenting out and other metaphors of this kind' a promise relating to a book called *Notable Metaphors*; your words were 'And so, although materials of this kind have some family relationship to proverbs, to pursue them in greater detail is not now my purpose, especially since this department has already been taken in hand by a native of Britain, Richard Pace, who is a young man expert alike in Greek and Latin literature, and possessed of unusual experience in the reading of authors in every subject. With the Muses' blessing, he has formed, as I say, and I believe is now engaged on, a project which (unless I am much mistaken) will be of great value to all who wish to make progress in polite literature; he intends to collect all the notable metaphors to be found in classical authors, with all the pointed and elegant phrases and other jewels and ornaments of style, and arrange them in a single volume.'

Pray do your best, eminent Sir, to see that this book, for which we have waited so long, may one day come into the hands of all lovers of literature. They need it very badly; night and day their cry is 'Georgius Precellius, why is your friend Erasmus' (for I claim you entirely as my own, I love and cherish and respect you as a father; whenever your name is mentioned, I exalt you above the starry height) – 'why,' they say, 'is he so slow in bringing out this little book of *Notable Metaphors*?' If only I could live to the day when I might at last behold it made available even in brief to the reading public! Farewell, our new Apollo and genius of eloquence.

Ulm, All Saints' house, 5 April 1516

Your friend, who loves you as himself, Georgius Precellius

* * * * *

398:4 Scenting out] *Adagia* I vi 81

9 Pace] Cf Ep 211:50–7. He is not known ever to have undertaken the kind of work here adumbrated.

399 / From Johann Witz — Sélestat, 11 April 1516

JOHANN WITZ TO MASTER ERASMUS

How right they are, the scholars of our native Germany, to love and respect you, my dear Erasmus, most scholarly of men! You have always regarded them with special affection, and your industry and learning contribute greatly to their prosperity; and this is why the devotees of literature flock round you from the whole of Germany in their devotion. Among their number is my friend Batt Arnolt, who by way of increasing his beatitude has formed the plan of visiting you, the most beatific of men, in hopes that he may easily succeed, if in your kindness you can somehow find time to see him. If you ask how I am, I divide my time as usual between school and domestic life, and grow no younger.

Farewell in haste, written at school, 11 April 1516.

Greetings to Beatus Rhenanus and all the Erasmians.

400 / From Pius Hieronymus Baldung — Ensisheim, 24 April 1516

Baldung (fl 1506–32) was the son of a physician to the emperor Maximilian, and was born in Swäbisch-Gmünd. He was educated at the university of Vienna, as Allen surmised from the fact that on one occasion Baldung referred to Conrad Celtis as 'communis praeceptor' to Vadianus and himself (*Vadianische Briefsammlung*, ed E. Arbenz and H. Wartmann (St Gall, 1890–1913) 394). He was registered in the Rhein Nation in the summer of 1504 as 'Hieronymus Pius Baldung utriusque iuris baccalarius' under Johannes Reuss' rectorship (Publikationen des Instituts für Österreichische Geschichtsforschung. VI Reihe: Quellen zur Geschichte der Universität Wien, Erste Abteilung. II Band 1451–1518 I.1 (Graz/Köln 1959) 319 col 1; Dr Astrik Gabriel, to whom I am indebted for this information, has confirmed the registration from photostatic copies of the *matricula* in his possession). On 5 February 1506 Baldung matriculated at Freiburg, and the following June succeeded Zasius in the chair of poetry. He received his doctorate in law in 1506 and in 1507 became dean of the faculty of law. He later followed his father's career of service to the emperor, and in 1517 became privy councillor to Maximilian. At the time of

* * * * *

399:7 Arnolt] Arnolt (1485–1532) was the son of an artisan of Sélestat and a graduate of the university of Paris with Beatus Rhenanus. After experience with the printers of Strasbourg, he became a secretary to Maximilian I and afterwards to Charles V.

Ulrich Zwingli
Hans Asper
Graphische Sammlung, Zentralbibliothek, Zürich

writing this letter he had been at Ensisheim in Alsace since 1510, as imperial councillor and agent. Cf Ep 319:27–31 and 27n.

HIERONYMUS BALDUNG TO ERASMUS

Most learned Sir, Lukas Klett, a cultivated man (if I may judge from a few hours' acquaintance) and devoted to good literature, has been with us on a short visit, and when your name was mentioned, as happens very often in the conversation of educated men, he told us briefly many things about you which were remarkable, but true nonetheless. This fired me, although I needed no kindling, with a desire to make myself somehow known to you. If with your habitual courtesy, honourable Sir, you think I have done right, I shall do all I can henceforward to see that Erasmus does not regret striking up some sort of acquaintance with my humble self. Farewell, in haste (as you can see), from Ensisheim, 24 April 1516.

Give my greetings to Beatus Rhenanus – this was my first intention, but the man gave me the idea of writing first to you. Once more farewell.

401 / From Ulrich Zwingli Glarus, 29 April [1516]

Zwingli (1484–1531) was at this time parish priest of Glarus, since his ordination in 1506. He came from the Toggenburg valley in the canton of St Gall, and had been educated at Berne, Vienna, and Basel, where he received his MA in 1506. At Glarus he had devoted himself to humanistic studies and, as can be seen, formed a great admiration for Erasmus. In 1518, two years after this letter was written, he took a position at Zürich, where his preaching on the New Testament in the following year really launched the Reformation in Switzerland. The text in the *Corpus reformatorum* is Egli VII no 13.

TO ERASMUS OF ROTTERDAM, THE GREAT PHILOSOPHER AND THEOLOGIAN, FROM ULRICH ZWINGLI

When I think of writing to you, Erasmus, best of men, I am frightened by the brilliance of your learning, which demands a more spacious world than that 'which all around we see,' but I am encouraged at the same time by the charming kindness you showed me when I came to see you at Basel not long after the beginning of spring; for it is no small proof of a generous nature that you did not disdain a man with no gift of speech and an author quite

* * * * *

400:2 Klett] See Ep 316 introduction.

13 the man] That is, Klett

401:4 spacious world] Reading *capaciorem* with a semicolon after *postulans*

unknown. Clearly this was a concession to my Swiss blood (for I seemed to detect that the nature of the Swiss is not wholly displeasing to you) and to Henricus Glareanus, whom I perceived to be your intimate friend. You may well have wondered very much why I did not stay at home, as at the time, unlike so many of your foolish visitors, I did not wish, much less ask, for the solution of any very difficult question; but when you think about it, and discover that it was that spirited energy of yours I was in search of, you will wonder no longer. It was your energy, in combination with the courtesy of your character and your well-regulated life, that I admired, innocently enough, though perhaps rather shamelessly, to such an extent that when I read what you write, I seem to hear you speaking and to see the courtly gestures of that small but far from ungraceful figure. For (if the phrase may be permitted) you are the favourite companion with whom we must first have some conversation, if we are to get off to sleep.

But why do I weary your exquisite ear with my tuneless chatter, when I well know that daws should feed on the ground? I should like you to know that I am far from regretting my journey to visit you (as Spaniards and Gauls did in olden days when they came to Rome to see Livy, as Jerome tells us); in fact, I believe I have made quite a reputation, simply by boasting that I have seen Erasmus, the man who has done so much for liberal studies and the mysteries of Holy Scripture, and who is so filled with the love of God and men that he considers anything done for the cause of the humanities as a personal service to himself. A man too for whom we are all specially bound to pray, that God may preserve him safe and sound, so that theology, rescued by him from barbarism and logic-chopping, may grow to full maturity and not suffer a harsh and unkindly upbringing, if deprived of such a parent while still of tender years. For my part, if I may at last unburden myself of the whole story, in return for this generosity of yours towards your fellow men, I have made you, though late in the day and on a lower level, the offering that Aeschines made to Socrates. Should you not accept a gift so unworthy of you, I will go one better than the Corinthians when repulsed by Alexander, and say that I never made such an offer before and never will again. If even so you will not accept me, it will have been benefit enough to have been rejected by you, for nothing so makes a man set his life to rights as finding he has not satisfied people like yourself. For

* * * * *

11 Glareanus] See Ep 440 introduction.

26 Jerome] *Epistulae* 53.1.3

38 Aeschines] Diogenes Laertius 2.34

39 Corinthians] They offered honorary citizenship to Alexander the Great, who refused it.

whether you will or no, I shall (I hope) be a better person when you return me to myself, after having made such use as you can of your very humble servant. Farewell and best wishes.

From Glarus, 29 April [1515]

402 / To Nikolaus Ellenbog [Basel], [April 1516]

This is a reply to Ep 395. It was printed by A. Horawitz *Erasmiana* I (Vienna 1878), and the manuscript source is in the Württembergische Landesbibliothek, Cod. hist. quart 99 f 213.

ERASMUS OF ROTTERDAM TO NIKOLAUS ELLENBOG, WHOM HE LOVES AS A BROTHER

Jerome will be finished by next autumn. The New Testament has been rushed into print rather than published, and yet the publication is such that in this class of work I have outstripped all my predecessors. You say you enjoy my things, such as they are. I love you for being so open-minded and appreciate the warmth of your feelings; for praise I care nothing. More welcome still would it be if you would commend me to Christ, whose approval is the true felicity. Your simple language, so clear and unspoilt and giving a picture of your mind, gave me very great pleasure. If you judge that the labour which I have spent on the New Testament may do good in the Christian cause, make others study it besides yourself.

Farewell, dearest Nikolaus.

403 / From Guillaume Budé Paris, 1 May [1516]

This letter was sent through the offices of Arnold Birckmann (d 1542), brother of the Cologne bookseller Franz Birckmann (cf Epp 258:14n; 437:3), and reached Erasmus on 19 June (cf Ep 421:2–3). It replies to an earlier letter of Erasmus now lost, the tone of which can be gathered from the opening of this reply. So begins an epistolary exchange between Erasmus and the man who is usually considered France's greatest humanist. It lasted for twelve years and left us fifty letters which tell us a great deal about the style and mentality of a humanist friendship.

Budé (1468–1540) was born at Paris, the fourth son of Jean Budé, *grand audiencier du roi*, and was privately educated for the most part; for his own account see Allen Ep 583:360ff. At about fifteen years of age he went to Orléans where he studied law and literature. He early became proficient in Greek and studied with Georgius Hermonymus of Sparta and with Johannes Lascaris. The first evidence of his mature scholarly achievement came with publication

Guillaume Budé
Jean Clouet
The inscription in the book, in Greek, reads,
'It may seem a great thing to realize one's desires, but truly the greatest thing is not to desire what one should not.'
The Metropolitan Museum of Art
Purchase, Maria De Witt Jesup Fund, 1946

of his *Annotationes in xxiv Pandectarum libros* (Paris: Bade 1508), a work of juridical and philological erudition, which was followed in 1515 by his important *De Asse*, a study of Roman money, which discussed fundamental questions about imperial finance. Like his earlier work it introduced many new and important texts and critical methods. His later works included a Greek lexicon and his *De transitu hellenismi ad christianismum* (Paris: Estienne 1535). He was one of those influential in persuading Francis I to found the trilingual *collège royal.*

It is possible that Budé and Erasmus met in Paris in the closing years of the fifteenth century, but their relationship is known to us in this prolonged literary exchange which seems to be the authentic expression of their friendship. It is an intellectual association sustained by erudition, ingenuity, reciprocal admiration, and rhetorical wit, and by the public and self-conscious indulgence of all of those qualities. In a correspondence in which the display of ornament and erudition are so conspicuous, the recourse of both writers to Greek is especially notable. In the twenty-five letters by Budé three are almost entirely in Greek; in those by Erasmus one is in Greek altogether; and in all the two writers strive constantly to show that the language is a fluent component of their learning and a complement to their customary Latin, thus indicating their membership in a tiny select society within the already select world of humanistic letters. The substance of the letters themselves is at once austere and rhetorical, moving to and fro from the refinements of philological and exegetical erudition to mutual praise and homage; in reading their exchanges one can only echo the comment of the most recent student of this correspondence, '*Ce sont politesses de rois.*' At the same time in this first letter from Budé there appears a significant divergence in their notion of the uses to which such highly esteemed learning is to be put, when Budé reproves Erasmus for his concern with 'trivialities' (lines 135–6).

This letter is almost half in Greek, half in Latin, but in the copy of it in the Deventer Letter-book (Deventer MS 91 f 192) the Greek is translated, probably for the benefit of the servant-pupil who was the scribe. The letter was printed by both Erasmus and Budé in *Epistolae ad Erasmum*, *Epistolae elegantes*, and in *G. Budaei epistolae* (Paris: Bade 1531). For an extended discussion of this entire correspondence see Garanderie.

GUILLAUME BUDÉ TO ERASMUS OF ROTTERDAM

'My dear Budé,' you say, 'I cannot tell you how much I wish to see you famous, and admire your learning.' That second phrase – do you really mean it? 'Yes, really,' you say. And you expect me to believe it? 'Of course.'

* * * * *

403:2 you say] Evidently in an earlier letter which is lost.

For my part I would gladly do as you say. Naturally so, for I believe you to be a fair-minded man – I think of you not as a theologian, but as one who has a reverence for the truth, and what has convinced me of this is *The Christian's Campaign* that you published some time ago. But I cannot say, nor predicate, nor even indicate, Erasmus dear friend of us all, – for you seem to me too great a man to be called my own friend, since single as you are you can be equal to the lot of us; besides which your writings have made you such a public figure that no one can claim you as his private property – I cannot express, I repeat, how wholly you have made me yours since I had your letter. It was delivered by the young man you recommended to me, who is now at the Sorbonne, or rather, sunk in that Sorbonian bog, for so we might well term that haunt of logic-choppers in its present state. So, when I got your letter and had read it two or three times, I decided then and there to take a holiday from business and devote my leisure entirely to you. The day after it came or the following day I began to read Seneca, to please you; for I supposed that was what you intended – if not, how could I testify to the skill of your printer? Anyhow, while I was poring over Seneca, lo and behold, news comes that the instrument of our salvation has arrived, Erasmus' edition, the bilingual text, that glorious work; for you had written to me about that too, recommending the printer to me.

The arrival of this book made me drop the Seneca that I already had in my hands. Reading your defence, your exhortation, and your preface I spent half of Sunday, the twenty-seventh of this month; for the book had been delivered the day before. Immediately after dinner I went to visit François Deloynes, a man of the highest learning and authority and a leader of the Parlement, who is both a most avid reader of your books and devoted to my books and myself. It was to him that I virtually dedicated my book *On the As*, when I introduced him near the end of the book in discussion with

* * * * *

7–8 *The Christian's Campaign*] The *Enchiridion militis christiani*. Budé's citation is in Greek.

19 Seneca] Erasmus' *Senecae lucubrationes* (Basel: Froben 1515); cf Ep 325 introduction.

22 instrument of our salvation] the *Novum instrumentum*, the title of the first edition of Erasmus' New Testament (Basel: Froben 1516)

27 this month] These words and the tone of this opening suggest that the letter was begun in April, although it is dated May.

28 day before] Conradus Pellicanus, arriving in Paris on 3 May, found the book on sale there the next day; cf *Das Chronikon des Konrad Pellikan* ed Bernhard Riggenbach (Basel 1877) 53 (Allen).

29 Deloynes] Cf Ep 494 introduction; a close friend of Budé.

31–2 *On the As*] *De Asse et partibus eius libri quinque* (Paris: Bade 15 March 1515); see introduction.

myself; for that suited my plan at the time, and in any case it was clear to me that the memory of a dedication in that form could never die except with the death of the book itself, while prefaces are often lost. Well, when I called on him, and he asked me whether I had any news, I replied that I had none. 'I on the other hand,' he said 'have something that touches you nearly, and that will give you pleasure.' I asked what it was. 'A eulogy of you,' was the reply, 'coming from an authority that you will consider equal to a decree of the Roman Senate. For you used to wish that we had three or four men like Erasmus in France (provided of course that one age could produce so many Erasmuses all at once), in hopes that one day you might be allowed to follow your own bent and give more free rein to your own modest abilities; for nothing, you used to say, is more tiresome than the way in which, just when your pen was warming to its work and a fresh breeze was blowing from the Muses, you were often forced to shorten sail and reduce the speed of your sailing to a level which the mental grasp of our fellow-countrymen could tolerate and welcome. Who could patiently endure the spectacle of half-educated men circumscribing the fulness of the Latin tongue to match the narrow limits of their own intelligence? So now you have this same Erasmus not merely reading your works but heralding their virtues.'

He finished speaking and, while I was waiting in suspense, produced your book, still unbound and fresh from the printer, and, showing me a passage in St Luke, 'This Erasmus of yours,' he said, 'now there is a real friend, with very good taste. You were speaking the truth, I can see, when you so often said you were a friend of his, and the kind things you said about him have not gone unrewarded. For my part,' he said, 'I used to marvel at the brilliance of his mind, but now I salute him, besides that, as most fair-minded. You, my dear Budé, who are always fired with ambition to equal the leaders of the world of letters, must now take particular care not to be outdone by a man such as this, when he puts you on your mettle by his generosity.'

That was what he said. And now I assure you, dearest of men, that you are to receive not less than what you have done for me. For on this point I could not endure to give way to you, and not recompense on equal terms a friend who had done me a service and, as far as in him lay, had made the name Budé immortal, especially when I have had so much kindness already from a better man than myself. To repay the debt with interest I would not

* * * * *

54 St Luke] Erasmus' note on Luke 1:4 describes how, at that point in the printing, Beatus Rhenanus showed him a translation of the opening verses of this Gospel by Budé in his *Annotations on the Pandects* (Paris: Bade 17 November 1508); see introduction. Erasmus then inserted in his annotations a long eulogy of Budé, reprinted by Garanderie app 1.

dare promise, seeing that I shall be very hard put to it to repay the principal. In fact, I feel that you have landed me in a tight place with this encomium, in which you have made me an elephant, as they say, instead of an ant. You know, I imagine, that if I pay adequately and in good faith what I owe – and I owe you everything in the way of exorbitant praise – I should immediately be thought to be returning one favour for another, at least among those who know what you have written, which means everybody. For who is there that does not read habitually everything that comes from you? If, on the other hand, in order to avoid this I touch on your praises, copious as they are, cautiously and with circumspection, I must inevitably be thought very mean, and grossly unfair towards you who deserve so much. So this is the kind of dilemma you have put me in by starting this wholly admirable practice of obliging a friend, when I ought to have forestalled you and landed you with the problem, since you would have been much cleverer at finding a solution for the difficulty. All the same, I hope to find some plausible way out, and to invent a satisfactory way of getting quit somehow of this obligation; but to be quit once and for all is more than I expect in my whole lifetime, for really the debt is larger than everything I possess. All the same, I would take on anything, rather than incur such a great burden of ingratitude.

Furthermore, I am most grateful to you, and gladly admit it, for your forgiveness in that matter of the word παρηκολουθηκότι. You gave me the most gentle treatment on that point, leaving me as you did to detect and amend my own error. I was wrong, I admit; I cannot seek to avoid the blame, only the penalty and the disgrace, and it is normal to let a man off these if he owns up. You had a perfect right to point out my mistake in a critical spirit, while still abstaining from censoriousness. If you take the phrase in question, I translated it as though Luke declared himself 'a follower of the eye-witnesses,' although in this passage παρηκολουθηκότι means the same as ἐφιγμένῳ, 'arrived at,' as you yourself seem to hold, although you seem to reject *assecuto* as the Latin equivalent of Greek words meaning 'reached' and 'arrived at' and 'correctly understood.' I am moved to accept *assecuto* by that sentence of Demosthenes in *Misconduct on a*

* * * * *

71 elephant] *Adagia* I ix 69

90 παρηκολουθηκότι] Luke 1:3

91 gentle treatment] Quintilian 11.1.70

99 *assecuto*] The Vulgate reading; Erasmus translated *persecutus* (misprinted *prosectus*), Budé *assectatori*. In his second edition (1519) Erasmus modified his translation and introduced Budé's citations from Demosthenes and Galen into his note; cf Ep 441 (Allen).

101 Demosthenes] *De falsa legatione* 257

Mission: 'that I, who know this man's misdeeds and have followed their whole course, may enjoy your full support as I accuse him.' How am I to understand this? Had Demosthenes uncovered all Aeschines' outrages and crimes and made careful enquiry into them and (as it were) followed up everything he said and did after the event, until in the end he fully understood them? Or was he present as a witness at all his misdemeanours, being his contemporary, a colleague in public life, and a member of the same foreign mission? In another place he says: 'You, gentlemen of the jury, will follow (παρακολουθήσετε) the whole story more easily'; nothing will escape you, but you will fully understand everything as I recount it. So Galen uses παρακολουθῆσαί τινι θεωρίᾳ, 'to follow by a kind of contemplation,' in the sense of perceiving in one's mind in such a way that the object does not elude the man who turns his mind upon it. You thought it referred to the order of procedure of a man writing a narrative. But if you are right, I wonder that he should have said 'to write it down for you in order,' for he had first to learn it all in due order and then write it. And yet both views mean the same thing; for you wrote *prosequi*, not *assequi*. Although you say this, you do not find it satisfactory. Certainly the passage is difficult to grasp.

Ἄνωθεν you have rightly rendered as 'from the beginning,' *retrorsus*. Far be it from me to set out to repudiate my debts instead of confessing openly how much I have profited. But on κατηχῶ I know that your memory has played you false, for your favourite Lucian uses it in the *Ass*: 'He handed me over,' he says 'to one of the young men in his household, a freedman, and told him κατηχεῖν, to teach me how I could most successfully amuse him,' the speaker being the ass, which he describes as having learnt to dance. In another place he puts κατηχεῖν for διδάσκειν, where the sense is 'instruct' or 'rebuke,' νουθετεῖν. Hence the word κατήχητοι in Dionysius the so-called Areopagite. Then again, you render κατήχηθης as though it were κατήχησο.

Apart from that, I could wish that you were yourself as well satisfied as I am with these grand and noble subjects; for now I want to speak to you seriously. To be perfectly frank, I often exclaim with astonishment when I see you misusing such eloquence and such intellectual gifts on the trivialities in which you sometimes give your mind a rest, as if the right course were not to leave ordinary and unimportant topics to men with minds of

* * * * *

109 In another place] *In Macartatum* 1

111 Galen] This reference has not been identified.

124 Lucian] *Asinus* 48

128 In another place] *Philopatris* 17

similar calibre. But you devote the same attention to subjects of the first rank and the third, and even lower, and could justly be criticized on two counts: first, that you step in and deprive lesser men of moderate attainments of their chance to shine, and second, that you waste your own divine fire on things unworthy of it; besides which you reduce the value men set on distinction of both language and thought – something like what the ancients used to call 'lèse-majesté.'

Finally I cannot say how pleased I am with you for your preface addressed to the Holy Father, whose dignity you display with great sense and cunning in the forefront of your book, like an amulet to ward off those stinging wasps, the self-styled divines. And so as to lose nothing meanwhile, although the book is already dedicated to him, you have contrived to involve the archbishop your benefactor in it at the same time, skilfully securing two strings to your bow, or (as they say in our country) acquiring two sons-in-law with only one marriageable daughter.

Steady on, I hear you say: you have come to the end of your paper. Right; I will now stop. You wrote to me in the old Laconic style, and I have replied in the Asianic, or anything there may be more verbose. But I am like that; if you can stand it, make the most of it. I write seldom and reluctantly, but when I do write, I write at length; once I have warmed to my work, I cannot take my hand from the paper. At the same time I urge you to reply, if ever you have the leisure to repay me in kind; use plenty of paper, I mean, for you can see I do not economize. At least you will let me know that you have received this letter and that at the moment I run no risk of being condemned for ingratitude; which I shall not believe until you tell me so. I envy you your leisure and your devotion to the Scriptures, which I have been promising myself this long time; but my spare time is devoted to family business rather than philosophy. How can it be otherwise when I have six sons to educate, brothers of my one small daughter, and am as devoted as anyone to my relations? So neglectful have I always been hitherto of the skills needful for a man with many children. Farewell, and do not cease to love me.

Paris, on Ascension day, on the eve of setting out on a votive pilgrimage

* * * * *

150 archbishop] Cf Ep 384:82ff.

151 two strings to your bow] Literally, to whitewash two walls out of one bucket; *Adagia* I vii 3

152 daughter] *Adagia* I vii 4

168 children] Reading *πολυπαιδίαν*, not *πολυπαιδεία*ν: with much education

404 / To Ulrich Zwingli

Basel, [c 8 May 1516]

The autograph of this letter is in the Staatsarchiv Zürich, E II 360 519–20, and the text in the *Corpus reformatorum* is Egli VII No 14. It was first printed by J.H. Hottinger *Historia ecclesiastica novi testamenti* VI (Hanover 1665).

ERASMUS OF ROTTERDAM TO ULRICH ZWINGLI

I was unusually delighted, both by your very kindly feelings towards me and by the eloquence of your letter, which was as lively as it was stylish. If I send a brief reply, you must blame it not on me but on these labours of mine, which I think will never finish. Often they oblige me to be less than polite to the last people I should wish to treat so, but the person I treat most rudely is myself, as I drain to the dregs my vital force, which draughts of quintessence itself could not restore. That my *Lucubrationes* are approved by a man like you, who yourself enjoy general approval, gives me the greatest pleasure, and on this ground at least I am less dissatisfied with them than I was. I congratulate the people of Switzerland, whose natures I do find most congenial, on having you and others like you to finish their education in the arts and the virtues and make them notable, with Glareanus as your leader and standard-bearer. He is a man I like not less for the outstanding range of his erudition than for his singular integrity and purity of life and character; and he is entirely devoted to you. I expect to revisit Brabant immediately after Pentecost, for business requires this. I shall be sorry to tear myself away from this climate. My dear Ulrich, mind you give your pen practice from time to time; this is the best way to learn to express yourself. I perceive that Minerva has given you the gift, if you will but exercise it. I have written this after supper to please Glareanus, to whom I can refuse nothing, even were he to bid me dance with nothing on. Farewell. From Basel

To the worthy Master Ulrich Zwingli, philosopher and theologian of great learning, whom he loves as a brother. In Glarus

405 / To Fridolin Egli

[Basel, 1516?]

Egli (fl 1514–21) was apparently a native of Glarus who matriculated at Basel with Glareanus and Aegidius Tschudi (cf Allen Ep 490:35n) in 1514. The note seems to have been written during the time Egli was a pupil of Glareanus,

* * * * *

404:8 quintessence] Cf Ep 225:12–15.

17 Pentecost] Or Whitsun, 11 May 1516

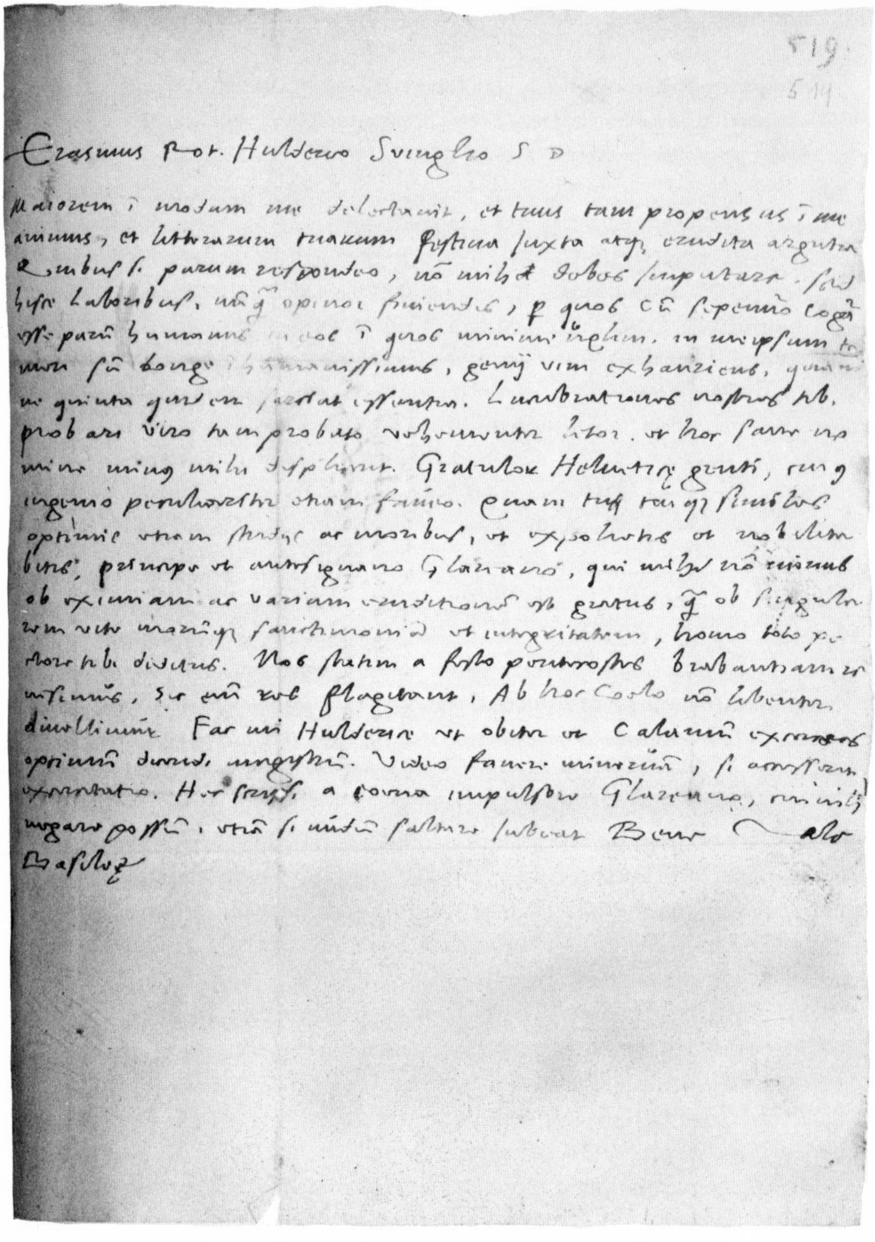
Erasmus Rot. Hulderico Zwinglio S D

Autograph letter, Erasmus to Ulrich Zwingli, Epistle 404
Staatsarchiv Zürich, MS E II 360 f 519

from 1515 to 1518. It survives as an autograph on a small scrap of paper in the Simmler collection in the Zentralbibliothek Zürich, MS S 3b, 15. It was first printed by Dr Emil Egli in *Zwingliana* I (1904) 344. The date is conjectural.

ERASMUS TO HIS FRIEND FRIDOLIN

'Evil communications corrupt good manners.' But you, my dear Hirudaeus, if you choose improving stories and read them to improve yourself, will not merely escape corruption, but will end up an even better man than you are now, especially if you have Henricus Glareanus as a first-rate guide on first-rate material. Farewell.

406 / From Udalricus Zasius — Freiburg im Breisgau, 9 May 1516

This letter was written in 1516, since Erasmus was in England in August 1515. It was first published in *Epistolae ad Erasmum*.

UDALRICUS ZASIUS, PUBLIC PROFESSOR OF LAW AT FREIBURG, TO ERASMUS OF ROTTERDAM

I catch your drift, my eminent friend, great man that you are, when you try to clear yourself of some negligible shadow of discourtesy. My good Sir, how will you persuade anyone that you suffer from the stigma of some duty inadequately performed, when you more than anyone in the world are distinguished above all other men for all good qualities, and exquisite courtesy among them? But I think I can guess what you are aiming at with this uncalled-for self-defence, as though by some kind of indirect fire. It is my discourtesy that is the target, I am the object of your writ of summons, because all this time while you have been a near neighbour I have failed to come and see you, and have never paid my respects to a man who stands first in the world of letters. And indeed this failure would richly deserve to be branded with the name of fault, if no help were forthcoming in the category of mitigating circumstances. But against the charge of discourtesy I am protected by my advancing years, for I have difficulty in walking round the town I live in, without setting off for other places. Besides which there is the heavy and continuous burden of my teaching in the civil law, to say nothing for the moment of the business that almost distracts me, so that you would find it easy to forgive a man who is anxious to excuse his fault; all the

* * * * *

405:2 good manners] 1 Cor 15:33

2 Hirudaeus] Hirudo = Blutegel; the identification is that of Egli.

406:16 advancing years] Zasius would have been in his fifty-fifth year, an advanced age by contemporary reckoning.

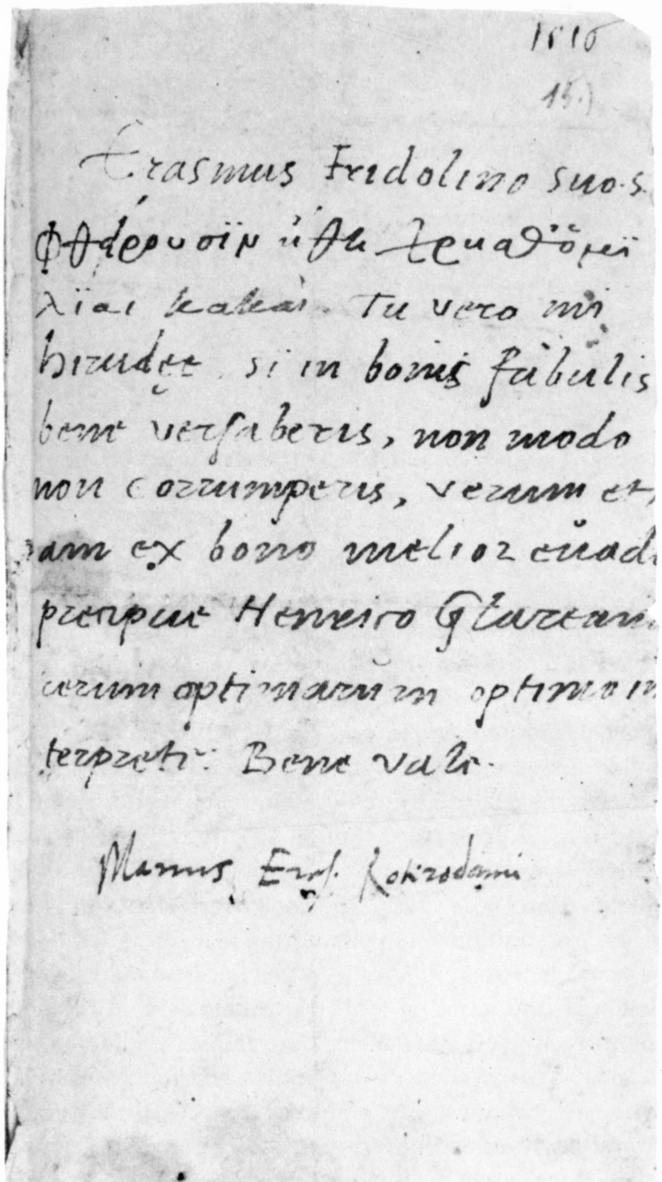

1516

15.)

Erasmus Fridolino suo s.

Φθείρουσιν ἤθη χρηστὰ ὁμιλίαι κακαί. Tu vero mi Fridoline, si in bonis fabulis bene versaberis, non modo non corrumperis, verum etiam ex bono melior euades, praesertim Henrico Glareano rerum optimarum optimo interprete. Bene vale.

Manus Eras. Roterodami

Autograph letter, Erasmus to Fridolin Egli, Epistle 405
A brief note on a scrap of paper, opening with a quotation in Greek from 1 Corinthians 15:33
Simmler Collection, Zentralbibliothek Zürich, MS S 3b Nr 15

more so, since you are a man so easily appeased, so agreeable by nature, all courtesy and kindness, as I hear daily from my dear friend Amerbach – just the man to turn even a black offence into something better, and surely not to reject what can in fact face up to the light, especially in a friend, against whom one cannot pass a hostile judgment without impiety.

You see the state to which I am reduced by your splendid rhetoric. The first aspect of your letter had power to move me to forgive your unkindness (of all unexpected things!). But as I thought it over, I found that I was laid under a heavy burden of defending myself; in fact, had I not detected your cunning art (and what is there of yours that is not full of art and wit?), I came close to exposing myself unexpectedly, in a fit of absurd self-satisfaction, to your extraordinary learning. As for the envious tooth of certain persons, of which you write, it is of no concern; Envy, as Emilius Probus says, is Glory's close companion. You need have no doubt that it is a proof of true and original scholarship and excellent learning if the popular scribblers get their teeth into you. I need say no more: you can learn this from your favourite, St Jerome.

After all this time, please come and see us, I beg you in the name of friendship. Your arrival will be welcomed by all men of good will, of whom you will find plenty here. I shall be your host, devoted, accessible, ready to the uttermost farthing; we shall inscribe my desk and the desks in the school 'Erasmus was here.' Farewell, and make much of my friend Bonifacius, who loves you like a deity; I wish he loved divinity and the gods above as much as he loves Erasmus, and I have already cast my vote for his future blessedness. So, glory of the world, farewell.

From Freiburg, 9 May 1516

Forgive my unpolished pen; the courier is at my elbow.

Your devoted Zasius

407 / To Willibald Pirckheimer — Basel, 12 May 1516

The year date is derived from the publications mentioned. Erasmus was about to leave for the Low Countries; cf Ep 410 introduction. It was first printed in *Pirckheimer* 1610.

ERASMUS TO HIS FRIEND WILLIBALD

I had nothing to say and no time to write to you, being already booted and spurred for my journey, and the labours of what is now so many months have virtually finished me off. But having the chance of someone to carry a

* * * * *

33 Probus] Cornelius Nepos 12.3.3: the *Lives* have come down to us under the name of Aemilius Probus.

letter, I could not fail to write to my dear Willibald. The New Testament for better or worse is finished. Jerome comes up breathless to the finishing line and will soon be in the hands of the public. The printer is now engaged on a short book on the education of a prince, together with some other things. We lesser men do what we can, and serve the cause of literature as best we may; you are in happier case, and thus can do greater things. Whatever part of the world I find myself in, I shall always carry you round with me in my heart. I beg you earnestly to say a good word to everyone for my annotations on the New Testament, for you know how much anything novel is exposed to ill will. Farewell, glory of the literary world. From Basel, Whit-Monday 1516

To the honourable Willibald Pirckheimer, councillor of the famous city of Nürnberg

408 / To Bonifacius Amerbach Basel, [c 12 May 1516]

The youngest [b 1495] and best known of the three Amerbach sons, Bonifacius matriculated at Basel in 1509, and became familiar with the scholars in his father's house who were working on the edition of Jerome. In 1514 he went to Freiburg to study law with Zasius with whom he remained until 1519. After further study with Alciati at Avignon (1520–4) he eventually succeeded to the professorship in law at Basel. He became a close friend and advisor of Erasmus, who appointed him executor of his will. His collections of manuscripts and letters are a principal source for the intellectual history of the time. The autograph original of this letter is in the Öffentliche Bibliothek of the university of Basel, MS AN III 15 69 (AK 552); and it was first printed in *Epistolae familiares*.

ERASMUS TO HIS FRIEND BONIFACIUS

If I have not written before, I know, my dear Bonifacius, that you are far too courteous to attribute this to discourtesy on my part; you will blame my quite exorbitant labours, which are not altogether unknown to you. I have great affection for you, and for all who bear the name of Amerbach. I have great hopes of you after reading your letter, which reminded me of Poliziano, or of that second Poliziano, Zasius. Go on as you have begun,

* * * * *

407:8 other things] Froben's edition of the *Institutio principis christiani* (cf Ep 393 introduction) included the panegyric *Ad illustrissimum principem Philippum, archiducem Austriae* (cf Ep 179 introduction) and translations from Plutarch (cf Epp 272, 297); cf Ep 393:67n.

408:7 second Poliziano] Cf Ep 307:23.

and win lustre for your family and your native place by being a really good and really well-educated man.

I was already booted and spurred for my journey, as I wrote this, and had no time to answer my dear Zasius' lively letter. When I have the leisure, I will move into the lead, with whole volumes perhaps. He seems to me the only German who knows how to express himself. Farewell. From Basel

To Bonifacius Amerbach, an accomplished young man richly gifted by the Graces. In Freiburg

409 / From Willibald Pirckheimer — Nürnberg, 20 May 1516

This letter is dated between the publication of the New Testament (Ep 384) and of the *Epistolae ad Erasmum* (October 1516) in which it first appeared; there is a MS version in the Deventer Letter-book, in which the postscript appears attached to Ep 527. Allen, who wished to place Ep 527 in 1517, transferred the postscript to this letter, arguing that it was perhaps written on a separate sheet and that the copyist mistakenly attached it to the wrong letter; cf Ep 527 introduction. This letter and Ep 527 follow one another immediately in the Letter-book.

WILLIBALD PIRCKHEIMER TO MASTER ERASMUS

I sent you a letter, my dearest Erasmus to whom I am devoted, about four months ago, but, having had no answer from you, I suspect that either my letter or your reply must have gone astray. In the meantime, however, your splendid publication, in which you have expounded the New Testament with flawless faith and piety, and yet with great success, took the place of a letter. You have protected your name against all the assaults of time, and completed a task as acceptable to almighty God as it is necessary and useful to all Christ's faithful people. Well done, well done indeed; you have achieved a result that has been denied to all men this side of a thousand years. But why do I try to extol your scholarship and learning, which is a task far beyond my powers, had I 'ten tongues, ten mouths, / Voice indefeasible and heart of bronze,' as the poet says? So it is better modestly to keep silence than to sing your praises inadequately; and if my treatment of them seems to you uninspired, this is a measure of my weakness, not my strength.

Enough of that. What are you doing? How is your state of health? What are you, in particular, getting ready for publication? I long to know, so

* * * * *

409:2 letter] Evidently a lost letter written since Ep 375

13 the poet] Homer *Iliad* 2.489–90

please write and tell me, if this is not too tiresome. I should then have some answer to give to the crowd of your unknown friends, who write to me daily, asking anxiously for news of our hero Erasmus. See, my dear Erasmus, how greedy we are – let me not say ungrateful – for anything from you: you have done very great things for us, far more than we had any right to expect, and we still ask for and more or less insist on something further. You must blame this on your own virtues, not on any vice in us. Farewell, light and glory of the human race.

Nürnberg, 20 May 1516

Stab, the court historian of the emperor, greets you once more, a good scholar and a good man. So do my two sisters, one the abbess of St Clare's and the other a votary of the same rule, who have your writings in their hands continually. They are particularly delighted with the New Testament, which appeals greatly to women who are more learned than many men who think they know something. They would write to you in Latin, if they did not think their letters unworthy of you.

410 / To Jean Le Sauvage — Antwerp, 1 June [1516]

With his work on the New Testament completed in March (Ep 384 introduction) and that on the letters of St Jerome in April (Ep 396), Erasmus left early in May for the Netherlands (Ep 407:1), knowing that his *Institutio principis christiani*, dedicated to Prince Charles, was shortly to emerge from Froben's press (Ep 393). He was concerned to pay court in the Netherlands, where he had been appointed to the prince's council (cf Ep 370:18n) and where he was more advantageously placed to deal with the problems surrounding the prebend at Tournai (cf Ep 388:32–65). He also intended to visit England to renew his contacts there and to collect his annuity (Ep 388:66–92). About the news contained in Ammonio's letter of the previous February (Ep 389) he had as yet no inkling (cf Epp 427; 429).

* * * * *

28 Stab] Johann Stab (d January 1522) was court historian to the emperor from 1503. He had studied at Sélestat and Ingolstadt, and in 1497 was made professor of mathematics at Vienna. His principal achievements were in the latter field.

29 two sisters] Charitas (d 1532) and Clara (d 1533), respectively abbess of the convent of St Clare at Nürnberg, and a nun of the same convent who succeeded her sister in the same office. The community also included two daughters of Willibald Pirckheimer. They were clearly learned ladies, and the Stadtbibliothek at Nürnberg contains some Latin letters written by Charitas and Clara.

At Antwerp, where he arrived on 30 May, Erasmus stayed with his old friend Pieter Gillis (cf Ep 312 introduction), the friend equally of Thomas More, whose letter of the preceding February Gillis delivered to him (cf Ep 412:35). From Gillis' house Erasmus wrote this letter to the principal minister of the young prince Charles, now king of Aragon and Castile; cf Epp 301:38n; 332:3n. He also took the opportunity to despatch copies of his recent publications to friends in England through the services of his familiar messenger and scribe, Pieter Meghen.

Jean Le Sauvage, heer van Schoubeke, who died in 1518, had been appointed chancellor of Burgundy in 1515, and in 1516 chancellor of Castile (see Epp 301:38n; 332:3n). From internal evidence of subject-matter and language it is clear that Epp 410 to 417 were written within a few days of one another. This letter first appeared in the *Farrago*.

TO THE HONOURABLE JEAN LE SAUVAGE,
CHANCELLOR OF HIS CATHOLIC MAJESTY,
FROM ERASMUS OF ROTTERDAM

At last I have detached myself from my labours in Basel, honoured Sir, later perhaps than I had wished and my friends had expected, yet almost in too much of a hurry to suit my work, for my book on the education of a prince was not finished when I left, although I greatly desired to offer it to the prince as a gift, and some things were still needed in my Jerome. In what remains I shall value your advice, as I do what needs doing.

I have left this letter in Antwerp on purpose, that if I do not have the good fortune to meet you in Brussels or Mechelen, this will at least give me some means of greeting your Highness. For I myself go to join Mountjoy, and from there mean to send someone to England to deliver the volumes of Jerome to the archbishop of Canterbury, to whom I have dedicated them, and at the same time to go and see the rest of my friends on my behalf, and collect my annuity for the past year. Once this is done, I come to see you next. Meanwhile best wishes to your Highness, incomparable as a man and eminent as a patron.

Antwerp, 1 June [1515]

* * * * *

410:7 not finished] Cf Ep 419:4–5.

12 Mountjoy] Lieutenant of Tournai and also of the castle of Hammes; see Ep 301 introduction.

16 annuity] Erasmus' income from the living of Aldington; cf Ep 255 introduction.

411 / To Remacle d'Ardenne Antwerp, 1 June [1516]

Remacle (1480–1524), a native of Florennes in the Ardenne, had studied at Cologne where he made the acquaintance of Cochlaeus. He made a career as tutor and school-teacher, finally procuring a post as secretary in the household of Prince Charles. He was teaching school in London in January 1512, and it was probably in London that he made the acquaintance of Erasmus. His literary reputation was as a poet. The letter was first published in the *Farrago*.

ERASMUS OF ROTTERDAM TO HIS FRIEND REMACLE

At last I have escaped from the workhouse in Basel, where I have got through six years work in eight months. It is surprising, my dear Remacle, with what warm feelings and what generous offers I have been received there in Upper Germany, and that part of the world attracted me in every way as much as any under the sun. I have left this letter at Antwerp on my way to Brussels for the pleasure of seeing you, with the intention that if, as luck would have it, we have no opportunity of meeting, it may greet my friends on my behalf, for I am delighted to find myself restored to them. Farewell, and if Luigi is there, be sure to give him my regards. Antwerp, 1 June [1517]

412 / To Thomas More [Brussels], [c 3 June 1516]

The month date and place are supplied from Tunstall's arrival (line 60n) and from the letter's position in the group Epp 410–17, whose content and language show that they were written within a few days of each other. In addition to the letters in this immediate group, Erasmus wrote by Pieter Meghen to Wolsey (Ep 424:75), Warham (Ep 424:29), Ruthall (Ep 437:1), Colet (Ep 423:2), Joannes Sixtinus (Ep 430:3), Watson (Allen Ep 450:1), Lupset (Ep 431:6, 10), and probably Bedyll (Ep 426). In reply Meghen brought back Epp 423–6 and 429–32, reaching Antwerp by 9 July; cf lines 47 and 61 below. The letter was first published in the *Farrago*.

ERASMUS OF ROTTERDAM TO HIS FRIEND MORE

Sick to everyone else, to you alone I am in good health. Heaven be thanked, I returned safely to Antwerp on 30 May. I had a plan to travel through

* * * * *

411:10 Luigi] Luigi Marliano of Milan (d 1521) was physician to the archduke Philip, and later physician and councillor to prince Charles. About 1517 he obtained the see of Tuy in Galicia. Cf LP II 1393, 1516, 2349, etc.

Lorraine, for I had got as far as Kaysersberg, a town in the mountains. But when I saw bands of soldiery everywhere, and the country people in many places moving from the country into the towns, and rumour had it that a large party was approaching, I thought better of it, and not so much avoided the risks as altered their nature. In Cologne I found some Italian envoys and finished my journey with them. We were a party of about eighty horsemen, and even so our journey was not free from peril.

The bishop of Basel, who is a very old man of high character and well read, has been extremely kind to me, although by repute he is not normally a very generous man; this is the blemish they find in so handsome a person. He invited me to his house, gave me a warm welcome, and spoke very highly of me. He offered me money and a position, and presented me with a horse which it was possible to sell on the spot for fifty gold florins when I was hardly out of the city gates. He had ordered a silver cup for me, but the goldsmith had deceived him, at which he was indignant. I can hardly say how much I like this Basel climate and the kind of people who live there; nothing could be more friendly or more genuine. The number of horses that escorted my departure; the emotion with which they bade me farewell! Not but what I was getting offers in other places that were by no means to be despised. I have sent you one letter, from which you can gather that I am not making all this up. The New Testament wins approval even from the people I thought most likely to malign it; the leading theologians are delighted with it. My *Enchiridion* is universally welcome; the bishop of Basel carries it round with him everywhere – I have seen all the margins marked in his own hand. But enough of this, or you will think me something of a boaster, although to a friend like you I will go so far as to talk nonsense without hesitation. But so many burdens weigh upon me that I cannot lift up my head. One or two blows of Fortune a man may learn to endure somehow, but I am unfortunate at all points. How hard it is to be sensible when our

* * * * *

412:4 Kaysersberg] In the Vosges, NW of Colmar

7 party] Cf Allen Ep 469:5.

11 bishop of Basel] Christoph von Utenheim (d 1527); cf Ep 598 introduction and line 26 below.

16 fifty gold florins] Probably Rhenish rather than Florentine or Burgundian florins. If so, then a sum worth, at official rates, about £8 10s 10d sterling = £12 1s 8d groot Flemish = £71 8s 0d tournois. Cf CWE 1 316–17, 338–9; CWE 2 327–45.

23 One letter] Evidently Ep 386

lady of Rhamnus is against one! Yet a spirit worthy of Hercules is my prop and stay.

I was pleased with the letter which Pieter Gillis delivered to me on my return to Antwerp. As for Maruffo, I cannot think what can have come into his head to make him talk such nonsense. I deposited one hundred and twenty nobles, first-class coin, with him, for which he gave me a receipt. But this business can be settled without any risk. I have written to the archbishop by this courier to say that that money has been repaid me by Maruffo's good offices. Maruffo should give this man his draft, against which I can get money in this part of the world, and when that draft has been deposited with you, let him collect his money from the archbishop. If that is not thought to be satisfactory, arrange to receive the money yourself, and write and tell your correspondents to pay it over to me here; and at the same time send me a document authorizing me to collect it. I will adapt my letter to the archbishop to make either course possible. At this point Pieter the One-eyed has suggested to me that it would be best to entrust the money to some German merchant, against whose draft I could receive it in Antwerp. And so I will say in my letter that he should give the money to you, and that through you it will soon reach me. I was delighted with your letter which showed your feelings towards me, and also made it clear how you have progressed in power of expression. Your defence of me I have not yet finished; I gather from it what Maarten van Dorp had written. I cannot think what has come into his head. But that is what this sort of theology does to people.

I have paid my respects to the chancellor. As it happened, that well-

* * * * *

33 Rhamnus] A famous Greek sanctuary of Nemesis; Erasmus often uses this phrase as an elegant synonym for Fortune personified.

36 Maruffo] Cf Ep 387:3n.

37–8 one hundred and twenty nobles] English gold coins, possibly the ryal or rose-noble, worth 10s 0d sterling, but more likely the angel-noble, worth 6s 8d sterling. If indeed the latter, this would have been worth, at official rates, £40 0s 0d sterling = £58 0s 0d groot Flemish = £341 6s 8d tournois. Cf CWE 1 312, 319 (plate), 325–6, 336–7; CWE 2 146 (Ep 214:4n), 327–45, 340 (plate).

47 Pieter] Meghen, the scribe; cf Ep 231:5n. His contribution to the Erasmian circle in England as both scribe and messenger was extremely important; cf McConica, and the article by J.B. Trapp 'Notes on Manuscripts Written by Peter Meghen' *The Book Collector* 24, 1 (spring 1975) 80–96.

57 chancellor] Jean Le Sauvage; cf Ep 410 introduction.

known figure, the provost of Cassel, was there to supper, a scholarly and friendly person. The bishop of Chieti is here too; and as I write this, Tunstall is expected. After greeting him I shall visit Mountjoy and the abbot, and spend some time with them, until this One-eyed returns. I shall soon open the question with the prince; but if I feel things are hanging fire, as is the natural attitude in Flanders towards learning, I shall go straight to Basel, unless you advise differently. Write fully and in detail, if there is anything relating to my future. If Pace is with you, tell him to send back by the bearer of this all my notes which I left with him at Ferrara. I have had a meeting with the bishop of Chieti, and took supper with him. He is full of affection and admiration for me, and is active with Prince Charles, whom he will accompany to Spain.

Today I had supper with Tunstall, who has, to put it in a nutshell, a strong likeness to you. Mind you recover, for I hear you have been very poorly.

[1518]

413 / To John Fisher

Saint-Omer, 5 June [1516]

Evidently Mountjoy, whom Erasmus had planned to visit at Hammes, was not there, so Erasmus went at once to Saint-Omer and enjoyed the hospitality of the abbot of St Bertin. The letter was first published in the *Farrago*.

TO THE RIGHT REVEREND FATHER IN CHRIST, JOHN, BISHOP OF ROCHESTER, FROM ERASMUS OF ROTTERDAM

Reverend Father, had my health permitted I should pay my respects to your Highness in person and thank you for all your kindness to me. Having originally intended the New Testament for you, why I changed my plan and dedicated it to the supreme pontiff I wrote and explained some time ago, and with your habitual generosity, not to say wisdom, you will I hope take

* * * * *

58 provost of Cassel] Georgius of Theimseke (d c 1536) was the most powerful member of an important family of Bruges. He was an influential ecclesiastic and diplomat, and an imperial councillor. See de Vocht *Literae*.

59 bishop of Chieti] Gianpietro Carafa; cf Ep 287:9n.

60 Tunstall] He arrived in Brussels on 3 June (LP II 2006); notice the postscript.

61 abbot] Antoon van Bergen at Saint-Omer; cf Ep 143 introduction.

62 the question] Cf Ep 370:18n.

66 my notes] Cf Ep 30:17.

413:6 I wrote] This letter is lost.

what I have done in good part. This work caused alarm before it came out, but now that it is published it is marvellously well received by all good scholars or sincere and open-minded men, not excluding theologians. The prior of Freiburg, who stands high among his own people (he is the author of *The Pearl of Philosophy*), after sampling the book said he would rather lose two hundred gold florins than be without it. Ludwig Baer, the Paris theologian, who was first of his year in the promotion (as they call it), greets it with enthusiastic devotion, and laments all the years he has wasted on the petty disputes of the schools. This is also the attitude of Wolfgang Capito, the public preacher at Basel, a much better Hebrew scholar than Reuchlin and also a man of great experience in theological disputation; and both of them are diligent students of Greek. I have found others very like him, a theologian at Mainz and at Cologne the suffragan bishop.

To say nothing of others, the bishop of Basel, who is a man of great age but of most upright life and very learned, has shown me every sort of kindness and offered me everything. When I refused it all, he insisted on my accepting a horse, which I could have sold as soon as I left the city for

* * * * *

11 prior] Gregor Reisch; cf Ep 308 introduction.

12 *The Pearl of Philosophy*] The *Margarita philosophica* (1503)

13 two hundred gold florins] Possibly Florentine but more likely Rhenish gold florins. If so, this sum would have been worth, at official rates, £34 3s 4d sterling = £48 6s 8d groot Flemish = £287 12s 0d tournois. Cf CWE 1 316–17, 338–9; CWE 2 327–45.

13 Baer] Cf Ep 488 introduction.

14 year of promotion] His graduating class

16 Capito] Cf Ep 459 introduction and Ep 386:6n.

17 Reuchlin] Erasmus was later brought to account for this hasty and unconsidered comparison by Ulrich von Hutten in his *Expostulatio* (1523). Erasmus replied in *Spongia* (LB X 1641C–E).

20 suffragan bishop] Theodoricus Michwael (sometimes Wichwael) de Caster or Castro (d 1519) of Calcar, near Cleve. He was an Augustinian who was prior of the monastery at Cologne 1495–1503, and at the same time a member of the theological faculty and regent of the Augustinian house of studies. In August 1504 he was appointed titular bishop of Cyrene and suffragan to the archbishop of Cologne. Humanistically trained and a friend of Agrippa von Nettesheim, he stood in opposition to the Dominicans and in support of Reuchlin. See A. Kunzelmann *Geschichte der deutschen Augustiner-Eremiten, Vierter Teil: Die kölnische Provinz bis zum Ende des Mittelalters* (Würzburg 1972); N. Teeuwen and A. de Meijer *Documents pour servir à l'histoire médiévale de la province augustinienne de Cologne* (Héverlé/Louvain 1961).

21 bishop of Basel] Cf Ep 412:11n.

fifty gold florins. Duke Ernest of Bavaria sent an emissary all the way to Basel for the express purpose of offering me two hundred gold pieces a year, besides the prospect of benefices and munificent gifts, if I would merely agree to live in Ingolstadt, the seat of the university of Bavaria. A certain German bishop, whose name at the moment escapes me, did the same. But I will stop boasting, although I could produce much more like this with perfect truth. I know that I deserve none of it, and yet I am delighted to know that my labours, such as they are, find some favour with men of good will. Many are taking this opportunity to read the Scriptures who would never read them otherwise, as they themselves admit; many people are beginning to take up Greek, or rather, this is now common.

St Jerome will appear complete at the next Frankfurt fair. At this moment I am sending the bearer of this, Pieter the One-eyed, on purpose at my own risk and expense to bring the four volumes of his letters to the archbishop of Canterbury, which he will readily give you access to. I had got as far as Saint-Omer with the intention of crossing to England, but I had a touch of fever and was unwilling to risk the voyage. When I have the chance, I will contrive somehow to show that I have not entirely forgotten your great and most generous kindness to me. Prince Charles is being sent for to take over several kingdoms (nine or ten, they say). A wonderful success, but I pray it may turn out well for our country and not only for the prince. After leaving Basel, when I was preparing to travel through Lorraine, I ran into soldiers everywhere and saw the country people moving their belongings into the nearest small town. Rumour had it that they were ready to attack Lorraine, but it was uncertain who sent them. I suspect they were men discharged by the emperor and looking for someone to pay them wages instead of him. What an extraordinary game these Christian princes play! We are in such a state of turmoil, playing dice all the time, and yet we consider ourselves Christians. But I and others like me can only lament this. Oh how I wish all pontiffs, cardinals, magnates, theologians would agree

* * * * *

25 fifty gold florins] Probably Rhenish florins. Cf above Ep 412:16n.

25 Duke Ernest] Cf Ep 386 introduction.

26 two hundred gold pieces] Probably Rhenish gold florins of the Four Electors. If so, a sum worth, at official values, about £34 3s 4d sterling = £48 6s 8d groot Flemish = £287 12s 0d tournois. Cf above Ep 413:13n.

39 archbishop of Canterbury] Cf Ep 439:6.

44 kingdoms] That is, Aragon and Castille; he was proclaimed king of Castile on 14 May 1516.

on this one object – to put an end sooner or later to these scandalous wrongs! But this will never happen unless they can rise above the passion for private gain and pursue solely the general good. The result would mean more prosperity for everyone. Farewell. I shall fare better myself, if you think I have earned a letter from you.

Saint-Omer, 5 June [1517]

414 / To Andrea Ammonio Saint-Omer, 5 June [1516]

This letter was first published in the *Farrago*.

ERASMUS TO ANDREA AMMONIO

I am delighted that the man you speak of should be released from his royal cage, and if this means some advantage for you too, I have a double reason to be glad. I admire Colet's truly Christian spirit, for I hear it was his doing alone that got him his freedom; and while Colet had always reckoned him among his closest friends, when his friend Colet was already being wrongly accused by the bishops, he sided with his enemies. The letters I wrote to Leo and the cardinals I have published, but in an expanded form. If there is any answer, or anything that you think I ought to know, please let me know by the bearer of this, Pieter the One-eyed, whom I have sent to England for this purpose at my own expense, and he will return here shortly; for a touch of fever that came on suddenly forbids me to cross, and there is something to be done to oblige Charles, which will take several days. Upper Germany I found so attractive in every way that I greatly regret having got to know it so lately. The bishop of Basel did all he could to show honour to your friend Erasmus, although he is a most sparing man by repute otherwise; he offered me money, offered me a position, made me accept a horse which I could have sold again for fifty gold pieces as soon as I had left the city. But if I

* * * * *

414:2–3 royal cage] That is, the chancellorship; Erasmus refers to Warham's resignation. Cf Ep 388:93; P.S. Allen 'Dean Colet and Archbishop Warham' EHR 17 (April 1902) 303–6; Allen later retracted the opinion expressed there that the present letter was a reply to Ep 389.

7 sided] Cf Ep 270:53n.

7 letters] In *Jani Damiani Senensis elegeia* (Basel: Froben August 1515)

13 Charles] Cf Ep 370:18n. Erasmus no doubt planned to have an audience in order to present a copy of the *Institutio principis christiani*.

18 fifty gold pieces] Probably Rhenish florins. Cf above Ep 412:16n, 413:25n.

am to turn Thraso like this, it had better wait until we meet. Farewell, and write at least to say how you are.

Saint-Omer, 5 June [1513]

415 / To Thomas Linacre Saint-Omer, 5 June [1516]

This letter was first published in the *Farrago*.

ERASMUS OF ROTTERDAM TO THOMAS LINACRE, PHYSICIAN TO HIS MAJESTY

There was nothing new in it, but it gave me the greatest pleasure to learn from More's letter that you have such warm feelings towards me, however little I deserve this. The New Testament gives such universal pleasure to educated people, even in the faculty of theology, that the uneducated are ashamed of themselves and keep quiet. A sudden attack of fever was the reason why I did not risk the crossing, especially as Ghisbert my physician was against it. I beg you urgently to copy out again and send me the prescription that I took on your advice when I was lately in London; my servant left the paper at the chemist's. I should be extremely grateful. My other news you will hear from More. Farewell. From Saint-Omer, 5 June

Croke is the great man in Leipzig University, giving public lectures on Greek. I wish your works would come out; everyone would then believe my praises of them, which I repeat constantly, both because they are well deserved, and to encourage my countrymen to study. If there is anything in this business in which I can do you any service, you will find me most ready to oblige. Farewell once more.

Give my greetings to Grocyn. So far am I from disliking him, heaven knows, that I sincerely respect and admire him. Farewell yet again.

[1514]

* * * * *

19 Thraso] The braggart in Terence's *Eunuchus*

415:4 More's letter] Cf Ep 388:174–7.

8 Ghisbert] Cf Ep 95:13n.

13 Croke] Cf Ep 227:31n. He went to Leipzig in 1515 and was retained there in response to a petition of the faculty of arts, supported by Duke George of Saxony. His Greek *Tabulae* were published there by Schumann in 1516, with a preface to the university dated 25 February.

14 your works] His *De sanitate tuenda;* cf Allen Ep 502:15n.

19 Grocyn] Cf Ep 350:8.

416 / To Christopher Urswick — Saint-Omer, 5 June [1516]

Urswick (cf Ep 193 introduction) was an active member of the humanist circle at the Tudor court, having been chaplain to Lady Margaret Beaufort, grand almoner to Henry VII, dean of York, and from 1495 dean of Windsor. He was one of the chief English patrons of Pieter Meghen along with John Colet; he died in 1522 at the age of seventy-four. Little is known about the life of Meghen, not even the dates of his birth and death, and most of what is known comes either from the colophons of his highly distinctive manuscripts or from the correspondence of Erasmus, as in the present letter. For Urswick's influence see McConica 70–2; see also Ep 412:47n. This letter was first published in the *Farrago*.

ERASMUS TO HIS FRIEND URSWICK

Your horse has brought me great good fortune. Twice has he carried me safely to Basel and back again, although the journey was most perilous as well as long. He is now at least as wise as Ulysses in Homer, who knew 'the cities and the minds of many men,' so many are the universities he has been to. While I was in Basel working myself almost to death for ten months, he in the mean time did nothing and grew so fat he could hardly move. That country of Upper Germany I found surprisingly attractive and that in many ways, and they seem surprisingly fond of your friend Erasmus. The New Testament you have no doubt seen. Jerome will shortly see the light as a whole, together with a small book on the education of a Christian prince. Four volumes of the Jerome I have sent to the archbishop of Canterbury by the bearer of this, your protégé Pieter the One-eyed, whom I found toiling so hard at copying books that he has almost worked himself to death. I think the poor man's end must be at hand, he has become so unlike his usual self; in fact he has almost turned abstemious and developed a dislike for wine, and hence his unusual pallor. Your kindness to me I shall always remember, whatever corner of the earth I may inhabit in the future. Farewell.

Saint-Omer, 5 June [1517]

* * * * *

416:4 Ulysses] Horace *Ars poetica* 142, copying *Odyssey* 1.3

13 protégé] On Meghen's connection with Urswick see McConica 70–2 and J.B. Trapp 'Notes on Manuscripts Written by Peter Meghen' *The Book Collector* 24, 1 (spring 1975) 82–3.

417 / To William Latimer

[Saint-Omer], 5 June [1516]

William Latimer (c 1460–1545) was an Oxford graduate and Fellow of All Souls College. He had studied Greek during extensive travel in Italy, and took an MA at Padua; cf Ep 208:25n. He was tutor to Reginald Pole, well known in the English humanist community, and a close friend of More and Pace; Erasmus himself was now to seek his assistance in revising his text of the Greek New Testament; cf Allen Epp 502:29; 520. This letter was first published in the *Epistolae ad diversos* (1521).

ERASMUS OF ROTTERDAM TO WILLIAM LATIMER

In the sacred name of literature, dear Latimer, kindest of men, I beg you for help with the New Testament. It has been published, considering how short of time we were, pretty correctly; but I had to spend much more time than I expected in correcting the printer's copy beforehand and then in reading proof, although two educated men had been hired for the purpose at great expense. The help I want is this: write and tell me what changes you think should be made, for I shall soon be preparing a second edition. Only mind no one gets wind of this for the printer's sake, for his volumes would all stay in the shop if the buyers knew of it.

Of the warm reception I have had from the whole of Upper Germany I will say nothing, for fear I seem to be showing off. My own country is wooing me too; but I am so far from hoping for that that I am actually ashamed of honour which I know I do not deserve. Yet I am delighted that sound learning should be on the increase, and hope the time will soon come when Erasmus will pass for a beginner. Farewell.

5 June [1517]

418 / From Johann Reuchlin

Stuttgart, 5 June 1516

The month is confirmed by the reference in Ep 419:3.

What a disappointment it was, my dear Erasmus, to receive your present, most holy and scriptural though it was, from the last fair, and my manu-

* * * * *

417:5 correcting] Cf Ep 421:54–60.

6 two educated men] Oecolampadius and Nikolaus Gerbel; cf Epp 384 introduction and 351:2n.

418:1 your present] Evidently the *Novum instrumentum*

2–3 my manuscript] Cf Epp 300:35 and 384 introduction.

script with it (I mean the book you have sent me, in two languages), without your usual pinch of salt, by which you are to understand a letter from you to confirm our more than ordinary friendship. For one letter from you, however laconic, would have aroused my sensations to pleasure far more exquisite than Vincent's whole *Speculum*, or a still more immense book, if there is one. Now you know your Pentateuch far better than anyone else (for I must pay a tribute to my beloved Moses; I call him mine, because with me he has taken the place of Cicero); you know, I am sure, that it says among the commandments that 'With every offering thou shalt offer salt,' which is the explanation of our professors of divinity for בכל המאכלים שיתן טעם. Your book, you see, is meat and drink to me, and a letter from you is the comfort of my mind; so do not rob me of these, I beg you, for I love you so well and read what you write with such enjoyment. You alone show us what the eloquence of the olden times was really like, and the rest of us are mere cyphers. Really, when I read you, I think so poorly of what I write myself that I often lay down my pen altogether for a time in some depression, rightly thinking that the great scale of your researches outdoes all the writers of our own age in every respect. Not, Heaven knows, that I grudge you the gifts that you owe to nature, industry, and fortune; but I lament my own circumstances, which allowed me no books and no teachers, and no kind of file, as it were, to put an edge on my speaking or writing, at the time when, as a young man, I might have done it. As things are, 'Now Moeris' very voice has left him.'

Never mind. Enough of my own wretched life and all this grumbling. Please, please, write to me soon and tell me how you are and what you are doing. My own news is that 'the case is still before the court.' My opponents have again borrowed a thousand gold ducats from the banks in Rome, as they have done twice before. Take my word for it, as long as there is one gold piece left, the whole thing hangs fire, everything tangled up in everything else, such is their appetite for anything they can get. For my part, I

* * * * *

7 *Speculum*] The gigantic encyclopaedic work, *Speculum historiale, morale, doctrinale, naturale*, of the Dominican writer Vincent of Beauvais (c 1190–1264). It was first printed at Strasbourg in 1473–6, in eight folio volumes.

11 salt] Lev 2:13

24 Moeris] Virgil *Eclogues* 9.53–4; cf *Adagia* I vii 86.

28 before the court] Horace *Ars poetica* 78

29 thousand gold ducats] Venetian gold coins. At official rates a sum worth about £229 3s 4d sterling = £1938 0s 0d tournois = £329 3s 4d groot Flemish. Cf CWE 1 314, 338–9, 342–4; CWE 2 327–45; and above Ep 388:86n.

30 twice before] Cf Hermann Busch to Reuchlin 30 September 1514, RE 192.

shall emulate the Hercules so skilfully portrayed in your third chiliad, and overcome this hydra of malignity by the patience I derive from my daily studies in philosophy. The day will come, I know it will, that will restore me to the sunshine. This is my one object: whatever anyone does or says, I must do what is right; as an emerald might say, whatever men do, I must be an emerald still. Virtue is never beaten. Farewell, my most excellent, most desired, Desiderius.

Johann Reuchlin of Pforzheim LLD
Stuttgart, 5 June 1516

419 / From Johann Froben Basel, 17 June [1516]

The date of this letter is established by reference to the brief of Pope Leo, which did not reach Erasmus until he had arrived in England; cf Allen Epp 457:37–8; 460:11–12. The famous printer, Johann Froben (c 1460–1527) was born in Hammelburg (Franconia) and perhaps studied at the university of Basel. In 1490 he became a citizen of the town and started printing, publishing his first book, a *Biblia integra*, on 27 June 1491. About 1495 he joined with Johannes Petri, and in 1500 with Johannes Amerbach. On Amerbach's death in 1513 he took over the press in conjunction with the three sons, and continued work on the great edition of Jerome. Froben's connection with Erasmus began in an unpromising manner, when in 1513 he virtually pirated the *Adagia* (cf Epp 283:182–96; 346 introduction). The enterprise surrounding the works of Jerome seems to have been the lure which caused Erasmus to break his ties with Josse Bade, the Parisian printer, and form his lasting association with the family in Basel. His epitaphs for Johann Froben are printed by Reedijk poems 116, 117.

Greetings. The letters that came for you in the days immediately after you left – a brief from Pope Leo, a copy of his letter of recommendation to the English king, and another with them, and letters from Reuchlin and Picheymer of Nürnberg – I have now sent on. Your book containing *Institutio principis christiani* and some other pieces is finished at our press. Jerome is nearing the end. We had trouble for some time with the supply of paper, the approach to Lorraine being closed to us, as you must have

* * * * *

33 Hercules] *Adagia* III i 1

419:1 letters] Epp 338, 339, 389

3 letters] Epp 409, 418

7 approach to Lorraine] Closed by the movement of troops; cf Epp 412:2–8; 413:46–50.

Johann Froben
Hans Holbein the Younger, c 1522–3
Hampton Court, Her Majesty the Queen
Reproduced by gracious permission of Her Majesty the Queen

discovered to your cost. But this will not cause us much delay, for Strasbourg will let us have enough paper, if the price (which is a little higher) is all right. The commentary on Canticles under Jerome's name which was being transcribed at Freiburg I am obliged to omit, because it is mutilated; several pages are missing both in the middle and at the end. So I am disappointed in my hope of producing something new, known hitherto to very few people. I will print your *Moria* with such care that in this edition I may fairly be said to have surpassed myself. All of us here are hoping for your return, and mean to show you every kindness. Lachner my father-in-law and his wife, and my wife Gertrude, and all our company send you their greetings. Farewell, dearest godfather. From our printing-house in Basel, 17 June [1515]

Johann Froben, printer in Basel

420 / From Bruno Amerbach

This letter has been redated and will now be found after Ep 337, as Ep 337A.

421 / To Guillaume Budé [Antwerp], [c 19 June 1516]

In this reply to Budé's charge that he spent too much of his energy on 'trivialities' (Ep 403) Erasmus manages not only to advertise the full scope of his current undertakings, but deftly to indicate the number of great personages who were impressed by, and indeed concerned about, his activities. The letter was first printed in the year of its composition, in *Epistolae ad Erasmum* (1516).

ERASMUS OF ROTTERDAM TO GUILLAUME BUDÉ

The courier was already booted and spurred when on my return from the prince's court to Antwerp I was given your letter, which was on 19 June; it had, if you please, been received at long last from Cologne. So, to answer

* * * * *

10 commentary] From a MS in the Charterhouse at Freiburg; cf AK 501, 535.

14 *Moria*] Probably the undated edition with a new title page; cf Ep 328:47.

16 Lachner] Cf Ep 305:198n.

17 Gertrude] Lachner's daughter married Froben in November 1510 as his second wife.

18 godfather] Erasmus was godfather to Froben's son Johann Erasmus or Erasmius.

421:3 court] At Brussels. Erasmus had arrived at Antwerp on 30 May 1516 and stayed there with his old friend Pieter Gillis.

laconically rather than not to answer at all: What is this I hear? Can Budé owe Erasmus anything? He the most fortunate and I the most unfortunate of all men? As for my mention of you in my annotations, I hoped to add a little lustre to my work from your famous name, and that was my selfish object; so far am I from thinking you owe me anything on that score. If you take what I have done in good part, it is I who owe a debt to you, on this ground as on so many others; and if you do not, I shall get the benefit of my piracy just the same. Whether what I did was well judged or no, it has at least one good result, for it was the occasion of such a learned, friendly, and long letter from you, whether I earned it or forced it out of you.

Nor is there any reason why you should be concerned about a *quid pro quo*. If in accordance with your usual kindly feelings towards me there was anything owing, your letter has paid the debt to the last farthing and with generous interest. If your mind cannot be set at rest any other way, you ought to repay any service I may have done you by correcting and instructing me, and not with compliments. When I sing the praises of my friend Budé, I get more than one advantage out of this. First, I am seen to have read your work and to recognize your outstanding intellectual gifts. Second, I secure the approval of all good scholars by sharing their opinion, for without exception they think highly of their Budé. Linacre himself, a good judge but a severe one, and one who does not lightly praise anyone, gives Budé full marks. I was as pleased as though I had won something when I heard that he entirely agreed with me, and was proud to think I had made up my mind about you long ago. He took the same line about Cop, whom he approves of without reservation. Maybe I have done no harm to the humanities by making your work more widely appreciated among men who, misled by affection I suppose, attach some importance to my opinion, worthless as it is; for I see that you have taken for your province the defence of liberal studies against the tyranny of those men whose knowledge is a form of ignorance, and the re-establishment in her old glories of our beloved Gaul – for why should not one and the same man be by jurisdiction

* * * * *

7 annotations] Cf Ep 403:54n.

24 Linacre] Cf Ep 388:174n. He had met Budé in Paris early the previous year; cf Ep 534.

28 long ago] Erasmus and Budé may have met in Paris, where both knew Fausto Andrelini (cf Ep 44:34n); see also Garanderie 13ff.

28 Cop] Cf Ep 124:18n; Allen Ep 618:40.

a German and a Gaul by the boundaries of the ancient geographers? And I only wish certain persons did not try to put asunder things that in their own nature should be united. A noble task indeed, for which no man could be as fit as Budé.

As for the points on which you partly disagree with me, partly agree, and partly suspend judgment and remain doubtful, I could not reply at the moment, being prevented in the first place by lack of time and second by having no text at hand, for before I answer there are some things I must reread. It shall be done on another occasion, and done soon. Meanwhile I will say this much in general: my Budé's opinion carries so much weight with me that if I find he seriously approves of something, I shall have no hesitation in recanting on any subject. Not but what in this work I have done what I usually do elsewhere. I had decided to treat the whole thing lightly, as I was to be concerned with minutiae, and merely to point a finger, as it were, at some passages in passing. Then, when the work was already due to be published, certain people encouraged me to change the Vulgate text by either correcting or explaining it. This additional burden would, I thought, be very light; but in reality I found it by far the heaviest part. Then they pushed me into adding rather fuller annotations; and very soon, as you know, everything had to be done again. And there was a further task: I thought correct copies were available in Basel, and when this hope proved vain, I was obliged to correct in advance the texts which the compositors were to use. Besides which, two good scholars had been engaged,

* * * * *

36 German] On Erasmus' German identity see Ep 302 introduction and Epp 306, 307, 334. Ep 399 from Johann Witz in the Deventer Letter-book is followed by a poem on the nationality of Erasmus, entitled *Ioannis Sapidi certamen de origine Roterodami quo duae nationes collitigantes introducuntur;* cf LB III 1556AB.

36 ancient geographers] The Rhine was traditionally the boundary of Roman Gaul; for another allusion to the same question see Allen Ep 1147:31–48. See Werner Kaegi 'Die Rheingrenze in der Geschichte Alemanniens' *Historische Meditationen* I (Zurich c 1942) 41–76.

40 disagree] The translation of Luke 1:3–4; cf Ep 403.

51 certain people] Since Erasmus' Latin version was in existence at least in part before 1509, he cannot have conceived of it now for the first time. An alternative explanation, proposed by Allen, is that he had not originally intended to publish it with the Greek text being prepared for Froben. He clearly wishes here to place responsibility for this decision on members of the Froben circle.

58 two good scholars] Cf Ep 417:6n.

one a lawyer and the other a theologian who also knows Hebrew, who were to be in charge of correcting proofs; but they had no experience of this and were unable to fulfil their undertaking, so it was necessary for me to take the final checking of the formes, as they call them, upon myself. So the work was edited and printed simultaneously, one ternion (which is the modern word) being printed off every day: nor was I able all this time to devote myself entirely to the task. At the same time they were printing off Jerome, who claimed a large share of me; and I had made up my mind either to work myself to death or to get myself free of that treadmill by Easter. On top of that we made a mistake about the size of the volume. The printer affirmed that it would run to thirty ternions more or less, and it exceeded, if I mistake not, eighty-three. And so the greatest part of my time was spent on things that were not really my business or had been no part of the original plan; and I was already weary and well-nigh exhausted when I came to the annotations. As far as time and my state of health permitted, I did what I could. Some things I even passed over of set purpose; to many I knowingly closed my eyes, and then changed my opinion soon after publication. And so I prepare the second edition, wherein I beg you urgently to help a man who is trying hard. Let people like you rebuke if they must and I shall take it as a friendly act. One thing you must please watch, my excellent Budé: do not let the public suspect this, or the copies of this edition will not move from the printing-house.

I was exceedingly grateful for such friendly advice, although when you speak of 'my trivialities in which I sometimes give my mind a rest,' I am not quite clear what you mean, except so far as I find everything of mine trifling, and often wonder in my own mind what there can be that some people praise so highly. For this is true even of some men in high place. How difficult it is to comply with everyone's standards! Some people pick a quarrel with me for my impudence in attacking such great subjects though a nobody myself. Take my *Enchiridion*: I have dared to differ widely from this age of ours, undeterred by any man's authority. In my *Chiliades*, which is a mass of detail, how I range over the territory of philosophers and theologians, and, as though I had forgotten my chosen theme, am carried far beyond what is proper to the subject! This will be clearer if you read the

* * * * *

62 formes] The type secured in the chase, ready for printing

63 ternion] A quire of three sheets, each folded in two

82 trivialities] Cf Ep 403:135–6.

proverb 'Be born king or fool if you can'; also 'You have drawn Sparta, make the best of it,' or 'War is sweet to those who have not tried it,' or 'The Sileni of Alcibiades'; for in 'The beetle is midwife to the eagle' I was being hardly serious. In my short book on the Christian prince I lay down principles on which no theologian dares lay a finger. Or do you call trivialities Lucian's dialogues and the tragedies of Euripides, on which I practised my pen? Nothing could be more trifling than the Cato, on which I spent one short day. But these light pieces, however trifling, I set above Scotus and all his quillets. Apart from that, I know well and do not deny that there are many trifling points in my New Testament, for so the course of the argument required. All the same, if anyone weighs up, or rather if he discovers by experience, what it means to translate these things and then discuss them, he will understand that a full-dress commentary could be written without much more effort than what it cost me to write those trifling trivialities.

And it is just these 'trivialities,' such as they are, that are welcomed by the most authoritative theologians, and they say they have derived a flood of light from them. Unless perhaps I am merely being made up to by all these highly reputable characters, whose names I could give and produce their letters, if I had not such a strong dislike of conceit. And in any case, if I were to measure myself by my own foot, I should undertake only trifling tasks, and avoid 'burdens too great for puny heart and frame.' Again I find it somehow more attractive to mix serious topics with my trifles than to show myself a trifler on great topics. And nothing seems to me a greater waste of time than to go on discussing the worthless questions which make so many theologians fancy themselves gods; for to you I can speak the truth. In fact, in this order of subject I think I have done better than all my predecessors in diligence at any rate, if not in erudition. Think how many almost frivolous notes there are in Jerome's treatment of the Psalter! Nor shall my resolution fail, if only life and strength hold out. I have written a preliminary piece on the psalm 'Beatus vir.' I shall attack St Paul. Jerome will come out entirely

* * * * *

93 'Be born ...] *Adagia* I iii 1; the other proverbs are, respectively, II v 1, IV i 1, III iii 1, and III vii 1. All are major pieces installed in prominent places in the edition of 1515.

99 Cato] In the *Opuscula aliquot* of September 1514 (NK 534). Martens published a reprint in September 1515 (NK 2603).

106 trivialities] Cf note to line 82 above.

113 burdens] Horace *Epistles* 1.17.40

122 psalm] In *Enarratio allegorica in primum psalmum* printed in Erasmus' *Lucubrationes* (Strasbourg: Schürer 1515). Cf Ep 327.

122 St Paul] Erasmus intended to do a commentary; cf Ep 301:21 and n.

reborn. These are such great tasks that the resulting unpopularity in certain quarters is almost insupportable. How great they seem to you, I do not know; too great at least for my capacities, I confess and am well aware. I have translated some of the essays of Plutarch, who seems to me all through a most important author. You must therefore be kind enough to explain which are the trivialities you wish me to avoid, in order that I may more securely follow your advice in this matter, which I am determined to follow everywhere as though it were an oracle.

As to the preface in which I dedicate the New Testament to Leo while joining with him none the less my great Maecenas the archbishop of Canterbury, I must say you make an uncommonly good guess. That was exactly what I had in mind at the time. When you congratulate me on my leisure and lament your own position, on this point, my dear Budé, I disagree with you absolutely. Your books are sufficient evidence that you are not wholly without leisure; although apart from that your remarkably ingenious and fertile mind could support any number of commitments. Then against your children, your wife, and your other household cares I set my one sole wife, that accursed Penury, whom I still cannot shake off my shoulders, such is her love for him that hates her. I adjure you by that immortality which assuredly awaits you and all your family: proceed with high and dauntless spirit on the way you have begun, to succour the humanities and by the great learning of your works to win undying glory for your native France. Be satisfied with this for the moment. The other points I will answer as soon as I have reread the passages. Farewell, and think well of your Erasmus, as I know you do.

There is a move in circles near the prince to cover me with gold. But somehow it happens that in my opinion nowhere is good literature held of less account than here; the reason: our quite uneducated rulers. But I have great hopes of Jean Le Sauvage, the chancellor of Burgundy, who is himself not only a great man and a very wise man but a very learned one, and what is more, a devoted supporter of all men who have distinguished learning to recommend them. If the gods in their goodness will but allow this great

* * * * *

126 Plutarch] *De tuenda bona valetudine precepta* (London: Pynson 1513; STC 20060); *Opuscula* (Basel: Froben 1514)

133 good guess] Cf Ep 403:145–52.

140 Penury] For a discussion of Erasmus' English income and expenditure see E&C 68–71, 146–7.

148 gold] A reference to the canonry of Courtrai which Jean Le Sauvage offered to Erasmus on 18 July; cf Ep 436.

man a long life, my hope is that in our country too men will come forward, the fruits of whose genius will bring honour and glory to the reign of a prince who has every other blessing. Farewell once more.

422 / From Guilielmus Brielis — 20 June [1516]

The writer of this letter of welcome, perhaps a monk, is otherwise unknown.

GUILIELMUS BRIELIS TO MASTER ERASMUS

As soon as I suspected that you had returned from Germany into Brabant, dearest Erasmus, I could no longer refrain from addressing you in absence by means of a letter, especially since I cannot do so face to face; for I had long wished to write to you and assail you with worthless words, had I not been prevented by distance, and by the rigorous solitude demanded by my vows. Let me say then what I wanted to say, and that briefly. If any room is still left in your list of friends, please ... Both by your singular learning and by your integrity of character and life you have won many patrons and many friends, who love you passionately as though you were a father or a brother. Happy are they who deserve to see and hear you face to face, and often enjoy your delightful conversation in the form of letters. Would that some day this might be my privilege too! Yet I will dare to assert (it may sound arrogant, but it is true) that my affection for you is no less than theirs, who value you so highly and love you so dearly. God is my witness, if I lie. And although I cannot enrich you in this life with preferment and the gifts of this world, seeing that I have left all in order that some day I may be rich in the poverty of Christ Jesus, yet I have done for you regularly, and still do, what I can, that is, to commend you warmly in my prayers to God, and specially in the most holy sacrament of the altar. And so, dearest Erasmus, let my prayer come before thy sight, and do not reject me from the number of your friends. But I would not wish to displease you by prolixity, so I will say no more. Farewell, Erasmus my delight, my treasure, and my second self. Consider how much you are in debt to me, for your name in this letter is so often on my lips, and from the abundance of the heart the mouth speaketh. Farewell once more.

From my secluded little cell of prayer, in haste, 20 June

* * * * *

422:17 left all] Matt 19:27

21 let my prayer] Psalm 118 (119):169

23 say no more] Horace *Satires* 1.1.121

25 abundance] Matt 12:34, Luke 6:45

John Colet, dean of St Paul's
Bust in plaster, probably by Pietro Torrigiano
Owned by St Paul's School, London
and presently on loan to the Victoria & Albert Museum

423 / From John Colet — Stepney, 20 June [1516]

This letter is an answer to a letter sent by the hand of Pieter Meghen; cf Ep 412 introduction. Colet was writing from his mother's home at Stepney. The manuscript of this letter in the Deventer Letter-book goes only to the mid-point of the fourth sentence, at which point the copyist broke off with the marginal explanation that the latter had been printed in *Epistolae ad Erasmum* (October 1516).

JOHN COLET TO ERASMUS OF ROTTERDAM

You cannot easily believe, dear Erasmus, how delighted I was to get your letter, which our one-eyed friend has lately delivered. I learnt from it where you are, which I did not know; and also you seem in it to expect to return to us here, which will be most welcome both to me and to the many friends you have here. I understand what you say about the New Testament. The copies of your new edition sell here like hot cakes and are read everywhere, and many approve your labours and marvel at them; some however disapprove and find fault, making the same criticisms that Maarten van Dorp makes in his letter to you. But these are theologians, of the kind you describe with as much truth as wit in your *Moria* and elsewhere, to be praised by whom is a discredit, and whose dispraise is praise. Personally I like your work and welcome your new edition, but in a way that rouses mingled feelings. At one time I am sorry that I never learnt Greek, without some skill in which we can get nowhere; and then again I rejoice in the light which is shed by your genius like the sun. In fact, Erasmus, I am astonished at the fertility of your intellect – you conceive so much, have so much in gestation, and bring forth some perfectly finished offspring every day – especially as you have no certain abode, and lack the support of any fixed, substantial endowment. Your Jerome is awaited here; he owes you a great debt, and so do we all, who can henceforth read him corrected and explained by you. You did well to write *Institutio principis christiani*. I wish all Christian princes would follow excellent principles. Their madness upsets everything. I want a copy of that book very badly, for I well know that, like everything else of yours, it will be a really finished performance.

What you say about Germany I can well believe; that you should remember my own remarks and quote my evidence from so long ago makes

* * * * *

423:9 Dorp] Ep 304

14 never learnt Greek] Cf Allen Epp 468:12; 471:27; and line 63 below.

22 *Institutio ... christiani*] Cf Ep 393.

27 my own remarks] Cf Allen Ep 1211:455n.

me wonder at your memory. You say you long for a peaceful habitation, and I wish you had one both peaceful and prosperous, such as both your age and your learning deserve. I wish too that you might ultimately settle among us, if we were worthy to harbour so great a man, but you have sampled our quality several times already; at least you have here men who are devoted to you. The archbishop of Canterbury, when I was with him recently, spoke much of you, and warmly expressed the wish that you were here. He is now released from all business, and living happily at leisure.

Your remarks about the pursuit of a Christian philosophy are perfectly just. There is no one, I think, in the Christian world of our own day better fitted for this business and profession than yourself, with the wide range of your learning; you do not say so yourself, I say it, because I really mean it. I have read what you have written on the first psalm, and I admire your *Copia*; I long to see the result of your work on the Epistle to the Romans. Do not hesitate, my dear Erasmus, but when you have given us the New Testament in better Latin, go on to elucidate it with your explanations, and let us have a really long commentary on the Gospels. Length from you will seem short. In those who love Holy Scripture the appetite can only grow, provided their digestion is sound, as they read what you have written. If you make the meaning clear, which no one will do better than you, you will confer a great benefit on us all, and make your name immortal. Immortal, did I say? The name of Erasmus shall never perish, but you will win for your name eternal glory, and as you toil in Jesus, you will win for yourself eternal life.

You lament your ill fortune: this shows a lack of courage. When you are engaged on some great enterprise, I mean the explanation of the Scriptures, Fortune will not dare abandon you; only put your hope in God, and he will help you more than all else, and will stir up others to assist you in these most sacred studies. I wonder to hear you exclaim that I am fortunate. If you speak of fortune, I have one, it is true, but it is not large, and barely covers my expenses. I should count myself blessed if in the depths of poverty I owned a thousandth part of your learning and wisdom, which you acquired without possessing wordly wealth, dispensing a learning to be found nowhere else in a new way, I know not how, that is special to yourself ... I will join you, if you will permit me, and will attach myself to your side, making myself your pupil even for the learning of Greek, although I am now getting on in years and am almost an old man. I have not forgotten that Cato

* * * * *

41 Romans] Cf Epp 301:21; 314:4–5.
52 ill fortune] Cf Epp 412:31; 421:6.

learnt Greek at a great age, and I know too that you, who are level with me in years, are now studying Hebrew. Continue to love me, as I know you do, and if you return to us, you will find me most devoted to you.

Farewell, from my mother's country house at Stepney. She is still alive, in a happy old age, and often speaks of you cheerfully and with pleasure.

St Edward's day, the feast of his Translation

424 / From Thomas More [London, c 21 June 1516]

More resumes the complicated matter of Erasmus' financial problems with Maruffo; cf Epp 388 and 412.

THOMAS MORE TO ERASMUS OF ROTTERDAM

You tell me, dearest Erasmus, to write to you fully about everything; and I am encouraged to do this all the more readily, because I see that you liked my earlier letter with its evidence of my affection for you. When you write that it pleased you also because it showed that my literary style is improving, it has the opposite effect: you encourage me to keep silent, for of course it is embarrassing to send you a letter when I see that it is carefully examined and assessed. When you praise the progress I have made, I am covered with confusion, knowing how much I lose every day of the little skill I used to possess. This must inevitably happen to a man who is continuously occupied in legal business which is so far removed from scholarship of every kind (for my course in life has landed me in this treadmill); I am now so much tormented by these inanities that I have no mind left for thinking or words for expressing myself with. So if you analyse what I write, if you test my powers of expression and count up my solecisms and my barbarisms (for that is what it amounts to), you instruct me to be silent. If however you are content to hear news of your affairs and mine in the first words that come to hand, here is some news first about your money, as that is a most important topic.

On receipt of your letter I sent at once for Maruffo, told him you had written to the archbishop to say that by his means you had received the money. 'Give me,' said I at once 'either the money, or a bill against which he

* * * * *

71 St Edward's day] The feast of the Translation of King Edward the Martyr, 20 June

424:22 a bill] A bill-of-exchange (*syngrapha*), to be redeemed or collected in Antwerp

can draw it in Antwerp.' 'I will do it with every care,' was his reply, 'as soon as I have had it from the archbishop; and after having heard from Erasmus in these terms, I have no doubt that he will pay for it on the spot.' 'But Erasmus,' I said, 'has written two letters: the one of which I spoke, which he said was not to be delivered except against receipt of the money or the bill, and another, which he said was to replace that one if the money was refused, in which he informs the archbishop that no money at all has yet reached him. Consider therefore what you think you should do.' When he heard this, the man was afraid of offending the archbishop, and at once wrote out a bill and gave it to me, receiving in return your letter to his Grace. This he sent off hastily together with a letter from himself in which, with the air of a man who expects to be thanked, he said he had long ago arranged for the money to be sent you, and had now at last had a letter from you in which you said you had received it; and that you had enclosed in a letter to the archbishop the quittance which stated that it had been paid to you (I had suggested this, since he demanded a quittance); therefore, if his Grace thought fit, would he please order payment to be made, since it was to please him that he had been out of his money for so long. The archbishop read this letter from Maruffo (for it so happened that he read it before yours), and then opened yours, and finding no quittance looked on the ground all round his feet, thinking it must have fallen out as he opened the letter. When it could nowhere be found, he told those who were there to bear witness that there was no quittance enclosed in the letter, and then, when he had read your letter, he gave up thinking that the quittance had arrived, because it was clear that the money had not. So he sent it to me immediately, with instructions to arrange for it to be remitted to you as soon as possible by the channel most convenient to yourself.

Next morning Maruffo was back again. He was beside himself. 'Hey, Master More,' he said, 'you have made a terrible mistake! You kept the letter which you ought to have sent to the archbishop, and sent the letter which ought at all costs to have been suppressed.' 'What's all this?' I said; 'that was certainly quite wrong. You see what it is to send a courier who has only one eye, for he made the mistake in distinguishing the letters, not I. You were given the letter which he said, and I have no doubt believed, was the right one.' 'Well,' he said, 'at least give me the other letter, so that I can restore my credit with the archbishop; for at the moment, either by your mistake or the courier's, I have almost none left.' 'But,' said I 'I have been

* * * * *

29 archbishop] Warham

too scrupulous over this. I knew that the letter which said that the money was still not accounted for was to be kept dark; and thinking it was the letter I had retained, in my anxiety to safeguard your position, alas, I put it in the fire.' At that point he exploded. I did my best to comfort him, and promised with the best will in the world that I would sort out all this confusion. So I told his Grace that he had written to you a long time ago, and told you to borrow the money against his credit, believing that you would do this; but that you had rejected the idea of borrowing the money, with the result that he thought you had had it, while you wrote to say that you had not. If this invention of mine is also refuted by your letter, I shall have to discover some other means of rescuing my credit with his Grace, which I have nearly sacrificed while trying to save somebody else's. In any case, I have given Maruffo back his bill; for I have placed the money more advantageously for you with another man. You will get for each pound of our money 30s 4d in Flemish money; Maruffo was giving 8d less in each pound.

My lord the cardinal received your letter and the books you had previously sent with a smiling face, and makes very generous promises, which I hope he will keep. I am delighted to hear you like Basel in so many ways, for your sake at any rate, for I should prefer things wherever you are to be according to your liking; but not to an extent that might rob us of your society, for, although we cannot do so much for you as they can, in affection, I do assure you, we yield to no one. I have read that little bundle of letters by men who, besides being good scholars, regard you with the deep respect which is your due; but I find nothing new in it. For they contribute nothing to your reputation (although they do all they can), which any country in the world would not be bound to offer that has any interest in humane studies. Pace has not yet returned, nor is it thought so far that he

* * * * *

73–4 each pound ... Flemish currency] By the bill of exchange £1 0s 0d sterling was to be redeemed for £1 10s 4d groot Flemish. That meant an exchange rate on the English pound sterling 4.04 per cent better than that indicated by the current mint par, or relative silver contents, of the two currencies or moneys-of-account. On such bills the mint par determined only the general level of the exchange rates. The specific daily rate was established by the two countries' relative balance of payments, the relative demand for and supply of commercial bills, and other credit instruments payable in (drawn on) each of the currencies. The current boom in the English cloth trade to Antwerp perhaps explains this favourable exchange rate on the pound sterling. Cf CWE 1 340–1, 345; CWE 2 327–45.

81–2 bundle of letters] Perhaps Ep 386 was a composite letter; cf Ep 412:23n.

will do so; I think you know that he is now our king's private secretary. I hear that you have been in Tunstall's company and have dined with him, since he was given the office of Master of the Rolls. I have nothing to say about my verses; you must do as you think best. What think you of my letter to Dorp? I very much want to know. Farewell, dearest Erasmus. My young man Clement greets you most warmly, etc.

425 / From William Warham — Otford, 22 June [1516]

This letter was first printed in the *Epistolae ad Erasmum*, but a manuscript version in the Deventer Letter-book is of better authority and contains a considerable passage omitted from the printed versions. Otford is a small village in Kent, three miles north of Sevenoaks, where Warham rebuilt the archbishop's palace. He writes now to acknowledge receipt of the New Testament volumes and of the Jerome dedicated to him; cf Ep 396.

WILLIAM, ARCHBISHOP OF CANTERBURY, TO ERASMUS GREETING

Greeting, most learned Erasmus. You have given my name some honourable mention, and thereby secured me an eternity denied to many famous emperors and kings, who have lapsed entirely from the memory of men except in so far as a mere list of their names, in the barest form, survives. What adequate recompense for immortality I can make you in this mortal life I do not see. I cannot forget how much you have done for me in every way; when present, by your conversation; in absence, by your letters; in general, by your published works; and this is more than I am able to support. You will rightly therefore think me most ungrateful if I do not bear your interests faithfully and constantly in mind, although what I can do is

* * * * *

87 private secretary] Pace was appointed principal secretary to the king in succession to Thomas Ruthall; at this time he was still on his mission to the emperor. Cf Wegg 98; G.R. Elton *The Tudor Revolution in Government* (Cambridge 1953) 56–9.

89 Master of the Rolls] Tunstall was appointed on 12 May 1516 (LP II 1882). The dinner presumably occurred in Brussels shortly after 3 June; cf Ep 412:58.

90 verses] Erasmus may have proposed to print More's *Epigrammata*; cf Allen Ep 461:20f.

90–1 letter to Dorp] Rogers Ep 15, 21 October [1515], from Bruges. It replied to Dorp's second letter to Erasmus (Ep 347, dated 27 August 1515) about the *Moriae encomium*.

92 Clement] John Clement; cf Ep 388:185n.

unequal and inferior to your deserts. If those sixty nobles have not yet reached you across the exchanges, this is Maruffo's fault, who undertook to see that the money should be made available to you where you are, not only these nobles but further sums as well. He averred that he had given you a letter of credit, on which you could draw the larger sum from the merchants anywhere in your part of the world. This news was brought to me again by Bedyll, whom I had sent more than once to see Maruffo and More on this subject. But that you may not be deprived any longer of the receipt of this sum, I have today sent it to More, as you wish; and he will arrange for its payment to you in Antwerp conveniently and without delay, I do not doubt.

Your publication on the New Testament I have shown to several of my brother bishops and some doctors of divinity, and all with one voice declare that you have done something well worth doing. I accept their verdict, and, regarding as I do all the products of your more than human gifts and wide range of learning as of the highest value, I count your book worthy of all praise, and so too the work on Jerome, which you are in a fair way to accomplish shortly. These works will secure you immortal fame among mankind, a divine reward in Heaven, and from me whatever I can conveniently provide. I received the volumes of your Jerome, which cannot be too highly praised, from the bearer of this letter; for these, and for the New Testament which you have also sent me, I owe you undying gratitude, bearing in mind the efforts which you have expended on these publications. In conclusion, may I ask you to see that this letter from me is delivered to my reverend and valued brother, the bishop of Basel, and to do your best

* * * * *

425:12 sixty nobles] Undoubtedly 'nobles' as the money-of-account = one half a mark (6s 8d sterling), so that this sum would have amounted to £20 0s 0d sterling = £29 0s 0d groot Flemish = £170 13s 4d tournois, by the official gold rates. (By the current rate on sterling at Antwerp, as indicated in Ep 424: 73–4n, it would have equalled £30 5s 0d groot Flemish.) Cf Ep 388:46n above; and CWE 1 325, 336–7, 340–1; CWE 2 146 (Ep 214:4n), 327–45. This was Erasmus' annuity from the Aldington living; cf Epp 225 introduction; 296:124n.

28 work on Jerome] Evidently a reference to the volumes of works other than the letters. Early in June Erasmus sent the four volumes he himself edited by Pieter Meghen; cf Ep 413:36–9. On 13 July he instructed Bruno Amerbach to send the remaining volumes; cf Ep 439:5–7.

32 letter] Evidently in answer to that mentioned by Erasmus in Allen Ep 456:154–5.

to overcome your ill health with all the more diligence, as I shall then hope to have the pleasure of seeing you soon.

Your much attached friend William Cantuar
Otford, 22 June

426 / From Thomas Bedyll Otford, 22 June [1516]

This letter accompanied that of Warham (Ep 425) from Otford, where Bedyll was in residence as the archbishop's secretary.

Most learned Erasmus, if it were as easy to give you good health as to wish it you, that insidious fever which troubles you would not intercept or postpone your return; for you are the one man above all others with whom I would gladly pass my whole life, if my fortune permitted. But you know how I am placed, worse than in a treadmill, turning my wheel continually and unable to diverge a hair's-breadth from my duty. And so I have often wished since the day we parted that I could become Daedalus or Menippus, and 'on oarage of my wings' flit over to see you and spend a few short hours in your delightful company, which I miss so much, before returning. But here we have neither eagles nor vultures, and no Mercury to transport me and bring me back. Please therefore, dearest friend, take great care to get better, and do not let us be tormented any longer by the wish for your society. And this you may believe as though it had been uttered by an oracle, that no visitor will ever be more welcome to my master the archbishop, who has and constantly expresses the highest opinion of you. He has it in mind to provide for you on your return as delightful a lodging as he can, in which you can grow old in comfort, after your Herculean labours, in a life of lettered ease, nor will there be anything else in reason that you will ask for and be refused. For your absence, in which you have achieved such great distinction, has increased his affection and his wish to see you (as is love's way); you know how unbroken familiarity with a person can make him less welcome, which has perhaps made me too common and of less account. So there is one thing you must do: recover your health, and return

* * * * *

426:7 Daedalus or Menippus] Daedalus (in Greek myth) and Menippus (in Lucian) are men who discovered how to fly. 'Oarage of wings' is Virgilian (*Aeneid* 1.301).

14 my master] Bedyll was Warham's secretary; cf 387 introduction.

to England as soon as you can. Others will take care of all the rest, and see that you lack none of the conveniences of life.

Farewell, from Otford, 22 June.

Thomas Bedyll

427 / From Andrea Ammonio London, 22 June [1516]

For the letters referred to see Epp 338 introduction and 389 introduction; Ep 429:1 describes the despatch of this letter.

ANDREA AMMONIO TO HIS FRIEND ERASMUS

My excuse must always be that I am too busy, as the man to whom I have given this note will perhaps be able to explain to you. I could not send an earlier reply to the letter which you wrote me recently from Saint-Omer; I did answer another letter, as you will see from the copy which I enclose with this. I wrote to our friend Pace, but I do not know whether the letter reached him; that you did not get yours is easily understood. The pope has sent a very friendly reply and holds out good hopes; he has also recommended you very warmly to the king here. I am keeping his letter, which they call a brief, for you, and hope to see you here as soon as possible. Take care as far as you can, dear Erasmus, to keep in good health, and do not forget your affection for me, in which I take great delight.

London, 22 June

428 / To Johannes Caesarius Antwerp, 23 June 1516

This is the preface to *Primus liber grammaticae institutionis Theodori Gazae … translatus per Erasmum Roterodamum* (Louvain: Martens July 1516; NK 3051). For Caesarius see Ep 374 introduction. Froben revised the book for a new edition in November 1516, and reprinted it in 1518 and in February 1521 with slight changes and the addition of the second book translated by Erasmus. Martens issued editions on 1 March 1518 (NK 962) and in May 1524 (NK 3054).

ERASMUS OF ROTTERDAM TO JOHANNES CAESARIUS OF JÜLICH, CHAMPION OF GREEK AND LATIN STUDIES

In every academic subject, my dear Caesarius, rules have by nature something disagreeable about them, but along with this element of tedium goes

* * * * *

427:5 copy] Cf Ep 389, written in February 1516 and sent to Pace in Switzerland to be forwarded.

a quality that makes up for it: they are so useful. And so I am always astonished when I see some people so particular that they take offence at anything at all unattractive, and from the outset reject the literary studies that might bring them so much profit for the rest of their lives; and equally I am filled with righteous indignation at those who add a tedium of their own making to a subject somewhat tedious already. For in order to display their own attainments they cram in on the very threshold of their work various complicated rules which should have been taught hereafter; and of course they make the raw pupil stupid and hostile, when they should have attracted him and drawn him in by a practical brevity and clarity and order and simplicity, and other beguiling features of the kind. To this there is one exception: Gaza. Gaza is always himself, which means that on every subject he is an expert craftsman; and he is equally judicious and reliable in giving the learner what he wants, his purpose from the outset being not to exhibit his own learning but to give his reader a chance to learn. In his first book it is truly astonishing how concise, how well-ordered, how clear a survey of grammar he gives us, as though he drew us a kind of picture of the whole.

Hoping therefore to make the subject even less tedious for some people, I have increased the practical element by my own industry in turning the book into Latin, except only for the examples. Besides which I have divided it up with cross-headings, and made it somewhat more lucid by adding brief notes, so that it can now be understood with the minimum of effort. Of the mistakes, I have removed only those commonly recognized as such. For what I heard long ago from good scholars who were acquainted with Theodorus and who had some concern with this business is clearly borne out by the book itself: several passages have been wrongly altered by smatterers impudent enough to display their cleverness on another man's work. For example, the way in which he excepts the comparative of the third declension; wastes so much space in repeating the present and imperfect of all moods, although here the passive forms agree at all points with the middle; gives the passives of verbs in *-mi* future and perfect tenses, although the rule that precedes has declared that they do not possess these tenses; elsewhere, in the declension of nouns, he sometimes confuses the vowels of primitive and derivative forms. And this element of error they

* * * * *

428:16 Gaza] Cf Ep 233:12n.

28 scholars] In Allen Ep 2291:51–2 Erasmus mentions having met in Rome a former secretary of Gaza; by that time Gaza had been dead for thirty-four years.

37 declension of nouns] Reading *nominum* for *horum*

attribute to Demetrius Chalcondylus, an honest man and a good scholar, but of average ability, by no means adequate to keep abreast of the precision and wide range of Theodorus' critical faculty.

How fortunate, my dear Caesarius, is our generation, in which we see Greek coming to life again everywhere! The neglect of Greek brought with it the universal decay of all sound learning and all elegant authors; we may hope that equally its revival will make them flourish too. There is one thing which often surprises me: while Russians, Scots, and Irishmen have for some time now welcomed Greek warmly and not without success, what fatal cause makes Cologne, that ancient and famous city, which should be among the leaders in such a noble enterprise, be uniquely reluctant to accept humane studies? For if the subjects which she now officially pursues are right, they will not be done away by the addition of Greek, but given fresh lustre; if wrong, all the more must one hope to see genuine replacing spurious and valuable replacing worthless, that, as in the famous exchange between Diomede and Glaucus, gold may be exchanged for bronze. What man in his senses would refuse to change good for better or bad for good?

This work, which cost me two days, I have decided to dedicate to you, although I am by no means unaware that this paltry gift is far below your deserts. A greater offering was due to your scholarship and your upright open-hearted personality, and a better one urgently demanded by our friendly intimacy; but for the moment your kind heart must do what you can with this, while I get ready something more worthy of your merits. Be it yours, my dear Caesarius, to press on with all you do for the good of literature and for your generation, and to add this crowning distinction to the university of Cologne. To that truly noble count Hermann von Neu or, if you prefer it in Greek Neaetius, that open-hearted Maecenas of the humanities, pray give my warmest greetings.

Antwerp, 1516, St John Baptist's eve

* * * * *

39 Chalcondylus] Chalcondyles (c 1424–1511) came to Italy from Athens in 1447, and taught at Perugia and (by 1463) at Padua, where he was professor of Greek. A few years later he removed to Florence where he succeeded Argyropoulos in the Greek chair; Grocyn and Linacre studied under him there. The last years he spent in Milan. Apart from several important editions, including texts of Homer and Isocrates, he published a Greek grammar (Paris: Gourmont February 1525). See Deno J. Geanakoplos 'The Discourse of Demetrius Chalcondyles on the Inauguration of Greek studies at the University of Padua in 1463' *Studies in the Renaissance* 21 (1974) 118–44.

53–4 exchange between Diomede and Glaucus] An exchange of arms in the sixth book of Homer's *Iliad; Adagia* I ii 1

64 count Hermann] Cf Ep 442 introduction.

429 / From Andrea Ammonio Westminster, 26 June [1516]

This letter, dispatched to Erasmus in the hand of Pieter Meghen, was first published in the *Farrago*.

ANDREA AMMONIO TO ERASMUS

Thinking One-eye had departed, I scribbled three lines to you, and gave them to a friend who was crossing the channel en route for Brussels, which I supposed you would visit, together with a copy of the letter I had written some time ago and sent by Pace, in which I enclosed what they call the brief addressed to you by the Holy Father. I kept a second copy by me, and now send it to you by the hand of your one-eyed friend; but the brief in which the pope warmly recommends you to the king I am keeping for you here, for even if you had it where you are now, you would certainly bring it back here, and if it travels around, it might get lost.

I long to hear the German gossip from you; although what wonder if you are attracted by the country which Tacitus calls 'ugly, with a severe climate, dreary to live in and to look upon, unless it were one's native land,' since you can make Riphaean mountains balmy and tame wild beasts and soften flint. If you get so far, you will have Haemus at your feet just as Orpheus did, of whom they can say nothing so superlative that it will not seem diminutive when compared with what you deserve.

But, as you say, a good gossip will come better face to face. You are warmly expected here not by me alone but by everyone. Larke himself, who has more influence than anyone with the archbishop of York, has a present ready for you as it happens. Meanwhile please take good care of yourself.

From Westminster, five days before the first of Quintilis (for I hate the names July and Julius)

* * * * *

429:2 three lines] Ep 427

5 brief] Ep 338; cf Ep 427.

12 Tacitus] *Germania* 2.2

14 Riphaean mountains] In the far north, proverbial for their savagery

15 Haemus] A mountain range in Thrace, the native country of Orpheus, who 'with his lute made trees and the mountaintops that freeze bow themselves when he did sing'

19 Larke] Cf Ep 283:198n.

23 Julius] A reference reflecting the opposition to war in the English humanist circle, and alluding both to Julius Caesar and Pope Julius II; see R.P. Adams *The Better Part of Valor* (Seattle 1962) passim.

430 / From Johannes Sixtinus London, 26 June [1516]

Sixtinus, or Sextun, was a native of Bolsward, West Friesland, who had followed a clerical career in England after study at Oxford; cf Ep 112 introduction; Emden BRUO III 1675.

JOHANNES SIXTINUS TO HIS FRIEND ERASMUS

I was very glad to see our one-eyed friend as an old acquaintance, but much more so because he brought the news of your safe return, which was as welcome and satisfactory to me as it was to everyone of any character or intelligence; for at this time of year travelling is so dangerous that I had little hope. So I am really delighted that you are back safe and sound, although your state of health makes me somewhat anxious, and I trust you will soon recover; Pieter told me your trouble was not serious. I continue as usual busy in the courts; the cases are tedious, but profitable, which makes them easier to bear. I will pass on your cheerful greetings to our friend John of Cologne tomorrow at any rate, for your letter did not reach me until today. I am glad you have met the chancellor and the bishop of Chieti; of whom the former since you left has acquired the power to do more for his friends than ever before, having to everyone's delighted approval been named Master of the Rolls. I certainly long to revisit the country where you are now, but I owe so much to our excellent, great, popular, and kindly king for all he has done for me, that compared with him I could easily give up my parents (were they alive again), country, brothers, kinsmen, everything. Your friends here are all in the best of health, and no doubt you will be hearing from them. My very best good wishes to your excellent self.

London, 26 June

You can trust the bearer if he gives you any message from me.

431 / From Thomas Lupset London, 28 June [1516]

Lupset had been with Pace in Italy and had only just returned to England; cf Ep 270:69n. His reference to the displeasure of Erasmus and Colet probably sheds light on the problem of the origin of the *Julius exclusus*; see Ep 502 introduction.

* * * * *

430:10–11 John of Cologne] This appears to be the only reference to this person.

12 chancellor] Tunstall was also vice-chancellor by virtue of his new appointment; cf Ep 424:89n; C. Sturge *Cuthbert Tunstal* (London 1938) 37.

12 bishop of Chieti] Cf Ep 335:264n.

TO MASTER ERASMUS FROM LUPSET

Although I learn from Parmeno in Terence that he is twice a fool who loves someone who he knows hates him, because he gives himself useless trouble and annoys the other fellow, yet (so help me God) I cannot fail to love and reverence and honour you. How you feel towards me I know only too clearly in part from your latest letter to me, and partly from a letter in which I am accused by Colet. I have done you no wrong in malice, but from thoughtlessness a great deal. I confess it, I am very sorry, I humbly beg your pardon; I am ready to suffer any punishment. I would have handed over to Pieter what I had kept back out of your papers, had I not thought it safer to hold them here for your return. When you are here again, I will give them all back without exception and, I do assure you, untouched. Farewell.

I would burden your ears with a longer letter, were I the man to do this neatly in good Latin, or if I thought you would enjoy reading anything written by me. Farewell once more, and love me if you can.

London, 28 June

432 / From John Fisher — Rochester, [c 30 June 1516]

This letter was apparently taken by Pieter Meghen in the same journey that brought Erasmus the foregoing communications from his friends in England.

JOHN, BISHOP OF ROCHESTER, TO HIS FRIEND ERASMUS

Although much impeded with business (for I am getting ready for a trip to Cambridge, where the college is now at last to be set on foot), I did not wish your man Pieter to return to you without a letter from me. I owe you enormous thanks for the New Testament newly translated by your efforts from the Greek, which you have given me. The moment I saw the notes in several places in which you pay most generous tribute to your patron the

* * * * *

431:2 Terence] *Hecyra* 343–4

10 Pieter] Meghen, the one-eyed scribe referred to frequently in all these letters; cf Ep 412:47n.

432:3 college] St John's College, Cambridge, whose foundation was arranged by Fisher at the behest of the Lady Margaret Beaufort. It was the first foundation of its kind in England to make serious provision for the new humanistic studies, done with a view above all to reformation of the English church. The charter was given on 9 April 1511, but the official opening was delayed until 29 July 1516. The statutes of the college are in *Documents of ... the University and Colleges of Cambridge* (London 1852) vol III and J.E.B. Mayor *Early Statutes of the College of St John ...* (Cambridge 1859) where the 1516, 1524, and 1545 version of the statutes all appear. See also McConica chap 4 esp 78–80.

archbishop of Canterbury, I went to wait upon him and showed him the exact passages. Having read them, he promised that he would do great things for you and told me that if I ever wrote to you, I was to urge you to return. Nor do I doubt that, if you do so, he will be more generous to you than he has been hitherto.

I wrote to Reuchlin; whether he had my letter, I do not know, but I shall write again without fail, for a letter from him did reach me, a good long one, to my very great pleasure. He seems to me, in comparison with everyone else whose works I have read so far, to be the best man alive today, especially in knowledge of the recondite field that lies between theology and philosophy and touches on both. Take care of your health, dear Erasmus, and come back soon, which will please everybody.

Farewell, from Rochester.

433 / From Alaard of Amsterdam — Louvain, 1 July 1516

Alaard of Amsterdam, who died in 1544, was a kinsman of Meynard Man, abbot of Egmond (Ep 304:16n). As a scholar and teacher Alaard lived at Louvain, although he was not a member of the university, and he is best known for his work on an edition of Rodolphus Agricola: *Rodolphi Agricolae lucubrationes, tomus posterior* (Cologne: Gymnicus [1539]).

ALAARD OF AMSTERDAM TO HIS FRIEND ERASMUS

Greetings and best wishes, my dear Erasmus, kindest and most learned of men. There is a story that Augustine, when he was composing his work on the Trinity, the one sole and true God, was walking along the seashore, and there found a small child very busily engaged in transferring the boundless ocean with cupped hands into a very small pool: and that he addressed the boy in these words:

Water on water thus why do you pour?
Will you soon drain the sea and flood the shore?

So when I had put together in verse the story of the child's project and St Augustine's conversation with him about the Trinity, I was not a little tormented for some time by the earlier history of this vision. First of all, I read all the books of the *De trinitate* over and over again, and yet I found nothing that threw any light on this story. And so without hesitation I

* * * * *

16 the best man alive] On Fisher's attitude to Reuchlin see Allen Epp 457:1–24; 471:14–15.

433:3 story] It is found in a slightly different form in the *Catalogus sanctorum* of Petrus de Natalibus of Venice (c 1406), first printed at Vicenza in 1493.

consulted your friend Dorp, who is a very gifted man with an enormous range of various knowledge, and then a number of divinity professors and also questionists and quodlibetics, of whom we have a very large supply, of course, in this town, and very able people. Immediately they all with one voice advised me to consult the Legends of the Saints, which I found a nonsensical and also very ill-written work, and have no use for. In the end, as I turned the pages of one historian after another, I found myself no better informed on the subject of this apparition than I was to start with. Now please, we all know how unspeakably kind and helpful you are: if you have ever read anything on this topic anywhere, either in Augustine himself or in any other author – and you will certainly have read it, for there is nothing however ancient and recondite that you have not read sometime – tell me what you think about this. I am almost reduced to thinking that it must be a fable or something like it; for I am convinced, and rightly as it seems to me, that the majority of mortals believe many things not because they seem to be true, but because other people believe them.

But I have said too much about this already. Some years ago, I began work on the theory of conciseness in writing. I wish that, for the love of our poor Holland that has so much to learn, you would make a list of authors and passages and topics which would help me to search out and pursue the principles of conciseness. In order to test my capacity I have made a translation of sorts of that poem of yours, which I send you on the understanding that you are to give it a good thrashing and send it back greatly emended. Please do not fail to give as much work as you can to assist the efforts which your friend Cornelis has expended on Jerome. I have some early pieces of yours and of your friend Willem, my old teacher, which I am keeping at home for you to use.

* * * * *

19 Legends of the Saints] The *Legenda aurea* of the Dominican theologian Jacobus de Voragine who died at Genoa in 1298. He was named archbishop of Genoa in 1292 by Nicholas IV. The *Legenda aurea* was extremely widely known in the fifteenth century, and was first printed about 1470.

32 theory of conciseness] There seems to be no work by him on this subject.

36 translation] This was Erasmus' Greek poem associated with his visit to Walsingham; see Ep 262:8n; and Reedijk 301–3. Alaard's version is printed in LB III 1561; the poem was first printed in Erasmus' *Lucubrationes* (Strasbourg: Schürer September 1515).

39 Cornelis] Gerard or Geraedts; see Ep 17 introduction. At this time he was engaged on a life of St Jerome.

40 early pieces] See Allen I 581, 610; Reedijk 131–5

40 Willem] Hermans; cf Ep 33 introduction. By this time Hermans had been dead for six years.

Farewell, dearest Erasmus, and please be sure of this, that no one in the world is dearer to me than you are.

Louvain, 1 July 1516

434 / From Josse Bade [Paris], 6 July 1516

This letter and the following (Ep 435) do not seem to have reached Erasmus until October; cf Allen Ep 477:9–10. It is dated between the publication of the New Testament and that of the *Parabolae* (line 3n).

JOSSE BADE TO ERASMUS

Dearest Erasmus, I have lately had two letters from you, and with the first a reprint of your *Parabolae*, which I accept as a token of friendship rather than a sop to Cerberus; but even so, since my friend Dirk van Aalst has printed it such a short time ago, I dare not entrust it to my press for fear of causing him to lose money. I set a much higher value on friendship than the gentlemen who reprinted the *Copia verborum* – which you had sent me as a handsome present complete with your preface – and not a little reduced the value of the work I had put into it. Or than that other lot who, having solemnly promised me your *Adagia*, sold them off for not less than a St Philip florin each which I had contracted to buy a year and a half before I received one copy

* * * * *

434:3 *Parabolae*] Probably the edition of Martens, who printed a revised version of Schürer's first edition at Louvain in June 1515 (NK 838). Schürer himself, having published the first edition of the *Parabolae* in December 1514, reprinted it in February 1516, with a page-for-page reprint in November 1516. The letters referred to no longer survive.

6 lose money] As Bade himself had done when Schürer reprinted the *De copia*; cf line 8, and Epp 311 introduction, 263. However Bade published an undated edition of the *Parabolae* not long after this letter, with a preface to Pieter Gillis dated 29 November 1516, in which Bade says it is reduced *in enchiridii modulum* (to the reduced size of a book for the pocket) to save space and money.

7 *Copia verborum*] For Schürer's editions see Ep 311 introduction.

9 other lot] Froben this time; cf Epp 219:4n; 263:22n. Bade had just published an edition of the *Adagiorum collectanea*, 21 June 1516.

10 St Philip florin] The Burgundian-Hapsburg gold coin currently worth 4s 2d groot Flemish = 3s 0d sterling = 24s 6d tournois. Cf CWE 1 318, 321 (plate), 336–9; CWE 2 327–45.

(for even now I have not had them all). I had planned to make good my loss by printing the New Testament in the same type, which I had acquired for quite another purpose; but I shall write it off and think no more of it in view of my friendship with you, dearest Erasmus, and our host. Your printers need have no anxiety about their earlier edition at any rate; I shall do them no harm. But I shall take it kindly, if they in their turn consider my interests.

But enough of that. I gave your letter to our friend Budé, and he has sent you the annexed reply. The same for Faber, who is devoted to you and sends his greetings. All good men do you honour, and the bad ones hardly dare speak a word against you; by bad, I mean the people who speak ill of humane studies. Please give my greetings to our hosts Jacob and Pieter and their charming womenfolk, and so farewell.

6 July 1516

435 / From Guillaume Budé Paris, 7 July [1516]

On the delivery of this letter see Ep 434 introduction. It was first printed in the *Epistolae elegantes* (1517).

GUILLAUME BUDÉ TO ERASMUS OF ROTTERDAM

Your letter reached me five or six days ago, and I should have devoured it eagerly had not the difficulty of reading it held me up; for you had despatched it so carelessly and negligently, the courier being, I suppose, already booted and spurred, and clamouring for it. Still, I feel this to be no small token of friendship and intimacy that you should write a great long letter fast and on the spur of the moment. I attribute this not to the

* * * * *

12 all] This reading differs from Allen's interpretation of the Latin in his note on this passage. If it is true that Froben sold off the 1513 *Chiliades* at a cheap rate, as Allen suggests, we should expect (line 10) *non pluris ac philippeo vendiderunt singula*. An alternative explanation which fits the Latin more closely is that Froben, uncertain of his market, gladly promised to let Bade have copies of the edition; but when he found that the book went very well ('not *less* than a florin each') he failed to deliver the promised copies in Paris.

15 host] Probably Pieter Gillis; cf line 22.

18 your letter] Ep 421, answered by Ep 435

19 annexed reply] Ep 435

19 Faber] Lefèvre d'Etaples; cf Ep 315.

22 Jacob] Perhaps de Voecht (Voogd); cf Ep 152 introduction. Pieter is presumably Pieter Gillis.

435:2 Your letter] Ep 421

confidence which you can derive, and ought to, from your mastery of style in speaking and writing, but to the openness of your character and your natural sincerity, which has no fear that a friend will misinterpret you; in fact, you judge other people by yourself. One thing however I cannot forgive: you wrote with no date and no year. So please torment me less in future, for I shall gladly read whatever you write, if only you will use the hand you generally use in your letters, which I know to be handsome and legible. You really sent me rough notes instead of a fair copy. You must take heed, if you go on writing in this careless fashion, or by this defect you may run yourself into serious trouble. For I do not merely lay up your letters among my literary treasures; I carry them round with me almost from door to door, because I think it good for my reputation that many people should be aware of my close relations with you. Besides which, I shall use your approval as a weapon against my detractors, if need arises; for I know that I have deserved to have many detractors, although whether I have or not, I do not yet know.

So much for that. As for what you wrote about your second edition, I will keep it a deep secret; for if I show off your letters to others, it shall be done without committing you. If I feel that anything has been entrusted to my bosom which you wish to keep dark, there is no risk of its becoming public through me, for when need arises I can be as silent as the grave. In such time as I can save from the imperious demands of business, I shall try to assist you to the best of my power, as a labourer helps a mason; whether I shall succeed, I do not know. When I read your preface and your defence of the New Testament, I did notice remarks on several passages. I have today ordered your latest proverbs from the bookseller, for your benefit. Previously I thought your old version was good enough for me, on the assumption that I did not read them through but consulted them like the Sibylline books when need arose; but I had read the *Sileni* and some other things in copies belonging to other people, the way one does, when I was in my friends' houses, for I kept hearing that these were the most popular pieces. Your friend Linacre – a most learned man, I think – I have spoken with here more than once, when he and I were exchanging visits. He seemed to me a man of high character, kindly, and devoid of all self-importance. I sent him

* * * * *

24 second edition] Of the New Testament; cf Ep 421:76–7.

33 proverbs] Probably the 1515 *Chiliades*; cf Ep 269.

34 old version] An edition of the *Adagiorum collectanea*; cf Ep 126.

36 *Sileni*] *Adagia* III iii 1; it appeared in the *Chiliades* for the first time. Cf Ep 421:93n.

a copy of my *De Asse*, since it came from the press about the time he left. He had said to me in the course of conversation that it was impossible in our generation to throw light on certain problems, which I am quite confident of having cleared up, and I had undertaken to do so, which surprised him. Having taken this opportunity to seek his friendship, I have entered it on my special list, where the name of Erasmus is on record in capital letters.

I wish you might have thought fit to take a few hours off sometime, so that you could have read some parts of my book with attention and I might have been able somehow to learn what you think of it. Among these is the passage where I reply, or let myself go rather, against those who attribute everything to the Italians, to the extent of saying that everyone else has been unsuccessful in their attempts at eloquence. When you have time, you will find this on folio 12, where I seem somehow to be putting the case in passing for educated men. But better on folio 90, where in opposition to those who argue against monarchs and their subjects I have not been afraid to accuse those in power. Although I would let you off this too without regret, if only you would run your eye over folio 146 and what follows to the end of the book, where I have tried to play the philosopher and obliterate Fortune and all its power, and to write something to encourage and incite those who are devoted to the study of the humanities, in order to remove a slur on philosophy as you understand it, which has a bad reputation on my account. You will find there something like, though not as good as, what you have written in your *Sileni*. But the book will shortly be reprinted with additions and corrections; for I have it in my hands at this moment that I am writing to you. But, although I wish you to have read it, I would not dare ask you to do so, for fear of being called selfish or importunate, if I behave in such a way as to summon you from serious or sacred things to attend to my own worthless work, to the public detriment. But this is a pretty thing that you try to persuade me to believe. 'First I let it be seen,' you say, 'that I have read your work and recognise your outstanding intellectual gifts.' I am to believe that you have read my work? – maybe one of your friends happened to mention the book in conversation, and read it aloud to you.

I come now to those 'trivialities,' a phrase which slipped from my pen I

* * * * *

42 *De Asse*] Paris: Bade 15 March 1515; cf Ep 403 introduction.

54 folio 12] On this and the following passages from the *De Asse* see the notes of Garanderie 65–6.

64 reprinted] The second edition was completed by Bade on 14 October 1516.

70 'First ...] Cf Ep 421:21–2.

74 'trivialities'] Cf Ep 421:82, referring to Budé's remark in Ep 403:135–6.

know not how; I meant to refer to certain short pieces, which even so will some day be thought to be spurious by posterity, if I may speak quite openly. Among these is one book, the *De copia*, which in my opinion and that of many good judges and supporters of yours does not live up to such a sounding title. By title I mean not only the word *Copia* but the name Erasmus. That book, however, and several others, I have not read with any care. But when I have heard other people speaking of them, I have sometimes said that I wished you possessed a spirit that was content with what is enough; for you were not content with having, and being seen to have, all-round learning, but you must be an all-round author too; and that seemed to me, I said, to get in the way of your better ideas. In this class are the *Parabolae* and even some translations of your making – a fact on which you prided yourself – which, if taken at their own valuation do not lack value, but, since you have drawn them from common sources, you might be thought to have snatched them from the grasp of lesser men. For it is commonly thought right that you and writers of your class should choose the subject on which you mean to shine from among special and exalted themes.

Such is my opinion of your 'trivialities,' since you are so much upset by the word. And I have kept a copy of my letter in draft, so that you cannot take too censorious a line, once a letter has been sealed and sent, if my pen has gone astray in one or two places. At this point too (for pity's sake!) you will say that you have edited the petty Cato, and do not regret it because it cost you only one day, besides some small things put together privately; as though all these trivial pieces could do your name no harm. You must make up your own mind on such a point. But I think it reasonable that you should give me leave to differ from you on this, begging your pardon, especially since I have others voting on my side. Apart from that, when you try to make your Budé a paragon of knowledge – shall we say a Boudaêmon? – I

* * * * *

86 *Parabolae*] The *Parabolae sive similia*; cf Ep 312.

97 petty Cato] 'Catunculus,' a perjorative diminutive form referring to the *Catonis praecepta* (cf Ep 298 introduction) or the *Dicta Catonis*, a widely known work of moral precepts, partly pagan, partly Christian, dating probably from the third century AD. This whole passage reflects the contrast between the humanist priorities of Budé, and those of Erasmus whose conceptions of scholarship were intimately linked with his concern to reform teaching methods and promote a revival of moral standards.

103 Boudaêmon] *Daêmon* is a Homeric word meaning 'knowledgeable,' 'experienced'; with the intensive prefix *bou-*, 'very,' put in front of it, the result is a word that begins with something very like 'Budé.'

cheerfully accept the irony, although I know I am being laughed at. What else can you expect, since you wish to persuade me of the truth of these two propositions, that you are a good judge, and that I have given you a good opinion of my intelligence?

When however I came to the end of your letter, I could not fail to regret both your position and my own, although you express regret for yours only, wherein I show myself a better friend than you. For bachelor as you are, you complain that you have a wife called Lady Poverty, who not merely sits at home but travels around with you, whom you cannot be quit of, range widely as you may, such is the devotion of your odious spouse; and you set off the tedium and disgust she causes you against all my household cares as a husband and a father, just as though in place of your Poverty I had a pretty boy called Wealth, in whom I could take pleasure to my heart's content. Let me make this quite clear: I am, it is true, your rival in the pursuit of Philology, but she whom you call your wife has been pretty much my bedfellow ever since I fell a victim to this crazy love of learning. The only difference is that you call her cursed Poverty in jest, and I in all seriousness the poverty that never leaves one's side; so true is it that all serious scholars (few enough!) are haunted by this rival to their mistress Philology, who sticks closer almost than a shadow. This results from the habits of our age and of earlier ages too; to this the love of learning tends by its very nature: those who have once become its enthusiastic followers must forgo worldly goods and credit in the eyes of ignorant men, while those who have begun or intend to be rich must forthwith cast away or lay aside the love of the humanities, as I fear we shall find true of you, if ever (as you hope) you are gilded o'er. As far as I am concerned, I accept and virtually comprehend my fate, to such a degree that neither love of literature nor its companion will ever leave me. This I endure with ease, but come to terms with Fortune I cannot. I have long been indignant with her because, besides that Poverty of yours, she has inflicted on me my habitual bad health, which for eleven years now has given me more trouble in the pursuit of letters than all the mishaps, of which I have suffered so many, although I have left no stone unturned to be rid of it. Both these troubles, indifferent health and loss of worldly goods, my friends and kinsfolk turn to my discredit, and lay the blame on Philology, simply because when I was a child I was lucky enough to be acquainted with neither of this precious pair. As for bidding farewell to literature – which my relatives, my friends, my doctors recommend,

* * * * *

111 Lady Poverty] Cf Ep 421:140.

118 Philology] Not of course the modern discipline, but the general science of letters, the foundation of eloquence

threatening me with dire penalties if I do not obey – I cannot bring myself to do it, no, not if Chance in person were to offer me, as the comic poet puts it, 'Plutus himself, and Battus' wealth of spice.'

As I write this I am fearfully busy, and preparing any moment to leave for the country and take the road. Do not think, however, that this means a holiday from household cares; for I am now building two country houses on two of my estates some distance apart, real seats in the Lucullan style, and I have to keep running back and forth between them, or pay the penalty of my neglect by heavy losses. How easy this is for a man who is a literary type to begin with, with no experience of such things, and above all, modestly provided with coin, you can imagine. Farewell. Best wishes for this plan to gild you, and may it answer all your hopes.

Paris, 7 July

436 / From Jean Le Sauvage — Brussels, 8 July 1516

This letter from the powerful chancellor of Burgundy introduces the troublesome issue of Erasmus' annuity from the living at Courtrai, which was doubtless intended to supplement his income as a non-resident incumbent. Le Sauvage's remarks do suggest that he hoped the living might encourage Erasmus to remain in the Low Countries.

JEAN, CHANCELLOR OF BURGUNDY, TO ERASMUS OF ROTTERDAM

Greetings master Erasmus, most learned of men. If you can come here at the first available opportunity, it will be to your advantage, because, if you have determined to remain in these parts and to live a peaceful and pleasant life in honourable leisure, as you could not hope to elsewhere without great effort, I will cause to be conferred on you forthwith a prebend or canonry of

* * * * *

143 Plutus himself and Battus] Aristophanes *Plutus* 925; Battus was king of Cyrene, which exported the valuable spice called *silphium*.

146 two country houses] One at Marly, west of Paris, the other at St-Maur-les-Fossés; cf Allen Ep 568:12n.

436:6 prebend] Erasmus planned to have the income from this living converted into an annuity; cf Ep 443. Allen noted, from Erasmus' correspondence with his banker Schets, that the annual value of this annuity a few years later was 130 florins; in a statement of 1533, however, Erasmus gave the income as 130 livres. Possibly Erasmus was merely using two common synonyms for the same Burgundian-Hapsburg money-of-account: the 'florin' (gulden) = livre de quarante gros = livre d'Artois = 40 Flemish silver groots. If so, this sum would have amounted to £21 13s 4d groot Flemish = £125 16s 2d tournois = £14 17s 11d sterling (in relative silver values). Cf CWE 1 322–3, 347.

Courtrai. Nor will that be the only thing you can expect with sure and certain hope from the generosity of his catholic majesty, my master.

Farewell. From Brussels, 8 July 1516

437 / To Thomas Ruthall Antwerp, 9 July 1516

This letter was first printed in the *Farrago*; the year date was added in the *Opus epistolarum* (1529) and is confirmed by internal evidence.

TO THE RIGHT REVEREND FATHER IN CHRIST, THOMAS, BISHOP OF DURHAM, FROM ERASMUS OF ROTTERDAM

My lord bishop, from Pieter the One-eyed, by whom I wrote recently to your lordship, I learn that my Seneca has never reached you. Franz admits that it is with Arnold, so pray demand it from him if you have not yet received it. I am better, Heaven be thanked, and shall soon, I hope, pay another visit to my long-standing benefactors. May Christ almighty vouchsafe that I find you all well. Best wishes to your lordship, to whom I profess myself entirely devoted.

Antwerp, 9 July 1516

438 / To Maarten van Dorp Brussels, 10 July [1516?]

This letter was printed as a complimentary introduction to Dorp's *Oratio in praelectionem epistolarum divi Pauli* (Antwerp: M. Hillen 27 September 1519; NK 739). The present dating follows both Allen and de Vocht (MHL 162–3, 371) and assumes that Erasmus heard of Dorp's forthcoming oration on his visit to Brussels (Ep 436), where he met Jean Desmarez, public orator of Louvain. Since the oration contained several favourable references to himself, it helped to effect a reconciliation after the differences between the two men; cf Epp 304, 337, 347; *Revue d'histoire ecclésiastique* 12 (1911) 115.

ERASMUS OF ROTTERDAM TO HIS FRIEND DORP

I heard with very great pleasure, my dearest Dorp, the news of you that our

* * * * *

7 Nor … thing] Cf Allen Ep 475:1–10 for the scheme to confer on Erasmus a bishopric in Sicily.

437:4 Seneca] Cf Ep 325 introduction.

4 Franz] See Ep 258:14n. Arnold is probably his brother, Arnold Birckmann, who acted as an agent for printers and publishers, and who conveyed Ep 403 from Budé in Paris to Erasmus in Basel. Cf Ep 332:7n.

common friend Desmarez had to tell – the spirit with which you condemn in your preface those who neglect sacred literature and grow old in meticulous and frivolous philosophical argument, and with what a clarion call you encourage your readers to the study of Holy Scripture. Oh blessings on your brave spirit! Right on the target! So men rise to the stars. You have bravely espoused a cause fully worthy of you: carry it through! And I, so far as I can, will be at your side. You are in the prime of life, you are able, you are fully equipped with all sound learning; you will support this great responsibility with valour no less great. I shall be most content to be put in the shade, if the poor lamp of my own reputation pales before the splendour of your glory.

What I learnt from Desmarez I passed on to Tunstall, the English envoy. Take my word for it, he jumped for joy when he heard that you were whole-heartedly taking up this business. You will earn Christ's blessing, you will make your name dear to the whole world, and do for all lovers of learning something highly satisfying, and leading also to salvation. Farewell, dear Dorp, most precious of all my friends.

Brussels, 10 July

439 / To Bruno Amerbach — Antwerp, 13 July [1516]

This letter is in the Öffentliche Bibliothek of the university of Basel, MS G II 13a 53, written in a contemporary hand and evidently a copy made after the letter arrived. See AK II Ep 559.

ERASMUS TO HIS FRIEND BRUNO

How goes our treadmill? What news of the cave of Trophonius? Have you by now successfully escaped and asserted your original liberty? At my end I have now run to earth a splendid prebend. Things are in train. The rest of

* * * * *

438:3 Desmarez] Cf introduction and Ep 180 introduction.

3 condemn] If so, the strictures were diplomatically omitted from the printed version.

7 rise to the stars] Virgil *Aeneid* 9.641

13 Tunstall] In Brussels at this time

439:2 Trophonius] A Greek hero, whose oracle in Boeotia was consulted by descending into an underground cave, an experience so unnerving that those who did so were said never to smile again; *Adagia* I vii 77. Hence this is an apt image for that dark treadmill, the Froben printing-house.

4 prebend] Courtrai; cf Ep 436:6n.

the story about my position in life you will hear from Ludwig Baer. Would you please add what was missing in the volumes sent to the archbishop, and also add the remaining volumes; and besides that, let Lachner send me seven sets of Jerome as soon as he can, one of which, if you please, I will take as a present and repay you some other way, but let him put a price on the others. I will see that you get the money faithfully in cash. It does not pay to be too generous, and I am anxious to support my fellow-godfather as far as I can.

Give my greetings to your brothers Bonifacius and Basilius, who are very dear to me too. See to it that no bookseller arrives here from the Frankfurt fair without a letter from you. Farewell.

Antwerp, 13 July

To Master Bruno Amerbach, expert in the three tongues

440 / To Henricus Glareanus [Antwerp, c 13 July] 1516

The recipient of this letter, Heinrich Loriti of canton Glarus (1488–1563), was a poet whose skills had attracted the admiration of Erasmus (Allen Ep 2651:58–9). He was a pupil of Hermann Busch and Johannes Caesarius at Cologne, where he took his MA in 1510; in 1512 he was laureated by the emperor Maximilian. He was a supporter of Reuchlin and as a consequence left Cologne, finding a new scholarly home at Basel in 1514. In time he opened an academy there which he later took to Paris; the previous March (Ep 394) Erasmus had commended him to Urbanus Regius for the post at Ingolstadt. Eventually he settled in Freiburg where he received a lectureship in poetry in 1529. For another complimentary appraisal by Erasmus within a year of this letter see Allen Ep 529:55ff. The manuscript of this letter was part of a collection made by J.H. Ott of Zurich and obtained by Allen, who first published it, from Ott's descendant Major-General E. Renouard James. It seems likely that

* * * * *

5 Baer] Cf Ep 488 introduction. Born in Basel in 1479, Baer was educated at Paris and returned to Basel in 1512 with his doctorate in theology. The letter here referred to is lost.

6 archbishop] Cf Ep 413:39.

7 remaining volumes] Erasmus seems to designate first the volumes published in June which were not included in the present for Warham, and those published since; cf Ep 425:28n.

7 Lachner] Cf Epp 419:16, 305:198n.

9 price] Marked on the copy as a precaution against fraud and as a protection for Erasmus; cf Ep 209:55.

11 fellow-godfather] Froben; cf Ep 419:18n.

it was subsequently destroyed; cf Leonard Forster 'A Calendar of the Correspondence of J.H. Ott 1658–1671' *Publications of the Huguenot Society of London* 46 (1960).

ERASMUS TO HIS FRIEND GLAREANUS

I wish very much that you were here. You could not have failed to secure a position, but I dare make no definite promises after so many disappointments. The prince is getting ready to sail to Spain about the end of the second week in August, although all is uncertain. Here too we have roving bands of soldiers, as lately there were around you. If you desire to escape by your own efforts, anything that a testimonial from Erasmus can do he will gladly provide for an old friend. Mountjoy listened eagerly to your praises. It would take too long to write to everyone separately about each separate thing, and so you will hear the rest of my news from Ludwig Baer. Of one thing, dear Glareanus, I would have you quite certain, that I am sincerely devoted to you, and that this is your doing.

Farewell, and let me have an answer longer than this, for I write this on return from court and on the point of setting out on another journey. Please give my greetings to all your pupils, and greet my friend Oswald also. Let me have the poem you wrote about me, and Busch's verses too. Farewell once more, and give my greetings to Rethus the physician.

[September] 1516

441 / To Guillaume Budé — Antwerp, 14 July [1516]

Erasmus was intending shortly to leave for England, where his chief business was final preparation of his appeal to Rome concerning his illegitimate birth (Ep 447). The appeal was left with Ammonio, after which Erasmus stayed with Fisher at Rochester for some ten days before returning to the continent. He

* * * * *

440:15 Oswald] Oswald Geisshüssler (Myconius) of Lucerne; cf Ep 861 introduction.

16 poem] *Ad Erasmum Roterodamum, immortale Belgarum decus, ἑκατόστιχον*; on this and other poems in honour of Erasmus, see Reedijk 80, 85.

16 Busch's verses] *Hermani Buschii Pasiphili in Erasmum Coloniam recens ingressum*, probably on the occasion of a visit from Erasmus on his return from Basel in this year. Little is known about the details of that journey.

17 Rethus] Hieronymus Artolf of Chur, who died in 1541, was a student of medicine at Basel whom Glareanus described in his *Elegiae* (Basel: Froben 1516) as 'medicus et musicus.' In time he became rector of the university of Basel (1538).

went directly to Brussels, no doubt to secure his claim to the prebend of Courtrai, and from there journeyed to Antwerp where for a month he stayed with Pieter Gillis.

The present letter is in effect a postscript to Ep 421; he had not yet received Ep 435. For the subject matter refer to Ep 403:89ff. The letter was first published in the *Epistolae ad Erasmum*. Written under some pressure and shorn of the literary flourishes that characterize so many of the exchanges between these two men, it reveals the kernel of matter-of-fact scholarly communication which was the practical burden of much humanist letter-writing.

ERASMUS TO HIS FRIEND BUDÉ

I have secured a copy and inspected the passages. When you regard παρακολουθεῖν and *assequi* as the same thing I do not entirely agree with you. If someone has grasped the course of a speech which was very difficult to understand, we shall rightly say that he has followed it, using *assequi*. But only the man who accompanies the speaker in his own mind with unbroken attention follows him closely in the sense of παρακολουθεῖ. I have noted many examples in good authors which support this, and even what you adduce yourself is on my side. Further, when you point out that everything should first have been verified in due order and only then written down, in the first place I give the rendering you wish, except that the printer chose to print *prosecutus* for *persecutus*. Apart from that, in my annotations I set forth both senses, so that we can refer παρηκολουθηκότι either to the successive acts of a man tracing out and learning the facts or to the succession adopted in his narrative. And both, I am clear, can properly be defended. But I defend neither; I have left the reader free to choose which he will.

Now for κατηχήθης, which I rendered as if κατηχήσο had been the word, a fact which seems to cause you some discomfort: the tense is, as you know, aorist or indefinite, non-committal (if I mistake not) between all forms of past, and so I rendered it by a pluperfect, in order to bring out more clearly that he had learnt these things before baptism. For the examples you give me of the verb κατηχεῖσθαι in various authors I am duly grateful. Not but what I do not agree that a man's memory has played him false, if he says that he does not remember; otherwise there is no one whose memory does not play him false, for with every man there are certain things which he does not remember. It is only the man who through forgetfulness writes

* * * * *

441:2 copy] Of the *Novum instrumentum*

3 *assequi*] Cf Ep 403:99ff

18 discomfort] Cf Ep 403:123–31.

and maintains something contrary to fact whose memory plays him false.

I touch on this briefly, since I am already booted and spurred for my journey, and weary after a spell at court. You can do me no greater service than to draw my attention like this to any other points, in the friendly way you do. Farewell, glory of France and champion of letters.

Antwerp, 14 July

442 / From Hermann, Graf von Neu — Cologne, 14 July [1516]

The writer (1492–1530) was also known as Comes a Nova Aquila and Neaetius; his territory of Neuenahr was west of the Rhine. He was a canon of Cologne even before he entered the university, where he matriculated 14 November 1504. While a student he was a pupil of Johannes Caesarius with whom he subsequently went to Italy in 1508–10. He lectured at the university of Cologne in Greek and Hebrew in 1517, and after abundant ecclesiastical preferment became chancellor of that university in 1524. Even apart from his own scholarship he was known as a supporter of humanism, and he was remembered in the dedications of many grateful scholars; cf Ep 428:64n.

TO THAT GREAT SCHOLAR AND EMINENT THEOLOGIAN, ERASMUS OF ROTTERDAM, FROM HERMANN, GRAF VON NEUENAHR

Your letter from Antwerp reached me on 1 July, and I perceived without difficulty how warm a supporter you are of one who deserves as little as myself to be praised by a man like you, and how great the kindness for which I am indebted to you, so that on both counts I must own myself defeated. But it is, I suppose, no disgrace to be beaten by Hercules in a contest of strength or by Apollo where the Muses are concerned. I owe you a great debt, my dear Erasmus, first because in praising me as you do you have allowed affection to override your usual fair-minded judgment, and second because, while I kept silence and hoped like Democritus to enjoy perpetual obscurity, you took the initiative; it was you, unprovoked by anything I had written, who thought it right that a man content to advertise his own ignorance should be put on his mettle. This was in character for a brilliant man like you; but I was so much dazzled that I could not see clearly in which direction I should turn. I know – who does not know? – how ready you are, with all your gifts, to think the best of everyone. I know how ordinary – say, rather, how feeble – I am myself; from which I suffer so

* * * * *

442:4 Your letter] Lost

much that I know I must shun competition with men like you. Yet on the other hand I am drawn by duty, moved by reason, inspired by affection. You may be certain therefore that the name of Erasmus can never be blotted out of my heart. He has won my devotion not by the vast edifice of his writings so much as by what I count the most important thing in a man, his generosity and kindness. Besides which, I am much drawn towards you by the affection we both feel for Caesarius; for inevitably, since you are attached to him, some part of that attachment must come my way too, if the old proverb speaks true, that friends have all things in common.

Your New Testament I highly approve of, as do all men of good will. How I wish the rest of the Bible translated after the same fashion were within our reach! An end to malice, to the money-grubbers and the logic-choppers, who have no use for anything but their own vomit, men of a really absurd, mean, and illiberal spirit! Away with them to perdition, those mercenary teachers who care only for earning their own bread and nothing for the character and training of their pupils, wasting the savings of the poor in every chop-house! I praise and honour the way of life that you have adopted, and wish I were as able as I am willing to follow it. I beg you of your kindness therefore to put me away in some corner of your friendship, for I would rather remain concealed than appear in false colours. I owe you undying thanks for having learnt to know my name. I did not think I should be recognised at Athens, as that wise philosopher once boasted had happened to him. But this is your generosity; my part shall always be to regard you with respect and affection. Farewell, therefore, my pride and joy.

From Cologne, 14 July

443 / From Pierre Barbier — Brussels, 18 July 1516

Barbier was chaplain and secretary to Jean Le Sauvage, and it is in that capacity that he writes to Erasmus concerning the latter's attempt to convert the prebend at Courtrai into an annuity. The purchaser of the prebend, Jan de Hondt, called Canius, was probably the purchaser recommended here by Barbier.

* * * * *

26 Caesarius] Cf Ep 374 introduction.

28 old proverb] *Adagia* I i 1

40 my name] Cf Ep 428:64–6.

41 philosopher] Democritus; Diogenes Laertius 9.36

PIERRE BARBIER TO THE MOST LEARNED MASTER ERASMUS OF ROTTERDAM

After I had sent your Reverence a letter from here, most learned Master Erasmus, and had also received your learned letter of 11 July, I discovered that the young man who had asked for the first prebend (you know to what I refer) and who was, I thought, next to yourself regarded with some favour by my master – I discovered, as I said, that he was unsuitable for the position. It is of such a kind as calls for an occupant in holy orders, which this young man is not, and cannot as yet be, from what I hear; so this will be to your advantage, if it is true that you will secure a much larger sum from the other candidate. I doubt, however, whether it is possible to go as high as thirty Flemish pounds; all the persons I have consulted say that a proper figure for this prebend would be a hundred St Philip florins. There is one man, however, who has offered me twenty-five Flemish pounds, to be charged on the abbey of St Michael's, Antwerp; and unless you can find someone who offers a good deal more, I recommend him warmly to your Reverence, both because there is the security of the charge, and because I have known him personally for some time.

It is quite definite that the archbishop of Saragossa has not yet passed away; but I hope that when some vacancy occurs, my master himself will not forget you. Please let me know what you think about the prebend, and I will carry out your instructions. Speed is desirable; you know how Opportunity, once let slip, is bald-pated, so that she cannot be caught at random. Farewell, Master Erasmus, whom I love as a father.

Brussels, 18 July 1516

* * * * *

443:5 prebend] At Courtrai; cf Ep 436:6n; the letters mentioned are lost.

12 thirty Flemish pounds] £30 0s 0d groot Flemish = £174 3s 10d tournois = £20 12s 6d sterling by relative silver values (mint par). Cf CWE 1 340–1, 345; CWE 2 327–45.

13 hundred St Philip florins] The Burgundian-Hapsburg gold coin. At official rates, which were then slightly less than the prevailing market rates for gold, this sum would have been worth £20 16s 8d groot = £122 10s 0d tournois = £15 0s 0d sterling. Cf CWE 1 318, 321 (plate), 336–9; CWE 2 310 (table 1), 327–45. Barbier was clearly bargaining for his nominee.

14 twenty-five Flemish pounds] £25 0s 0d groot Flemish = £145 3s 3d tournois = £17 3s 9d sterling, by relative silver values (mint par).

19 Saragossa] Alfonso of Aragon (1478–1520), at this time regent of Aragon on the death of Ferdinand, as Ximénes was regent in Castile

20 vacancy] The implication is that Erasmus was mooted for promotion to a see, presumably as a non-resident bishop; cf Allen Ep 475:4n.

22–3 Opportunity] *Adagia* I vii 70; *Disticha Catonis* 2.25

444 / From Pierre Vitré Paris, 2 August 1516

Vitré was apparently a former pupil of Erasmus at Paris; cf Ep 66 introduction. He had been teaching at Calais and had returned to Paris seemingly at the urging of Erasmus, who may also have used his influence on Vitré's behalf.

PIERRE VITRÉ TO THE MOST LEARNED ERASMUS HIS TEACHER

Although I have seldom written to you before this, kindest of teachers, I shall not try, as most other people do, to invent some loophole of excuse; I would rather honestly confess the truth. I have often made the attempt and begun a letter to you, but I was dissatisfied with all my efforts, and shame often made me desist. And so in hopes of someday writing something that might not be wholly unsatisfactory, I wasted a long time in the search. All the same, not a day has passed without affectionate memories of you; but to a man to whom I owed everything (and you know that I owe my whole self to you) I was ashamed to send a reply unworthy of such a distinguished recipient, the more so as you had done so much for me. I cannot do what I should; you are a tolerant man, you must do it for me. You can say I am as sluggish as a tortoise, and not without reason; you can say you have been fobbed off with tricks and trifles. I do not deny it; this letter that I make bold to send now is only trivial, I know. Such as it is, though, you must read it with your usual kindness towards me. I would hardly dare to put pen to paper, did not your incredible generosity give me strength and courage. Long ago, when I was dead and buried, you restored me to the light of day, and not only restored me, but set me up in my native country and made me immortal with a generous tribute; and I hope that now my weakness will receive your friendly support. And so I beg you, by your great patroness Minerva, by every Muse and every god, do not despise or abandon that poor Vitré, who is really yours.

What I could promise you, since I am wholly yours, I do not see, unless it were a mind sincere and frank and simple, that always finds in you its refuge. I therefore offer you, next to immortal God, my first and chiefest love and worship and affection; you are my patron, you my teacher and my father, you my divinity on earth, and would that I might add, immortal and eternal! And why should not your more than human writings, your truly

* * * * *

444:14 tricks and trifles] Martial 14.1.7

19 native country] Cf Allen Ep 528:10ff.

20 tribute] Cf Ep 66 introduction.

godlike mind, and your immortal spirit make you immortal and eternal in reality? And so, my kind beloved teacher, if you have any leisure from your sacred studies, spare a thought sometimes for your friend Vitré. The tribute that you paid me was very onerous as well as very honorific. If you will write me even the briefest letter, so that men may not think you have deserted me, it will be much easier for me to live up to your praise; if I once know that a humble letter from me does not displease you, you will find my future diligence more than a match for earlier failure.

About my present circumstances I write nothing to you here and now; my resources are adequate to my modest situation, but I hope for better things and a more interesting reason for a letter. I will only say this much. When I first arrived here, I was poor and needy, as you may well suppose, and I at once opened a school and began to give public instruction in the Lombard college, with some success, as I may say without arrogance. But I was very soon lured away with great entreaties and boundless promises to the Collège de Navarre by the master of that institution, who gave me students from Paris to teach, which was undoubtedly a very tedious and burdensome affair. And so, since I am more tied by that business than I could wish, I decided once again to resume my freedom. As for the treatment I met with in England, I hope no one else may ever be subjected to it, or be willing to endure it.

If there is anything I can do for you, I should find nothing more delightful than to carry out your commissions with the greatest care. On another occasion I will write you a longer letter. Meanwhile please give these few lines a kindly reception. Fausto and Lefèvre send you their greetings. If you wish your friend Vitré to be in good health, look after your own health as best you can.

Paris, 2 August 1516

* * * * *

43 Lombard College] A college in Paris founded in 1334 for Italian scholars by Andrea Ghini of Florence, bishop of Arras and Tournai

45 Collège de Navarre] Founded in 1304 by Joanna, queen of Navarre and consort to Philip the Fair

45 master] Pierre Duval, grand master of the Collège de Navarre from 1503–18, and a canon of Notre Dame; cf Renaudet *Préréforme* 619.

49 in England] *Apud Britannos*; apparently meaning Calais; cf Ep 528.

54 Fausto] Andrelini; cf Ep 84 introduction.

54 Lefèvre] Lefèvre d'Etaples; cf Ep 315 introduction.

445 / From Thomas Grey

Paris, 5 August [1516]

Grey and Vitré (Ep 444) were old associates and pupils of Erasmus in Paris (cf Ep 66 introduction).

THOMAS GREY TO MASTER ERASMUS

Although I cannot express my feelings towards you, dear friend, in a letter, on account of your many acts of kindness and the unspeakable goodness and generosity you have always shown to my unworthy self, not to mention my own lack of knowledge and of literary skill, yet I will put my trust in your exceptional humanity, and reply without misgivings. To start with, I must express most sincere thanks – more thanks than anybody can imagine, although all the same they are far less than you deserve. What can one invent that can be equal to your deserts, when you are so good and so generous? Quite simply, nothing. Not to mention what you had done before, I simply cannot express how much the delightful letter you lately sent me from Basel added to the heap of your goodness to me; for in it I could see clearly that our old relationship was as strong as ever, that you were in good health, and enjoying the respectful admiration of all the leaders of society and unusual popularity among the common people as a whole. All of which was not only very pleasant hearing, but a complete answer to my prayers. I say nothing of the delicious letter I have had from Beatus Rhenanus, which I owe to your more than paternal influence with him, and which was as salutary as it was learned at all points; I have answered it somehow, but not as I wished. For, as St Paul says, to will is present with me, in this matter as in others, but how to perform what is good I cannot discover. If my capacity were equal to my desires, I would return thanks to you in the first place, and to him also. And then I cannot but be quite delighted and congratulate you on your being so well thought of both by the much-respected bishop of your diocese and by your most noble prince Charles. For this be glory to almighty God, and to our Lord Jesus Christ, who has chosen you to serve him to such good purpose, and so

* * * * *

445:11 letter] Apparently lost

13 old relationship] Cf Ep 58.

18 Rhenanus] For Grey's reply to this letter see Allen Ep 460:15–16; for his acquaintance with Beatus Rhenanus cf Allen Ep 581:24–5.

20 St Paul] Rom 7:18; Grey's Latin reflects Erasmus' translation of the New Testament: 'Novi enim quod non habitet in me, hoc est in carne mea, bonum: nam velle adest mihi, at ut faciam bonum, non reperio.'

25 bishop] Christoph von Utenheim

armed you for the task that you cannot be turned aside by any of the charms of this world and its specious honours. Take my word for it, this is no mean gift, to be able so easily to despise such things, to take on these great labours of your own accord, and (what I think best of all) to be as vigorous in mind now as if you were in the flower of your youth.

For in many men of your age, although they are not worn out by frequent nightly vigils and continual toil, I see the powers of the mind begin to slow down, as happened some time ago to Lefèvre d'Etaples. He has told me to send you his most cordial greetings, and the only reason why he does not write is that he cannot compose anything up to his own standard in either prose or verse; he, I repeat, feels the warmest affection for you, he speaks of you in any company as the most learned and most industrious of men, and as far as I can gather, he loves you sincerely. For he often expresses the wish that you might meet in Christian charity, and although you have sometimes rebuked him, he does not resent that at all as a carnal man would, but owes you immortal thanks as a truly spiritual man, asserting that he himself had noted some of your points long ago, and would have printed them, had you not forestalled him. And then it is on your account that he gives me too such a kind reception and talks with me so freely; although it is true that he shows many signs of weakness both in ordinary speech and in scholarship, so much so that he can now hardly explain any doubtful point. I have put many questions to him, but his answers have been little to the point, and often he asks a pupil named François, who is really not quite up to it yet. But the nearer he approaches to the death of the body, the more he lives for the spirit. At least he listens gladly to anything I ask him, and when he knows the answer, he gives it readily; if he does not, he openly confesses that he has forgotten it. And so I beg you urgently, if you do write to him, to express thanks to him on my

* * * * *

35 Lefèvre d'Etaples] Cf Allen Epp 460:16–17; 493:447–50; he was now about sixty years old, and was to survive to the age of eighty-two.

51 François] Identified by Herminjard with François Vatable (d 15 March 1547), who was to be professor of Hebrew in the *collège royal* from its foundation in 1531 until his death. A native of Gamaches in Picardy, he was an intimate of Lefèvre in this period. See Herminjard I 23 2n, 45 19n; and Rice introduction to Ep 83.

52 death of the body] In the light of this extended account of failing powers, it should be remembered that Lefèvre would yet publish his commentaries on the Gospels (1521) and the first complete translation of the Bible into French (1530); cf note to line 35 above. On the other hand, contemporary attitudes to age made Lefèvre by this time a very old man. See A. Renaudet *Humanisme et Renaissance* (Geneva 1958) 209–16.

account; for he told me to tell you what friendly feelings he has towards me for your sake.

Your *Enchiridion* printed in Strasbourg I do not know how to trace here; I suppose it has not yet reached us. When you say that I should abandon my hopes of learning to write well, I think I see pretty well what you mean: you know I cannot succeed, and as a kind friend, would not have me waste my time scrubbing bricks. One last point: I gave your greetings to Master Roger, as you told me to, and he is indignant with you for not answering his letter as well as mine; but he sends you his greetings in return, seriously enough. If at any time, God willing, I am allowed to enjoy your society, which I desire so much, and to pluck ripe fruits for my soul's salvation from the source whence came in the old days such sweet life-giving seed, I should have nothing more in life to wish for. So if in future this should be possible in any convenient way, be sure to let me know. And if by the favour of Heaven it does come about, I and my children will look after you most faithfully, with no less cheerful compliance than if my father and mother and all my other friends were restored to me in you alone.

In taking the trouble to send back my letter with corrections, you played the part of a most indulgent teacher, and by this kind act you have made me, who was already devoted to you, still more (if that is possible) attached to you. I beg you for my own profit to undertake something of the sort for this letter too. I have long been expecting a kind letter from you from Brabant with no common eagerness. So please answer as soon as you can. Farewell, second hope of my soul, and remember me as I do you.

Paris, 5 August

* * * * *

58 *Enchiridion*] Probably the edition published by Schürer at Strasbourg, September 1515, of the *Lucubratiunculae*. His reprint of June 1516 must also have been near publication when Erasmus wrote the letter to which this replies.

62 scrubbing bricks] *Adagia* I iv 48

63 Roger] Perhaps Wentford; cf Ep 196 introduction.

THE EARLY PUBLICATION OF ERASMUS' LETTERS

Erasmus' controversial works often took the form of 'open letters' which lived their own life in the public domain, and form part of his works rather than his correspondence; a good example is the *Letter to Christopher bishop of Basel on the eating of meat*, 21 April 1522, of which fifteen editions were published in the first two years, with German and English versions as well. And from the summer of 1517 onwards, if not earlier, individual letters were put out either in Latin or in the vernacular, usually for propaganda purposes, as a rule outside Erasmus' control, and sometimes to his great annoyance. The best known case is perhaps Ep 1033 of 19 October 1519, addressed to the archbishop of Mainz: a dozen editions appeared in pamphlet form, nearly all in Germany, in 1519–20.

From these individual letters it is easy to distinguish the collections, nearly all published with Erasmus' connivance if not actually under his own eye, of which an invaluable account is given by Allen in appendix VII in his first volume. Erasmus himself tells us in Ep 1206 that unofficial selections from his letters were in circulation in manuscript as early as 1509, and that he did what he could to suppress them. However in the summer of 1515, when he arrived in Basel from England and found Froben printing *Jani Damiani Senensis ad Leonem X pont. max. De expeditione in Turcas elegeia*, 4°, August 1515, he seems (the suggestion is Allen's) to have taken the opportunity to circulate four important letters written earlier that year, Ep 335 addressed to Leo X and two associated with it (Epp 334 and 333), and his long answer to Maarten van Dorp's strictures on the *Moria* (Ep 337), which was in future to be printed regularly with the *Moria* and not with the *Epistolae*. These letters had no preface; they seem to have been reprinted, perhaps at Louvain by Thierry Martens later in the same year (NK 2938) and at Leipzig by Valentine Schumann in 1516.

The next collection to appear was the *Epistolae aliquot illustrium virorum ad Erasmum Roterodamum, et huius ad illos*, published at Louvain by Thierry Martens in October 1516 (NK 2939), with a dedication by Pieter Gillis, who supervised the work. Writing to Budé in February 1517 (Allen Ep 531:525ff), Erasmus disclaims responsibility, but indicates that he knew something was afoot and could have stopped it if he had wanted to. The book, a quarto of 38 leaves, is not rare. It contained twenty-one letters, of which only seven were by Erasmus, and of these three had appeared in 1515.

The same editor and publisher were responsible for the *Aliquot epistolae sanequam elegantes* (Louvain: Martens April 1517; NK 819), a quarto of 66 leaves, with a preface by Pieter Gillis addressed to Antonius Clava. This contained four letters from the 1516 volume and thirty-one new ones, of which over half were written by Erasmus during his recent stay in Brussels and Antwerp. Gillis admits in the preface that his action will not please Erasmus, and Erasmus himself confirms this in Ep 730 (6 December 1517); but he has the sense to make the best of it. It is therefore hardly surprising to find Rutgerus Rescius, who was working for Martens as a learned corrector and copy editor, writing direct to Erasmus when the copy of a letter he had written while staying with Gillis in Antwerp ten days before does not make sense (Ep 546 of 8 March 1517). Rescius further asks for something to fill the space left by the printer for preliminary material which had fallen short; and when Erasmus responded with a copy of Ep 529, which was in fact too long, we can still see how Martens used every possible abbreviation, and even added two lines to one page, in order to fit it in.

At this stage the whole picture alters. Froben in Basel seriously enters the field with a stout quarto of 272 pages, which, under the same title *Aliquot epistolae sanequam elegantes* (Basel January 1518), reprints all the letters printed in the early editions except that to Dorp about the *Moria*. The book has an epigram by Gerard Geldenhouwer on the last page, but for a preface it merely reprints that by Pieter Gillis. It must have commanded a good market, and was reprinted, like other successes, by Matthias Schürer in Strasbourg (February 1519).

Meanwhile Froben, using as he so often did the talents of Beatus Rhenanus, was preparing a supplement, the history of which purports to be given by Beatus in a dedication to Michael Hummelburger. This was the *Auctarium selectarum aliquot epistolarum*, which appeared as a quarto of 224 pages in August 1518. Schürer was not slow to follow suit, and his reprint of the *Auctarium* appeared in April 1519; volumes still exist in which his *Epistolae elegantes* of the previous February and the April *Auctarium* are bound together. But he seems not to have spoilt Froben's market, for a Froben reprint of the *Auctarium* (mainly, but not exactly, page-for-page) appeared in March 1519, and seems to be a commoner book today. Neither of them seems to have found much of a sale in Italy. As late as February 1524 the Venetian printer Gregorius de Gregoriis, working for the publisher Laurentius Lorius, republished the *Auctarium* (with a supplement of twenty-one letters taken from Froben's *Epistolae ad diversos* of 31 August 1521); and the editor Marcus Abstemius tells us in his preface that the *Auctarium* was printed from the only copy in Italy, kindly lent by Fridericus Nausea (cf Ep 1577).

But it is clear that by now the public demand for Erasmus' letters was not to be resisted. Froben no doubt wished to repeat what had proved a prosperous undertaking, and from the words of Erasmus himself at the start of Ep 1206 it seems that other publishers may have been willing to enter this field. There is no reason to suppose that his own expressed reluctance was other than perfectly genuine; but beneath his often quite unrealistic expectations of the way other people ought to behave, Erasmus was seldom out of touch with facts, and he complied. Not being in Basel himself, he seems again to have relied on Beatus, and sent him a quantity of letters (many, it seems, with dates newly added) to choose from and emend for publication. The result was the *Farrago nova epistolarum ... admixtis quibusdam quas scripsit etiam adolescens*, a folio of 410 pages published by Froben without a preface, and dated October 1519. Erasmus found the editing very unsatisfactory,[1] but the book sold out at once.

Henceforward the publication of Erasmus' letters wears two different aspects. On the one hand, there is the series of folio collections which runs from the Froben *Epistolae ad diversos* dated 31 August 1521[2] right through to the Leiden edition of 1703; on the other, the long series of selections from the correspondence intended for use in schools, which begins with Baerland's first edition (NK 820) in December 1520 (see Allen III appendix XII). These selections (we know of over thirty editions, and no doubt there are more) have not yet, so far as we know, been explored; and they may serve as evidence which, though humble, is not unimpressive of the influence exercised by this inexhaustible correspondence.

RABM

Prefatory Letters[3]

TO THE HONOURABLE CASPAR VAN HALMALE,
DOCTOR OF CIVIL AND CANON LAW
AND SHERIFF OF THE NOBLE CITY OF ANTWERP,
FROM PIETER GILLIS, SECRETARY OF THE SAME CITY,
GREETING

Words fail me, noble Caspar, counsel most learned in the law, to express either in writing or in speech the dismay that overcame me when I heard that you were suffering from a fever, and I pray heaven to bring it to the end that it deserves and restore you safe and sound. Your health I value as I

* * * * *

1 Ep 1066; for the printing cf Allen IV 9. The errata page is headed *Tertia epistolarum recognitio*.

2 Cf CWE 1 xx.

3 The Latin texts are reprinted in Allen II app XI.

would my own; for you have been very dear to me ever since boyhood, and I could not but groan in spirit as was meet and right.

And so, as I wondered how I might relieve your sickness by some antidote, for beyond question it presses hard upon me too, I thought of selecting a certain number from a great pile of letters written by Erasmus of Rotterdam, the famous theologian who by common consent knows more and writes better than all others, to eminent and famous men, or by them to him – but a few only, such as I guessed would give you pleasure, although I know you enjoy everything that comes from Erasmus' pen, and your affection for the writer, as he well deserves, is unsurpassable. Indeed, his great gifts are so well known to the whole world, so highly spoken of in letters from distinguished men, so entirely approved by the authority of the pope himself, that they need no man's testimony, while he himself is by temperament entirely averse from any such assistance. But to give you something that you might enjoy, I have collected these letters for you and, knowing your warm affection for the man himself and the delight you feel when anything by Erasmus is put into your hands, I hope and pray that they may restore you to your original good health. See to it therefore that we may soon behold you fit and well. Farewell.

Antwerp, 26 September 1516

From the *Epistolae ad Erasmum* (Louvain: Martens October 1516)

TO ANTONIUS CLAVA, A DISTINGUISHED MEMBER OF THE COUNCIL OF FLANDERS, FROM PIETER GILLIS, GREETING

Your request, my honoured friend, is one that I receive from several people every day. You have published, they say, a number of notable and learned letters; pray do the same in respect of other letters written later, in which the standard of scholarship is even higher, those which contain a most friendly confrontation between Erasmus and Budé. Inasmuch as I enlist in this task the aid of printers instead of scribes – for scarcely could a hundred copyists satisfy so great a demand – I will do a service to many people, but Clava shall be the only name it bears. Yet on this count I shall not be very popular with my friend Erasmus, who is reluctant to see such trifles, as he calls them, published, for fear they give a handle to those who enjoy finding fault. I know that scholars everywhere, and you in particular the best scholar of them all, will greatly enjoy the spectacle of these two paladins of learning, one from France and the other our own countryman, matched as it were in some tournament of eloquence, each of them of such outstanding, although diverse, merit that you might well wonder which you would prefer, but must admire both as of the highest class. Farewell, most learned Clava.

Antwerp, 5 March 1517

From the *Epistolae elegantes* (Louvain: Martens April 1517)

BEATUS RHENANUS TO
MICHAEL HUMMELBURGER OF RAVENSBURG,
A LEARNED LAWYER AND A LATIN AND GREEK SCHOLAR,
GREETING

Listen, my dear Michael, to the bold undertaking I have planned these last few days. Erasmus, our incomparable champion of liberal studies and of the theology that was so nearly dead, has been robbed – by me! 'Heavens!' you will say; 'what news is this? Perhaps you are making game of me.' Not so, I mean it. Here is the story in brief. By a stroke of luck I chanced upon several bundles of correspondence from Erasmus' library here, out of which I chose forthwith a number of letters, the outstanding letters in fact, of which some are his and some are answers to them from the greatest scholars of our generation. I was encouraged to purloin them by the thought that the very rich who are well supplied with everything do not notice if a few things are actually removed; for I thought likewise that Erasmus who is so richly endowed with all the treasures of the Muses would not detect it if I had removed something. Besides which, that great man loves me so sincerely – little as I deserve it – that even if I do him some serious wrong he will surely make allowances. You see what confidence sincerity in friendship can encourage. In the Muses' name I reckon our native Germany fortunate, and France and Britain too, for each of them now possesses distinguished authors and scholars of outstanding attainments. Who could know more or write better than Erasmus? whose style more polished, more elegant, more truly Attic than Budé's? whose more free-spoken, more compact, more finished in every way than Tunstall's? – to say nothing for the moment of the others.

After Erasmus' departure I handed these letters to Froben to be printed, partly that I might have something to send you, for in your last letter you showed such a desire to be sent something by Erasmus or Budé; partly to be of some use to those who wish to improve, for I know they will gain not a little from the reading of these letters. And, further, the literary circles of this city, as they read them, will be relieved of the sadness they have lately felt because of the great man's departure, or at least will have some consolation. They will think they still hear his voice as they read his letters with their universal brilliance of style, and those who admired so lately the eloquence of his conversation will now enjoy the elegance of what he writes. Farewell, and pray take a kindly view of my enterprise.

Basel, 22 August 1518

From the *Auctarium* (Basel: Froben August 1518)

TABLE OF CORRESPONDENTS

WORKS FREQUENTLY CITED

SHORT TITLE FORMS

INDEX

TABLE OF CORRESPONDENTS

WORKS FREQUENTLY CITED

This list provides bibliographical information for works referred to in short-title form in the headnotes and footnotes to Epp 298–445. For Erasmus' writings see the short-title list, pages 363–6. Editions of his letters are included in the list below.

Adam	Paul Adam *L'Humanisme à Sélestat: L'école, les humanistes, la bibliothèque* 2nd ed (Sélestat 1967)
AK	Alfred Hartmann ed *Die Amerbachkorrespondenz* (Basel 1942–)
Allen	P.S. Allen, H.M. Allen, and H.W. Garrod eds *Opus epistolarum Des. Erasmi Roterodami* (Oxford 1906–58) 11 vols and index
ASD	*Opera omnia Desiderii Erasmi Roterodami* (Amsterdam 1969–)
Auctarium	*Auctarium selectarum aliquot epistolarum Erasmi Roterodami ad eruditos et horum ad illum* (Basel: Froben August 1518)
Benzing	Joseph Benzing *Die Buchdrucker des 16. und 17. Jahrhunderts im deutschen Sprachgebiet* (Wiesbaden 1963)
BHR	*Bibliothèque d'humanisme et renaissance* (Geneva)
Bopp	Marie-Joseph Bopp *Die evangelischen Geistlichen und Theologen in Elsass und Lothringen von der Reformation bis zur Gegenwart* (Neustadt a.d. Aisch 1959)
BRE	A. Horawitz and K. Hartfelder eds *Briefwechsel des Beatus Rhenanus* (Leipzig 1886; repr 1966)
CSEL	I. Hilberg ed *Sancti Eusebii Hieronymi epistulae* in *Corpus scriptorum ecclesiasticorum latinorum* vols 54–6 (Vienna/Leipzig 1910–18)
CWE	*The Collected Works of Erasmus* (Toronto 1974–)
Damiani elegeia	*Jani Damiani Senensis ad Leonem X pont. max. De expeditione in Turcas elegeia* (Basel: Froben August 1515)
DNB	*Dictionary of National Biography* (Oxford and London 1917–)
E & C	H.C. Porter ed and D.F.S. Thomson trans *Erasmus and Cambridge: The Cambridge Letters of Erasmus* (Toronto 1963)
Egli	E. Egli, G. Finsler, W. Köhler, O. Farner, F. Blanke, L. von Muralt, E. Künzli, and R. Pfister eds *Huldreich Zwinglis sämtliche Werke* in *Corpus reformatorum* vols 88 and ff (Berlin 1905–)
EHR	*English Historical Review*
Emden BRUO	A.B. Emden *Biographical Register of the University of Oxford* (Oxford 1957–74) 4 vols
Epistolae ad diversos	*Epistolae D. Erasmi Roterodami ad diversos et aliquot aliorum ad illum* (Basel: Froben 31 August 1521)
Epistolae ad Erasmum	*Epistolae aliquot illustrium virorum ad Erasmum Roterodamum et huius ad illos* (Louvain: Martens October 1516)

Epistolae elegantes (1517)	*Aliquot epistolae sanequam elegantes Erasmi Roterodami et ad hunc aliorum eruditissimorum hominum* (Louvain: Martens April 1517)
Epistolae elegantes (1518)	*Aliquot epistolae sanequam elegantes Erasmi Roterodami et ad hunc aliorum eruditissimorum hominum* (Basel: Froben January 1518)
Epistolae familiares	*Epistolae familiares Des. Erasmi Roterodami ad Bonif. Amerbachium* (Basel: C.A. Serin 1779)
Farrago	*Farrago nova epistolarum Des. Erasmi Roterodami ad alios et aliorum ad hunc: admixtis quibusdam quas scripsit etiam adolescens* (Basel: Froben October 1519)
Garanderie	Marie-Madeleine de la Garanderie ed and trans *La Correspondance d'Erasme et de Guillaume Budé* (Paris 1967)
HE	E. Böcking ed *Epistolae Ulrichi Hutteni* in *Ulrichi Hutteni opera ... omnia* vol I (Leipzig 1859; repr 1963)
Herminjard	A.L. Herminjard ed *Correspondance des réformateurs dans les pays de langue française* (Geneva/Paris 1866–97) 9 vols
Knowles	Dom David Knowles *The Religious Orders in England* III: *The Tudor Age* (Cambridge 1959)
LB	J. Leclerc ed *Desiderii Erasmi Roterodami opera omnia* (Leiden 1703–6) 10 vols
Lefftz	Joseph Lefftz *Die gelehrten und literarischen Gesellschaften im Elsass vor 1870* (Heidelberg 1931)
LP	*Letters and Papers, Foreign and Domestic, of the Reign of Henry VIII* ed J.S. Brewer, J. Gairdner, R.H. Brodie (London 1862–1932) 36 vols
McConica	J.K. McConica *English Humanists and Reformation Politics under Henry VIII and Edward VI* (Oxford 1965)
Mackie	J.D. Mackie *The Earlier Tudors 1485–1558* (Oxford 1952)
Metzger	B.M. Metzger *The Text of the New Testament* 2nd ed (Oxford 1968)
NDB	*Neue deutsche Biographie* (Berlin 1953–)
NK	W. Nijhoff and M.E. Kronenberg eds *Nederlandsche Bibliographie van 1500 tot 1540* (The Hague 1919–)
Opus epistolarum	*Opus epistolarum Des. Erasmi Roterodami per autorem diligenter recognitum et adjectis innumeris novis fere ad trientem auctum* (Basel: Froben, Herwagen, and Episcopius 1529)
Opuscula	W.K. Ferguson ed *Erasmi opuscula: A Supplement to the Opera omnia* (The Hague 1933)
Phillips	M.M. Phillips *The 'Adages' of Erasmus* (Cambridge 1964)
Pirckheimer	M. Goldast ed *Bilibaldi Pirckheimeri opera* (Frankfurt 1610; repr 1969)
PL	J.P. Migne ed *Patrologiae cursus completus ... series latina* (Paris 1844–1902) 221 vols
RE	L. Geiger ed *Johann Reuchlins Briefwechsel* (Tübingen 1875; repr 1962)
Reedijk	C. Reedijk ed *Poems of Desiderius Erasmus* (Leiden 1956)
Renaudet *Italie*	A. Renaudet *Erasme et l'Italie* (Geneva 1954)

Renaudet *Préréforme*	A. Renaudet *Préréforme et humanisme à Paris pendant les premières guerres d'Italie (1494–1517)* 2nd ed (Paris 1953)
Renouard	*Imprimeurs et libraires parisiens du XVIe siècle: ouvrage publié d'après les manuscrits de Philippe Renouard* Histoire générale de Paris: collection de documents publiée sous les auspices de l'édilité parisienne, tome deuxième (Paris 1969)
Rice	E.F. Rice jr ed *The Prefatory Epistles of Jacques Lefèvre d'Etaples and Related Texts* (New York 1972)
Ritter	François Ritter *Histoire de l'imprimerie alsacienne aux XVe et XVIe siècles* (Strasbourg-Paris 1955)
Rogers	E.F. Rogers ed *The Correspondence of Sir Thomas More* (Princeton 1947)
Rossi	V. Rossi *Il Quattrocento* (Milan 1933)
Schmidt	C. Schmidt *Histoire littéraire de l'Alsace* (Paris 1879; repr 1966) 2 vols
STC	A.W. Pollard and G.R. Redgrave *A Short-Title Catalogue of Books Printed in England, Scotland, and Ireland and of English Books Printed Abroad 1475–1640* (London 1926)
de Vocht CTL	H. de Vocht *History of the Foundation and the Rise of the Collegium Trilingue Lovaniense 1517–1550* Humanistica lovaniensia 10–13 (Louvain 1951–5) 4 vols
de Vocht *Literae*	H. de Vocht *Literae virorum eruditorum ad Franciscum Craneveldium 1522–1528* Humanistica lovaniensia 1 (Louvain 1928)
de Vocht MHL	H. de Vocht *Monumenta humanistica lovaniensia* Humanistica lovaniensia 4 (Louvain 1934)
Wegg	J. Wegg *Richard Pace* (London 1932)
Winterberg	Hans Winterberg *Die Schüler von Ulrich Zasius* (Stuttgart 1961)
WPB	Emil Reicke ed *Willibald Pirckheimers Briefwechsel* (Munich 1940, 1956) 2 vols (containing letters to December 1515)

SHORT TITLE FORMS FOR ERASMUS' WORKS

Acta contra Lutherum: Acta academiae Lovaniensis contra Lutherum
Adagia: Adagiorum chiliades 1508 (Adagiorum collectanea for the primitive form, when required)
Admonitio adversus mendacium: Admonitio adversus mendacium et obtrectationem
Annotationes de haereticis: Annotationes in leges pontificias et caesareas de haereticis
Annotationes in Novum Testamentum
Antibarbari
Apologia ad Fabrum: Apologia ad Iacobum Fabrum Stapulensem
Apologia ad Carranza: Apologia ad Sanctium Carranza
Apologia adversus Petrum Sutorem: Apologia adversus debacchationes Petri Sutoris
Apologia adversus monachos: Apologia adversus monachos quosdam hispanos
Apologia adversus rhapsodias Alberti Pii
Apologia contra Latomi dialogum: Apologia contra Iacobi Latomi dialogum de tribus linguis
Apologia contra Stunicam: Apologia contra Lopidem Stunicam
Apologia de 'In principio erat sermo'
Apologia de laude matrimonii: Apologia pro declamatione de laude matrimonii
Apologia de loco 'omnes quidem': Apologia de loco 'Omnes quidem resurgemus'
Apologiae duae
Apologiae omnes
Apologia invectivis Lei: Apologia qua respondet duabus invectivis Eduardi Lei
Apologia monasticae religionis
Apophthegmata
Argumenta: Argumenta in omnes epistolas apostolicas nova
Axiomata pro causa Lutheri: Axiomata pro causa Martini Lutheri

Carmina
Catalogus lucubrationum
Cato
Christiani hominis institutum
Ciceronianus: Dialogus Ciceronianus
Colloquia
Compendium rhetorices
Compendium vitae
Conflictus: Conflictus Thaliae et barbariei

De bello turcico: Consultatio de bello turcico
De civilitate: De civilitate morum puerilium
De conscribendis epistolis
De constructione: De constructione octo partium orationis
De contemptu mundi
De copia: De duplici copia verborum ac rerum
Declamatio de morte

Declamationes
Declamatiuncula
Declamatiunculae
Declarationes ad censuras Lutetiae: Declarationes ad censuras Lutetiae vulgates
De concordia: De sarcienda ecclesiae concordia
De immensa Dei misericordia: Concio de immensa Dei misericordia
De libero arbitrio: De libero arbitrio diatribe
De praeparatione: De praeparatione ad mortem
De pronuntiatione: De recta latini graecique sermonis pronuntiatione
De pueris instituendis: De pueris statim ac liberaliter instituendis
De puero Iesu: Concio de puero Iesu
De puritate tabernaculi
De ratione studii
Detectio praestigiarum: Detectio praestigiarum cuiusdam libelli germanice scripti
De tedio Iesu: Disputatiuncula de tedio, pavore, tristicia Iesu
Dilutio: Dilutio eorum quae Iodocus Clithoveus scripsit adversus declamationem suasoriam matrimonii

Ecclesiastes: Ecclesiastes sive de ratione concionandi
Enarratio in primum psalmum
Enchiridion: Enchiridion militis christiani
Encomium matrimonii
Encomium medicinae: Declamatio in laudem artis medicae
Epigrammata
Epistola ad fratres: Epistola ad fratres Inferioris Germaniae
Epistola consolatoria: Epistola consolatoria in adversis
Epistola contra pseudevangelicos: Epistola contra quosdam qui se falso iactant evangelicos
Epistola de apologia Cursii: Epistola de apologia Petri Cursii
Epistola de esu carnium: Epistola apologetica ad Christophorum episcopum Basiliensem de interdicto esu carnium
Epistola de modestia: Epistola de modestia profitendi linguas
Exomologesis: Exomologesis sive modus confitendi
Explanatio symboli: Explanatio symboli apostolorum sive catechismus

Formulae: Conficiendarum epistolarum formulae

Hyperaspistes

Institutio christiani matrimonii
Institutio principis christiani

Julius exclusus: Dialogus Julius exclusus e coelis

Liber quo respondet annotationibus Lei: Liber quo respondet annotationibus Eduardi Lei
Lingua
Liturgia Virginis Matris: Virginis Matris apud Lauretum cultae liturgia

Lucubrationes
Lucubratiunculae

Methodus
Modus orandi Deum
Moria: Moriae encomium, or Moria

Novum instrumentum
Novum Testamentum

Obsecratio ad Virginem Mariam: Obsecratio sive oratio ad Virginem Mariam in rebus adversis
Oratio de pace: Oratio de pace et discordia
Oratio de virtute: Oratio de virtute amplectenda
Oratio funebris: Oratio funebris Berthae de Heyen

Paean Virgini Matri: Paean Virgini Matri dicendus
Panegyricus: Panegyricus ad Philippum Austriae ducem
Parabolae: Parabolae sive similia
Paraclesis
Paraphrasis in Elegantias Vallae: Paraphrasis in Elegantias Laurentii Vallae
Paraphrases in Novum Testamentum
Paraphrasis in Matthaeum: Paraphrasis in Matthaeum, etc.
Peregrinatio apostolorum: Peregrinatio apostolorum Petri et Pauli
Precatio ad Virginis filium Iesum
Precatio dominica
Precationes
Precatio pro pace ecclesiae: Precatio ad Iesum pro pace ecclesiae
Progymnasmata: Progymnasmata quaedam primae adolescentiae Erasmi
Psalmi: Psalmi (Enarrationes sive commentarii in psalmos)
Purgatio adversus epistolam Lutheri: Purgatio adversus epistolam non sobriam Lutheri

Querela pacis

Ratio verae theologiae
Responsio ad annotationes Lei: Responsio ad annotationes Eduardi Lei
Responsio ad annotationem Stunicae: Responsio ad annotationem Iacobi Lopis Stunicae
Responsio ad collationes: Responsio ad collationes cuiusdam iuvenis gerontodidascali
Responsio ad disputationem de diuortio: Responsio ad disputationem cuiusdam Phimostomi de diuortio
Responsio ad epistolam apologeticam: Responsio ad fratres Germaniae Inferioris ad epistolam apologeticam incerto autore proditam
Responsio ad epistolam Pii: Responsio ad epistolam paraeneticam Alberti Pii

Responsio adversus febricitantis libellum: Responsio adversus febricitantis cuiusdam libellum
Responsio contra Egranum: Responsio apologetica contra Sylvium Egranum

Spongia: Spongia adversus aspergines Hutteni
Supputatio: Supputatio calumniarum Natalis Bedae

Vidua christiana
Virginis et martyris comparatio
Vita Hieronymi: Vita diui Hieronymi Stridonensis

Index

This book

was designed by

ALLAN FLEMING

and was printed by

University of

Toronto

Press